ROGER ASCHAM

Lawrence V. Ryan

ROGER ASCHAM

STANFORD UNIVERSITY PRESS
STANFORD, CALIFORNIA
LONDON: OXFORD UNIVERSITY PRESS

Stanford University Press
Stanford, California

London: Oxford University Press

© 1963 by the Board of Trustees of the
Leland Stanford Junior University

Library of Congress Catalog Card Number: 63-10735
Printed in the United States of America

First published 1963
Second printing, 1964

FOR

Patricia Ann Ryan

Acknowledgments

ALTHOUGH I am indebted to many persons for help and inspiration in preparing this study of Roger Ascham's life and works, I wish particularly to thank the following for their exceptional assistance and kindnesses:

Professor Virgil Heltzel, for first suggesting the worth of this endeavor and for being the "teacher of all the little poor learning I have."

The trustees of the John Simon Guggenheim Memorial Foundation, for a yearlong fellowship, and the trustees of the American Philosophical Society, the Henry E. Huntington Library, and Stanford University, for research grants that enabled me to complete my investigations and writing.

The librarians and members of the research staffs of the British Museum, the Public Record Office, the Folger, Huntington, and Pierpont Morgan Libraries, the libraries at Cambridge, Harvard, Oxford, and Stanford Universities, and the Library of Congress; especially Mr. H. S. Bennett of Emmanuel College, Dr. R. Vaughan of Corpus Christi College, and Mr. Norman Buck and Mr. Malcolm Pratt of St. John's College, all of the University of Cambridge; Mr. W. O. Hassall, Keeper of Western Manuscripts in the Bodleian Library; and Miss Mary Isabel Fry of the Huntington Library—all of whom generously assisted me in my research and led me to new discoveries about Ascham.

Professor George Parks of Queens College, for graciously turning over to me the manuscript notes of his own investigations concerning Ascham's earlier years.

Mr. Kazimierz Dubinski, of Brantham Hall, Suffolk, for a delightful tour of Sir Humphrey Wingfield's manor house, followed by a memorable tea and a picnic in the fields where the young Ascham probably learned to manage his longbow.

Mr. J. G. Bell and Miss Pauline Wickham of the Stanford University

Press, for their patient and careful editing of my manuscript and for culling out, if not all, at least the worst, of its excrescences.

Above all others, my wife, to whom this book is dedicated—though she typed not a page, checked not a single reference, and had nothing to do with the index or the proof—because she bore with me cheerfully and did everything possible to keep up my spirits during the many years of its gestation.

Stanford, California   L.V.R.
January 2, 1963

Contents

ROGER ASCHAM

CHAPTER ONE

☙❧

Introduction

ON DECEMBER 30, 1568, a fever-wasted little man died in his home near
Newgate in London. When the news reached Queen Elizabeth, it is
said that she was deeply moved. The blend of genuine sorrow and
melodramatic demonstration with which she often reacted to the loss
of faithful servants and old friends appears in her alleged response to
the message: "I would rather have cast £10,000 in the sea than parted
with my Ascham."[1] For the person whose death evoked this hyperbolic
yet characteristic tribute from the queen was the Cambridge humanist
Roger Ascham, one of her girlhood tutors and her Latin secretary during the first ten years of her reign.

It would be hard to say how keenly Elizabeth did feel the loss of
this man whom she, like many of his contemporaries, claimed to love
well for his remarkable learning and gentle, friendly behavior. The
evidence suggests that Ascham may have been less a real favorite of
the queen than has sometimes been assumed by her biographers and
certain historical novelists. Nor was his death a real blow to Elizabethan letters; for in no fair estimate can he be ranked among the outstanding writers of this golden age. He was, rather, one of those lesser
but surprisingly influential men who, more by their typicalness and
their frank revelations about themselves than by the remarkableness of
their writings or lives, afford posterity an intimate view of their times.
It is, after all, Pepys the diarist of the commonplace, rather than the
historian Clarendon, through whom most readers come to know something of the life of seventeenth-century England.

Ascham's appeal to later periods has stemmed mainly from two of
his books, both written in the vernacular. Although his other writings,
including his extensive and historically important correspondence and

his third work in the vernacular, *A Report and Discourse of the State of Germany*, are not widely read, his *Toxophilus* and *The Scholemaster* have gained a large audience. Most students of English literature have at least a passing acquaintance with these two works, and much has been written about their place in the development of modern English prose. *The Scholemaster*, a popularization of widely-held Renaissance ideals, has immortalized Ascham among historians of educational theory; and *Toxophilus*, a dialogue on shooting with the longbow, has made his name a legend among archers.

The two books have inspired a number of memorials to his fame. English bowmen have remembered him through the creation of the Toxophilite Society, which shoots in Regent's Park, and his surname has been given to the wooden case or cupboard in which archers store their gear. As a scholar and educator, he has been honored by monuments both in his old college at Cambridge and elsewhere in England. The visitor to St. John's may find his coat of arms in stained glass in a window of the hall, a portrait carved in wood in the library, and a statue, handsome and dignified, in an exterior niche of the new chapel. (Unfortunately, neither the woodcarving nor the statue is authentic, since no portrait of Ascham is known to exist.) In the city of Cambridge, the stroller comes upon Ascham Road, at the end of which stands an elementary school that has recently been renamed in his honor. In his native village, a stained-glass commemorative window has been installed behind the altar of the parish church. And some years ago at Eton, the masters formed a social club in his memory and dubbed it with his name.[2]

The impressive record of Ascham's relationships with historically significant people is another reason for perennial interest in his writings. Besides Queen Elizabeth, about whom he has given us several revealing anecdotes, he is a valuable source of information on Henry VIII, Edward VI, Mary Tudor and her consort Philip II of Spain, Lady Jane Grey, the Emperor Charles V, Cardinal Pole, Archbishop Cranmer, Lord Burghley, Robert Dudley, Earl of Leicester, and Bishop Stephen Gardiner—all of whom he knew personally. He was, besides, one of the best-known members of that circle of Cambridge humanists and religious reformers who figured prominently in the intellectual, ecclesiastical, and political life of England from the time of Henry VIII's break with Rome until the close of the Tudor period. His travels abroad and his connections at Cambridge and the English court put him in touch with several of the leading Continental scholars of his generation, including Peter Ramus, the reformer of dialectical studies at Paris; the medical pioneer Vesalius; the Strasbourg educator Johann Sturm; the theologian Martin Bucer and the Protestant historian Johannes Sleidan; Peter Nanninck (Nannius) of Alkmaar, the leading contemporary humanist at Louvain; Jeronimo Osorio, the celebrated Portuguese churchman and Ciceronian; George Buchanan, the ablest Scoto-Latinist of the age, and a number of less famous, yet noteworthy, Neo-Latin authors. His letters, consequently, have provided historians and biographers with valuable contemporary information about political events, intellectual currents, and prominent figures of the middle years of the sixteenth century.

Because of the extent and highly informative content of his correspondence, Ascham is also one of the Englishmen of his time for whom the autobiographical record is most complete.* In reconstructing the story of his life, one finds in the letters not only the educational reformer, the experimenter in vernacular prose, and at times the naïve and pedantic Cambridge don, but also an enthusiastic antiquarian, an insatiably curious traveler, a devoted husband and father, a generous friend, an unfulfilled historian and political philosopher, something of the gallant and lover, even a touch of the *bon vivant*. On the less attractive side, and it was the seamier side of many of the best men of the times, he reveals himself as importunate seeker after patronage and place in university and court, chronic grumbler against fortune, sometimes obtuse breeder of discord and faction in his college, temporizer for personal

* The Latin epistles, principal source of information about Ascham, were first edited by Edward Grant (London, 1576). Extensive contemporary interest in this correspondence may be surmised from the number of early editions. Besides the original one, Grant brought out further editions at London in 1578, 1581, and 1590, with epistles of Sturm and others to Ascham added in the last of these. In the early seventeenth century, three editions were printed abroad, at Hannover in 1602 and 1610, and at Geneva in 1611. A number of the letters were widely copied and translated into English as models; several appeared, for example, in Abraham Fleming's *A Panoplie of Epistles* (London, 1576), pp. 427–48. The eighth edition of the Latin correspondence, overseen by William Elstob, appeared at Oxford in 1703. The most complete collection of the correspondence is that in Giles's edition of *The Whole Works*. In the present century the Latin epistles have been translated by Maurice A. Hatch, "The Ascham Letters: An Annotated Translation of the Latin Correspondence Contained in the Giles Edition of Ascham's Works," unpub. diss., Cornell, 1948, and the English correspondence has been carefully edited by Albert McHarg Hayes, "The English Letters of Roger Ascham," unpub. diss., Princeton, 1934. While I am deeply indebted to both Hatch and Hayes for their helpful annotations, all translations from the correspondence that appear in this book are my own.

advantage, and apparent weathercock shifting with the winds of scholarly and religious opinion. If the portrait emerging from the letters, especially in his ambitious early period and in his hard-pinched last years, seems to emphasize these less appealing features, one must honestly admit their existence. The preservation, moreover, of so many epistles of excuse or petition was due in large measure to the prominence of the addressees and the keen interest of Ascham's contemporaries in successful and imitable examples in this useful kind of correspondence.

The proper image to be drawn, then, is that of a man in whom aspiration for both worldly success and self-perfection ran high. But although his promise was considerable, he ended his life with few of his expectations realized. Sometimes his disappointment was due to illness, political change, and other accidents of fate, but sometimes, too, it arose from conflicts within himself, ambition exceeding honest self-appraisal and capacity for performance. His attempt, nearly but not quite successful, to combine the careers of academician, courtier, and author is typical of his age. Allowing for the superficial changes of time, it is even a striking prototype of the career of a certain kind of professor today, the man who tries to combine the functions of teacher, government servant, and author of popular books on scholarly subjects.

In all three respects, though Ascham fell just shy of success, the achievement was sufficiently remarkable to justify his contemporary and later fame. Probably he was disappointed most by the ultimate failure of his academic career. He made a brilliant start at Cambridge and soon acquired a reputation as a humanistic scholar worthy to follow his master Sir John Cheke. Surrounded at St. John's College by men devoted to the new learning, he set out to excel them all in both Greek and Latin. Even the most cursory review of his writings shows the breadth of his acquaintance with classical literature. Nor was his familiarity based, as was often true of his less ambitious contemporaries, upon mere tags and stock quotations culled from volumes of *florilegia*. In his early twenties, however, a succession of chills and fevers, possibly malarial, began to trouble him, and caused a temporary slackening of zeal for study from which his reputation never recovered. Apparently the logical successor to the regius professorship of Greek when Cheke left the university to tutor Edward VI, he was passed over and remained a low-salaried reader of the language in his own college. Yet in spite of this blow to his prestige, he managed to leave his mark upon classical studies at Cambridge. In the next generation, Gabriel Harvey, Thomas

Nashe, and the author of *The Pilgrimage to Parnassus* mention his scholarship with pride, while in a famous passage in *The Advancement of Learning*, Sir Francis Bacon pays him a negative tribute by deploring the pernicious, yet admittedly widespread, effects of his teaching.[3] Further, if Ascham left no scholarly editions of the classics or Latin commentaries on ancient authors, he supplied a livelier memorial to humanistic learning in his own original works in the English language.

Disappointed at his own failures and at partisan religious and intellectual strife within his college, he departed from Cambridge thrice to try his fortune among courtiers. Twice, and for brief periods, he reluctantly turned back to the university that he loved but in which he could never find contentment. Ironically, his ventures into public life were no more satisfactory. He first took leave from his college in 1548 to tutor the fifteen-year-old Princess Elizabeth. In spite of the persistent legend of his immediate and great success with his apt royal pupil, a legend that leaves a mistaken impression of long tenure in that capacity, he remained with her less than two years. Then, having apparently quarreled with other members of her household, he resigned, or was dismissed, and returned to Cambridge. Soon afterwards, he spent three years as secretary to the English ambassador at the court of Charles V. His time abroad left him with a widened outlook and new friends and acquaintances on the Continent, but did little to quiet his chronic restlessness. Nor did it procure him the slightest advancement upon his return to the university, though it did open the way to minor preferment at court. During the final years of his life, which he spent as Latin secretary to both Tudor queens, he gained no public office of major responsibility, and he died, after more than fourteen years at the side of Mary and Elizabeth, with neither riches nor marks of dignity for his service.

Living in a world of expanding opportunity, at least for so many others, Ascham may be excused for complaining repetitiously of his various disappointments. If there was a main chance for him, somewhere he missed it: yet once again relative failure had its compensations. Out of his travels and his years at court came the knowledge of public life that makes his epistles a rich source of information about his times. Had he lacked this experience beyond the college walls, he would never have been able to attempt his *Report of Germany*, nor might he even have undertaken the work for which he has been chiefly remembered by later generations, *The Scholemaster*.

His career as a writer follows a similar pattern, though literary immortality has compensated somewhat for the disappointments of the author living. With characteristic Elizabethan ambition, he projected far more than he was able to accomplish. Of all the larger works he planned or embarked on, only *Toxophilus* ever reached print in completed form. He sometimes championed, moreover, what turned out to be hopeless literary causes, such as the making of quantitative verses in English or the perpetuation of Latin Ciceronianism. In no respect was he a brilliant or original thinker or a literary innovator. Scarcely anywhere does he express a thought that cannot be traced to some earlier writer. Still, his contemporaries, interested less in novel matter than in ingenious treatment of the thoroughly familiar, esteemed him for successfully popularizing some of the best things from the common stock of ancient and contemporary wisdom. And to the modern reader who finds *The Scholemaster* congenial and instructive reading, it signifies little that Ascham is merely reworking ideas that Erasmus, Juan Luis Vives, Sturm, Sir Thomas Elyot, Cheke, and other humanists had already in their turn adapted from the classics. In fact, for the reader to notice his extensive borrowing would have meant to Ascham that he had succeeded admirably in the respected practice of literary imitation. Similarly, he would have welcomed praise from readers of *Toxophilus* less for the newness of his subject matter than for his masterly assimilation of venerable literary forms and techniques to an original design. It is one of the main contentions of this biography, as it would undoubtedly have been Ascham's own, that much of his success as a writer is due to his conscious and deliberate following of classical models.

Apart from the frequency with which he was cited and in his own turn imitated by others, the number of early editions of Ascham's works affords additional evidence of his contemporary success as an author. *Toxophilus,* first published in 1545, was twice reprinted during the sixteenth century. Apparently Englishmen found in it both a stirring appeal to their patriotic nostalgia for the longbow and an excellent pattern for the technical treatise. *The Scholemaster,* received even more enthusiastically than the earlier work, was issued in four new editions within twenty years after its first appearance in 1570. Scarcely a notable English discourse on educational theory that appeared during the following century is unmarked by its influence. And besides disseminating the most universally approved humanistic theories, it helped to give form to national awareness in the midst of the growing crisis with Spain.

The Scholemaster also exerted an important influence, beneficial in some ways, in others perhaps not so salutary as that of *Toxophilus* had been, on the development of a mature expository prose style in English. Among those who profited from Ascham's example was Sir Philip Sidney, whose *Defence of Poesy* owes far more to him, intellectually as well as stylistically, than has been generally granted or noticed by the critics. Even the English prose of Bacon, despite his contempt for Cambridge Ciceronianism, echoes more of Ascham's style in the early *Essays* and *The Advancement of Learning* than their author would have cared to own. Finally, *The Scholemaster* is noteworthy in the history of criticism for Ascham's theories concerning the drama, for his pioneering attempts at systematic analysis of literary style, and for his popularization of the doctrine of imitation.

With regard to Ascham's other works, his Latin correspondence seems to have been in remarkable demand. It went through four posthumous editions in Elizabethan England, plus three more in Germany early in the seventeenth century. No other Tudor writer, with the possible exception of St. Thomas More, received such acknowledgment of his quality as a Latin epistolist. The *Report of Germany* and the remainder of his published writings, the latter consisting principally of occasional verse and theological works in Latin, were never reprinted and were not so widely known. Still, the *Report*, though fragmentary in its surviving state and restricted to a single undated edition, is the most promising bit of English historiography to appear before the works of Bacon and Sir John Hayward. Finally, Ascham's theological tracts and few efforts in Latin verse, while not otherwise remarkable, at least add illuminating details to his own biography and to the record of the circle of Tudor scholars and statesmen among whom he lived.

Despite his considerable stature as a literary and historical figure, Ascham has been dealt with only in partial studies by modern scholars. Except for Alfred Katterfeld's volume in German, published more than eighty years ago, no critical biography has ever been attempted. In English, the most significant account of his life and writings has been Samuel Johnson's *vita*, written anonymously in 1761 to help sell the Reverend James Bennet's edition of Ascham's *English Works*. The following biography is an attempt to present the story of Ascham's life accurately and sympathetically, to trace the generation of his three principal English works from his reading, his personal experience, and his letters, and to assess his contribution to the intellectual heritage and prose literature of Elizabethan England.

❧❦

CHAPTER TWO

In That Most Worthy College
of St. John's

ASCHAM WAS BORN in either 1515 or 1516 at Kirby Wiske, a tiny village six miles south of Northallerton in the North Riding of Yorkshire.[1] Of the village as he knew it, nothing but the parish church remains; yet its character seems to have been little altered by time. Separated from the main road to Northallerton by the broad bottomlands of the River Wiske, its two quiet streets with their mere score of buildings winding away from the ancient church and grammar school, it gives an impression of unchanging remoteness. Besides Ascham, it has produced only two other men of note, the seventeenth-century scholars and bishops George Hickes and William Palliser.

As obscure as his birthplace are Ascham's ancestry and family connections. Formal parish registers were not maintained in Kirby Wiske before 1615, nor does the surname Ascham occur in those that were kept subsequently.[2] Edward Grant, in the earliest account of Roger's life, reports that his father, John Ascham, was steward to Henry, seventh Baron Scrope of Bolton (III, 307). Scrope, whose formidable castle at Bolton in Wensleydale was later to hold Mary Stuart after her flight from Scotland, fought at Flodden and once more against the Scots in 1522.[3] Thus, to the small son of his overseer, Scrope may have been a living symbol of the military prowess of the English, whose invariable victory over their northern enemy by means of the longbow is celebrated in *Toxophilus*.

Roger's mother, according to Grant, was named Margaret and was "related in descent and blood to many gently-born men" (III, 307).

Who these relations were Grant does not tell, nor does Ascham anywhere identify them. They may have been a family named Conyers,
since for a time Ascham shared his rooms at Cambridge with a wellborn relation of that name.[4] But whether his mother was herself a Conyers is not certain, for nowhere is there mention of her maiden name.
Only once does Ascham give any clue that he had important family connections. Early in his career he wrote a note of thanks for a benefaction
to an unnamed kinsman; the language and tone of the letter, though it
ends on a note of familiarity, suggest that he was addressing someone
who was not only a benefactor but also his social superior.[5]

Grant attributes to John Ascham genuine concern for the good breed-
ing and education of his children. He praises him, too, for "integrity of
life, gravity of manners, honesty, prudence, and modesty" (III, 307).
Although such characterization of the parent is conventional in the
demonstrative oration extolling a famous man, it is supported by the
pious respect and seriousness with which Roger heeded his father's
counsel during a crisis in his university career.

In material matters, however, the elder Ascham was less help to his
son. The one surviving fact about his business affairs concerns his difficulties in running a farm that he had leased at Newsham, directly across
the river from Kirby Wiske. For several years before Roger's birth, a
spate of bad luck left him hard put to meet the terms of the lease. In
1508, his landlord, Robert Lascelles of nearby Breckenbrough Castle,
asked the executors of his will to come to some fitting agreement for
the tithes with John Ascham, who in "times past" had sustained "loss,
and had no corn in the fields."[6] Apart from this, we know nothing about
the family's fortunes; one can only surmise from Roger's continual search
for patronage during his years at Cambridge that he could look for small,
if any, ready money from home. According to his own account, moreover, his sole inheritance upon his parents' death consisted of "a very
small legacy" (I, 67).

Besides several sisters, Roger had two brothers, one older and one
younger than he, both of whom also went to Cambridge. Thomas, the
elder, was admitted to St. John's College soon after its foundation in
1516, around the time of Roger's birth. He took the degree of bachelor
of arts during the academic year 1521–22 and was elected fellow of the
college in 1523. He seems to have resigned his fellowship in 1527 to
take up residence at Gray's Inn.[7] By 1543, or at the latest by early 1544,
he had died; he was, Roger declared in a letter to his friend John Cheke,

THE FAMILY OF ROGER ASCHAM

This genealogical table has been constructed from the scattered available evidence; the facts upon which it is based appear in the relevant places throughout the text. Thus far it has proved impossible to trace Roger Ascham's ancestry beyond his parents, or his descendants beyond his two known grandsons.

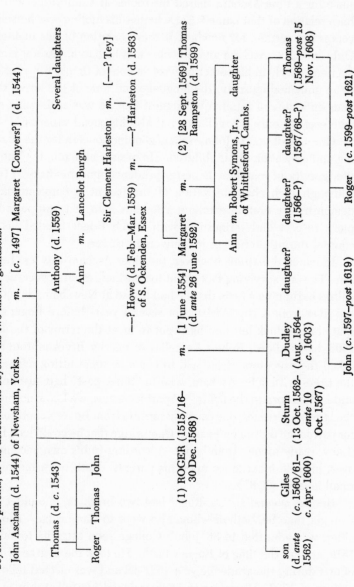

"such a brother as not only our family, but England, had scarcely ever produced" (I, 47). Thomas left three sons, Roger, Thomas, and John. In September 1544, the younger Thomas matriculated, like his father and uncle before him, at St. John's College. Nothing further is known of these nephews of Roger Ascham.

Roger's younger brother, Anthony, may be identified with fair certainty as the Cambridge physician and astronomer who wrote *A Little Herball* (1550), *A Lytel Treatyse of Astronomye* (1552), and several almanacs. This Anthony Ascham entered the university in 1532 and studied medicine for eight years, receiving his baccalaureate degree in the year 1539–40. During the same academic year, Roger Ascham offered pledges to the proctors of the university in order that Anthony might be exempted from the requirement of delivering a course of lectures, presumably in medicine, in the schools.[8] In 1552, Edward VI appointed Anthony vicar of St. Lambert's Church in Burneston, a village four miles from Kirby Wiske. In the same year, he received a second benefice, the rectorship of Methley, near Leeds.[9] Anthony continued to publish almanacs until 1557 and died in 1559.[10] He seems to have married and left at least one child, for later in the century one Ann, daughter to "Antony Askham," is recorded as the wife of Lancelot Burgh, of Brompton-on-Swale, Yorkshire.[11] Apart from the assurance that Roger put up for the exemption from lecturing and, in 1551, a request that a friend at St. John's deliver a letter for him to his brother, no further information exists about the relations between the two Aschams.[12]

II

In keeping with his reputed zeal for the proper education of his sons, John Ascham seems to have placed Roger at an early age in a local grammar school, perhaps under the tuition of the parson at Kirby Wiske, Robert Wensley. Here the small boy would have begun his study of Latin according to the traditional method of rote learning and "making Latins without book" that he later attacked in *The Scholemaster.* "I remember, when I was young," he recollects, "in the North they went to the grammar school little children; they came from thence great lubbers, always learning and little profiting; learning without book every thing, understanding within the book little or nothing" (III, 170).

By singular good fortune, he escaped emerging a "great lubber" himself, for his father was able to place him in the model household of Humphrey Wingfield, a Suffolk lawyer and royal commissioner, future knight and speaker of the House of Commons. Sir Humphrey, a member of one of the most considerable landholding families in East Anglia, was uncle to the better-known privy councillor Sir Anthony Wingfield, with whom he has been confused by several of Ascham's biographers, among them Grant (III, 308). He was distantly connected with the Scropes, the widow of one of his numerous brothers having married John, fifth Baron Scrope of Bolton.[13] Further, Elizabeth Scrope, daughter of John Ascham's employer, held Nayland Manor, which stood within ten miles of Humphrey Wingfield's holdings in southeastern Suffolk.[14] Possibly his duties as steward would have taken the elder Ascham on journeys to this estate, in which case the connection may have helped him to place his son in the Wingfield household.

Roger's new home was situated near the village of Brantham, either at a house called Bridge Place or at the moated manor of the Wingfields known as Brantham Hall.[15] Here, in pleasant farm lands sloping southward to the estuary of the Stour, Sir Humphrey saw to the education of his own and other men's children. The establishment had an excellent reputation among contemporaries. Children sent there from other families were treated as the equals of Sir Humphrey's own sons, and the household was evidently patterned after that of the master's professional associate, St. Thomas More.[16] The children studied Latin and some Greek under a capable tutor named Robert Bond. Since the name does not occur during the sixteenth century in the published records of either university, this may have been the Robert Bond who received a bachelor's degree at Cambridge in 1492–93.[17] Whatever his background, Bond was specified as "clerk" in official documents in which he was mentioned. In recognition of his abilities, he was made rector of Carleton and Martelysham in Suffolk, and in July 1532 was designated a royal chaplain. Perhaps as an acknowledgment of his value as a tutor, he was permitted, at Sir Humphrey's request, to remain in the Wingfield household in spite of his appointment at court.[18]

In this favorable environment, young Roger Ascham seems to have flourished. Besides taking eagerly to his regular lessons, he developed, says Grant, a keen taste for English books and read as many of them as could be come by in a Suffolk manor in the 1520's (III, 308). What this reading consisted of can only be surmised. In his own writings, Ascham mentions few English authors, and not many of these were in print during his boyhood. The two with whom he shows most familiarity are Chaucer and Malory, and it may be that already as a boy he had come to appreciate that talent for lively description and insight into character for which he praises Chaucer in *A Report of Germany* (III, 6). At this time, too, he may have chanced upon *The Four Sons of Aymon*, the memory of which returned to him in 1550, when he visited Cologne cathedral and heard again the legend of the part taken in its erection by Reynaud of Montauban, hero of this popular prose romance.[19] And perhaps among the volumes in Sir Humphrey's library he found the *Boke of St. Albans,* which included "The treatyse of fysshynge with an angle," one of the models for his own *Toxophilus.*

Whatever the nature and extent of this childhood reading, it acquainted Ascham early and quite thoroughly with English literary prose, and it was largely his awareness of both its possibilities and its shortcomings that prompted him to write in the vernacular, rather than in Latin, the first of the books upon which his own fame now rests. Without this youthful predilection for literature written in his native tongue, he might have been turned away from English by his later enthusiasm for classical studies and, like his friend Walter Haddon, who did choose to write in Latin, have been forgotten by later generations.

Besides providing an excellent tutor and a supply of books for the children entrusted to his care, Sir Humphrey concerned himself personally with their physical training. "At term-times," Ascham reports, "he would bring down from London both bow and shafts; and, when they should play, he would go with them himself into the field, and see them shoot; and he that shot fairest, should have the best bow and shafts; and he that shot ill-favouredly should be mocked of his fellows, till he shot better" (II, *Tox.*, 135). Ascham never forgot and could not sufficiently praise this benefactor who so humanely brought up his charges to be skilled "in the book and the bow." Not only did Sir Humphrey teach him the meaning of gentleness in education by providing instruction that was both effective and pleasant, but he instilled, at least in this one boy from Yorkshire, an abiding interest in archery that led to his first published literary effort.

III

Ascham does not tell how long he remained in these congenial surroundings, but at the age of fourteen or fifteen he left the Wingfield household to enroll in the university. Cambridge, in 1530, was just beginning to come of age. Already forming was that group of scholars who were to bring it the great reputation it enjoyed during the middle years of the sixteenth century. Had Ascham come upon the scene a generation earlier, he would have found himself in a far less stimulating atmosphere. At the close of the Middle Ages, most of the intellectual energy of the university was still being expended on analysis of Scholastic texts and commentaries upon Aristotle.[20] Those Cantabrigians who had traveled abroad during the fifteenth century to continue their studies on the Continent had been interested mainly in civil and canon law. They seem, most of them, to have been either oblivious to the progress of the new learning at such universities as Bologna and Ferrara, or else unconcerned with the possible effects its introduction might have on the intellectual life of their own academy. Certainly they returned with few of the books that had set the minds of their Italian counterparts on fire. Apart from two recorded copies of Petrarch and one of Ficino's commentaries on Plato, the university and college libraries at the opening of the sixteenth century boasted practically none of the works associated with current humanism.[21] Still in greatest evidence were the standard professional works: service books, Bibles, Aquinas, the commentaries of Duns Scotus and Alexander Hales, and the codes of civil and canon law. Only a few scholars owned copies of Virgil or Seneca, Galen and other medical writers were hard to come by, and it was equally difficult to obtain access to the texts of Aristotle.[22] While Oxford, through the efforts of Latimer, Linacre, Grocyn, More, and Colet, was becoming noted as a center of the new learning, Cambridge apparently remained content with the old studies and was unmoved by, or contemptuous of, the excitement occasioned by the introduction of Greek at the sister university.

By the 1520's, the atmosphere had altered. Erasmus, it is true, had met with little immediate success when he attempted to read Greek publicly during his tenure as Lady Margaret professor of divinity from 1511 to 1513. And only a small, unreceptive audience had come to hear him lecture on the grammars of Manuel Chrysoloras and Theodorus Gaza.[23] Yet in spite of his personal failure to arouse interest in Greek, within six years of his leaving Cambridge a salaried reader in the language had been appointed. By this time, familiarity with his *Novum Instrumentum* (1516), which demonstrated the advantages of Greek for scriptural studies, prompted students of theology to attend the new lectures in earnest.

During the same period, other humanistic studies were beginning to attract notice. In her statutes for Christ's College (1506), the Countess of Richmond included a specification that lectures were to be given "on the works of the poets and orators."[24] In 1518, Sir Robert Rede established a university lectureship in Terence.[25] And soon after, John Fisher, Bishop of Rochester, revised the original statutes for St. John's by providing salaries for readers of Greek and Hebrew in the college—several years before Henry VIII founded university professorships in the same languages.[26]

Also in the 1520's, the Reformation was gaining its first supporters in Cambridge. Since the new doctrines were unorthodox and could not be discussed openly in the schools, small groups of scholars were meeting secretly in their chambers, or at inns, to examine the teachings of the Lutheran reformers. The members of this new religious party in the university, contemptuously dubbed "Germans" by their colleagues, soon became quite numerous and were quietly promoting the cause of the Reformation in the colleges long before the official breach with Rome in 1534.[27]

Such were the first stirrings of the intellectual and religious changes that were to take place in Cambridge during the second quarter of the century. Although the traditional curriculum and religion continued to be officially maintained and to have strong support among the resident scholars, the predominant mood of the university at the time of Ascham's arrival was one of innovation and change, an atmosphere that he thoroughly enjoyed. Throughout the 1520's, Thomas Bilney of Trinity Hall, Thomas Cranmer of Jesus College, and Hugh Latimer of Clare Hall had been preparing the ground for religious reform. By 1530, Matthew Parker, later Archbishop of Canterbury, and Nicholas Ridley, Ascham's future friend, were also inclining toward the party of reformation. At the same time that religious controversy was stimulating intellectual activity, classical studies were attracting some of the best minds of the university. Already on hand, or soon to arrive, were a group of scholars who did much to stir up interest in the learned tongues: the Wakefield brothers, Robert and Thomas, in Hebrew; John Redman, Walter Haddon, and George Day, in Latin; Thomas Smith, John Cheke, and again Redman, in Greek. With all these men Ascham became well acquainted, and through his friendship with Cheke, Smith, and especially Haddon, he came also to know, though less intimately, Thomas Wilson, the author of a pair of vernacular treatises on Ascham's favorite subjects, rhetoric and dialectic.

IV

Undoubtedly the most flourishing society in the university at this time was the College of St. John the Evangelist. St. John's had been established by the will of Margaret, Countess of Richmond and mother of Henry VII. In 1516 her confessor and executor, Bishop Fisher, formally opened the college, after persuading Henry VIII to observe his grandmother's wishes for its foundation. In his first statutes, Fisher called for an eventual total of fifty members, fellows and scholars, to live on the endowment. One-half the fellows and one-half the scholars were to be Northerners. Fisher, himself a Yorkshireman from Beverley, thus helped to establish at Cambridge a means to preferment for many able North countrymen like Ascham. By the same token, his provision inadvertently prepared the way for the strife between northern and southern members that plagued the college throughout the sixteenth century.[28]

Despite its newness, St. John's rapidly acquired a reputation for intellectual leadership. The list of members who distinguished themselves in Tudor times is impressive. There are twenty-six, perhaps twenty-seven, bishops, among them Edwin Sandys, Archbishop of York, and the elder Thomas Watson, one of Ascham's closest friends and a writer of Latin tragedies. Several members rose to prominent positions at court, the most successful of all being William Cecil, later Lord Burghley; others were Sir Anthony Denny and Sir Ambrose Cave, both of whom, like Cheke, eventually became privy councillors. Among literary men one finds, besides Ascham, the poet Sir Thomas Wyatt, who was one of the earliest scholars of the college; Sir Thomas Hoby, friend of Ascham and Cheke and translator of Castiglione's *The Courtier*; Abraham Fraunce, author of *The Arcadian Rhetorike*; Thomas Drant, Latin poet and translator of Virgil; and the writers Robert Greene and Thomas Nashe. Other members of note were the preachers Thomas Lever and Thomas Cartwright, and the scientist William Gilbert.

The greatness of St. John's is extolled in Nashe's preface to Robert Greene's romance *Menaphon*, in the same passage in which he pays tribute to the scholarship of Ascham. Borrowing his phrasing directly from *The Scholemaster* (III, 235), Nashe describes the college as "an university within itself" and the prime fountain of learning in contemporary England. Not content with maintaining her own excellence, this "pitying mother" also sent forth sons "to supply all other inferior foundations' defects"; Trinity College, for instance, was "aptly termed [by Ascham] *Colonia deducta* from the suburbs of Saint John's." It was, Nashe continues, the work of Cheke, Watson, Lever, Ascham, Redman, and their kind that established true scholarship in Cambridge, for their efforts "repurged the errors of arts, expelled from their purity, and set before our eyes a more perfect method of study."

The man under whose guidance St. John's thus flourished was Nicholas Metcalfe, archdeacon of Rochester, who held the office of master from 1518 to 1537. Metcalfe, though not a scholar himself, was evidently an ideal administrator and moderator for the college, united as it was by its members' zeal for learning and yet divided by their religious, intellectual, and regional differences. He was quick to see promise, and his talent for recognizing ability in others led the seventeenth-century antiquarian Thomas Fuller to compare him to Themistocles, who although he "could not fiddle, yet could make a little city a great one."[29] Educated himself in the old school and a staunch Catholic throughout his life, Metcalfe was nevertheless sympathetic toward the new Greek learning of the Renaissance, a discipline that many of his contemporaries of similar background associated with the spread of heresy. Whatever their religious leanings, he encouraged promising younger scholars and was often their anonymous financial benefactor. In his manner of bestowing charity, says Ascham in an elegiac passage in *The Scholemaster*, "this worthy Nicolaus followed the steps of good old St. Nicolaus, that learned bishop" (III, 234).

Within a few years of Metcalfe's appointment, St. John's showed a fivefold increase in its income, and its fellows had made an excellent record in theology, medicine, and logic. The college was also justly proud of the accomplishments and reputation of the men who held Fisher's readerships in Hebrew and Greek, Robert Wakefield and Richard Croke. Among those who would have heard Croke lecture were three men who had much to do with shaping the intellectual development of Roger Ascham: Robert Pember, John Cheke, and the highly regarded theologian and Latinist John Redman.

It was Pember, according to Grant, who first directed Ascham's reading in Greek at Cambridge and brought out his gift for the language (III, 310). Ascham's official tutor was a young fellow of the college named Hugh Fitzherbert, who supervised his pupil's prescribed reading and instructed both him and Pember, even though the latter was several years his senior, in sacred scripture. Both mentors respected Ascham's diligence and abilities, and the three continued to study together until Fitzherbert's untimely death in 1537. Thereafter, Ascham and Pember remained intimate even though the older man never gave up his support of Catholicism. They shared an enthusiasm for antique coins and other memorials of the classical world, and when Ascham traveled abroad in later years, he sent his colleagues descriptions of the Roman relics he had seen so that Pember could share in the excitement of his discoveries (I, 261, 280, 316–17).

Some measure of the happy relationship between Ascham and his two tutors may be gathered from Grant's oration. Under the guidance of Fitzherbert and Pember, Grant says, Ascham applied himself not only to philosophy, rhetoric, and "the sweetness of histories," but to drawing, singing, and playing musical instruments. Grant also quotes a letter of Pember's commending Ascham on the excellent epistolary style he had developed in Greek as well as on his beautiful penmanship (for which he is still remembered by calligraphers). The same letter provides further testimony of Ascham's proficiency in Greek, for in it Pember encourages him to continue the practice, begun while still under tuition himself, of instructing his fellow students in the language. The benefit of such teaching, Pember explains, is that "a single fable of Aesop thoroughly analyzed by you is more to your advantage than the entire *Iliad* even if you had heard it expounded in Latin by the most learned men" (III, 311). Ascham's precociousness soon came to the notice of the master and fellows of the college. They gave formal approval to his giving lessons in Greek and immediately saw that his penmanship was put to good use. From 1532 onward, as he boasted later, he invariably transcribed the official letters written by the senate of the university to the king and other eminent persons.[30] Even before he took his bachelor's degree, then, it seemed as though he were assured of a distinguished and prosperous future in the university.

V

If Pember gave him the initial encouragement, Cheke, Redman, especially through his application of Greek to scriptural studies, and, later, Thomas Smith of Queens' College, led him to real proficiency in the language. Redman, somewhat older than the others, had been an important pioneer of humanistic studies. Celebrated at Cambridge as the restorer of Cicero, his example had inspired in both Cheke and Smith their own zeal for the ancients (I, 294–95). Smith, too, was a brilliant and respected teacher, in some regards the best among English scholars of this period, though in contemporary opinion a lesser man than Cheke, the cynosure of the new learning in Cambridge. Borrowing an idea from Plato, Ascham describes the energy and accomplishments of this one man as transmuting the intellectual life of the university, much as the example of a single virtuous citizen may reform the thought and morals of an entire commonwealth.[31]

Even before his nomination to a regius professorship in 1540, Cheke had "read publicly without stipend," as Ascham wrote to Richard Brandisby, an absent fellow of the college, "through all of Homer, all of Sophocles, and that twice: all of Euripides, and almost all of Herodotus" (I, 26). In addition, he read Thucydides, Xenophon, Isocrates, and Plato privately to his friends (II, *Tox.*, 67). Upon his appointment as professor, he planned to lecture in the schools "on all the Greek poets, historians, orators, and philosophers." According to the same letter from Ascham to Brandisby, this ambitious undertaking was abandoned on account of an altercation with Bishop Stephen Gardiner, chancellor of the university, but not before Cheke had aroused true ardor for learning in his audience. So much was the study of Greek prospering that mere lads were now reading Plato and Aristotle in the original. Brandisby would scarcely recognize the university if he were to return, for now "Sophocles and Euripides are better known, than Plautus was in former times when you were here. Herodotus, Thucydides, Xenophon, are spoken of more and borne in more hands, than was Titus Livius then." Moreover, Ascham goes on, the same is true of Demosthenes and Isocrates, who were now receiving more attention than was once paid to Cicero and Terence. Nor was Latin meanwhile neglected, all of the best writers of the golden age of Rome being eagerly studied. Allowing for some rhetorical exaggeration, Ascham seems to be giving a fair picture of the revival of interest in classical literature that occurred under the stimulus of Cheke.

The dominant figure in the university, Cheke was also the strongest individual influence in shaping Ascham's taste in authors, educational views, ideals for Latin and English prose, and critical attitudes. There is more than flattery in his assertion toward the end of his life that John Cheke was responsible for all the learning he ever had (III, 83). The effect of their early association is everywhere present in Ascham's writings. Both were ardent Hellenists, and Ascham's preferences among the Greeks clearly echo his master's. Both hailed Aristotle as the wisest of philosophers and Demosthenes as the most accomplished of orators. Cheke educated Edward VI according to Aristotelian ethical and political principles and managed to satisfy Ascham that the *Nicomachean Ethics* was more suitable for the young king than even Xenophon's *Cyropaedia* (I, 226). So firm was Ascham's conviction of Aristotle's worth that he considered anyone who disliked his works to be well on the road to heresy and treason (III, 176–77). Again, though his own writings reflect more the style and thought of Isocrates, Ascham concurred in Cheke's wholehearted endorsement of Demosthenes. To make his work available to those who could not read it in the original, Cheke, according to his biographer John Strype, translated into Latin the orations in favor of the Olynthians, and those against Philip, Leptines, and Aeschines. His example led Ascham to bring up his own pupils, including Queen Elizabeth, on the last-mentioned of these famous speeches. And what Ascham claims to have regretted most about Cheke's eventual departure for court was that it prevented him from crowning his academic achievements at Cambridge with the lectures he had meant to give on these two authors (II, *Tox.*, 67–68).

Ascham's preference for Athenian over Roman dramatists also owed as much to Cheke's inspiration as to his own pride in being associated with the Hellenists. Cheke's lectures, supplemented by frequent conversations between them about the drama, introduced Ascham to both Euripides and Sophocles and led to one of his earliest literary efforts, a translation into Latin of the *Philoctetes*. Similarly, Cheke influenced Ascham's choice of reading in the Christian fathers. Whereas most of their colleagues admired St. Augustine above all other patristic writers, Ascham and Cheke preferred St. John Chrysostom. Soon after Cheke had rendered two of St. John's homilies into Latin, for example, Ascham seems to have undertaken a similar exercise. Early in 1544, he asked Cheke in a letter to return his copy of Chrysostom, which he needed in order to get on with some projected translation of his own.[32]

Further evidence of Cheke's role in Ascham's intellectual life may be seen in their mutual admiration for Herodotus and Xenophon. Ascham admired Xenophon for his vivid and pure style and for the wisdom of the educational system outlined in the pseudobiographical *Cyropaedia*; Cheke admired him so much that he made a practice of awarding copies of his works to outstanding pupils.[33] It is not known whether Ascham, who did receive other gifts from Cheke for scholarly accomplishment, was among those who benefited from this particular method of reward; but that he derived his great esteem for this author from Cheke seems likely. The same is true for Herodotus. Apparently, it was hearing his friend read from the descriptions of Egypt and the campaigns of Xerxes in the *Histories* that first gave Ascham the urge to travel (I, 221). He also adopted and maintained throughout his life Cheke's view that Herodotus was a superior historian to Thucydides. He took this stand because, like Cheke, he was at heart a rhetorician and based his preference on stylistic grounds. Though he admired Thucydides for exceptional skill in portraying "the inward disposition of the mind," he disapproved of the manner in which he ordered his materials and, citing Cheke's opinion as confirmation of the soundness of his own judgment, the artificiality and "outlandishness" of his diction (III, 6, 61, 264, 269).

Although Ascham's intellectual life centered in the new learning and in the brilliant companions at St. John's who were among its most distinguished exponents, he was not permitted to neglect the standard curriculum leading to the bachelor's degree. The traditional course of grammar, rhetoric, and especially logic, along with some philosophy, a bit of arithmetic, geometry, geography, and music, remained the principal academic fare in the schools and colleges. In the statutes for Christ's College, upon which those for St. John's were based, the typical program is outlined. Four lectures were given daily in the hall, one each on dialectic, logic, philosophy, and "the poets and orators." The texts normally expounded in Ascham's time were Priscian's grammar; Boethius, Cicero, and Aristotle on rhetoric; and for logic, the *Parva Logicalia* of Petrus Hispanus, based on the Aristotelian system. In the third and fourth years, students also heard natural and moral philosophy and some metaphysics, again with Aristotle as the prescribed text. Most of the lecturers, however, read not from Aristotle's own works, but from such commentators as Scotus and Hales, or from abridgements like Thomas Bricot's *Cursus optimarum questionum* (Basel, 1492) and *Logicales questiones* (Paris, 1494). Among the poets and orators, as the letter to Brandisby suggests, were Plautus, Terence, and Cicero, and probably something of Ovid and Virgil as well.

Every Monday and Wednesday at noon students engaged in "oppositions," or debates, on questions of Scholastic logic. On Monday, Tuesday, and Wednesday exercises in sophistry occupied one hour of the afternoon; at the same time on Friday a problem in philosophy was assigned. Every Friday morning from nine to eleven there was "a disputation in grammar."[34] For those who were interested, private readings in the Vulgate Bible and in Greek completed the weekly round of studies.

Limited though it may have been in scope and quality, the curriculum seems not to have proved distasteful to Ascham. Naturally he took greater pleasure in the Greek he learned privately, but only once, and that long after his Cambridge days, did he criticize the offerings of the schools. The passage occurs in *The Scholemaster*, where in elaborating his favorite theme that theories and principles are difficult to comprehend without concrete illustrations, he remarks that "Cambridge, at my first coming thither, but not at my going away, committed this fault in reading the precepts of Aristotle without the examples of other authors" (III, 232). The objection, it should be noted, is not to the dominance of Aristotelian thought within the university; it is rather against an error in method, the failure of lecturers to provide apt instances and analogies to clarify the more difficult passages in Aristotle's writings.

Yet even this fault, Ascham concludes, was soon corrected by the efforts of men like Cheke and, he might have added, himself. "The humanists," writes a recent historian of the English universities, "making grammar and rhetoric equal in importance to logic, shifted the balance among the subjects in the trivium, gave the arts course more content, and began the process which was to elevate it from the position of a handmaid to metaphysics and theology to one of a mistress in her own household."[35] The aim, therefore, of the reforming group with which Ascham became associated was not to destroy entirely the old learning at Cambridge, but rather to rejuvenate it by reintroducing into the curriculum those humane arts that the preoccupation with logic had virtually banished.

CHAPTER THREE

Some Worthy Manner of Living

IN THE AUTUMN of 1533, Ascham began his tenth term in the university. Having attended lectures and engaged as a "sophister," that is, disputed publicly in logic, for the prescribed length of time, at the end of the term he became a "questionist," the final step before receiving the baccalaureate. As a questionist, he stood available every weekday for a month to dispute logical problems with any challenger before the university examiners. Apparently he survived this preliminary exercise without undue difficulty, for on February 18, 1534, at the customary pre-Lenten exercises, he was admitted bachelor of arts.[1] Shortly thereafter, he was nominated for a fellowship in his college.

Considering his promise as a scholar, there should have been little question of his election. But during the same Lent, Dr. Simon Heynes, vice-chancellor of the university, and John Skip, future Bishop of Hereford, were appointed by the king to preach at Cambridge against the papal supremacy. Ascham, by this time clearly on the side of the "German" party, welcomed such evidently official support for his own opinions and, according to his account of the affair in *The Scholemaster*, ventured—among friends—"to speak against the Pope." In so doing, though he had the crown on his side, he impaired his own cause with several members of the college. The master and a number of the most influential fellows vigorously opposed the Reformation; even after the break with Rome several of them remained staunch Catholics. Some of them, consequently, found Ascham's temerity offensive and regarded his nomination with disfavor. The account of his close escape from rejection is a fine glimpse into the character of the master, Metcalfe, and into the inner workings of academic politics. "My talk," writes Ascham, came to Dr. Medcalfe's ear: I was called before him and the seniors; and after grievous rebuke, and some punishment, open warning was given to all the fellows, none to be so hardy as to give me his voice at that election. And yet for all those open threats, the good father himself privily procured that I should even then be chosen fellow: but the election being done, he made countenance of great discontentation thereat. This man's goodness, and fatherly discretion used towards me that one day, shall never out of my remembrance all the days of my life. And for the same cause have I put it here in this small record of learning. For next God's providence, surely that day was, by that good father's means, *dies natalis* to me, for the whole foundation of the poor learning I have, and of all the furtherance that hitherto elsewhere I have obtained (III, 234–35).

Obviously Metcalfe was not one to deny a fellowship to a promising scholar because of religious differences. But he may have had an additional reason for favoring this brash candidate, though Ascham emphasizes his absolute impartiality, in that they were both Yorkshiremen.[2] Whatever its motivation, the master's maneuver resulted in Ascham's election on March 26, 1534.[3] Perhaps this kindness of Metcalfe, along with that of another unwavering Catholic, Pember, was partly responsible for the tolerance and sympathy Ascham later displayed toward old friends who remained uncompromising foes of the Reformation.

Ironically enough, shortly after this episode, several changes that were already taking place in the religious and intellectual life of the university received official sanction. For one thing, Henry VIII's ecclesiastical reforms, limited as they were, did make life easier for the rapidly growing Protestant party. Then, in 1535, Bishop Fisher, imprisoned for refusal to take the oath of supremacy, was replaced by Thomas Cromwell as chancellor of the university. Although Fisher himself had not been opposed to the new learning, it is striking to note that as soon as he was gone, changes came in favoring the supporters of reform.

The altered spirit of the times was reflected in a series of injunctions issued by Cromwell in the name of the king. These injunctions required each college to maintain at its own expense daily lectures not only on Latin texts, but also on Greek literature. Divines were forbidden to read publicly from that standby of the Scholastic curriculum, the commentaries on the *Sentences* of Peter Lombard. Theological studies were to be based strictly on the text of the Old and New Testaments; every student was permitted to read the Bible privately and attend lectures on the scriptures. Since rejection of papal authority invalidated much of the canon law, the injunctions abolished lectures on the subject. Finally, they prescribed the "new Aristotle," along with such works as Rudolf Agricola's *De inventione dialectica* and Philip Melanchthon's commentaries upon Aristotle, as replacements in the arts curriculum for their Scholastic counterparts.[4] According to Grant, these changes, repugnant to many conservatives, enabled the religious and academic reformers to go direct to the fountains of learning, there "to drink plentifully, rather than follow up the rivulets derived from them" (III, 313).

For the next several years, the atmosphere was exceedingly favorable both to Ascham's own progress in Greek and Latin letters and to the furthering of his career. His chief objects of study were, not surprisingly, Plato, Aristotle, and Cicero; these three authors, Grant tells us, "he imitated wisely . . . and admired almost to the point of amazement" (III, 312). Under the stimulus of Cheke and Redman, he also spent much time with Caesar, Thucydides, Herodotus, Demosthenes, Isocrates, and sacred scripture, particularly the Pauline epistles. His tastes, in other words, conformed exactly to the ideals of the new humanism. Plato, Aristotle, and Cicero he read for the language and for their ethical and rhetorical doctrine; next in importance for eloquence were the historians and orators; St. Paul was the obvious choice for a friend of the Reformation. Nor did he neglect belles-lettres, in which he inclined, no doubt through the influence of Cheke and Watson, toward the drama rather than other forms of poetry.

During this time, Ascham continued tutoring his fellow students. Then, on July 3, 1537, he paid the university proctors the usual "grace," or fee, of five shillings and received his master of arts degree.[5] He now automatically became a "regent," and as such delivered a required course of lectures in the schools. This he did for a year, possibly for longer, since, owing to a shortage of lecturers, a statute enacted in 1538 specified that regents serve for two years after taking their degrees.[6]

Nowhere does he mention on what subject he lectured during his first year as a regent. By the summer of 1540, he had given three public courses, in dialectic, mathematics, and Greek, but which of these constituted his inaugural series is uncertain. Dialectic seems the likeliest choice, not only because of the emphasis at Cambridge upon logical studies that Francis Bacon was to find so irksome, but also because Ascham seems always to have been intensely interested in the subject. In 1538–39, moreover, he complained in a letter to Watson that other burdens thrust upon him by the university might require his asking a colleague to complete the final week of the lectures in dialectic for him (I, 6). Or possibly his special flair for Greek may have afforded him the chance to undertake a regular course in that language. A few years later he did claim that he had been "handsomely enough paid" to read it for several terms in the schools (I, 52).

Although it is not clear whether he delivered his first lectures on Greek as a regent master of arts or as an additional undertaking, the principal writer whose work he expounded is known. Sometime afterward, Sir Thomas Smith, who had been one of his predecessors as a lecturer, recalled that Ascham dealt chiefly with the Athenian orator Isocrates.[7] His memory is doubtless correct, for the influence of Isocrates is strong in both Ascham's English and Latin writings. Some corroboration of Smith's testimony appears in a letter Ascham wrote an unnamed friend, apparently in the latter part of 1538. He cannot thank the addressee enough for the loan of a copy of Isocrates, as well as for certain commentaries (made or owned by the friend's brother) on the rhetorician Hermogenes.[8] From these bits of evidence, it seems clear that Ascham's reading in Greek concentrated on the rhetoricians and orators, who, along with the dialecticians, remained his principal interest throughout most of his life.

In the same letter to Watson in which he mentions the course in logic, Ascham indicates that he also delivered at least one full series of lectures in mathematics. His many other academic duties considered, this evidence of a third course of public readings suggests either an abundance of talent and energy, or else a willingness, in his eagerness to get ahead, to assume far more responsibility than was wise in a promising young scholar. For besides lecturing, he continued as amanuensis to the academic senate, began tutoring regularly in his own college, and served as one of the university examiners of candidates for the baccalaureate degree.[9] This last office proved very irksome to him and led him to complain to Watson that he had been "practically coerced, rather than enticed" into accepting it, and that it constituted a real hindrance to his reading in dialectic. He seems, nonetheless, to have sought the third lectureship, for he mentions that if the recent election of a vicechancellor had not come out favorably, his "hopes about the mathematics had either been in vain or next to nothing" (I, 5). At any rate, his suit for the lectureship succeeded, and during each of the three terms of 1539–40 the proctors recorded payment of the sum of "twenty-six shillings eightpence to Master Ascham for the mathematical lecture."[10]

His lectures on mathematics need not be taken as evidence of an exceptional proficiency or interest in the subject. A regent master was expected to be capable of lecturing on any subject in the arts curriculum. Ascham does not mention the course either in a later enumeration of his services to the university (I, 50–51) or in the first letter he wrote to acquaint Johann Sturm with his personal character and scholarly interests (I, 183). His writings even suggest an aversion for mathematics. In *The Scholemaster*, for example, he maintained that excessive devotion to such studies rendered men solitary and "unapt to serve in the world" (III, 100). His three terms as a mathematical lecturer may thus indicate nothing more than willingness to try his hand at almost any task during an energetic and diversified early career.

In 1540 his teaching in the schools came to an end. During that year his lectureship in Greek was rendered superfluous by Henry VIII's establishment of a professorship in the language. Upon Cheke's appointment to the chair, Ascham retired to St. John's, there to serve as college reader in Greek for another ten years. This office provided him with an annual stipend of £3, a tiny sum compared with the £40 Cheke received as regius professor. Yet added to his fees for transcribing documents and official letters, plus the £6 allowed for his maintenance as a fellow of the college, it gave him an adequate, if not a handsome, living. At this stage of his life, he appears to have been in much the same position as his twentieth-century counterpart, the promising young instructor or assistant professor with many irons in the fire, seemingly boundless energy for a variety of tasks, and a sharp eye out for the main chance, a senior appointment and the security of an endowed chair.

II

In most respects, he found this a happy and rewarding time. He had every reason to expect a prominent academic or, should he take orders, ecclesiastical appointment. From his letters it appears that he was outstandingly successful as a reader and tutor, and that he was continually widening his circle of friends within the university. According to Grant, he was quick to win people's affection, for "he was gentle in character, frank and ingenuous in spirit; by nature he was mild and placid, affable in company, most faithful to his friends: honorable in his life, a man born for making fast friendships with good and learned persons, and especially adapted to winning over and conquering the affections of men" (III, 313–14).

Grant's characterization, of course, is again idealized to suit his purpose of inspiring the boys of Westminster to take Ascham's life as a model for their own. Considered in conjunction with other testimonies to his gentle and friendly nature, the portrait is probably correct enough in outline, but his letters and actions suggest that Ascham could occasionally show a less attractive side. For example, by modern standards (though not at all by Renaissance ones), his constant hunting after patronage and his flattery of those to whom he looked for favors is distasteful. Moreover, though in general a mild man and usually quite ready to conform to prevailing opinion, he displayed on occasion a surprising contentiousness, notably when he allowed himself to be caught up in religious controversies. He could also plunge into collegiate politics without considering the effect his conduct might have on his colleagues. More than once ill-timed outspokenness, when he talked against the papacy, involved him in difficulties.

Yet despite these occasional displays of rashness and quick temper, apparently no blunder he made, nor trouble he stirred up, ever led to the permanent loss of a friend or patron. Protestants appear not to have been put off by his open and affable association with Catholics, nor Catholics by his few tirades against the Roman "Antichrist." Curiously, during his earlier years, when he was aligning himself with Protestantism, he tended to be most intimate, his relationship with Cheke apart, with adherents of the old faith. Among his closest friends, even after they left St. John's, were Watson, Brandisby, and John Seton, all three uncompromising and outspoken supporters of Rome.

Seton, a fellow Northerner, was an older man than Ascham, and what drew them together was probably their mutual interest in dialectic. In contrast with his later accounts of conversations with Cheke and Watson, Ascham records nothing of those he must have had with Seton, who remained his correspondent until the 1550's. Yet if he gives no direct proof that he was a disciple of Seton in logic, the content and emphasis of Seton's widely used text, the *Dialectica*, could not have failed to provoke his interest and approval. Since the Latin eloquence he professed was regarded as complementary to dialectic, he would have found Seton's concentration on the arrangement of arguments a welcome supplement to other treatises, most of which had emphasized the initial logical and rhetorical step of *inventio* (finding the topics, or grounds, for disputation or proof).[11] As *Toxophilus* and *The Schole-master* amply demonstrate, Ascham possessed an exceptional talent, which Seton's doctrine may have helped develop, for logical and effective ordering of literary subject matter.

Another link between the two men was their mutual friendship with Watson (I, 60). Watson, apparently at this time the closest to Ascham of his three Catholic friends, shared with him an enthusiasm for the ancient drama and for composing English verses in classical meters. About 1540, while still in residence at St. John's, Watson translated Sophocles' *Antigone* and some passages from Homer. He was also the author of an original Latin play entitled *Absalom*, historically significant as the only surviving tragedy written in England before *Gorboduc*. Apparently a perfectionist, he circulated this work only among friends and would never allow its publication or performance; according to Ascham, Watson was dissatisfied with the play "because *in locis paribus, Anapaestus* is twice or thrice used instead of *Iambus.*" Ascham goes on to claim that, setting aside George Buchanan's *Jephtha*, Watson's was probably the only tragedy of modern times that could "abide the true touch of Aristotle's precepts and Euripides' examples."[12]

Although his good judgment may be doubted, Ascham did not make this extreme claim for his friend's work through want of knowledge or experience. During this period at Cambridge he had frequent opportunities of seeing revivals of classical plays, and there were sufficient performances of new plays to enable him to measure them against ancient practice and the observations made by Aristotle in the *Poetics*. For several weeks after Christmas, the colleges staged dramas regularly and sometimes quite elaborately. Upon Ascham, who had an appreciative eye for color and spectacle, these performances made a lasting impression, for when he visited Antwerp in 1550, he wrote that the city exceeded in splendor all others that he had ever entered "as far as the hall of St. John's exceeds its usual self when decorated after Christmas in the manner of a theatre" (I, 212). Although he nowhere mentions what plays he saw acted in that hall, he may have been present when Aristophanes' *Plutus* was given in Greek in 1536. He may also have arrived at the college early enough to see performances of Thomas Arthur's lost moralities, *Microcosmus* and *Mundus plumbeus*.[13] Still another production he may have attended was that of *Jephtha*, a tragedy in Greek written about 1544 by another of his friends, John Christopherson.[14] Then almost certainly he knew about, though he may not have read or seen, Thomas Kirchmayer's antipapal *Pammachius* (1538), the performance of which at Christ's College in 1545 incurred a rebuke from Chancellor Stephen Gardiner and another from the privy council.[15]

During these golden Cambridge years, as Ascham recalls toward the end of his life, he and Watson and Cheke held "many pleasant talks together" on the relative merits of the various ancient playwrights, the nature of dramatic imitation, and the possibility of writing respectable English poetry in quantitative meters instead of rhymed verse (III, 241, 249). Through Watson and Cheke, Ascham became familiar with all the available Greek and Roman drama, as is evidenced by widespread and frequent quotation in his earlier writings. It was also conversation with them that inspired him in 1542 to attempt his own Latin version of the *Philoctetes,* a fitting enterprise for an enthusiastic archer and the future author of *Toxophilus.*

His own comment regarding his method of translating this play is worth citing. Since he was rendering the work into Latin, he set out to imitate the Roman dramatist Seneca (presumably in style and diction); at the same time he endeavored to follow in every verse the exact meter employed by Sophocles (I, 32). His success cannot be judged, for the translation, if ever he did complete it, was never published, and no record of a manuscript containing such a play exists.[16] Yet the effort and his comments on it are of some significance. Besides anticipating the Elizabethan predilection for Seneca, he gives a preview of his later concern with the doctrine of imitation as expounded in *The Scholemaster.*

Finally, it seems to have been his friendship with Cheke and Watson that led him to the *Poetics.* Thus, these conversations among the three men are something of a landmark in the history of English literary criticism; for Ascham's observations on Watson's *Absalom* are the earliest reference in English to this work of Aristotle's and the earliest effort to apply its principles to a tragedy composed in England.

III

If Ascham's first ten years at Cambridge were on the whole a time of reasonable hope based on youthful precociousness, the ensuing four years brought almost nothing but disappointment. Much like one of the metaphorical trees by which he characterizes the overready of wit in

The Scholemaster, he had apparently turned out to be one of those "that show forth fair blossoms and broad leaves in spring-time, but bring out small and not long lasting fruit in harvest-time; and that only such as fall and rot before they be ripe, and so never, or seldom, come to any good at all" (III, 99).

He began, for one thing, to taste some of the bitterness of academic politics. Although his personal experiences and relationships had been generally fortunate, he did not escape entirely the consequences of the growing faction at St. John's. Foreshadowings of subsequent ills had already appeared in the elections of the two immediate successors to Metcalfe in the mastership. After the break with Rome, Metcalfe's position became increasingly difficult, especially since he had been closely associated with Bishop Fisher. In July 1537, probably under pressure because of his unflinching Catholicism, he resigned to make room for a master more acceptable to the court. Henry VIII nominated George Day, a fellow of the college and public orator of the university. Day was a logical choice, since he had a fair reputation for scholarship, and he had publicly maintained the crown's right to supremacy over the English church. Yet in spite of his obvious suitability, his colleagues chose to ignore the king's will, electing instead Metcalfe's friend Nicholas Wilson, a Yorkshireman and staunch anti-Protestant. When Wilson, alert to the dangers of assuming office under such circumstances, wisely declined, the fellows became aware of their imprudence and hastily altered their vote in favor of Day.[17] Within the year, however, they again had to "choose" a new master, for Henry VIII decided to make Day provost of King's College. The privy council then ordered the election of John Taylor of Queens', future Bishop of Lincoln. On July 4, 1538, the fellows grudgingly cast a unanimous vote for the new candidate, not daring to cross the royal will again and asking only that their new head "be allowed to preside over the college in person."[18]

At first Ascham was impressed by Taylor's qualities as master, praising him in particular for the gentle and prudent methods by which he managed to keep the restive society quiet.[19] But Taylor was not able to maintain peace for long between the opposing parties. An avowed Protestant, he was hardly acceptable to the large body of Northerners in the college, who remained firmly conservative in their religious views; a kindly and moderate person, he lacked the forcefulness to keep the more hot-tempered radicals in check.

In spite of his expressed approval of Taylor, Ascham himself helped on more than one occasion to make trouble in the college. Early in 1540, four candidates, among them a pupil of his named John Thomson, were nominated to fill a vacated fellowship. Although Cheke favored Thomson, several of Ascham's other friends, among them Redman, Seton, and Watson, had recommended another man to fill the vacancy. In order to secure the necessary votes for his protégé, Ascham appealed in writing to several of the fellows, and went so far as to look for extramural support. Two of the letters have been preserved; one of them is to Taylor himself. In the other, to his colleague Henry Cumberford, Ascham maintains that although all the candidates are worthy men, there is one compelling argument in favor of his own: the others, in particular the man backed by Redman, Seton, and Watson, will be able to gain suitable preferment elsewhere, whereas Thomson will be left destitute unless he is elected (I, 12).

In the end, Thomson secured the fellowship, but it was a Pyrrhic victory for Ascham. However innocent his intentions may have been, he had helped to create new bitterness in the college, and into the bargain, he lost for some years the good will of John Redman.[20] Nor was this the only time that Ascham added to Taylor's numerous difficulties. Four years later, as he confessed to Cheke, he caused further trouble by proposing another pupil of his, William Grindal, for one of the readerships in the college. But this time the campaign was unsuccessful (I, 53–55).

Ascham did manage, however, to escape entanglement in the bitterest contest between Taylor and his opponents among the fellows. Finding himself unable to maintain order by means of gentleness and compromise, Taylor at length expelled three members of the college who were backed by the Catholic party. In April 1542, the supporters of the expelled men, among them Seton and Watson, retaliated by asking Thomas Goodrich, Bishop of Ely, in whose jurisdiction the college lay, for a visitation. Goodrich came to the college at the beginning of May to investigate the situation. His recommendations led to a truce, under which Taylor managed to remain in office until 1547, when he willingly resigned in favor of a close friend of Ascham's named William Bill.[21]

Although he was on hand for the unpleasantness of the investigation, Ascham had missed the outbreak of this dispute owing to an enforced absence from the college. During the winter of 1540–41 he left Cambridge to visit his parents.[22] Only once previously, in 1537, had he gone back to Yorkshire since matriculating at the university (I, 2). Either before he left Cambridge on this second visit to the north, or during his stay at home, he became seriously ill. Unable to shake off the attacks of a quartan fever, an affliction that was to plague him for the rest of his life, he remained with his parents for nearly two years. He was thus spared the unhappiest part, if not the consequences, of the strife between the fellows and master of his college. On the other hand, as he complained more than once, he was forced to languish in Yorkshire, cut off from "serious studies and all the delights of the Muses" (I, 25). In his own view this long absence marked the downturn in his academic career, causing him to miss precious opportunities for advancement (I, 18). If the letters he wrote do not grossly exaggerate his predicament, not only did he now lack the means to continue his studies; he could not even raise sufficient money for the journey back to Cambridge (I, 21).

In these straits, he sought help from two prelates, Robert Holgate, Bishop of Llandaff, and Edward Lee, Archbishop of York. To Lee (remembered now chiefly for his attack on Erasmus, who had satirized him in the *Colloquies,* and for his controversy with William Tyndale, translator of the Bible), Ascham offered the service of his literary talents. He would be glad to help with any work the archbishop might desire to have edited or translated. There were, if his grace wished to have them at hand, excellent Greek *scholia* on the Pauline epistles worthy of being turned into Latin. On these Ascham wished to try his style, for his own benefit and for the advantage of others who could read no Greek (I, 19). Holgate's reaction to Ascham's request for assistance is not recorded, but Lee responded in the autumn of 1541 with the assurance of an annual pension of forty shillings. This was not a large sum, but when one considers that Ascham's stipend for reading Greek at St. John's was only £3, it seems in comparison not a mean one (I, 44, 58). No great obligation, moreover, appears to have been attached to the grant; Lee's reason for making it is not given, and Ascham had to try to "invent" services by which he might express his gratitude to the archbishop.

Sometime after returning to Cambridge, he began to prepare a suitable gift for his new patron. During his convalesence, he had evidently spent part of the idle time in studying St. Paul's epistles with the aid of various books of commentary. One of these was a *catena* of excerpts from Greek patristic writers made by, or at least attributed to, Oecumenius, a tenth-century Thessalian bishop. Oecumenius, besides his collection on St. Paul, reputedly wrote commentaries on Acts, the Apocalypse, and the catholic epistles; the *editio princeps* of his works had appeared at Verona in 1532. Ascham probably had turned to these recently published glosses because they helped his study of Greek and because the new theology that he favored relied heavily on the Greek fathers' interpretation of Pauline doctrine. Oecumenius's collection was a representative anthology in this kind, with selections from a number of well-known authorities, chief among them St. John Chrysostom.

Finding the collection to his liking, Ascham decided to try out his Latinity on the passages dealing with two of the briefer epistles, those to Philemon and Titus. The former he offered as a New Year's gift to John Seton at the close of 1542. The latter he had already dedicated sometime after the preceding May to Thomas Goodrich to commemorate a private conversation they had had during the bishop's visitation of St. John's.[23] Now, after having asked Seton's advice in the matter, he decided to rededicate the Titus to Lee, and accordingly carried a fine new copy of his translation to the archbishop's residence in London (I, 27–29, 43). Finding his benefactor ill and unable to receive him, Ascham sent in the manuscript with the following rather extravagant compliment: "May you, most illustrious bishop, receive the ancient bishop Titus, who I judge will be the more readily acceptable to you under that title because, as the church of Crete was once so well governed by Titus, so in our time we have discerned with what like care your lordship oversees that of York" (I, 28).

There can be no mistaking Ascham's aim in making this translation: as a demonstration of his beautiful penmanship and his mastery, by contemporary standards, of Ciceronian style, it might incline the archbishop to offer him some preferment. That this was his sole purpose is clear from the dedicatory letter in Seton's copy of the commentaries on Philemon. There he shows concern only with questions of style, certainly not with theological niceties, when he boasts, for example, that he has "followed Erasmus in all things, save only that instead of *rogo* I use *deprecor*, having that supreme authority M. T. Cicero, who says that we *deprecamur* when we do not excuse our deed, but ask forgiveness for transgression" (I, 24). Moreover, the epistle to Titus seemed to offer no major difficulties of interpretation, and Ascham, so far as he could judge himself, had interposed no controversial material. He had even tried to forestall any misunderstanding of his purpose by promising that if there were anything displeasing in the translation, he would "gladly acknowledge" his error.

But in spite of the inoffensiveness of the exercise, Lee was not at all pleased with it. As Ascham later informed John Redman, the archbishop did make him a gift of money, but he also returned the manuscript with the advice that the translator look to the comment made in the text upon I: 6. This is the verse in which Paul advises Titus to consider in choosing a bishop whether the candidate "be blameless, the husband of one wife, having faithful children, not accused of riot, or unruly." The offending passage, which Ascham was certain Oecumenius had quoted from the unimpeachable St. John Chrysostom, simply asserts that St. Paul regarded as heretics those who abhorred marriage and that he considered a married man perfectly capable of giving proper attention to his ecclesiastical duties. Evidently the conservative Lee objected to any mention of the existence of married clergy, even in the earliest centuries of the church, when, as Ascham suggested cautiously in his account of the affair to Redman, "certain things were allowed out of necessity, which, as the church matured and so to speak reached its nobler age, were rescinded in the councils of its prudent guardians" (I, 44).

In order to regain the good will of so important a patron, Ascham twice wrote letters of apology. He begged forgiveness for the error on the ground of ignorance, claiming, though disingenuously, that he was unacquainted with any writings which advanced the new religious teachings and that he "had never made use of any book concerning the Christian religion excepting the Psalter and the Greek New Testament" (I, 35). He promised to stay away from theological works and apply himself in the future exclusively to humane letters (I, 32). As proof of his sincerity, he offered to send his translation of the *Philoctetes*, but the archbishop seems to have given him no encouragement. He did not cancel the forty-shilling pension, but after this incident Ascham found it increasingly difficult to collect. More than once payment was overlooked at the specified times, and he was forced to beg for what was his by right. Early in 1544, he pleaded with Redman, who had the ear of Archbishop Cranmer, to help him secure the amount that had become due on the preceding Michaelmas, and expressed misgivings about his chances of receiving the forthcoming spring installment (I, 44).

Another source of discouragement was the blow suffered by Greek studies at Cambridge during this period. For several years Smith and

Cheke had been advocating a system of pronunciation that differed from the one used at Oxford and in the universities on the Continent. Italian, French, and German, as well as Oxford scholars, followed the pronunciation that had been brought to the West in the fifteenth century by such pioneer teachers as John Argyropoulos and Manuel Chrysoloras, who pronounced classical Greek as they would the Greek of their own times. The disadvantage of this manner of pronunciation lay in the fact that the spelling of classical texts had not altered to accommodate the sound changes that had taken place over the centuries, and, as a result, the letters and diphthongs η, ι, υ, αι, and οι had all acquired the approximate sound of *iota*.

Although many scholars uncritically adopted the pronunciation they heard from the lips of contemporary Greeks, Erasmus, in 1528, and Smith, taking up his ideas about seven years later, urged that every vowel and diphthong be assigned distinct phonetic values, on the ground that such values must have existed in ancient times. The suggested change, they hoped, would eliminate the confusion resulting from the accepted pronunciation. The work in which Erasmus framed his proposal was *De Recta Latini Graecique Sermonis Pronuntiatione Dialogus* (Basel, 1528), written in the form of a dialogue between Ursus and Leo, who discuss the values to be given to the vowels in both classical tongues. Erasmus goes into the matter thoroughly, even digressing to comment on the way in which peculiarities of modern European languages have affected the sounding of Greek and Latin in various countries.

Despite Erasmus's reputation and the reasonableness of his argument, little came of his proposal on the Continent. At Cambridge, however, Smith managed to introduce his reformed method successfully. He gained the support of some of the best scholars in the university, including Cheke, Redman (who gave prestige to the system by following it in his lectures on divinity), and John Ponet of Queens' College (Ascham's immediate predecessor as reader of Greek in the schools). Unexpectedly, Ascham at first sided with the "iotacists" and for some time refused to follow the new pronunciation in his public lectures. According to Smith, he even disputed its suitability with Ponet, though with a certain reluctance that was due, perhaps, to the commanding reputations of Ponet's confederates, Smith and Cheke.[24] Eventually the innovators did win him over, and then, as Smith says in a phrase which is the earliest recorded suggestion that Ascham inclined to be something of a weathercock in matters intellectual, he became "a most vehement defender" of the new system.[25]

The reformed pronunciation having been in use for some time, Bishop Gardiner, chancellor of the university, finally got wind of it. Rumors also came to him that the innovation was stirring up contention among the scholars. The truth appears to be that Smith's method had been widely accepted and that a few undistinguished opponents, perhaps members of the "Troyan" party that regarded everything about the new Greek humanism with suspicion, misrepresented its consequences to the chancellor. Whatever the merits of their accusation, in May 1542 Gardiner suddenly forbade use of the new pronunciation and threatened those who persisted in it with severe reprisals.

Smith's adherents were shocked and disheartened by this unexpected rebuff. As Ascham wrote in his letter to Brandisby, the interdiction had hindered Cheke's grand design of lecturing on all the extant Greek authors, and "practically all the ardor for mastering the Greek tongue has been utterly extinguished in our spirits." No one could now hope to understand the language when it was spoken or read aloud, all its sounds having been reduced once again to the single sound of *iota*; all would sound like "the idle chirping of sparrows or the hissing of serpents." Ascham's metaphor was doubtless appropriate and his complaint just. In an age when many students still lacked the texts themselves and depended on lectures for almost all their information, the approved, but far less distinct, pronunciation constituted a serious hindrance to the comprehension of works being read aloud and expounded. What made the prohibition even less intelligible was that it came from Gardiner, whose scholarship and authority the members of the university respected. Although the reformed pronunciation was eventually to prevail in England, for the moment the cause seemed lost, since, as Ascham punningly laments, the scholars may have had the better arguments, but Gardiner had the "superior" (that is, the winning) ones.

The ban on the new pronunciation could not but add to Ascham's growing uneasiness about his own future in the university. It is possible, though not at all certain, that he even contemplated leaving Cambridge. The antiquarian Anthony à Wood has made the unverifiable but tantalizing assertion that in the summer of 1541 Ascham petitioned the University of Oxford for incorporation as a master of arts; a later source places the request in the following year.[26] No other evidence of this petition has ever been found, and Ascham nowhere alludes to hav-

ing made such a gesture. Yet if Wood's claim is true, it could be taken
as an indication of an even earlier starting point for Ascham's discontent with his lot at Cambridge.

His restlessness was at its height by 1544, when he learned that both
his parents had died on the same day after having lived together hap-
pily for forty-seven years (I, 47, 272–73). The news was the more
shocking because his elder brother Thomas had also recently died. The
loss of his father moved him deeply and led him to question the fitness
of his life at St. John's. Before his death, John Ascham had somehow
learned of the new dissensions in the college. In a letter to Cheke,
Roger tells how his father, writing the Christmas before, had virtually
made him promise to leave Cambridge and dedicate himself "to some
worthy manner of living." He had further warned Roger that he and
his colleagues "by their contentions were exciting God's most deep
wrath and displeasure." Since these were, so to speak, his father's dying
words to him, Ascham took the admonition seriously. He confessed to
Cheke that he could discern only two courses open for him if he were
to show filial obedience. If peace could be restored, he might remain
in his college, for then in effect he would no longer be living in the contentious Cambridge to which his father had objected. But if the troubles
over religion and intellectual matters should continue, he would feel
obliged to withdraw at the earliest opportunity (I, 48–49).

V

In spite of his apparently troubled conscience and distress over the
condition of the university, Ascham was not really prepared to exchange
the academic for some other mode of life. At the time, neither church
nor court, the chief avenues to preferment for learned men in Tudor
England, attracted him. Though he once or twice contemplated taking
orders, he seems never to have considered at length the possibility of
an ecclesiastical career; as for the courtier's life, he feared its insecurity
and its allurements to idleness and vice. Nor was he at all inclined, as
he admitted himself, to relinquish the freedom and leisure he enjoyed
as a scholar to wait attendance upon some nobleman. His own accidental misfortunes and the present state of the university apart, he still
found his chief delight in study and in the companionship of learned
men.

Nevertheless, the ambivalence of his attitude toward Cambridge is apparent in two letters written at roughly the same time that he wrote to Cheke about the death of his parents. Early in the same year, Redman had come to him with an attractive proposal from Charles Blount, fifth Lord Mountjoy. Mountjoy wished to bring Ascham into his household in a double capacity, to serve him at court, possibly as secretary, and to tutor his children. Since Mountjoy stood high in Henry VIII's favor, joining his retinue might have proved the first step to a successful public career. The tutorship, too, promised unusual opportunities. Mountjoy was himself well-educated and owned an enviable private library. His father, a noted patron of scholars and a former pupil of Erasmus, had given the household a reputation for learning that was unrivaled, according to Ascham, except by "that one household of the Medici in Italy" (I, 36).

The chance to tutor under such conditions, particularly for a scholar unhappy in his college but not wanting too radical a change from his accustomed manner of living, was not to be despised. Yet Ascham firmly, though with cautious politeness, declined the offer. His excuse to Mountjoy was that he could not bring himself to trade the quiet and free way of life of the university for the bustle of the court and the burdens, however light, of service. To avoid giving offense by his refusal, he also pleaded prior obligations. Nothing, he claimed, could have attracted him so much as instructing Mountjoy's children, had he not committed himself two years previously to serving the Archbishop of York (I, 36–37).

In explaining his refusal to Redman, though he repeats the same excuses, he reveals his motives more candidly. Had he really wished to accept the offer, his vague commitment to Lee would have been no impediment. One real objection was that Mountjoy had not offered a stipend tempting enough to make the change worthwhile. Ascham granted that it was a reasonable salary and that money was not with him the fundamental consideration. Still, he said wrily, he had grown so hardened to poverty at Cambridge that he did not mean to sacrifice the leisure and freedom of university life for an income that could maintain him only slightly better while making greater demands on his time.

He had, perhaps, an even stronger personal reason for declining. Mountjoy had suggested that he come to court for a few months to see how he liked it. But Ascham was wary and hinted to Redman that if he were to return to Cambridge after a brief absence, people might

chide him for capriciously accepting an office in which he did not in-
tend to continue (I, 42). This concern for his reputation may account
better than anything else for his decision; in a single telling phrase he
betrays his worry that some of his colleagues are beginning to find him
wanting in serious purpose. "I have betaken myself for some years to
learning," he remarks, "if not with very great profit, yet with no small
pleasure" (I, 41). Apparently doubtful that he had lived up to the
promise of his youth, he dared not risk failure now in a new and uncertain enterprise.

He offers, finally, an excuse that seems almost incredible. Ascham,
who had been teaching for more than ten years, and who professed to
regard educating the young as the most rewarding and important task
anyone could undertake, denied his own fitness for the position. To instruct boys in grammar, he protests, when he had learned scarcely anything about it himself, was far beyond his powers and inclination (I,
42).

This excuse seems odd coming from the man who was to be tutor to
Elizabeth I and author of a treatise that bears the subtitle "Plain and
perfect way of teaching children, to understand, write, and speak, the
Latin tongue, but specially purposed for the private bringing up of
youth in gentlemen's and noblemen's houses." Yet in 1544 Ascham's
determination not to leave Cambridge on such terms was evidently
strong, for about the same time he also declined an offer to instruct the
children of Margaret Roper, best-loved daughter of Sir Thomas More.
He responded to Mistress Roper's proposal no more satisfactorily than
he had to Mountjoy's, though he did submit to an interview at the
home of her kinsman Giles Alington. The interview, however, was
apparently a mere courtesy, since some years later he told the Ropers'
daughter, Lady Anne Clarke, that at the time nothing on earth could
have induced him to depart from the university.[27]

Despite these protests, Ascham was not so enamored of his scholarly
leisure or so content with his meager income as he claimed in these
letters. He concludes his apology to Redman, in fact, by expressing an
eagerness to go abroad, perhaps as secretary to some ambassador. Lest
this be thought, he adds, a rash, adolescent dream, he would have it
clear that the desire had been in his mind for a long time, that he had
pondered the implications seriously, and that he really hoped that Redman would believe him and find him some such position (I, 45–46).
Nothing appears to have come of the hint, and Ascham began immediately to seek other means of advancement.

A few months after receiving Mountjoy's offer, he learned that Cheke was about to be appointed one of the tutors to the six-year-old Prince Edward. The appointment was confirmed on July 10, and Cheke assumed his duties soon after. Much as he regretted his friend's departure, Ascham saw in it a possible advantage for himself. With Cheke gone, presumably his regius professorship would become available, and people now began to speculate who his successor would be, a decision that lay with the king. Thomas Smith, who already held the professorship of civil law and was beginning to spend a fair amount of his time at court, was apparently out of the running. There were two other candidates, both with influential backing, but certain persons, Ascham claims, persuaded him to go to London to present his own qualifications for the chair.

When he arrived at court, he felt himself to be "the least known among the unknown" and had no idea where to turn for help. But just then Sir William Paget, secretary of state and currently the councillor highest in the king's favor, returned from a successful embassy to Charles V. Observing the honor with which he was received, Ascham decided that this man had appeared on the scene to be his own *deus ex machina.* So he wrote to Paget, setting forth as qualifications for the professorship his various services to the university and to his college, especially his long tenure as a reader in Greek (I, 50–53). Although the letter, even by Renaissance standards a masterpiece of commendation and supplication, seems to have impressed Paget favorably, at the time he was powerless to help Ascham. Cheke was allowed to retain the chair *in absentia* and did not resign it until 1547. Then, instead of Ascham, a Catholic scholar named Nicholas Carr received the appointment. To add to Ascham's chagrin when he was finally passed over, the fellows of St. John's would not let him occupy Cheke's more commodious rooms in the college, even though the chancellor of the university supported him in this request (I, 149).

As evidence of his talents, Ascham had mentioned in his epistle to Paget that he had in press a book *"de re Sagittaria,"* which he hoped to present to Henry VIII before the royal departure for the wars in France. The treatise would prove the usefulness of archery to the English in both peace and war and would teach them how to perfect themselves in this skill. He hoped that the effort would be "neither unworthy of my love for my country, nor an insignificant testimony of my inconsiderable learning" (I, 52). With these words he first describes his *Toxophilus* as it stood in a preliminary draft. On July 14, however, before the printing could be finished, Henry set sail for Boulogne, and Ascham called back the manuscript to revise it once more before the king's return.

This miserable year of 1544 ended for him as bleakly as it had begun. Shortly after Cheke's departure, Ascham's best-loved pupil, William Grindal, was nominated for a Greek readership in the college. The two men had long shared the same chambers, were constantly together in public, and were such good friends that their intimacy provoked a certain amount of envious criticism from their colleagues (I, 62). As Ascham recounted the affair of the election to Cheke, Grindal was supported by several of the "worthiest" fellows and seemed assured of the readership. But an opposition group suddenly formed, and as he claims, out of spite for the authority Ascham held in the college and jealousy of his deep affection for Grindal, had the impertinence to declare "that without our help they could and would appoint by their own free will whomever they wished" (I, 54). Accordingly, Grindal was passed over.

Ascham, feeling obligated to provide for his young friend, who could not subsist on his fellowship alone, tried to find him some other position. With Cheke's help, he eventually secured for Grindal the office of tutor to the eleven-year-old Princess Elizabeth. The appointment, though a great honor for the recipient and a vindication of Ascham's confidence in his abilities, did have one unhappy feature. It took Grindal away from Cambridge at a time when Ascham desperately needed his companionship to make his life endurable in the university (I, 74). So many of his friends had left to take up other appointments that he now had no near contemporaries to whom he could look for comfort.

He therefore turned for friendship to his younger pupils. He attached himself to his kinsman Thomas Conyers, who shared his chambers, and especially to his charges William Ireland and Edward Raven. In Ireland and Raven he strove to realize *pietas litterata,* the educational ideal of Christian humanism that he had inherited from men like Erasmus and Sturm (I, 74). As might be expected from the earlier discussion of his own literary interests, this meant that he exercised them chiefly in the writings of Plato and Cicero. For he held the common belief of the humanists that almost all learning is contained in the Greek tongue, "Cicero only excepted," and that among the Greeks, Plato was the greatest of philosophers (III, 134). Then, in order that the two young men might not become learned merely in pagan letters without acquiring true piety, he set them to comparing with the original Cheke's

Latin translation of St. John Chrysostom's six orations *De providentia Dei ac de Fato*.[28] By this procedure, resembling the method of imitation and double translation advocated later in *The Scholemaster*, he hoped that Raven and Ireland would not only improve their own Latin style and command of Greek, but also profit spiritually from exposure to the soundest and most eloquent of the fathers of the church.

VI

Meanwhile, he continued to think of his own career and to search for means of attracting the notice of influential patrons. On September 13, 1544, Archbishop Lee died, and Ascham was deprived of his one small pension. Looking now to the highest possible sources of patronage, he composed two poems in Latin, in honor of the Prince of Wales and the king, respectively. The exact date of the poem to the king is not known, but it was almost certainly written during the same autumn.[29] The poem to the prince, a song for his seventh birthday, may never have reached the court because Ascham, as he wrote to Grindal, was diffident about the merits of his literary "trifle" (I, 74). The poem links the birth of Edward with the beginning of a new cycle of years and the dawn of a golden age in Britain. "The Roman beast and its dogmatic filth" having been driven out, joy awakens, and the tabernacle of peace is restored to the land. The young child is a terror to the Scots and French, but he is the glory of his own people and his father's delight. The song concludes with prayers for a long and prosperous Christian life for the prince, as well as the hope that he may prove a benefactor to learning, especially to the University of Cambridge.

It is obvious that in composing his poem Ascham had in mind Virgil's "To Pollio," or at least the recurrent Neo-Latin theme of *Saturna regna*. Still, the little birthday song can scarcely be labeled Virgilian. Neither the imagery nor the language owes anything directly to the fourth eclogue, and the verses are not even in classical meters. Ascham instead employs a tail-rhymed stanza that is common in medieval Latin *cantilenae* and secular lyrics as well as in vernacular carols. He does, in fact, speak of his own effort as a "rime in the measures of the old carol *My little pretty one*," apparently a vernacular lullaby of the fifteenth or sixteenth century. Further, although most of the poem echoes the language and phrasing of sacred hymns, the opening lines curiously recall the spirit of the old drinking songs that Ascham had undoubtedly sung as a student at St. John's:

Profani cedite,
Procul hinc jam naeniae,
Procul hinc querimoniae,
        Luctus et odia.
Salibus et joculis
Fabulis et poculis,
Dapibus et epulis,
        Sint plena omnia.[30]

It is strange that Ascham, self-conscious humanist that he was, should have chosen rhymed, accentual verse for a poem meant as a compliment to the royal pupil of John Cheke. Not only did he write all the rest of his Latin verse in classical meters, but he also advocated and demonstrated their use in English. The later Ascham had only contempt for "rude beggarly rhyming," which he regarded as a pollution first brought in "by Goths and Huns" (III, 249). Possibly this fact accounts for his withholding the poem, and for his hesitation about showing it even to such a close friend as Grindal.

Of no greater literary merit, though more correctly classical in form and diction, is the other poem, "Ad Potentissimum Principem Henricum Octavum, Angliae, Franciae, et Hiberniae Regem." The dating of this poem rests on the reference to the king's golden sceptre as having "broken all your enemies," almost certainly an allusion to the sack of Edinburgh in May 1544 and the taking of Boulogne four months afterward. The poem extols Henry above all the famous ancient monarchs, since England's king unites all the royal virtues in his person. He excels all the pagan rulers even as Christ excels Jove. Indeed, after that of Jesus, no human condition is more worthy, and no authority more sacred, than that of Henry. Under God's providence, he has dispelled the "Babylonian plague" and restored to his people the holy gospels, "which long lay hidden in the shadows." He is divinely favored, for "Christ sits upon his sword, and upon his countenance." His subjects pray that he and his queen (Catherine Parr) may long reign over England (III, 277–78).

In these poems Ascham expresses an attitude toward the Tudors that had already been formulated by such historians as Polydore Vergil and Edward Halle, and that was just now beginning to make its appearance in the Latin verse of Walter Haddon and the antiquarian John Leland.[31] The poems of Ascham and these friends of his reflect a change that had occurred in English humanism after the Reformation: from the international movement it had been to More and his circle, it had become a Protestant and national concern. Learning, even more emphatically than for their predecessors, meant for Ascham and his contemporaries a preparation for devoted service to religion and the commonweal; for although the Reformation had brought about a decline of ecclesiastical influence in the government, religion and country were now more closely identified than at any previous time in English history. It had now become the function of the schools and universities not only to prepare young men for the church, but to train them for secular life as well, to imbue them with the piety, learning, and moral qualities necessary for serving God and England well. Hence Ascham's two poems, though conventional panegyrics with little else in them worth remarking, place him among the pioneers of this emerging messianic ideal that was to reach its climax in the far greater patriotic works of the Elizabethan literary giants.

Besides making this gesture toward the royal family, Ascham turned to the prelates Gardiner and Cranmer. Shortly after Lee's death, he asked Seton, who had become one of Gardiner's chaplains, to write a letter in his behalf, "in either Greek or Latin, or," since he wanted a special compliment paid to the Bishop of Winchester's learning, "in both the tongues." Although he could not have foreseen its consequences at the time, turning to Gardiner, along with the earlier inspiration to approach Paget, proved an extremely fortunate move. Before another year passed, these men would bring him to the presence of King Henry; upon Mary Tudor's accession, moreover, their support would gain him protection and advancement at a time when he might have expected little of either in view of his known adherence to Protestantism.

Early in 1545, he also approached Cranmer. The specific occasion for his doing so was a request he wished to make for exemption from the laws of abstinence during the coming Lent (I, 63–70). Like Erasmus, Ascham could not abide fish, and after his protracted siege of illness, he found the prospect of seven weeks of such a diet more than he could face.[32] In supporting the request, he draws cleverly upon his classical and patristic learning. He reminds Cranmer that abstinence from flesh meat on specified days is not a divine ordinance, but rather an ecclesiastical discipline founded upon custom; it is, besides, the antithesis of a religious observance recorded in the second book of Herodotus. According to Herodotus, the priests of ancient Egypt, men also dedicated to study and contemplation, were forbidden to taste fish, "lest the force and excellence of their wits be extinguished by some frigid humor, which the eating of fish engenders."[33]

While cautiously acknowledging that the Egyptian practice was a mere superstition, Ascham at the same time uses it to good rhetorical purpose in pleading his own case. Since such proscriptions can be traced through human, rather than divine, institutions, he hopes for exemption on what, according to the theory of the humors, are solid medical grounds: namely, that the wet spring season is the worst time for a scholar to eat fish. If the practice was interdicted in the arid Egyptian climate, how much more harmful must it be in fenny places like Cambridgeshire, how "unwholesome to the course of our studies, noxious to my melancholy disposition, and ever distasteful to my stomach." In order to avoid scandal, Ascham promises to use the dispensation discreetly. This favor he seeks not out of fastidiousness or greed, but solely out of a desire to rid himself of his melancholy and to build up his strength again. This he must do, for his health has become so decayed through his sedentary way of life, feeble constitution, and long illness that he can no longer pursue his studies with proper diligence.

What Ascham wrote is of course more than a plea for dispensation from the Lenten abstinence. Not that the request was only a pretext for writing; but the letter, unusually lengthy for a simple petition, gave him a chance to mention his abilities and at the same time to suggest that he would welcome patronage. Since he was unknown to Cranmer, the citation of Herodotus was a neat way of implying his intimate acquaintance with Greek authors. Lest the archbishop miss the point, however, Ascham offers to discuss the current state of learning in the university. In doing so, he manages along the way to cite the epistles of Cicero, the difference between the views of St. Augustine and the modern Catholic apologist Albert Pighius on predestination, and, in much the same manner as in the earlier letter to Brandisby, the superiority of several of the best Greek authors to their Latin counterparts. Although he gives all credit for the flourishing of scholarship at Cambridge to Cheke, he hints that were it not for two obstacles, others, himself included, might be making similar progress in their own scholarship. Unfortunately, their more recent pupils were lacking in zeal, and their colleges had become poor because certain persons apparently objected to the idea that any royal funds should go to the relief of needy scholars, again, obviously, like himself.

The supplication evidently achieved its purpose. Not long afterward Ascham wrote again to Cranmer, thanking him for the kindness with which he had received the petition, for granting the dispensation, and, perhaps most importantly, for relieving his poverty with a handsome gift of money (I, 72).

There is no reason to believe that Ascham was exaggerating his weakness of body and melancholy of mind. He seems really to have been struggling to regain his health, for fear of breaking down completely. Besides seeking a proper diet, he had begun to devote a considerable amount of time again to his favorite recreation, archery. Ever since his boyhood days in the Wingfield household he had kept up the practice in the fields near Cambridge, and even in open competition with townsmen elsewhere.[34]

As a means of rehabilitation, archery was a choice that any sensible physician, Renaissance or modern, might have recommended. Yet Ascham's return to it apparently supplied ammunition to certain people who had begun to snipe at him about the falling off in his scholarship. Not only did he seem to be neglecting his books, but now he was also wasting precious time on an exercise unbecoming to a master of arts of the university. There is no means of determining the source or the precise nature of this criticism, since Ascham is vague on the subject and shows only that he had suddenly become keenly sensitive to it. Further, his own worry at the time about his inability to concentrate on study after the illness in Yorkshire may simply reflect an excess of melancholy brought on by a discouragingly long convalescence.[35] For he was still reading widely, if sometimes indiscriminately, and during the same year mentions several books that he had been perusing in addition to the standard list given in the letter to Cranmer.[36] His correspondence also affords ample evidence that his especial enthusiasm for Greek had not waned.[37]

Nor does the fact that he published no edition of, or commentary upon, any classical or Christian writer prove him guilty of indolence or dilettantism. Neither specialization nor publication seems to have been an important criterion of accomplishment among his Cambridge contemporaries. In this respect, the output of even the most distinguished of his colleagues, including Cheke and Wilson, is negligible. A scholar's reputation depended, rather, upon his success as a teacher, whether by diligent tutoring or effective public reading he managed to inspire his pupils. After assimilating the best qualities of the ancients to his own manner of thought and expression, it was his duty to prepare his students, through the study of scripture and humane letters, for distinguished service to religion and the realm. To a large extent, the same was true on the Continent, scholars concerning themselves mainly with pedagogy and its immediately practical results. Though a number of the outstanding humanists, Erasmus, Budé, Scaliger, and Sturm among them, wrote learned treatises and edited or commented indefatigably upon classical texts, almost all of them claimed that their main function was teaching. Much of their publication, moreover, assumed the form of dialogues designed to introduce schoolboys to the mysteries of Latin, to treatises on education, and to grammatical, rhetorical, and epistolary manuals and source books.

Thus Ascham may have had somewhat less need and incentive than a modern university professor to vindicate himself by publishing an important work of scholarship. Still, in order to restore his own faith in himself by giving some public evidence of his attainments, he began working hard to prepare his treatise on archery for the press. Besides having failed to get it into print before the king's expedition to France, he had been caught short once again by the unexpectedly swift victory of the English army and Henry's sudden return home at the end of September 1544. But by mid-February 1545 he was well on with the task of revision. As he wrote to Grindal, he had even given up reading his favorite author, Herodotus, in order to speed his book to publication (I, 75).

CHAPTER FOUR

Toxophilus

TOXOPHILUS, *the schoole of shootinge conteyned in two bookes,* came from the press sometime during 1545.* Since one of his avowed ends was to gain some new and more generous patron to succeed Archbishop Lee, Ascham sent copies to a number of influential people at court. He dedicated the work to the king, from whom he hoped for a pension or, preferably, leave and maintenance to study "for some years in Italy and other transmarine lands" (I, 80–81). Other recipients were the Prince of Wales; William Parr, brother to Queen Catherine and Earl of Essex; the Lord Chancellor, Thomas Wriothesley; Sir Anthony Denny; Bishops Day, Gardiner, and Nicholas Heath; and probably Cranmer, Paget, and Prince Edward's young Irish companion, Barnaby Fitzpatrick.[1]

---

* The first edition (*STC* 837) was published at London by Edward White-church. Some earlier bibliographers speak of a 1544 edition (e.g., Robert Watt, *Bibliotheca Britannica*, Edinburgh, 1824, I, 49a), but their assumption seems to follow from a misreading of Ascham's report to Paget that his work was at the printer's during that year. On the title page of the second edition, moreover, appears the correct, but misleading, information, "written by Roger Ascham. 1544." Physical differences among copies of the 1545 edition suggest that parts of the work may have been typeset at different times during the course of publication, with certain gatherings in some copies left perhaps as they stood before Ascham recalled the manuscript upon Henry VIII's departure for France.

In 1571 Thomas Marsh brought out a new edition, apparently in two printings (*STC* 838 and 838.2 [W. W. Bishop, *Checklist of STC Books,* 2d. ed., Ann Arbor, 1950], since fols. D_1, D_2, D_7, and D_8 of some copies are set in a different type from that used on corresponding leaves of other copies. After Abel Jeffes published a third edition (London, 1589), *Toxophilus* did not appear again until James Bennet edited Ascham's *English Works* (London, 1761). The fourth separate edition was that of John Walters (Wrexham, 1788; reissued 1821). Since that date the treatise has been reprinted frequently, and extensive excerpts have appeared in books on archery and anthologies of English literary prose. In *English Works of Roger Ascham* (Cambridge, 1904), William Aldis Wright accurately reproduces the 1545 text.

Still honored by archers as the seminal treatise on their sport, and by literary historians as the most successful of early attempts to write a formal prose discourse in English, *Toxophilus* shows the touch of a man skilled in both his book and his bow. This twofold distinction was quickly noted by his friends. "He is not less illustrious with the bow," asserted his former tutor Pember in a Latin distich composed for the occasion, "than he is in both the tongues; thus he gives honor to, thus benefits his fatherland."[2] And in Latin lines prefixed to the work, Walter Haddon wrote: "The author is Ascham, whom Apollo made great in his art, and Minerva in hers. A skilled hand, a learned mind brought forth this little book."[3] Pember and Haddon hit upon the just compliment, for Ascham did want men to regard this endeavor both as an authoritative work on his favorite pastime and as a worthy product of his long devotion to humane letters.

The treatise, which is divided into two books, is a Platonic or, better, Ciceronian dialogue between the scholars Philologus, lover of study, and Toxophilus, lover of the bow. The first book is an extended apologia for shooting; the second, a description of the equipment and technique of the sport. In Book One, prompted by his friend's amused skepticism, Toxophilus defends his predilection for this pastime by showing it to be the most honest and advantageous of exercises. Citing numerous authorities and examples from modern and classical times, he demonstrates that all worthy nations, and especially the most highly civilized ones, have placed great value upon archery because of its benefits in peace as well as in war. The Persians, for instance, considered it essential in the upbringing of their princes and noblemen, as did Plato in the training of his ideal citizen. Its use is particularly recommended to scholars, who should take to it as an antidote to their sedentary manner of living. No other recreation, walking, or more strenuous and boisterous sports, or even music itself, is either so healthful or so proper for students. Its wholesomeness, its moderation, and the fact that it takes men out into the fresh air make it an ideal corrective for the temptation to spend their leisure hours in vicious pastimes such as "unlawful games and namely cards and dice."

This much of the argument, occupying half of the first book, is patently designed to meet the objection that Ascham's excessive devotion to shooting had been detrimental to his scholarship. The rest of Book One, concerned with the value of archery in warfare, adds further proof that he had by no means neglected his studies, but rather had put the knowledge acquired through extensive reading to the service of the commonwealth. Citing many of the most highly approved authorities, scriptural, classical, medieval, and contemporary, Toxophilus notes that from the earliest recorded times peoples skilled in archery—Persians, Greeks, Jews, Romans, Goths, Normans, Turks—have won military renown. No nation has been more celebrated for this art than England, which owed some of its greatest triumphs on the battlefield, even in Ascham's own lifetime, to the mighty longbow. This portion of the dialogue ends with Philologus capitulating and asking his companion to explain how a tyro may become master of so useful an art.

In the second book, Ascham continues, through Toxophilus, to display his classical learning, as well as his detailed knowledge of the craft itself. He writes lucidly and authoritatively, from personal experience rather than simply from reading, of the requisites for becoming a competent archer. This book, also divided into a pair of main sections, professes to contain all that is necessary to achieve the end of the sport; namely, hitting the mark by "shooting straight, and keeping of a length."[4] The first part deals with "things belonging to shooting," both those "proper for every sere [individual] man's use" and those "general to all men." Proper to the individual archer are the items of equipment —bracer, shooting glove, bowstring, bow, arrows. Upon the comparative merits of different materials used in making the gear, especially the bow and arrows, Toxophilus comments in loving detail. Since the principal matters common to all archers, studying the weather and sighting the mark, belong to the technique of shooting, he defers treating them until the final pages.

In the second part of Book Two, he discusses mastery of the process itself, which he calls "handling things belonging to shooting." The five basic steps are standing, nocking (fitting the arrow to the bowstring), drawing, holding (and sighting), and loosing the shaft. The final topic is the psychological disposition of the shooter, who must possess "bold courage" and inward calmness.

Dispersed throughout the work are digressions on politics, morals, and education, several of which are as appropriate today as they were in Ascham's time. In the first book there are four major digressions: on the state of music in Tudor schools, on the sharp rise of gambling and other forms of vice, on the growing threat of the Turks to a divided

Christendom, and on the desirability of union between England and Scotland. Of the digressions in the second book, that on the lack of judgment shown by parents when deciding which of their children to send to the university is most significant because it anticipates educational views elaborated later in *The Scholemaster*.

In the stricter sense, none of these passages is a digression, since each is ingeniously woven into the main thread of the dialogue. In the first of them, Ascham manages to develop a line of thought that runs counter to the main argument without impairing its force. He laments the decay of proper musical training in the grammar schools while, at the same time, Toxophilus is contending that music is too sedentary a recreation for the scholar, who, like Elyot's or Castiglione's ideal nobleman, should be accomplished in body as well as in mind. The account of card sharps and dice players in the second digression, as lively and informed an exposé of the underworld as any in the later Elizabethan cony-catching pamphlets, underscores the official concern at the time over the decline of wholesome physical exercise and of public and private morality. The digression on the Turks stresses the need for Christian unity against the common foe, who may be defeated, Toxophilus declares, only by superior archery. Finally, the passage on uniting with Scotland argues that after centuries of warfare in which the English longbow has invariably decided the issue, the only reasonable course for the future is to weld the two nations into a single Protestant state under the rule of Henry VIII and his successors.

Both apologia and technical exposition are presented attractively. Yet it may seem odd that Ascham, in attempting to secure royal patronage and vindicate his career in the university, should have chosen to do so by expounding this almost "mechanical" skill rather than some liberal art. There were already a few quite successful specimens of prose discourse in the vernacular, such as Sir Thomas More's *Richard III* and *Four Last Things*, or his English writings, before his fall, in defense of the established church. There were also Sir Thomas Elyot's popular treatises on medicine and education. But in spite of these precedents, Ascham had good reasons for choosing a different kind of subject.

One was that his detractors were blaming archery for whatever deficiencies they claimed to find in his scholarship. Nor, in the manner of some authors, did he fabricate this story of opposition within the university merely as a pretext for writing. Many of his contemporaries at

Cambridge, whose profession as scholars exempted them from the royal statutes requiring men to be proficient in the skill, associated archery with such rough, unseemly exercises as bowling, wrestling, dancing, tumbling, and football. Worse still, from their viewpoint, was the fact that men sometimes forgathered to shoot upon wagers, rather than for any honest purpose. Official academic disapproval appears in the fifteenth-century statutes of King's College, which expressly forbid "the games of dice, hazard, ball and all noxious inordinate unlawful and unhonest sports, and especially all games which afford a cause or occasion for loss of coin, money, goods or chattels of any kind whatsoever, whether within King's College or elsewhere within the University."[5] These activities were considered suitable only for yeomen and clowns, not for men of learning, who had neither time nor money to fritter away on such vanities.

The inference to be drawn from Ascham's apology is that certain of his fellow scholars associated him with those who indulged inordinately in "unlawful sports." That their criticism really harmed his reputation and pricked his self-esteem is clear from what he says elsewhere in his writings. Long after he published *Toxophilus*, he admitted in a letter to Sir William Cecil that his shooting had proved, even after he had virtually given it up, a continuing source of mistrust of his intellectual seriousness (I, 351). It was thus only natural that he concern himself at this point with defending archery as the pastime most suitable and beneficial for a man in his station in life.

He could also justify the technical matter of the book, even if shooting ranked with the mechanical and not the liberal arts, as worthy of scholarly treatment. In all ages one might find treatises and dialogues on sport and kindred subjects by the most eminent authors. There were, for example, the *Hippiké* (on horsemanship) of Xenophon, the *De Falconibus, Asturibus, et Accipitribus* of St. Albertus Magnus, and the dialogue "De Venatione" (on hunting) in the second book of the *De Philologia* of Guillaume Budé, the greatest of contemporary French humanists.[6] With such respected predecessors, Ascham could readily justify his own undertaking. He believed, too, that he would be making not only a worthwhile but a totally original contribution to the literature of sport. For although many authors had written in praise of archery, they had not described "how it is to be learned and brought to a perfectness amongst men."[7] He meant, therefore, by reducing its

principles to writing, to perpetuate its method for patriotic Tudor Englishmen, whose attitude toward shooting was not to be measured by the
objections of a handful of dyspeptic academics.

II

In the popular and official mind, the longbow still occupied a place
of honor and affection. Throughout the long dynastic wars in France,
in the frequent border skirmishes and occasional pitched battles with
the Scots, in the still vividly remembered Wars of the Roses, English
armies had relied heavily on their "artillery," then consisting principally
of bowmen. Crécy, Poitiers, and Agincourt, the most celebrated triumphs of medieval English arms, had been decided by the marksman-
ship of the nation's yeoman archers. More recently, the bow had played
its part in the rout of the Scots at Flodden (1513) and again in 1542 at
Solway Moss. On Flodden Field, the chronicles reported, the unfortunate James IV had dropped at the feet of the Earl of Surrey, mortally
wounded by arrows. Then, in the marsh at Solway, the English bowmen had carved up a force of several thousand floundering and panic-
stricken Scots. Antiquarians asserted that both the Saxons and the Normans owed their conquests of the island in large measure to the terror
caused by their swift-flying shafts, and that Harold might have driven
William of Normandy back into the Channel had he not been slain at
a decisive moment by an arrow.

By Ascham's time, cannons and handguns were already becoming a
more important and lethal part of English ordnance than the longbow.
The last land engagement in which a body of archers was to shoot with
effect took place just two years after the appearance of *Toxophilus*,
when Lord Protector Somerset overcame the Scots at Pinkie Cleugh.
Yet if their growing dependence on other kinds of "artillery" was causing them to leave their archer's gear to rot in forgotten corners, the
subjects of Henry VIII maintained their strong sentimental attachment
to the trusty bow of yew. And of all the men in the realm, the king
himself seemed most attached to this, the characteristic weapon of true-
born Englishmen.

Henry proved his interest in archery by both legislation and example. Early in his reign, in order to root out "unlawful games" that
bred vice and effeminacy, he confirmed the old statutes of Edward III
requiring every man and boy to own a longbow and shoot regularly.

In 1541–42 he reconfirmed the same laws and prescribed in detail how they were to be observed.[8] A contemporary manual issued for the guidance of justices of the peace shows that though they were not usually observed, the statutes had been re-enacted in earnest, and that the justices were expected to enforce their provisions. They applied to all men under the age of sixty, except the physically unfit, clergymen, jurists, scholars, and others whose profession exempted them. Fathers and children's guardians were expected to see that their male offspring and wards between the ages of seven and seventeen learned to shoot. The fine for not having the prescribed gear ready at all times was 12*d*. In every city and town, butts were to be erected, and the inhabitants were ordered to shoot on holy days and at other convenient times. No alien was allowed to use the longbow (so deadly was the national weapon considered), or to convey one out of the realm. Any Englishman discovered shooting with a crossbow or handgun, instead of a longbow, was subject to a fine of £10 unless he or his wife had an income of at least 300 marks a year.[9]

Small wonder, then, that Sir Humphrey Wingfield, himself a justice of the peace, had followed the statutes to the letter in exercising the children of his household. Small wonder, too, that Hugh Latimer, in a sermon before Edward VI (1549), looked back with pride on the days when fathers still gave their sons bows and supervised their shooting. On Sundays, Latimer recalled, men and boys "were wont to go abroad in the fields a shooting; but now it is turned into glossing, gulling, and whoring within the house."[10]

A competent bowman himself, Henry VIII encouraged his courtiers as well as his lesser subjects to practice archery. In 1537–38 he issued a patent for the Fraternity of St. George, a group of courtiers who met regularly to practice shooting with crossbows, handguns, and longbows.[11] Hence there was more than flattery in Ascham's tribute to the royal attitude toward archery: "Again, there is another thing, which above all other doth move me, not only to love shooting, to praise shooting, to exhort all other to shooting, but also to use shooting myself; and that is our King his most royal purpose and will, which in all his statutes generally doth command men, and with his own mouth most gently doth exhort men, and by his great gifts and rewards greatly doth encourage men, and with his most princely example very often doth provoke all other men to the same" (II, 25). There was obviously small risk that such a monarch, born at the close of a century when the bow still proved at times a more effective weapon than the gun, would scorn a book in commendation of archery. Besides, if Henry required any further convincing, the time finally selected for publication of *Toxophilus* was opportune. For during the weeks in which Ascham began his last revision of the manuscript, the king was in a good position to note how in skirmishes around Boulogne the long-memoried French troops still quailed before the stalwart English bowmen (II, 79).

Ascham, moreover, though he made the conventional disavowal of the worth of his treatise, claimed that it would profit his countrymen in two ways. First, in writing on "this English matter, in the English tongue, for Englishmen" (II, 2), he hoped to demonstrate the capabilities of vernacular prose, in his mind still an unproved literary instrument. Second, the subject was a valuable one, since in his opinion archery was a vital feature of the national life, contributing to the physical, moral, and intellectual welfare of its practitioners in all classes of society. Though others might place it among the less honorable crafts, Ascham undoubtedly would have endorsed the claim made a century later by Thomas Fuller that "above all Shooting is a noble recreation, and an half Liberall art."[12]

Such, in summary, are the contents and motivations of a treatise that was to succeed as a work of literature far beyond the author's expectations. Though one may, if one chooses, regard Ascham's alleged reasons for writing as purely conventional, in particular the claim of seeking order for English prose, the truth is that he did accomplish everything he promised to his readers. Further, *Toxophilus* caught the fancy of his contemporaries, and even helped to develop the English nostalgia for the longbow that persists to the present day. British and American archers still quote Ascham with respect—a recent manual[13] refers to him as "the 'father-in-archery' of us all"—and regard as basic his five steps of standing, nocking, drawing, holding, and loosing.[14]

Elizabethan and Jacobean writers on shooting and kindred topics frequently show indebtedness to his work. Edward VI's cousin, Sir John Smith, devoted the greater part of his treatise on military weapons to a similar apology for the longbow.[15] His attempt to maintain this anachronism of ordnance, though sharply criticized in a rejoinder by Humphrey Barwick, was supported by the historian Sir John Hayward who, taking his cue from Ascham, questioned the weather-worthiness of such undependable modern inventions as the arquebus and the caliver.[16] Another writer on military science, Gabriel Naudaeus, remarked in 1637 that Ascham's discourse excelled anything that had been written since on shooting or related matters.[17] In 1596 a certain "R.S." liberally quoted and paraphrased sections of Book One in his essay *A Briefe Treatise, to proove the necessitie and excellence of the use of archerie.* And in 1625, William Neade, in a curious pamphlet entitled *The Double-Armed Man,* urged the advantages of adding a longbow to the pikeman's standard equipment in an argument closely patterned after that of *Toxophilus.*

Poets, too, looked to *Toxophilus* whenever they found occasion to celebrate the bow of yew. The playwright Anthony Munday borrowed from it several details for the passage on shooting in his poem *The Paine of Pleasure.*[18] Richard Robinson's "A Threefold Assertion friendly in favor and furtherance of English Archery at this Day"[19] is based closely upon Ascham, and so, to a lesser extent, is Richard Niccols's *Londons Artillery* (1616), a heroic poem written in praise of the Honourable Artillery Company.

Ascham's treatise was honored by plagiarists as well as more scrupulous imitators. In 1634, the notorious and prolific pamphleteer Gervase Markham took over large parts of it in his own work *The Art of Archerie* without troubling to credit his source for a single detail. His opening chapters are simply the first book of *Toxophilus,* severely abridged and eliminating the dialogue form. The remainder of his work he lifted from Book Two without rearrangement of any of the material and only the slightest alterations in diction. In 1676, Robert Shotterel and the dramatist Thomas D'Urfey collaborated on a poem entitled *Archerie Reviv'd; or, the Bow-Man's Excellence.* These two associates in the Theatre Royal, neither of whom appears to have had any great personal knowledge of the sport, simply converted large chunks of *Toxophilus* into mediocre heroic couplets—again without acknowledgment.[20]

Among more eminent authors who show familiarity with Ascham's book are Shakespeare, Samuel Daniel, Michael Drayton, Ben Jonson, Robert Burton, and Milton. The most notable instance of Shakespeare's borrowing is King Lear's observation, "That fellow handles his bow like a crow-keeper; draw me a clothier's yard" (IV, vi, 87–88), a direct echo of Ascham's description of an ungainly archer: "Another cowereth down, and layeth out his buttocks, as though he should shoot at crows" (II, 141). In *The Civil Wars,* Daniel's enthusiasm for the longbow—"peculiar Ingine of our Land"—reiterates Ascham's, while the passage on Robin Hood's men in Drayton's *Poly-Olbion* contains technical information about arrows that harks back to the second part of *Toxophilus.*[21] Jonson picks up the simile about the mind's need, like that of the finest bows, for unbending.[22] Burton cites Ascham in recommending various exercises as cures for melancholy.[23] Milton sets down in his commonplace book Ascham's anticipation of his own belief in the necessity of union with the Scots.[24] Perhaps most flattering of all to Ascham would have been the analogy Queen Elizabeth drew from his treatise in a letter of political admonition to her successor, James VI of Scotland: "I hope that you will remember that who seeketh two strings to one bow, he may shoot strong, but never straight."[25]

More significant than these various borrowings was the effect of *Toxophilus* on formal treatise-writing during the half-century following its publication. As Francis R. Johnson has noted, it shared with the works of Elyot and Robert Recorde the major role in establishing "the vernacular tradition for technical and scientific exposition."[26] It became a standard authority on physical training as an essential part of education: later writers draw frequently upon its contents. The anonymous author of *The Institucion of a Gentleman* (London, 1555) commends Ascham for having "taken pains to set forth a book of the right order of shooting" and urges the wellborn to adopt archery as a regular exercise. He also imitates the passage attacking dice-play and, in his prologue, begs the reader to amend the faults in his book even as a master archer instructs his pupil by taking the bow in hand and hitting the mark himself.[27] Others who regarded *Toxophilus* as the finest available discourse on physical exercise were Richard Mulcaster, who praised Ascham "both for training the archer to his bow, and the scholar to his book"; James Cleland, who lifted most of his discussion of this topic from the *Institucion*; and Henry Peacham, who refers his reader to Ascham as the chief authority in these matters.[28]

In his English version of John Leland's *Assertio inclytissimi Arturii Regis Britanniae*, published in 1582, Richard Robinson provides an interesting sidelight on another kind of influence exerted by Ascham's book. "I could at large here call to mind," he writes, "the commendation of this peaceable practice of shooting which once I as a raw scholar read over in *Toxophilus*, and at times by taxed lessons interpreted in Latin here and there."[29] Who set him to "making Latins" of Ascham's work Robinson does not say, but his statement is evidence that at least one Elizabethan schoolmaster regarded it as a model of prose style for his pupils.

Not the least of Ascham's achievements was his demonstration of the effectiveness of prose dialogue as a vehicle for expounding the principles and techniques of an art or craft. Indebted to him in this respect, though with amusingly diverse subjects, are such works as Christopher Clifford's *The Schoole of Horsmanship* (London, 1587) and Thomas Morley's *A Plaine and Easie Introduction to Practicall Musicke* (London, 1597).[30] Though composed originally in Latin before it appeared in an English version, Everard Digby's treatise on swimming, *De Arte Natandi, Libri duo* (London, 1587), is also in the line of descent from *Toxophilus*. Since Digby was a fellow of St. John's, it is not surprising to find that among Elizabethan treatises his most closely resembles Ascham's in form. Another group of writers, incidentally, who manifest a debt to Ascham for his exploitation of dialogue and vigorous, colloquial prose are the pamphleteers with their exposés of the "art" of "cony-catching." Not only is the description in *Toxophilus* of the shifts of cheaters at gambling one of the earliest passages of this kind in English; but with so respectable an example before them, the later pamphleteers could pretend to a similarly high moral purpose in setting forth their sensational "discoveries" of contemporary roguery.

One final example of the influence of *Toxophilus* is the recently discovered *Arte of Angling, 1577,* itself a work of considerable accomplishment.[31] Though descended from such humble medieval progenitors as the section on fishing in the *Boke of St. Albans, The Arte of Angling* is also the offspring of Ascham's treatise. It opens with an encounter between Viator, who resembles the genially skeptical Philologus in character, and Piscator, like Toxophilus a pious, learned, and engaging spokesman for the sport in question. The discourse covers the usual topics for a work of its kind—the origins and virtues of the sport, its equipment and technique, and the good moral qualities it develops in the practitioner. With even greater literary finesse than Ascham, the anonymous author works his technical exposition into the dialogue, while Viator and Piscator wait for Cicely, the latter's understandably unsympathetic spouse, to finish the perennial wifely chore of cleaning and frying her husband's catch for supper. Since *The Arte of Angling* is almost certainly the immediate source of Izaak Walton's more famous work, *Toxophilus* appears as a direct ancestor, albeit an unacknowledged and possibly unrecognized one, of *The Compleat Angler* and its numerous literary and subliterary progeny.

III

Apart from the freshness of its content and treatment and the thoroughgoing Englishness of its tone, the success of *Toxophilus* seems to have been due to the vigor and appropriateness of its language and the excellence of its construction. According to Ascham, he was trying to point out to other writers in the vernacular the certain way to effective composition. With the copy of the treatise that he sent to Gardiner, he included a Latin epistle in which he claims that, in contrast with the artistic license then prevalent in works of vernacular prose, he had

taken pains to depart far and differ from almost the entire rout of English authors: not because I take it ill that anything is written in English but because I perceive that commonly unlearned and temerarious men have made attempts at this kind of undertaking. But they pursue matter either idle or unsuited to their capacity, in which circumstances, they forsake appropriate and clear vocabulary, and do not understand which words are used figuratively and are fitted to true adornment; they are unskilled, besides, and ignorant of all proper arrangement. For indeed they have a sufficiency of neither dialectic for reasoning nor rhetoric for the embellishment of style; and thus in our vulgar tongue they strive to be, not familiar and appropriate, but rather outlandish and strange. Now I know this to be too true: I feel very distressed that Englishmen, though empty and devoid of faculty, yet hastily and rashly, with so little reflection, undertake the writing of English. The reason is that for some years only the bolder, not the more competent ones have usually thrust themselves into this business: which fact has both introduced great confusion into our language and filled up this realm with most trivial books of all sorts. I have dealt with a subject, neither unsuited to my capacity nor pernicious and hurtful to anyone . . . (I, 79–80).

A flourishing native prose, in other words, was possible only if someone possessing superior dialectical and rhetorical skill would undertake its fashioning. Capacity for choosing clear and appropriate language presupposed a firm grounding in the art of eloquence; proper arrangement demanded the exercise of carefully disciplined logical powers.

This belief in the need of the writer for both kinds of training is echoed in pronouncements by several of Ascham's friends. Shortly before the publication of *Toxophilus*, Johann Sturm, who next to Cheke exerted the strongest intellectual influence of any contemporary upon Ascham, brought out his *De amissa dicendi ratione* (Strasbourg, 1543). In this treatise, Sturm insisted that in addition to training in rhetoric, constant practice in style, and imitation of the best models, a knowledge of dialectic was necessary for the recovery of the lost art of eloquent composition. Dialectic and rhetoric, he pointed out, were in fact inseparable, particularly in the matter of *inventio*, or the devising of arguments appropriate to the subject in hand.[32] And also, Ascham could have added, in the matter of *dispositio,* or arranging the "invented" topics in the most effective order. For as his colleague Seton made clear in the third book of his *Dialectica,* which had been circulating in manuscript for some time at St. John's and first appeared in print in the same year as *Toxophilus,* successful proof or demonstration is impossible without careful attention to arrangement. Finally, according to Thomas Wilson, an author well schooled in rhetoric and reasoning should be capable of managing any subject that presents itself to him: "Now a wise man that hath good experience in these affairs, and is able to make himself a *Rhetoric* for every matter, will not be bound to any precise rules, nor keep any one order, but such only as by reason he shall think best to use, being master over art, rather than art should be master over him, rather making art by wit, than confounding it by art."[33]

The implication of the boast to Gardiner, then, is that if Ascham has proved himself up to the task, not only has he vindicated himself before his critics as a diligent student of the liberal arts; he has also, for the first time, given the vernacular a specimen of prose composition in which the author is indeed "master over" his art. The remainder of this chapter will attempt to show just how he did surpass the works of nearly all of his predecessors in English, in the suitability and flexibility of his style and vocabulary as well as in the masterly fitting of his design to the nature of his subject. *Toxophilus* is the work of an academic author conscientiously following the best examples and rules for composition, but performing his task, none the less, in an inventive and original manner.

In spite of the vigor of his protest to Gardiner, Ascham did not actually scorn the efforts of all of his forerunners. Although he drew principally upon the classical models and handbooks that had constituted the stuff of his own university education, he profited too from the example of both learned and popular works in the vulgar tongue. He was not above taking hints for organizing his matter from such earlier treatises on sport as *The Master of Game,* a translation by Edward Plantagenet, second Duke of York, of Count Gaston de Foix' *Livre de Chasse,* or the humble "Treatyse of fysshynge wyth an angle," which had first appeared in the second edition (1496) of the *Boke of St. Albans.* But above all other English predecessors, he owed most to Sir Thomas Elyot, for the actual inspiration to write on archery, for several ideas incorporated into his own treatise, for the incentive to render his native tongue a worthy literary instrument for spreading the benefits of learning.

Although Ascham nowhere explicitly acknowledges his many obligations to Elyot for ideas in both *Toxophilus* and *The Scholemaster*, he
had profited much from the older man's example and from a personal
acquaintance sufficient at least to have involved them in conversation
on a recondite point of historical information. On one occasion, apparently while *Toxophilus* was in the making, Ascham asked Elyot "if he
at any time had marked any thing, as concerning the bringing in of
shooting into England" (II, 77). Elyot, who had recently been reading
British antiquities for a projected work "De rebus memorabilibus Angliae," had an instance ready to hand. He recalled a passage in a certain "exceeding old chronicle" which mentioned that in the days when
Vortigern was ruling the island, the Saxons had overcome the Britons
principally by means of their bows and arrows.

This conversation, the only one recorded between the two men, confirms the extensive internal evidence in Ascham's writings of his indebtedness to Elyot.[34] It also links *Toxophilus* with *The Governour*, a hint
in which gave Ascham the inspiration for his own work. Almost half
of the first book of Elyot's treatise deals with the physical training of
the future courtier or magistrate, and its final chapter is entitled "That
shooting in a longbow is the principal of all other exercises." Elyot
argues the commonplace that moderate bodily exertion is essential to
a man's physical, intellectual, and moral well-being. Most exercises are
either too mild or too full of "beastly fury and extreme violence" for
the wellborn. Archery, however, achieves a desirable "measure" and
has two additional advantages: it is the surest means for bringing down
one's quarry in the chase, the sport most appropriate to noblemen, and
for centuries it has given Britain military supremacy over her neighbors.
Now, to the reproach of Englishmen, shooting is on the wane, so that
in spite of the statutes ordering its restoration, one may well ask "Who
effectually putteth his hand to continual execution of the same laws and
provisions?"[35]

Besides affording this suggestion of a motive and a scheme for writing, the influence of *The Governour* is most evident in Ascham's digressions. Elyot, too, lamented the irrational behavior of parents who took
away from schoolmasters "their aptest and most proper scholars, after
they be well instructed in speaking Latin" and either sent them to court
to become lackeys or pages, or else apprenticed them to tradesmen.[36]
Again, although Elyot does approve of music in the education of his

ideal gentleman, his approval is contingent upon the qualification that the playing of instruments be "moderately used and without diminution of honor, that is to say, without wanton countenance and dissolute gesture." For by too "exact knowledge" of music, one may "be illected [allured] to wantonness, abandoning gravity, and the necessary cure and office, in the public weal, to him committed."[37] Finally, *The Governour* contains a diatribe against idle pastimes, the ugliest being dicing, which involves "vehement chiding and brawling, horrible oaths, cruel, and some time mortal, menaces."[38] Ascham's own digression on dicers and card-players, though a more vivid piece of writing than Elyot's, is simply an amplification and dramatization of this passage in *The Governour*.

Elyot's wish to make his native language an eloquent means of spreading knowledge also seems to have inspired Ascham. "The Proheme" to Henry VIII in *The Governour*, with its hope "that men which will be studious about the weal public may find the thing thereto expedient compendiously written," is almost certainly the model for Ascham's own prefatory epistle. And as Ascham the professional scholar felt obliged to justify his use of the vernacular rather than a learned tongue, so Elyot the scholarly amateur had felt the need to justify the same practice in his works. Some readers appear to have caviled at the vulgarization in *The Governour* of knowledge formerly locked up in the classical languages and at Elyot's careful effort "to augment our English tongue."[39] Hence, in a revised "Proheme" to the 1541 edition of *The Castel of Helthe*, he chides those professional men who scorn their native language and try to screen learning from the prying eyes of the untutored many. "But if physicians be angry," he protests, "that I have written physic in English, let them remember, that the Greeks wrote in Greek, the Romans in Latin, Avicenna, and the other in Arabic, which were their own proper and natural tongues." If these writers had meant to conceal precious medical knowledge from the vulgar mob, certainly they would have "devised some particular language, with a strange cipher or form of letters, wherein they would have written their science."[40] Elyot clearly stood for the humanist aim of spreading useful knowledge as widely as possible, a patriotic goal that could be achieved only by perfecting the vernacular.

In taking up the same cause, Ascham made valuable contributions of his own. Elyot had concerned himself primarily with expanding and elevating the language. This end he hoped to achieve by judicious borrowing from foreign tongues. The results, despite an occasionally infelicitous importation or coinage, were on the whole salutary. Many of his neologisms have enriched the language permanently, and he did prove that English could be readily adapted to the requirements of discourse on a variety of scientific and philosophical subjects. Ascham, in contrast, wanted not so much to expand the native vocabulary as to show that its existing resources could be used with precision and decorum. His especial virtue lay in demonstrating that current English was adequate to treat significant matter without awkwardness, affectation, or strangeness of expression.

In this respect, Ascham shows greater discernment than Elyot; for there is little excuse for such pedantic borrowings and coinages in *The Governour* as "adminiculation" (aid), "conglutinate" (joined), "demulced" (coaxed), "illecebrous" (enticing), and "propice" (suitable).[41] To Ascham, such diction violated the rhetorical principle of decorum. If one is truly interested in informing one's reader, eloquence consists in clarity and plainness of expression. Stylistic beauty does not mean gorgeous verbal dress, but rather proper decking out for the occasion. The language, he observes in a later work, should rise or fall in splendor and evocative power according to the immediate aims of the author and the magnitude of his subject (III, 6). As his friend Wilson put it a few years after *Toxophilus* was published, "Among all other lessons, this should first be learned, that we never affect any strange inkhorn terms, but to speak as is commonly received: neither seeking to be over fine, nor yet living over-careless, using our speech as most men do, and ordering our wits as the fewest have done."[42]

In their desire for perspicuity and their preference for current speech rather than importations from the learned or Romance tongues, Ascham and Wilson reveal their sympathy with, though not uncritical concurrence in, Cheke's campaign for an unadulterated native English prose. Cheke's position, illustrated in his own partial translation of the Gospels, is spelled out in a letter that he wrote shortly before his death in 1557 to Sir Thomas Hoby. After having amended some of the diction in the manuscript of Hoby's translation of *The Courtier,* Cheke asserted that he was "of this opinion, that our own tongue should be written clean and pure, unmixed and unmangled with borrowing of other tongues, wherein if we take not heed by time, ever borrowing and never paying, she shall be fain to keep her house as bankrupt." Not realizing how his inept metaphor betrays the illogical extremity of his recommendations, Cheke would have English mature as a literary language solely by developing her own resources, using "plainly her own" ancient vocabulary, borrowing only when no native roots or compounds are available to "serve us to fashion a word of our own."[43]

An example of what Cheke's anglicizing movement could produce may be found in the *Arte of Reason, rightly termed Witcraft* (London, 1573) of Ralph Lever, a fellow of St. John's College. In this first vernacular treatise on logic in England after Wilson's *The Rule of Reason* (1551), one finds awkward native compounds substituted for even the most intelligible and current terminology. Thus "preface" becomes "forespeech," "conclusion" becomes "endsay," and "definition" becomes "saywhat"; a "declarative" proposition and a "conditional" proposition become, respectively, "showsay" and "ifsay."[44]

Ascham, though up to a point sharing their views, was no "Saxonist" like Cheke and this zealous disciple. In *The Scholemaster* he does echo Cheke's dislike of Sallust and Thucydides for their "outlandish kind of talk" as well as their irregular grammatical constructions and obscurity; like Cheke, he prefers the current and "more natural" language of Xenophon and Demosthenes.[45] And in the preface to *Toxophilus* he remarks that to write well one "must follow this counsel of Aristotle, to speak as the common people do, to think as wise men do, and so should every man understand him, and the judgment of wise men allow him. Many English writers have not done so, but using strange words, as Latin, French, and Italian, do make all things dark and hard." With an especially apt anecdote, he drives home his point: "Once I communed with a man which reasoned the English tongue to be enriched thereby, saying, 'Who will not praise that feast where a man shall drink at dinner both wine, ale, and beer?' 'Truly (quoth I) they be all good, every one being taken by himself alone, but if you put malmsey and sack, red wine and white, ale and beer, and all in one pot, you shall make a drink neither easy to be known, nor yet wholesome for the body.' "[46]

Ascham avoids the extremes of Cheke's and Elyot's positions by employing diction that affects neither excessive borrowing nor unrelieved nativism. Perhaps in *Toxophilus* he did enjoy a certain advantage over Elyot, for in being the first to expound this craft of unlettered yeomen, he was unhampered by any tradition of a learned vocabulary. Thus when he set out to write better English prose than any of his predecessors, he was able to show how he could "think as wise men do" in the homely language of archers themselves. A few archaic words aside, his diction is free of any quaintness. It is everywhere apt and clear, with all but a rare sentence relatively succinct and firmly molded.

The style of *Toxophilus*, in fact, conforms quite well to the invariably avowed but too seldom realized ideal of Ciceronian oratory, namely the truly Attic manner. For the Attic style, as Cicero describes it in providing Brutus with a portrait of the perfect orator, is always pure, plain, and clear; it seeks what is fitting to the occasion. Indulging but moderately in figurative display, it tries to avoid rhythmical artifice, though it may indulge in some metaphor "since all speech makes frequent use of it, not only that of citizens but also of rustics as well." It is sparing of neologisms, abounds in maxims, is salted with humor and wit. Nor does the Attic orator, though customarily direct and simple, always constrain himself within the bounds of the plainest sort of language; as his matter increases in importance, he adjusts the level of his speech accordingly, sometimes rising to the middle style, and at times even to the high style.[47] Or, as Ascham expresses the same principle, even as the proper arrow must be selected for the individual archer and occasion, so nobody "can appoint any one kind of words, of sentences, of figures, fit for every matter; but even as the man and the matter requireth, so the fittest to be used" (II, 118).

For the parts of his treatise offering instruction or technical exposition, therefore, Ascham followed classical theory and wrote in an almost unadorned, though by no means frigid or attenuated, style. Whenever Toxophilus is explaining technique or describing the archer's gear in the second book, or when he and Philologus are defining issues in the first, the language is invariably plain, the metaphors homely, the sentences largely devoid of rhythmical artifice. When his matter, on the other hand, "rises" to ethical generalizations, condemnation of current immorality and irreligion, climactic attempts at persuasion, apostrophes or addresses to the mighty, Ascham deliberately elevates the diction and figures of speech, and expends greater ingenuity on the rhythmical casting of his sentences. As might be expected, the dedication to Henry VIII and the preface are in a style much higher than that found generally in the body of the treatise.

A typical instance of his spare instructional manner is the passage on the function of the bracer:

A bracer serveth for two causes, one to save his arm from the stripe of the string, and his doublet from wearing; and the other is, that the string gliding sharply and quickly off the bracer, may make the sharper shot. For if the

string should light upon the bare sleeve, the strength of the shoot should stop
and die there. But it is best, by my judgement, to give the bow so much bent,
that the string need never touch a man's arm, and so should a man need no
bracer, as I know many good archers which occupy none (II, 100).

When he does wish to lend gravity to a passage or to make it more
memorable in its phrasing, Ascham is more generous with rhythmical
and figurative devices: "Where is comparison, there is victory; where
is victory, there is pleasure; and where is pleasure, no man careth what
labour or pain he taketh, because of the praise and pleasure that he
should have in doing better than other men" (II, 82). Here one finds
not only alliteration and careful balance among the members of the
sentence, but also the figure of *gradatio*, or building to a climax by
carrying over key words from one phrase to another. The intent, as
with the use of similar devices in the passage quoted earlier concerning the king's beneficence in fostering archery, is to underscore the idea
and impress it firmly upon the reader's memory.

Yet in general the interlocutors stick to a homelier manner of speaking (even though Ascham knew well how to manipulate the intricate
schemes and figures outlined in the handbooks of rhetoric), and thus
he avoids the musty flavor of the schoolroom by relying instead upon
metaphors and analogies drawn from everyday experience. He appears
to be keeping in mind Aristotle's dictum that well-chosen metaphors,
besides giving one's style "smartness," help men to learn more readily,
provided they are suitable and not far fetched.[48] Thus when Toxophilus
explains why it is wiser not to buy an apparently perfect bow, but rather
to select one that requires trimming and cutting as the owner gets its
"feel," he goes to daily life for his analogy: "For every new thing must
always have more than it needeth, or else it will not wax better and
better, but ever decay, and be worse and worse. New ale, if it run not
over the barrel when it is new tunned, will soon lease [*lose*] his pith
and his head afore he be long drawn on" (II, 110). He makes a political moral more striking by taking an image from a familiar trade: "And
surely an awl of lead is not so unprofitable in a shoemaker's shop, as an
unfit minister, made of gross metal, is unseemly in the commonwealth"
(II, 151–52). One of the liveliest figures of all is the central simile of the
digressive passage on the Turks. In deploring the moral and political
insensitivity that has rendered Westerners almost incapable of resisting
the advance of Islam, he compares Christendom to "a man that hath an
itch on him, and lieth drunk also in his bed, and though a thief come
to the door, and heaveth at it, to come in and slay him, yet he lieth in

his bed, having more pleasure to lie in a slumber and scratch himself where it itcheth, even to the hard bone, than he hath readiness to rise up lustily, and drive him away that would rob and slay him" (II, 72).

Accuracy of observation and ability to set down whatever he has seen in racy, colloquial language also appear in Ascham's straight descriptions, as in his account of the antics of certain inelegant shooters after they have released their arrows:

Some will take their bow and writhe and wrench it, to pull in his shaft, when it flieth wide, as if he drave a cart. Some will give two or three strides forward, dancing and hopping after his shaft, as long as it flieth, as though he were a mad man. Some, which fear to be too far gone, run backward, as it were to pull his shaft back. Another runneth forward, when he feareth to be short, heaving after his arms, as though he would help the shaft to fly. Another writhes or runneth aside, to pull in his shaft straight. One lifteth up his heel, and so holdeth his foot still, as long as his shaft flieth. Another casteth his arm backward after the loose. And another swings his bow about him, as it were a man with a shaft to make room in a game place. And many other faults there be, which now come not to my remembrance (II, 142–43).

Anyone who has even casually observed archers, golfers, bowlers, or, best of all, players of electric pinball machines at their disport may readily appreciate the humor and truth of this passage of "antic" description.

But the touchstone of his mastery of vernacular style is Ascham's explanation of how wind may play havoc with even an expert shooter's aim. The excerpt, though long, deserves quoting in full, since it demonstrates why *Toxophilus* is regarded as one of the first triumphs of modern English prose and why its author has been favorably compared with such a practiced observer of nature as Thoreau.[49]

To see the wind with a man his eyes it is unpossible, the nature of it is so fine and subtile; yet this experience of the wind had I once myself, and that was in the great snow that fell four years ago. I rode in the high way betwixt Topcliff-upon-Swale and Boroughbridge, the way being somewhat trodden before, by way-faring men; the fields on both sides were plain, and lay almost yard-deep with snow; the night afore had been a little frost, so that the snow was hard and crusted above; that morning the sun shone bright and clear, the wind was whistling aloft, and sharp, according to the time of the year; the snow in the high way lay loose and trodden with horses' feet; so as the wind blew, it took the loose snow with it, and made it so slide upon the snow in the field, which was hard and crusted by reason of the frost over night, that thereby I might see very well the whole nature of the wind as it blew that day. And I had a great delight and pleasure to mark it, which maketh me now far better to remember it. Sometime the wind would be not past two yards broad, and so it would carry the snow as far as I could see. Another time the snow would blow over half the field at once. Sometime the snow would tumble softly; by and by it would fly wonderful fast. And this I perceived also, that the wind goeth by streams, and not whole together. For I should see one stream within a score on me; then the space of two score, no snow would stir; but, after so much quantity of ground, another stream of snow, at the same very time, should be carried likewise, but not equally, for the one would stand still, when the other flew apace and so continue sometime swiftlier, sometime slowlier, sometime broader, sometime narrower, as far as I could see. Nor it flew not straight, but sometime it crooked this way, sometime that way, and sometime it ran about in a compass. And sometime the snow would be lift clean from the ground up to the air, and by and by it would be all clapt to the ground, as though there had been no wind at all, straightway it would rise and fly again. And that which was the most marvel of all, at one time two drifts of snow flew, the one out of the west into the east, the other out of the north into the east. And I saw two winds, by reason of the snow, the one cross over the other, as it had been two high ways. And, again, I should hear the wind blow in the air, when nothing was stirred at the ground. And when all was still where I rode, not very far from me the snow would be lifted wonderfully. This experience made me more marvel at the nature of the wind, than it made me cunning in the knowledge of the wind; but yet thereby I learned perfectly that it is no marvel at all though men in wind lose their length in shooting, seeing so many ways the wind is so variable in blowing (II, 154–55).

IV

Though not the only successful example of vernacular prose from early Tudor times, *Toxophilus* won particular acclaim from Ascham's contemporaries because it stood without a native rival in its kind. No one had previously brought so much learning or literary talent to the writing of a treatise on a pastime. Nor had any author created more vivid passages expressing his delight in observing the marvels of his immediate surroundings. And, even more significantly perhaps, Ascham had achieved his aim of showing other Englishmen how to order the matter of prose discourse in the most effective manner.

In arranging his material, he relied on three interrelating and mutually reinforcing structural patterns, all deriving from classical theory and example. Basically, he depended upon a three-part arrangement characteristic of treatises on sport ever since the divisions were first suggested by the *Cynegeticus,* a discourse, attributed to Xenophon, on hunting the hare. The second ordering pattern, since his end was to persuade men of the value of shooting, he took from rhetorical theory, the first half of *Toxophilus* being constructed upon the recommended scheme for the deliberative oration. Finally, he cast the work, in imitation of Platonic and Ciceronian examples, as a dialogue, a form eminently suited in the humanist view to both deliberative thought and technical exposition. Before him no writer in English, not even Elyot or More, had fully realized the capabilities of dialogue for such purposes. Ascham blends all three patterns, moreover, with such apparent ease that the reader, as should be the case whenever art succeeds in concealing art, is seldom fully aware of the intricacy of the artifice.

Yet because he did turn to the most familiar classical doctrines and resources, some scholars have objected to Ascham's book as "a conventional exercise," smacking a little too strongly of the schools.[50] The use of conventions, however, is not in itself a criterion; it is the manner and circumstances in which an author uses them that measure the presence or absence of originality and imagination in his artistic make-up. Applied to an author in the succeeding generation, when at least a few of the more competent writers of prose had acquired some facility and sophistication in handling the vernacular, the jibe of "school exercise" might have a somewhat greater appearance of justice. But even the most celebrated of Elizabethan prose treatises, Sir Philip Sidney's *Defence of Poesy*, was painstakingly drawn up according to the classical principles governing the demonstrative oration, and it abounds, despite its appearance of *sprezzatura* or "masterful negligence," in figures of style and other rhetorical devices recommended in the schools and ancient manuals.[51] Besides, revival of the classical prose dialogue was one of the principal contributions of humanism to literature, among the best things in the kind being *Utopia* and *The Courtier*. Now in the 1540's, when English formal prose still had no firm foundations, it needed exactly the sort of discipline supplied by Ascham's effort. His careful attention to the basic principles of rhetoric and his studied, though in no way slavish, following of classical models demonstrate the beneficial rather than the pernicious effects of subscribing to the Renaissance doctrine of literary imitation.

Despite the lavish use of classical models and rhetorical trappings, Ascham's apology for shooting is far more than a showy academic exercise. A certain display of erudition, after all, was hardly out of place in an author who felt that his learning had been impugned and in an age when a capacity for drawing upon the ancients was the hallmark of both scholarship and competence in formal controversy. Hence, rather than detracting from the work, Ascham's ingenious use of both his models and the rhetorical tradition contributed much to the literary success of his "little purpose of shooting."

The three conventional divisions of this kind of treatise deal, successively, with the venerable origins, the commodity, and the equipment and techniques of the art or sport in question.[52] In *Toxophilus*, Book One covers the first two topics, and Book Two deals with the third. Of especial significance for Ascham's purpose was the nature of the arguments usually presented under the heading of commodity. The author of the prototypical *Cynegeticus*, for instance, urges that hunting improves the sportsman physically, mentally, and morally, so that he becomes a braver soldier in war and a better citizen in peace. Hunting keeps men from base pleasures and roots out foul desires and the evil of political ambition. Nor, in contrast with certain pastimes, does it cause one to neglect one's domestic affairs, a claim which may seem dubious to the skeptical, but which Ascham, having such eminent authority behind him, likewise advances for shooting.[53]

Equally cogent arguments are put forward under the heading of commodity in those two important English precursors of Ascham's work, *The Master of Game* and the "Treatyse of fysshynge wyth an angle." The former lists the same advantages to be derived from the chase as the *Cynegeticus*, with modifications appropriate to the structure of medieval society. So long as hunting does not prevent a man from rendering due service to God and his master, it cannot but add to his physical and spiritual well-being. It keeps him from the seven deadly sins, for it is enemy to idleness, the mother of vice. The huntsman feels himself to be a better man when he rides forth, "more alert and more at ease and more undertaking." He is inwardly joyful; he will live longer and enjoy better health than the non-hunter; his life in the woods is a kind of prelude to paradise itself.[54]

The "Treatyse of fysshynge wyth an angle" adds yet another dimension to this traditional praise of the sport under consideration. Its author extols angling above hawking, hunting, and fowling, the other field sports treated in the *Boke of St. Albans*, because it confers superior physical and psychological benefits. It is the most salubrious of recreations because it provides a man with three properties of which he may make his own "leech and medicine." These are enjoyment, moderate exercise, and a healthful diet consisting of what the angler takes by his own cunning with hook and line. He enjoys good spirits because he rises early and walks in the sweet fresh air of the open countryside. Fishing is therefore the ideal recreation for the man who truly cares to be hale in body and mind.[55]

Ascham, proceeding on a similar pattern, adjusts to his own purposes the significant modifications introduced in these two late medieval treatises. Although he nowhere alludes to either, there can be little doubt that he was familiar with their contents. Both were widely known in his time, and a new edition of the *Boke of St. Albans* had appeared as recently as 1540. In defending his own favorite pastime, he offers arguments closely paralleling those of *The Master of Game*. Shooting, too, keeps men from idleness and vice by bringing them out into daylight and open air where honest deeds are done; it, too, gives its practitioners more alert minds, stouter hearts, and longer lives than their sedentary fellows. In claiming for it effectiveness as an antidote for vice, Ascham is more specific than Plantagenet, who mentions the deadly sins only in passing. Shooting, according to Toxophilus, may serve to rid the community of a specific evil; namely, gambling in dark, dirty corners with cards or "the bitched bones two." Again, this time following the arguments of the treatise on angling, Ascham commends his chosen exercise particularly for its moderation and for its properties as the finest preventive medicine for maintaining one's health (II, 33–34). The long-established formal traditions of the genre, supplemented by the novel arguments that he adapted from these two fifteenth-century predecessors, thus provided him with the general outline for his work.

For his principal objectives, however, these delightful but crude vernacular forerunners were only partially adequate models. He needed some further guide on how best to exploit the tripartite structure as a means of persuasion, at the same time creating a really substantial specimen of well-ordered prose discourse. The necessary guidance he found in the principles established by the ancients for the deliberative oration, in which the aim of the speaker is to convince the audience that by adopting a certain course of action they will gain both honor and advantage.[56] According to Wilson, in an expansion of the definition that is usually given, the end of deliberative speaking is to "persuade, or dissuade, entreat, or rebuke, or dehort, commend or comfort any man." One of its principal functions is "to advise our neighbor to that thing, which we think most needful for him or else to call him back from that folly, which hindereth much his estimation." To achieve any of these aims, it was customary to establish that the recommended course of action was necessary, profitable, and possible. Or, as Wilson amplified and subdivided these terms, to establish whether it was "honest, profitable, pleasant; safe, easy, [or] hard; lawful and meet, praiseworthy, necessary."[57]

Since Ascham's avowed intention was to persuade his readers to take up archery, his method of "inventing" arguments in *Toxophilus* was to concentrate on the topics of "honor" and "advantage" as most proper to a treatise in this kind.[58] It is noteworthy, too, though he was writing several years before *The Arte of Rhetorique* appeared, that he makes a point of commending archery at some length under every one of Wilson's headings. Shooting is honest, especially in contrast with card-playing and dicing, the dishonorable pastimes of a decadent age. It is profitable to the kingdom in both peace and war, and pleasant to those who use it for recreation. Its praiseworthiness is manifest from its illustrious history and good repute among the noblest peoples. It is lawful and meet, not only for temporal men, but also for scholars, for whom it is necessary lest they fall off in their studies through lack of proper exercise. Both men and boys may engage in it without fear of overstraining the body. Finally, though its mastery requires sound instruction and continual practice, it is possible to achieve the end of the sport, to shoot and hit the mark.

A slight rearrangement of Wilson's triads of topics shows further that the groups of terms closely parallel the three typical divisions of the treatise on sport. Whatever is ancient and long-established among good men must perforce be lawful and praiseworthy; whatever is honest, profitable, and pleasant is obviously commodious; and whatever is safe and easy (or, if difficult at least possible) can be taught and practiced according to rule and method. Awareness of this affinity between the principles of rhetoric and the structure of earlier works on sport gave Ascham a second guide for exercising control over his matter.

He was careful, also, to design *Toxophilus* so that it would include, insofar as they could be accommodated to his subject, all the quantitative parts prescribed by rhetorical theory for the deliberative oration. Although the names and number of these formal divisions vary slightly from one authority to another and even from one work to another within the canon of a single author, Cicero's *De Inventione* supplies a typical and widely followed system. The six principal parts are the *exordium* (introduction), *narratio* (statement of the facts of the case), *partitio* (an outline of the issues to be considered), *confirmatio* (evidence of the soundness of the pleader's cause or, at least, of his good character), *refutatio* (rebuttal of the claims of the opposition), and *peroratio* (conclusion). Cicero also mentions, though hardly with approval, that Hermagoras and certain other rhetoricians considered digressions among the formal divisions of the speech.[59]

Since Ascham meant to convince the indifferent and the skeptical of the value of archery, it is not surprising that although he pays due attention to each of the stipulated parts, he concentrates on sections corresponding to the *exordium, confirmatio,* and *refutatio.* Now the function of the *exordium,* according to both Aristotle and Cicero, is not so much to provide information as to secure a hearing from one's opponents and to put the matter into proper perspective for the audience. The speaker, consequently, must find means of removing immediately whatever prejudices may disincline the audience from listening to his cause.[60] Similarly, in the *confirmatio* and *refutatio* he must bring to bear all the available means of persuasion. According to Aristotle, the three modes of persuasion proper to the rhetorician's art consist in the speaker's establishing his own good character, evoking the desired emotional responses from the listeners, and presenting convincing arguments in behalf of the truth or at least the apparent truth.[61]

In *Toxophilus,* Ascham avails himself of all these three modes of persuasion. In addition, he places the more important digressions—on gambling, on music, on the Turkish threat, and on the desirability of union with Scotland—in critical places within the *confirmatio* and *refutatio.* He inserts them, in other words, not merely to display his erudition, but to add to the persuasiveness of his case. Although they were technically not a formal division of the oration as Hermagoras had claimed, Quintilian and other authorities recognized digressions as most helpful in winning over the audience. They were particularly advantageous if, as Ascham makes them do, they treated such topics as religion, public duty, and the evils of greed and licentiousness, and if they grew out of the main subject in such a manner as not to seem digressions at all.[62]

V

Choice of the dialogue form, however, was probably Ascham's finest literary stroke. This device enabled him to disarm criticism by masking his *exordium, confirmatio,* and *refutatio* within an apparently casual conversation and by diverting attention from his own person to that of his spokesman, the impeccable scholar Toxophilus. It also enabled him to present his case for archery under the guise of a seemingly thorough investigation by the speakers of all available evidence on the subject. Further, the creation of the two likable Cambridge interlocutors gave the treatise vitality and a sense of character interplay.

His ultimate models are the Socratic dialogues and two different types of Ciceronian dialogue. Several of Plato's works are devoted, in part when not entirely, to the sort of inquiry with which *Toxophilus* is concerned. The *Ion, Philebus,* and *Phaedrus,* to cite a few, contain discussions on the nature, utility, and formal principles of, respectively, poetry, dialectic, and rhetoric. In the Latin West, this special function of philosophical dialogue prevailed, since the tradition drew its main inspiration from the writings of Cicero, particularly the much admired and widely imitated *De Oratore,* itself a work modeled loosely on the *Phaedrus.* The first half of *Toxophilus,* treating the nature and origins, utility, and ethical and political significance of archery, stands squarely in this tradition of literary dialogue.

Ascham, in fact, borrows the setting of the *Phaedrus,* though he does modify it to fit the different circumstances of his own interlocutors.[63] In both dialogues the speakers meet by chance in the country at a warm hour of the day. Before settling down to talk in a shady place, Socrates and Phaedrus begin their conversation with a pleasant stroll, tracing their way, in a scene charmingly depicted by Plato, along the banks of the Ilissus, in whose refreshing waters they occasionally cool their feet. Ascham alters this opening slightly by placing his interlocutors in an appropriate Cambridge setting and by leaving out the almost ubiquitous stage prop of Plato's Renaissance imitators, the famous plane tree under which Socrates finally reclines. As in the *Phaedrus,* the time spent in talking extends from shortly after noon until the cool of early evening, even though the division of *Toxophilus* into two books might have tempted Ascham to follow Cicero's *De Oratore* and stretch the conversation beyond the period of a single day. In addition to the good impression it was meant to make on the reader, this imitation of Plato lends Ascham's dialogue unity not only of time, place, and action, but of atmosphere as well. Rural fields and the afternoon hours are suited to wholesome exercise and hence to an inquiry into the nature and ends of recreation. The mood induced by evening as the long discussion ends is one of calm and repose after the exertions, whether physical or intellectual, of the brighter and warmer part of the day. As evening brings coolness and ease, so the successful resolution of differences takes the heat and agitation from men's spirits, leaving them relaxed and satisfied after work well done.

In the second part of his book, where the purpose and character of the conversation are somewhat different, Ascham goes to another pattern of dialogue for his model. One might distinguish this second type from its more philosophical counterpart by labeling it the "catechetical" or "master-pupil" dialogue. The prototype is Cicero's *De Partitione Oratoria*, an elementary handbook on rhetoric in which the beginner (Cicero's son) asks questions about the parts and terminology of oratory, and the expert (Cicero himself) supplies the answers.[64] Owing to the authority of Cicero's name, the master-pupil dialogue was widely used in the Middle Ages and the Renaissance for teaching the terms and processes of both the liberal and the mechanical arts, including the pastimes of the field.[65] It suited the character of the second half of *Toxophilus* ideally, even as the philosophical type had suited the first. Hence the decision to use both kinds of dialogue was well taken. Alone, either might have proved inadequate: the philosophical would have seemed pretentious for describing the equipment and procedures of a common sport; yet the technical was ill-adapted to discussion of first principles and the nobler functions of the art.

The long afternoon's conversation between Toxophilus and Philologus takes place in the fields of ripening wheat close by Cambridge, immediately after dinner on a warm, sunny day, presumably late in the springtime.[66] Though it is the hour for recreation after the midday repast, Philologus discovers his friend intently reading a book as he strolls along; he is surprised that Toxophilus is not with a group of shooters who have just passed by on their way to the butts. Then he warns him that he may be injuring his health by reading now, "for we physicians say, that it is neither good for the eyes in so clear a sun, nor yet wholesome for the body, so soon after meat, to look upon a man's book" (II, 11). What has been absorbing the attention of Toxophilus is, appropriately enough since this encounter is itself imitated from that particular dialogue, Socrates' fable in the *Phaedrus* which tells "how some souls, being well feathered, flew always about heaven and heavenly matters; other some, having their feathers mowted away and drooping, sank down into earthly things."[67] He is glad, nevertheless, of the interruption, and is sorry to have missed an excellent chance for exercise and sport. But shooting, objects Philologus, is hardly a fit occupation for a scholar, who ought to remember Cicero's dictum that men are born, not for play, but for grave conduct and weighty studies.[68]

At this point, as happens several times in the dialogue, Toxophilus proves himself too well-read to be deceived by quotation out of context. He recalls that in the very same passage Cicero speaks of the necessity of wholesome recreation amidst the more earnest tasks of life. Possibly that is so, Philologus grants, but the field of "fair wheat" near which they are walking reminds him that industrious husbandmen "have fatter barns in harvest, than they which will either sleep at noon-time of the day, or else make merry with their neighbours at the ale" (II, 13). Again, if Philologus thinks to prevail in argument with a mere analogy, however apt, Toxophilus is too skilled a rhetorician to lose the opportunity of turning the figure neatly back upon him. Good minds, he replies, need recreation even though dull ones may not. Perhaps his friend has forgotten that at times even rich fields must lie fallow. Or, to draw a comparison from music, that the treble minikin string of the lute, which produces a fine, clear note, must always be loosened when one is not playing upon the instrument. Or, looking to archery itself, that whereas a heavy, clumsy bow may be left strung without suffering much damage, a fine one must be unbent when stored in order to keep it from warping. Similarly, intelligent men must have their unbending lest they go stale from overwork. And shooting, Toxophilus concludes triumphantly, is not only the best exercise physically, but the one that above all others "hindereth learning little or nothing at all, whatsoever you and some others say, which are a great deal sorer against it than you need to be" (II, 15).

With the contention that shooting is no hindrance to study, Philologus disagrees. Yet because they both have leisure, he offers to listen to any arguments that may be advanced in its behalf, since he can recall no one else who has thought this art worth either defending or expounding. In the face of this direct challenge, Toxophilus eagerly takes up the role of advocate.

This opening interchange in effect performs the main function of an *exordium*: that is, to gain the attention and good will of the audience. It also serves to establish the reader's confidence in Ascham's spokesman, who obviously represents the author. Through this persona, whose good character and homely, forthright manner are certain to win favor and attentive hearing, Ascham imputes to himself the same excellent qualities and manages to suggest that a pastime engaged in by so admirable a person can scarcely be as noxious as its opponents claim.

As foil for Toxophilus and stimulator of the discussion, Philologus is also attractively drawn. His model in real life is not identifiable, though some commentators have assumed arbitrarily that it must be Cheke.[69] As the most celebrated scholar in the university, Cheke would appear to be the likeliest candidate, were it not that Toxophilus refers to him as having already left Cambridge, to the sore detriment of learning (II, 67). Unless Ascham is nodding in this passage, he would scarcely permit Toxophilus to lament Cheke's departure and address him as interlocutor all in the same breath. Other possible originals of the character are Smith, Watson, and Grindal. But Philologus, though he is a rhetorician (II, 118), calls himself a physician at the outset of the dialogue. Since the one Cantabrigian of the time who was accomplished in both medicine and rhetoric, Nicholas Carr, did not take a medical degree until several years after the publication of *Toxophilus*, it is unlikely that Ascham had him in mind. Philologus thus seems to be no identifiable member of the Cambridge circle, but rather a composite critic, invented as a questioner to enable Ascham to argue his own case.

In a sense, Philologus is the wise fool who has inhabited philosophical dialogue ever since Plato created that profound yet comic character Socrates. The difference is that, unlike Socrates, Philologus does not lead his friend on by hiding his greater knowledge under a sham of ignorance. Only briefly, toward the close of the first book when Toxophilus admits his own inability to teach anyone how to shoot perfectly, does Philologus become another Socrates, subtly drawing forth from his companion the correct implications of his own answers (II, 92–94). But his normal function is to set up objections for his opponent to demolish neatly, to provoke him to draw upon his learning in a manner that proves the ardent toxophilite a most humanely learned scholar. By representing the argument as a friendly, even-tempered debate between two such agreeable speakers, Ascham was able simultaneously to flatter the opposition, provide his cause with an acceptable advocate, and divert attention from his own person and intracollegiate animosities to the real issues involved.

Within the space of little more than a page, Philologus's speeches serve to bring out in several different ways Toxophilus's (that is, Ascham's) zeal for learning. The opening words of Philologus, "You study too sore," immediately set the tone. Then, Toxophilus is so absorbed in his book that he has disregarded the advice of physicians not to read in the sunlight or immediately after meals (a glance, perhaps, at Ascham's claim to have kept up his studies despite his recent years of poor health). For when deeply engrossed in Plato, the best of all the pagans, he becomes oblivious to everything else. He is occupied here with that divine author's *Phaedrus*, which treats the most profound of philosophical subjects, the nature of the human soul. It is a dialogue, moreover, that embodies significant commentary on Ascham's own main professional interest, the rhetorician's art. Again, by completing the misappropriated quotation from the *De Officiis* and thereby wittily turning its edge back upon his friend, Toxophilus-Ascham manifests his intellectual alertness and intimate knowledge of his sources. These introductory hints thus prove the author as well as his persona to be thoroughly versed in the writings of Plato and Cicero—for the Renaissance humanist the patterns of all true wisdom and eloquence. A final point in Toxophilus's favor in this skillfully devised *exordium* is his having been discovered with his attention so concentrated upon a worthy book that his head has begun to ache. Through this one detail the reader is prepared to react sympathetically when Toxophilus soon afterward insists upon the scholar's need for exercise and diversion from his studies.

His having in hand the *Phaedrus* also helps to link the opening pleasantries with the serious business of the dialogue. The step is almost inevitable from Plato's "well-feathered" souls to the feathered arrows of Ascham. Philologus is in fact prompt to trade upon the association in order to support his own mild opposition to shooting: "I suppose it be a great deal more pleasure also to see a soul fly in Plato, than a shaft fly at the pricks" (II, 12). Toxophilus reacts to the suggestion by arguing that Plato too had taught the necessity of exercise for serious students. He offers at this point to show that archery is far more venerable and beneficial to mankind than his skeptical friend may think.

"Let us go forward," Philologus then agrees, "and examine how plentifully this is done that you speak; and, first, of the invention of it; then what honesty and profit is in the use of it, both for war and peace, more than in other pastimes; last of all, how it ought to be learned amongst men, for the increase of it" (II, 17–18). This request for enlightenment, summarizing in correct order the topics with which the remainder of the dialogue is concerned, corresponds quite evidently to

the *partitio,* or division of the issues, of a deliberative oration, while at
the same time conforming to the typical pattern for the treatise on sport.
It helps the reader, moreover, to follow the way in which Philologus
manipulates the ensuing discussion so that every one of Ascham's objectives in writing the treatise is realized. The rest of Book One includes all the recommended means of confirming the honor and advantages associated with shooting; it also refutes all counterclaims against
its primacy as a form of defense and recreation. Halfway through the
dialogue Philologus admits that he has been won over by his companion's persuasive arguments and expresses an ardent desire "to become
a shooter" (II, 89). Since the debate is now concluded, Book Two is
simply an exposition of how archery "ought to be learned amongst
men."

Whereas the first part of *Toxophilus* conclusively demonstrates
Ascham's ability to use all the best resources available to the rhetorician, the second part, though in a less intricate manner, proves his capacity as a logician. It is an extremely well-managed technical discourse, presenting in "natural" rather than "artificial" language and
order the essential information about the archer's craft. The nature of
the subject and the shift to master-pupil dialogue gave Ascham some
opportunity to display his skill in dialectic. Having done all that was
possible in the way of allusion and citation to dispose of any suspicion
that shooting had made him neglect his literary studies (*grammatica*),
or had impaired his development as a *rhetor,* he sets out at length to
prove his mastery of the third of the basic liberal arts. When Philologus asks his friend to instruct him in archery, Toxophilus ironically
pretends that "my much shooting has caused me study little, so that
thereby I lack learning, which should set out the art or way in anything. And you know," he slyly concludes, "that I was never so well
seen in the *posteriorums* of Aristotle as to invent and search out general demonstrations, for the setting forth of any new science" (II, 90).

Undoubtedly Ascham's sole reason for mentioning this work from
the *Organon* is to forewarn his readers that the remainder of the book
will demonstrate his mastery of Aristotelian logic. For the *Posterior
Analytics,* though concerned mainly with the newly invented syllogism
and with the requirements for accurate definition, also treats of the
method of discovering the first principles and distinguishing the essential characteristics of the various sciences. Philologus will therefore have
none of Toxophilus's diffidence, for he knows him to be well enough
schooled in this Aristotelian treatise to understand what is required in

expounding any new art or science. When he further points out that Socrates and Cicero did not disdain to instruct others in useful arts, even when they were not themselves perfect in them, Toxophilus finds himself no longer able to deny the request. He asks only that his friend, whom he regards as the abler rhetorician and dialectician, assume primary responsibility for guiding the course of the discussion by means of a proper method of questioning.

Here again Ascham has anticipated and disarmed possible criticism by having Toxophilus defer to the supposedly superior knowledge of the other speaker, though Philologus, of course, is likewise the creature of his author's imagination. Through this exchange, furthermore, Ascham ironically makes him rather than Toxophilus responsible for the existence of the technical half of the treatise. A disquisition on a mechanical art, however skillful, may still have seemed a dubious undertaking for a scholar. But since the demand is made by the irreproachable Philologus, his "reluctant" companion may scarcely in courtesy refuse.

Is *Toxophilus*, then, merely an ingenious literary exercise? Not if one remembers the combination of reasons for which it was written, and not if one is receptive to the intricate and many-layered construction of so much Renaissance art, whether literary, musical, or plastic. The Tudor mind loved elaborate structure and multiplicity of detail; it inhabited a universe made up of involved correspondences and complicated interrelationships that unified in one grand design all conceivable varieties of forms and levels of being. Hence it preferred its works of literature, whether an *Arcadia*, a *Faerie Queene*, or a *Laws of Ecclesiastical Polity*, to imitate both the intricacy and the logical unity of the cosmic order. Ascham, despite the ingenuity he expended upon it, actually wrote as economical a book as the occasion and his intentions permitted. Within its complex, imitative pattern, a classical simplicity and clarity of language and organization remain evident, as the experience of generations of readers who have been charmed by the forthrightness and deceptively casual manner of the work attests. For such an achievement in an age when English literary prose was still creeping on all fours, the grateful reader might wish to say to the man who showed it how to go upright, as Philologus says to Toxophilus at the close of the dialogue, "How well you have handled this matter . . . I may not well tell you myself now; but, for your gentleness and good-will towards learning and shooting, I will be content to show you any pleasure whensoever you will" (II, 163).

≈≈≈≈

CHAPTER FIVE

Shadows Eclipsing Our Studies

REWARD FOR *Toxophilus* came to Ascham promptly. The privy council received the work favorably (I, 79), and he was summoned to Greenwich for an audience with the king. Regrettably, no record survives of what passed between them, but as a result of the interview Ascham was granted a royal pension, secured through the good offices of Gardiner, Paget, and the Duke of Norfolk (I, 398). Gardiner, when Ascham met him afterward in the gallery of the palace and told him that the sum was to be £10 per annum, thought it too small and offered to ask for more. But Ascham, satisfied with the amount and with the distinction of the audience, implored him rather to "reserve that goodness to another time" (I, 412). To the bishop's credit, he remembered this request, and some eight or nine years later helped Ascham in a far more meaningful way. Ascham now enjoyed most of the personal advantages that he had sought in writing his book. The annuity of £10 more than doubled his income, and he had won the regard of influential people capable of helping him to future preferment. Nor could his scholarship and devotion to archery be called in question now that his treatise had won him a royal pension and an audience with the king.

A second triumph came in the following year. Sometime after the trip to Greenwich, he again became seriously ill, probably through a recurrence of his old quartan fever. Once more he was forced to spend a long period, this time the greater part of a year, away from Cambridge, and he bitterly lamented the new interruption of his studies (I, 94). Nevertheless, soon after his return in 1546 he was elected, out of respect for his polished Latin epistolary style, to succeed Cheke as public orator. The office added an annual stipend of forty shillings to his income, and remained his until 1554, when he resigned it in favor of a career at court.¹ In part this appointment compensated for the failure to obtain the regius professorship of Greek, and he was pleased to be able to inform Paget, who had already helped him on trust as a scholar of promise but unknown merit, that his colleagues had conferred such a distinction upon him (I, 94).

The public oratorship, however, came too late to restore his enthusiasm for his life at Cambridge. Although no good opportunity outside the university had presented itself, the unsettled nature of the times made him feel more strongly than ever the urge to move. Possibly his restlessness was intensified by the obligations of his new office, for he found himself composing letters to prelates and noblemen about the various difficulties of the university and its imminent decline as a center of learning. In spite of the improvement in his personal fortunes, he seems to have shared the feeling of his colleagues, though the evidence is not overwhelmingly on their side, that prospects for scholars were deteriorating and learning was falling off, with few signs of hope for its restoration in the immediate future.

One source of uneasiness was the attempt of various lay groups to strip the university of certain of its ancient rights and endowments. Throughout the 1540's the academic senate was kept busy forestalling encroachment upon its privileges, not only by royal officials, who sometimes disregarded the statutes and attempted to impose special taxes and military levies on the university, but also by opportunistic courtiers and "impudent" townsmen. Because of the extremely broad privileges of the university and the policing and judicial powers of its officers over citizens as well as academics, relations between the local residents and the scholars had always been strained; but if one may credit the protests of several of his contemporaries, they were never worse than during the years that Ascham was at Cambridge.

In the mid-1530's, conflict over university prerogatives reached such a pitch that finally, in 1537, a sharply worded royal letter to the town officials and a hearing within the Star Chamber were required before order could be restored.² By 1540 the reprimand seems to have been forgotten, for the townsmen began once more to foment trouble. Over the following seven years Ascham, first as paid scribe and then in his role of public orator, drafted numerous complaints about the "unseemly behavior" of the local people. The earliest among his preserved official letters, for example, is a request made to Bishop Thirlby in 1541 for prompt assistance against the townsmen, who were threatening the privileges of the scholars in their usual contumacious manner (I, 16–17).

Despite repeated attempts at arbitration, the strife continued. In 1546 and 1547 Ascham drew up several more complaints of fresh disputes between town and gown. To Gardiner, as chancellor of the university, and to Lord Chancellor Wriothesley he reported that on one occasion feeling was running so high that it had proved impossible to find two aldermen in Cambridge who would swear, as royal statutes prescribed, to maintain the peace (I, 102, 104). Again, upon Edward VI's accession, the senate appealed for the king's support of its privileges against the usurpations of the townsfolk. If peace is the best thing a monarch can offer his people, runs the argument of the letter, it should especially be guaranteed where it is necessary for the promotion of useful arts and sound learning (I, 117). To impress upon the privy council the need for maintaining order, in the autumn of 1547 the senate instructed Ascham to draft petitions to Cranmer, Somerset, Warwick, and several other councillors, for reaffirmation of the prerogatives of the university as soon as King Edward's first parliament should convene.

The appeals convey a certain note of desperation, for in September a near-riot had occurred following an arrest made by the university proctors at Stourbridge Fair. At this famous and ancient fair, held annually on a common about a mile northeast of the center of town, the university maintained a right of supervision and of levying a tax on all edibles sold. This tax, which had always annoyed the townspeople, had aggravated them even more in recent years because several colleges had recently established their own kitchens and bakeries, thus depriving the local victuallers of the custom of these very tax-collectors. Stourbridge Fair, therefore, invariably threatened to produce friction. At the current fair, as Ascham, writing for the senate, reports the incident to Paget, a number of people had become disorderly. In their function as supervisors, the proctors were called upon to arrest the offenders. Suddenly, however, the mayor of the town became obstinate and refused to have the prisoners lodged in the Tollbooth. The proctors, having no alternative, locked them up in the old castle, which stood within the jurisdiction of the university. An hour or two afterward, the mayor's son, urged on, Ascham alleges, by his father, led a rescue party to the castle and freed the prisoners. The senate, refusing to look upon these small-town heroics as mere high spirits, begged Paget to use his influence to suppress such impudence, lest the domestic tranquillity of the university be utterly destroyed.[3]

Another vexing incident recorded among Ascham's official letters occurred in the spring of 1546, when a fishmonger named Maxwell misused a warrant permitting him to requisition horses whenever he was conveying fish for the king. Ascham's account of the matter to Gardiner and Wriothesley recreates a lively, farcical scene, though to him, or at least to the academic council, the affair was in no way humorous. For this Maxwell (according to Ascham, "a most quarrelsome burgher, fashioned for the life of a jailbird or a bearkeeper") had outrageously flouted scholarly privilege (I, 96). On the occasion in question, even though horses owned by men not connected with the university were standing nearby, Maxwell, without a by-your-leave and over the vigorous protests of the college groom, had appropriated a horse belonging to the master of Peterhouse. Nor was that the only rub: he took the creature simply as a mount for his own servant, not to help draw the cart bearing the king's fish, for which he already had beasts in harness. This may not seem, the petition admits, a major encroachment upon the ancient rights of scholars, but if such small offenses against law and right (*contra jus et fas*) pass uncensured, they will eventually lead to disturbances of a more serious nature (I, 99–100).

This stubborn resistance of town to gown, if filled with the cunning and wrath of the ignorant, was at least out in the open where it could be met and overcome. A threat apparently more dangerous to the university, and requiring more subtle countermeasures, was the greed of royal favorites. Having profited from the suppression of the monasteries, these acquisitive courtiers began to turn lustful eyes on the rich lands and endowments of the Oxford and Cambridge colleges. Ironically, even as various societies within both universities were seeking a share of the spoils of the recently dissolved monastic foundations, land-hungry courtiers were in turn working on the king and council to dissolve the colleges themselves as remnants of the age of idolatry. The current parliament, moreover, was enacting legislation that served the interests of the would-be despoilers. The first Chantries Act of 1545, for instance, had given into the royal hands for arbitrary disposition all income and property of ecclesiastical foundations, not exempting universities and colleges, that had been designated for obituary masses, votive candles, and other such relics of the "superstitious past." Another statute, later amended, ordered the dissolution of all colleges within the universities, the sponsors hoping no doubt to profit from the ensuing confiscation of lands.[4]

The plight of the colleges is spelled out in a group of letters composed by Ascham at the time. Early in 1546, he addressed pleas for help to Smith and Cheke, both of whom were becoming influential at court. Thus, when a commission for investigating the revenues of the Cambridge foundations was formed, Smith managed to persuade the king to compose it of university, rather than court, officials. When the report of the commissioners came in, Henry, though asserting that it was his duty to find new means of rewarding those who had served the realm faithfully "in wars and other affairs" (in less flattering words, his predatory favorites), expressed surprise at the large number of people "so honestly maintained in living by so little land and rent" in the colleges. Although he promised no definite relief, he at least made it clear that there would be no further encroachment on university revenues. Moreover, the amended Chantries Act of the same year did exempt the property of the colleges from confiscation. The worst threat to their existence, at least for the time being, was thus averted.

Constant vigilance in protecting their interests was nonetheless required of the scholars. Despite the exemptions that had been granted, royal procurators and assessors continued to harass the universities. Again, toward the end of 1547, Ascham protested to Gardiner that learning was now certain to decay because a recently issued order would deprive the societies of the right to elect their own fellows (I, 151). His own college, furthermore, was engaged in a struggle to keep intact the land attached to the school at Sedbergh in Yorkshire. The founder of this school had assigned to the corporation of St. John's the right to choose the headmaster, along with a handsome endowment of £1,000 to maintain eight undergraduates and two fellows in the college itself. Since Sedbergh was a source of northern scholars and the only grammar school in the sparsely settled country along the border between Yorkshire and Westmorland, its importance was obvious. Between 1544 and 1550 Ascham wrote no fewer than ten letters to various bishops and privy councillors, asking them or thanking them for assistance in preventing loss to the school of its lands, especially of a "little farm" that helped support the master. To the council he sent one appeal that should have stung the consciences of at least a few of those present at its reading: if even the property of a school so necessary and useful to the commonwealth cannot be protected, "charity will wax cold, seeing that not even a time of reformation can repress plunder."[5]

Although earlier attempts to pluck away the master's farm were thwarted, mainly by the vigilance of Sir Anthony Denny, in 1549 a syndicate of purchasers was granted Sedbergh lands. In a letter to the Marquis of Northampton protesting the award, Ascham foresees the imminent ruin of public schools in England if such depredation should continue.[6] His gloom was matched by that of Thomas Lever, who preached a sermon before the king soon after this transaction in which he expressed the opinion that Sedbergh School was already "sold, decayed, and lost."[7] Fortunately Ascham and his friend were poor prophets, for Sedbergh, in spite of the inroads made into its properties, is still flourishing and sending scholars up to Cambridge, while St. John's College continues to play its role in the governing of the school.[8]

However serious these threats to their estates may have been, the university and the colleges did manage to come through this trying period with relatively small loss.[9] Still, having to compose numerous letters on this dismal subject could not but intensify Ascham's melancholy. Further, there is no doubt that Cambridge was in fact in a difficult financial position. Scarcely any of the colleges, even those with large revenues like St. John's, could make ends meet in the face of rising costs, inflation of the coinage, and declining or unaltered income from endowments. Nor, in this period of private acquisitiveness, in which ecclesiastical and other charitable foundations were rapidly disappearing into the sticky hands of royal favorites, could the universities look for many new bequests. The living conditions of scholars, never luxurious, were worsening alarmingly, at least by their own accounts. At St. John's, for example, fellows were supposed to receive slightly under 4*d.* per day for their subsistence. Pupils were apportioned half as much. Even at the time when Fisher had designated these sums, the allotments were, while adequate, frugal; now scholars complained that inflation had made them pitifully small.

Since academicians have chronically protested their indigence, such complaints might be suspect. The attitude of outsiders, however, confirms the fact of the scholars' relative poverty, as the following anecdote from the life of St. Thomas More illustrates. After he had lost the favor of Henry VIII and his perquisites as Lord Chancellor, More called the members of his household together to explain why he was asking them to tighten their belts. His biographer, William Roper, quotes him as conceding that "many grave, ancient, and learned Fathers live continually" on the subsistence provided at the universities. "But," More goes on, "by my counsel, it shall not be best for us to fall to lowest fare first. We will not therefore descend to Oxford fare, nor to the fare of New Inn. But we will begin with Lincoln's Inn diet, where many right worshipful and of good years do live full well."[10] No one, of course, would have expected a fellow or scholar of a Tudor college to dine like a Lord Chancellor, but More's comparison speaks much about the contemporary view toward conditions in the universities.

Nor did conditions improve during the 1540's. Lever, preaching at Paul's Cross on December 14, 1550, attempts to arouse sympathy for the poor scholars of Cambridge, who

be not able to tarry and continue their study in the university for lack of exhibition and help. There be divers there which rise daily betwixt four and five of the clock in the morning, and from five until six of the clock, use common prayer with an exhortation of God's word in a common chapel, and from six unto ten of the clock use ever either private study or common lectures. At ten of the clock they go to dinner, whereas they be content with a penny piece of beef amongst four, having a few porridge made of the broth of the same beef, with salt and oatmeal, and nothing else.

After this slender dinner they be either teaching or learning until five of the clock in the evening, when as they have a supper not much better than their dinner. Immediately after the which, they go either to reasoning in problems or unto some other study, until it be nine or ten of the clock, and those being without fire are fain to walk or run up and down half an hour, to get a heat on their feet when they go to bed.[11]

Possibly Lever exaggerates, but his words ring sincerely.

Ascham, too, had depicted the woes of the university in his long letter to Cranmer asking for exemption from the Lenten abstinence. Many students, the letter reports, were reading divinity or studying the learned tongues, thanks mainly to the efforts of Cheke before he went to court. Yet lately unprofitable controversies about original sin and predestination had done much harm to theological studies. Not enough men of sound learning and authority were staying on at Cambridge to give the proper intellectual and moral guidance to the younger scholars. Besides, even though their numbers continued to increase, the students who now came to the university were not so diligent as those of former years. Too many were sons of noble and wealthy families, some of whom, simply through their powerful connections, had begun to usurp the scholarships created originally for poor boys. Few of these sons of the rich were genuinely interested in learning, and almost none of them intended to remain or take holy orders. They came to while away their time until called, after a minimum of preparation on their part, to important positions at court or elsewhere in the kingdom. Yet at the same time many deserving fellows in the colleges lacked maintenance. The result was what might have been expected; sound learning was decaying at the roots (I, 68–70).

Ascham appears, however, as a rather paradoxical witness to the supposed academic predicament of this decade. Both he and his friend Haddon could deplore the emptiness of the schools and the poverty of the colleges in one breath, and in the next proclaim, with matching eloquence, the flourishing state of the university. In delivering the baccalaureate address at the commencement exercises of 1547, Haddon launched into a spirited, if conventionally worded, attack on "ivory-towerism." True to the Tudor humanistic ideal, he speaks of the need for scholars to carry their learning forth into public life, as a possession to be used for the benefit of the commonwealth rather than hidden away in dark and musty corners. Yet he fears that the Cambridge lecture halls and schools will become deserted in the process. "Never," he observes, "was the university more prosperous, never in my memory more populous than it is now; never were the schools more abandoned, never more solitary. For they have been reduced to such straits and to such an extraordinary paucity, that scarcely one auditor has been left to each master."[12]

Ascham could likewise write to Sturm of the marvelous flourishing of studies at Cambridge, even though he had unfolded the gloomier side of the picture to Archbishop Cranmer. Strangely enough, both views seem to accord with the facts. The university had been growing in size and reputation, and to a certain extent the desertion of the schools merely reflects the expansion of college tutoring at the expense of the traditional system of lecturing by regents. Still, it is true that the roll of eminent and devoted scholars was rapidly shrinking, for few promising younger men, despite the increase in their numbers, stayed on at the university. In the troubled period from 1542 to 1548, only two hundred students advanced to the bachelor's degree; during the next six years, in spite of an increase in matriculations, the number did not rise significantly.[13] The situation was no better at Oxford, where the number of new bachelors and masters likewise declined.

The training of the clergy fell into similar neglect. So few people took orders that Ascham, Haddon, and others wondered how the reformed religion was to be kept alive in England's ill-shepherded parishes. In another of his sermons before the king on the abuses of the times (April 6, 1549), Hugh Latimer expresses serious concern over the decrease in ordinations. These sons of great ones, he complains, will not be preachers, while most of those already in orders have deserted the poverty-stricken university. So few persons are studying theology that there are scarcely enough lecturers for the schools (a questionable assertion if the schools were as empty of auditors as Haddon had claimed). It may soon become impossible, Latimer warns, to hold up true divinity against superstition and keep out "the supremacy of the bishop of Rome."[14]

That conditions were by no means so black as Ascham and his colleagues sometimes painted them is beside the point. What does matter is that the prospect appeared dismal to the scholars themselves. Because they could foresee little good for the universities in the years ahead, it is small wonder that many of them began to think seriously of forsaking the academic life. As for Ascham himself, the old discontent could only have been heightened by his growing conviction that Cambridge was in a bad way. It was also increased by a recurrence of religious dissension in his own college, and by the suppression of open discussion, in his view the only means of clearing the atmosphere.

II

Theological differences within the English church began to define themselves more sharply upon the death of Henry VIII, who had been no friend to doctrinal change, and upon the accession of a boy-king expected to prove more sympathetic toward further alterations in ritual and dogma. In 1547 the Reformation was far from safely established in England. A number of the bishops, among them Thirlby, Day, Tunstall, and Gardiner, were still Roman in belief if not in name and remained opposed to further tampering with the church. In the universities, men whose sympathies lay with the old religion were still numerous. At St. John's, in some respects a center of radical new thinking, they seem to have constituted a majority, at least among the fellows. Even among the reformers in the college, several were fairly moderate. John Redman, for instance, appeared to be such a doubtful friend of the "Germans" that his deathbed affirmation of several fundamental Reformation doctrines in 1551 created a sensation.[15]

Further, until their repeal late in 1547 and even afterwards, the Six Articles of 1539 kept the doctrine and practice of the English church relatively close to orthodox Catholicism. The dogmas reaffirmed in the articles were deplored by such Continental reformers as Melanchthon, who disliked their "popish taint" and their severe punishment of dissenters.[16] All the articles were intrinsically distasteful to the more liberal reformers, but the most annoying, even to conservative Protestants like Ascham, was that maintaining the doctrine of transubstantiation in the Eucharist. Yet because of the extreme penalties prescribed under the act, it was not until after Henry VIII's death that anyone could risk open discussion of the theological issues involved.

During 1547, however, the Protestants gradually began to speak out. Early in that year word came to Bishop Day, then provost of King's College, that the fellows had started to engage in open debate about religion, and that they were refusing to offer private masses for the repose of their deceased benefactors. Immediately he sent the college a reprimand. The members then chose Haddon, their best epistolist and a worthy match for Day, to compose a reply. Ingeniously skirting the obstacle presented to his case by the Six Articles, Haddon managed to make it appear that the provost's, and not the fellows', stand on private masses was contrary to the accepted practice of the reformed church. He defended freedom of scholarly investigation by calling attention to the statutes of the college, which granted "that in the cause of seeking truth all of us may search into the corners of all controversies, if only pertinacity be absent and gentleness present amongst us."[17] The outcome of this affair suggests that the religious climate was already beginning to change. Not long afterward Day, realizing that the fellows meant to stand firm against his will, resigned the provostship, to be succeeded early in 1548 by a more zealous friend of the Reformation, John Cheke.[18]

The situation at King's, where the Protestants apparently dominated, was quite different from that at St. John's, where the reformers were in the minority. Ascham reports that in his college informal discussions had also begun during 1547 over such matters as private masses and transubstantiation. Although he claimed, as had Haddon for those at King's, that the debates were conducted decorously, the heat they generated probably touched off a notorious act of sacrilege in the same year. In September a young Frenchman attending upon Cardinal Pole's nephew, Lord Robert Stafford, who was then in residence at St. John's, secretly cut down the pyx for the eucharistic host from its position over the altar in the college chapel. The master, William Bill, committed the offender to Archbishop Cranmer's authority, expressing his fear, in an accompanying letter composed by Ascham, that the affair would cause scandal. Even if the archbishop could handle the matter without commotion, the Protestants feared that "certain men, who are exceedingly angry at the decline and fall of superstition, and are attempting at this time to spread darkness over the shining gospel by whatever means they can, may want to misapply this his deed towards diminishing the dignity of the college" (I, 118–19).

In spite of this scare, the reformers, headed by Lever, continued throughout the autumn to discuss within the college the controversial issues of the mass and transubstantiation. One of their number, a man named Fawden, even began to teach the new beliefs to the younger scholars, though according to Ascham he did so with discretion, "quietly and piously at break of day" (I, 154). In November, Lever and a colleague of similar convictions named Roger Hutchinson openly discussed whether the mass was the same ceremony as the Lord's Supper. At this point Bill, though a Protestant himself, became worried about the possible consequences of allowing the discussions to proceed. Absent from the college at the time, he sent a letter rebuking the fellows for persisting in their unauthorized investigations and controversies.[19]

The reprimand went down hard with Ascham, for if not himself a zealot, he had been doing his share on the side of reform. As president of the society and, apparently, acting master, it was his responsibility not to let matters get out of hand (I, 156). He replied to Bill that the entire debate, since Hutchinson and Lever were both "grave, learned, and good men," had been conducted reverently, and that no unseemly quarreling had ensued. He protested further that the truth of God's word can spring up only if its seeds are sown at the right time on properly prepared soil rather than unseasonably tilled ground. What riper time, then, for sowing than the present, and in what better place than the university, where men are gathered expressly to seek out God's truth? We shall not stop, he declares, no matter how the papists fulminate against us. Yet we are much disturbed to hear that these troubles have made you consider resigning the mastership. If you do not wish to be identified with the reformers, we will say so publicly unless, of course, you prefer not to be named by us at all. But when you consider the relative merits of the two parties, is it not we who give more credit to the college by our learning, our zeal in teaching the young, and the modesty and decorum of our lives? If one or two Protestants are rash and vehement, the fault should not be laid to all the rest. Still, though a number of men here are discontented at the shape of recent events and care little whether or not they remain in the college, we promise to obey your wishes cheerfully "for the Lord's sake." We shall ask God, at the same time, to perfect the good work that he has begun in our midst (I, 153–56).

Elsewhere in the University men were naturally curious about the controversy at St. John's. For this reason, and because of Bill's wish to have them discontinued, Ascham arranged to have the disputations transferred to the schools (I, 154). In doing so he hoped, as he explained to Cecil, "that freely and without bashfulness we might learn from informed men, what could be drawn from sacred scripture in support of the mass, which not only usurps the highest place in religion and in the consciences of men, but also has driven out almost all faithful service of God's word and the sacraments from the observance and custom of Christians" (I, 156). The disputants had gone about their work in a modest and scholarly manner. Scripture had been their guide and authority; canons of the primitive church, decisions of councils and decrees of popes, and opinions of ancient theologians and of "all the modern writers we were able to bring in, both Germans and Romans" had been judiciously sifted in a sincere effort to resolve the matter.

The public debates had not gone far before Cranmer and Somerset heard of them. Although neither interfered directly, they were not pleased. Ascham attributed Cranmer's disapproval to misrepresentation of the facts by the opposition (I, 157). With the Lord Protector it was simply that he objected to interference in what he intended henceforth to be the business of parliament alone. He advised the academic senate that scholars should keep to their proper studies and leave issues of state and religion to those responsible for governing the kingdom (I, 146). Before the proceedings could go any further, therefore, the vice-chancellor, Dr. William Madew, suspended them.

Ascham's own part in the matter went considerably beyond his effort to have the discussions transferred to the schools. In his letter to Cecil he mentions that he is in process of completing a book on the subject of the controversy. He hopes to present the work to Somerset when it is finished, unless Cheke and Cecil should consider it inadvisable to do so.[20] The book to which he alludes is quite certainly a treatise published later by Grant under the title *Apologia . . . pro caena Dominica* (A Defense of the Lord's Supper).* The subject of the published work is identical with that of the debates, and the title page announces that it had been "in Academia olim Cantabrigiensi exercitationis gratia inchoata." Further evidence that the *Apologia* grew out of the disputations is afforded by Ascham's explicitly submitting his opinions in it to the judgment of the king, Somerset, and "the most renowned fathers and very learned men" of the university.[21] Finally, there is a direct allusion in the text to "this most famous College of St. John."[22]

Ascham may have conceived this treatise as a means of putting his learning to the service of state and church according to the ideals expressed in Haddon's baccalaureate address. That he did have such an intention is strongly suggested by a passage in which he speaks of Somerset, the Duke of Suffolk, and other privy councillors as having been raised up by God to drive out the superstition of the priests and confirm in law the evangelical religion of Christ.[23] Edward's first parliament, moreover, was sitting at the time and was facing the difficult problem of religious settlement. Among the most vexing matters in legislating for the church was finding a satisfactory definition of the essential nature of the Eucharist. One of the first parliamentary acts, after the repeal of the Six Articles, was a cautionary measure directed against those who might "irreverently speak against the sacrament of

---

* The treatise, dedicated by Grant to the Earl of Leicester, was published at London in 1577 (*STC* 825). Bound in the same volume were two other works by Ascham, his earlier translations from Oecumenius and his *Themata Theologica*, a collection of exegetical exercises upon various sentences taken from scripture and the church fathers. No further editions of this volume appeared, though W. T. Lowndes and H. T. Bohn mistakenly cited a second edition of 1587 (*The Bibliographer's Manual of English Literature*, London, 1864, I, 78). The work seems to have attracted little notice, although Anthony à Wood and Gabriel Harvey show familiarity with its contents. Harvey, in fact, reproduced Grant's dedicatory poem as part of his tribute to Leicester in *Gratulationum Valdinensium, Libri Quatuor* (London, 1578), fol. D₇ʳ.

the body and blood of Christ." The act authorized the laity to receive this sacrament of bread and wine in both species and guardedly alluded to the fact that the Communion was "called in Scripture the supper and table of the Lord." Yet at the same time that it took this definite step toward Protestantism, the act deftly avoided the issue of transubstantiation.[24]

Ascham and his reforming friends, having had in their own little society enough experience of the consequences of uncertain definitions of doctrine, must have been disappointed when parliament was prorogued just before Christmas without having proceeded further on the question. If Somerset, whom they considered a sincerely religious man, could be swayed by their arguments, he might, instead of leaving matters so ill-defined, call for settlement of the issue at the next convening of parliament. Conceivably, then, Ascham hoped to produce some direct results by presenting his treatise to the Protector.

The *Apologia* opens with an allegorical attack on papal abuses in which the church is portrayed under the familiar exegetical image of a ship (or ark). By treachery, the mutinous Satan has seized command and now sails the vessel as he pleases, with a conniving pilot (the pope) and willing oarsmen (the Romish bishops). This ungodly crew now go fishing to ensnare the souls of men, for whoever teaches anything in religion besides the veritable doctrine of Jesus is a fisherman for the devil. The bait of the papists consists of vain superstitions, idols, and sacramentals, a service consisting of "symphonies instead of hymns," and, above all, the mass, "in which, in the midst of mimic and histrionic trickeries, superstition and idolatry are offered for sale to the onlookers for the sake of lucre." This farcical performance has been substituted in the churches for the Lord's Supper, which is the true seal of mankind's salvation. The private mass, with its celebrant in his actor's robes, reading words from the missal that contradict the explicit instructions of the New Testament, making apelike gestures, turning his back on the people, mumbling to himself who knows what sort of nonsense, giving Communion to none but himself, certainly this cannot be the Supper of the Lord instituted in the Gospels. The papistic teaching, moreover, that the mass is a re-enactment instead of a simple memorial of the immolation on Calvary is manifestly absurd. Christ offered his body but once, in order that believers might eat, not sacrifice, his flesh again and again. Having set forth these "Romish abuses" of the sacrament, Ascham proposes to maintain the ceremony of the Lord's Supper by the authority of the New Testament and the fathers of the church, in whose writings he professes to find no support for the institution of the mass.

Although he claimed in his letters to Bill and Cecil that the debates had been carried on piously and without rancor, one questions his candor upon discovering in his own book abusive and even irreverent language, especially when he undertakes to refute contemporary apologists for the Catholic doctrine. Probably out of respect for the Bishop of Rochester's memory in the college, he nowhere mentions Fisher's *De Veritate corporis et Sanguinis Christi in Eucharistia* (Cologne, 1527), even though the treatise must have provided ammunition for his and Lever's opponents. But when he comes to Albert Pighius (Pigghe), whose opinions concerning the Eucharist, though not really pleasing to the Catholic hierarchy, were apparently being cited as authoritative by the Roman party at Cambridge, his contempt is unbounded. Of St. Thomas More's "mockeries" on the subject he is equally scornful.[25] In one place, furthermore, Ascham is guilty of the irreverence cautioned against in the recent act of parliament. The battle cry at the end of his introduction is a parody of the *Agnus Dei*: "Behold the mass of the pope, which takes away the supper of the Lord: behold the foxes of the pope, which devour the Lamb of God: behold the heathen idol of the pope, which adds to the sins of the world."[26] The sole excuse for such writing is that it comes from an age in which invective and scurrility were only too often enlisted in the cause of religion.

Ascham attacks not only private and votive masses, but the ceremony itself as conceived by Catholics: their conception of the mass as a sacrifice, their veneration of the sacrament, and, though he prudently avoids speaking against transubstantiation, their opinion concerning the real presence of Christ in the elements of bread and wine. In doing so, he sets up a curious pattern of argument that may account, as much as official discouragement or lack of time, for his failure to complete the treatise. He offers to demonstrate that the mass is opposed to every commandment in the decalogue. The virtuosity required to carry off such an argument may have been beyond his powers, for the work suddenly breaks off, after a rather absurd attempt to explain how the mass violates the injunction "Thou shalt not kill."

Even a cursory reading of its series of "proofs" shows the *Apologia* to be more an exhibition of its author's knowledge of Greek, an exercise of his Latin style, and an effort to sway by misapplied rhetoric than a soundly reasoned treatise in theology. Though Grant claims in the dedicatory epistle that Ascham proves by scripture, patristic authority, and irrefutable argument that the mass is not identical with the supper instituted by Jesus, he nevertheless admits that the principal virtue of the work lies in "the worthiness of the writing and the attractions of the language."[27] Certainly the *Apologia* affords little evidence of Ascham's command of divinity or skill in theological disputation. He shows small acquaintance with the opinions of the major contemporary controversialists; in addition to More and Pighius, he mentions only one other recent author. Never a Genevan himself, he nevertheless cites with approval Calvin, whose views on doctrinal questions had been solicited by Cranmer.[28] The rest of his citations come mainly from the Bible and from earlier theologians, among them St. Augustine, St. Jerome, St. John Chrysostom, St. Anselm, and Nicholas of Lyra. Yet his familiarity with these writers seems to be superficial, since he makes little use of their judgments in supporting his own arguments. The one exception is the "Master of the Sentences," whom he admires as "the best and most learned of all the papists." His fair knowledge of Peter Lombard, however, is hardly evidence of any great learning in divinity, since up to the Royal Injunctions of 1535 the *Sentences* was the standard textbook at Cambridge for students in theology.[29]

Ascham writes with more conviction when he argues that few religious abuses have been corrected since the break with Rome and that the sabbath is no longer kept holy in England. No other worship takes place on Sundays, he laments, except the mass, which the priests, who are ignorant of everything else, supposedly offer for the benefit of the people. Yet the laity for their part attend without interest. Honest preaching has been abandoned and, once the mass is over, all decent behavior is forgotten while for the rest of the Lord's day men occupy themselves with unseemly pastimes. Although everybody now mocks at the pope, the clergy, by not preaching God's word and by maintaining the old liturgy, keep the people in a world of fantasy. Thus, whether intentionally or not, they continue to uphold the superstitions of papistry. The only solution is to rid the kingdom of these deceitful "mass-makers" (*missatores*) and replace them with sincere ministers of the gospel.[30]

In dealing with the mass as a violation of the commandments "Thou shalt not take the name of the Lord thy God in vain," "Honor thy father and thy mother," and "Thou shalt not kill," Ascham depends almost entirely for effect on his Latin prose style, on wit and word-play, in-

cluding syllogistic equivocation, and on his knowledge (available to
anyone familiar with the trend of recent controversy in religion) of
the Greek equivalents for various terms found in the Vulgate Bible.
The "proof" that the mass violates the commandment of taking the
Lord's name in vain typifies his juggling with words. Throughout the
entire ceremony, he claims, God's name is taken in vain because the
priests pronounce it in a strange tongue which they themselves, let
alone the people, scarcely understand. They say, "Ite, missa est," yet
no one goes; they say "Dominus vobiscum," but this is meaningless
except at the time of Communion (a peculiar charge for Ascham to
make, since it immediately follows his own argument for worship in
the spirit, rather than through corporeal things).

Another of his devices is fallacious use of the syllogism; Ascham
seems to have forgotten in this slightly later work the lessons in dialectic
that his spokesman in *Toxophilus* had been able to give his companion.
Scholastic disputation, at the time still the dominant mode of argument
at Cambridge, demanded that the syllogism be used according to the
accepted laws of reasoning. Yet Ascham is not above equivocating, and
in at least one instance is patently guilty of begging the question. Under
the heading "Thou shalt not kill," his major premise, valid in theology
because authenticated by scripture, is that they who eat Christ's body
unworthily are guilty of his blood. The minor premise is that the mass
is unworthy (which the treatise has still to prove). The conclusion is
that those who celebrate masses are therefore guilty of Christ's blood.[31]
Had Ascham argued in this manner as an undergraduate, Pember or
Fitzherbert would certainly have taken him to task.

When logical arguments fail in divinity, philology sometimes may
help. In the tradition of the new learning, Ascham makes it clear that
he considers a knowledge of Greek essential in theological debate if one
is not to appear "insolent and inept." By citing parallels between passages in scripture and the works of Demosthenes, Isocrates, and Cicero,
he tries to show how the noblest thought of the ancient pagans, though
admittedly not a source of revealed truth, often conforms remarkably
to Christian teaching. More important, however, is the manner in which
a knowledge of Greek can open up the true sense of scripture. To prove
that the priests who claim to be "sacrificers" in the mass are in error,
he offers to compare a number of Latin terms with their Greek counterparts, not, he protests, to show off his erudition, but only to set forth
the truth. How can the papists claim that the mass is a true sacrifice,
he wonders, when in the Greek New Testament the word *hilasmós*

(propitiation) is never applied except to Christ himself? Why do they not inquire into the right meanings of words they have abused, such as *leitourgía* (which never meant a sacrifice for the living and the dead, but simply a charitable ministration), *epískopos* (a visitor or watchman), *diákonos* (a distributor), *presbúteros* (a minister)? Why, indeed, do they reject the name "minister," invariably used by St. Paul in preference to the odious term *sacerdos,* which, properly applied, refers only to priests who are also kings? He concludes with the charge that the papists, albeit unwittingly, by their sacrifices, their vestments, their very titles, are perpetuating Judaism rather than Christianity.[32]

The *Themata Theologica,* published in the same volume as the *Apologia,* are eleven in number. Nine are commentaries on scriptural verses. Of the remaining two, the first tries to explicate the saying from St. Augustine's *De Doctrina Christiana* that "Sin consists not in the thing done but in the intention of the doer." The other seeks to resolve the paradox of the *felix culpa*: whether more evil resulted from Adam's fall than good from the redemption by Christ. Some of these exercises may date from Ascham's earlier years at Cambridge; others, since he incorporates passages from them into the *Apologia* with little alteration, he apparently wrote, or at least reworked, about the time of the controversy over the mass. Grant assumes as much in remarking that he "composed some of them in private in his own chamber, and some of them he debated in the schools."[33]

Because they deal with random quotations, the *Themata* do not constitute a unified work. They do present, on the other hand, a consistent doctrinal viewpoint, and much as they smack of the school copybook, reveal, far better than the *Apologia* itself, what Ascham's religious beliefs at this time of his life really were. They show him to be, though definitely antipapal and an upholder of the basic new doctrines, a relatively conservative Protestant. He is unwilling to entangle himself in fruitless speculations over whether the human will is free or enslaved before conversion. He insists that all the spiritual good performed by man comes from God; at the same time he stresses the importance of leading a righteous life based on one's natural capacities as well as grace. Rather surprisingly he includes in the church militant all sorts of Christians, papists and heretics as well as "true evangelical believers." In the spirit of the not yet formulated Thirty-Nine Articles, he would maintain all customary practices of the church not manifestly contrary to the word of God, and he upholds the right of civil magistrates to exact obedience from all their subjects, redeemed Christians having no special prerogatives in this respect. He is opposed, clearly, not only to the "Romish abuses" that he attacks in the *Apologia*, but also to the excesses of certain extremists among the reformers. Objectionable papal dogmas he sees as "filths of that Roman cesspool," and the pope to him is a servant of the Antichrist. Then, too, "that traitor" Cardinal Reginald Pole is "infamous" for daring to suggest that a naturally (though not a supernaturally) good life might be led *extra Christum*. Equally abominable are those rash Protestants who would reject absolutely the freedom of the will, so that men may disregard the need to strive for a pious and upright life. He despises those who would strip the church of all its nonscriptural laws and ceremonies, and of its God-given authority to teach, and those who would deny the right of secular power to legislate in temporal matters for regenerate Christians.[34]

In several of the *Themata* he concerns himself with this last point, and hence identifies himself with the belief that the monarch is God's vice-gerent and that service to God and service to the Christian state are in practice inseparable. He stresses the rights of national churches by declaring that the lawful heads of Christian churches "after Christ, are the kings."[35] Then, as examples of ways in which men can observe St. Paul's injunction to "be angry, and sin not" (Ephesians 4:26), he asserts that princes and magistrates may exercise the wrath of correction, parents and teachers the wrath of monition, without moral culpability.[36] In support of this conclusion, he advances a curious argument in the first *thema*, on the *felix culpa*. Through the redemption, he claims, God not only gave man bliss greater than the evils brought into the world by Adam's fall, but in his inscrutable wisdom and goodness he made the ills themselves beneficial. Even fear and toil have been sanctified by Christ. Fear provides teachers with tractable pupils, and rulers with obedient subjects. Toil teaches that good comes only to him who strives; without work to occupy him, man soon falls into evil ways.[37]

The *Themata Theologica*, not one of his more important works, has at least the value of correcting the notion, sometimes derived from passages like the diatribe against Italy in *The Scholemaster*, that Ascham belonged to the advanced Reformation party and even inclined rather strongly toward Puritanism.[38] An occasional outburst against Rome apart, at least in these early exercises he appears as a quite moderate Protestant. He also reveals his conviction as an experienced teacher that the best in men must be brought out by strict self-discipline combined with proper moral guidance and, in the final analysis, the advantages of Christian corporate life. There is little, in fact, even in his later writings to suggest that the Marian restoration of Catholicism drove him toward the more extreme doctrines of Zürich or Geneva, the direction taken by many English Protestants during that period. And, finally, the views he expresses here on the moral obligation of all men to obey their prince help to account for the readiness with which he served Mary's government in spite of his well-known Anglican commitment.

Yet it was probably well for him that neither the *Themata Theologica* nor the *Apologia* was published at this time. The unmistakable, though relatively conservative, Protestantism of the two works, along with the slighting remarks on Cardinal Pole, would have proved embarrassing when Pole returned as papal legate to England. Nor would it have been wise to go through with the plan of dedicating the *Apologia* to Somerset. Whether Cheke or Cecil dissuaded Ascham, or whether he himself thought better of the matter after the Protector's stern admonition against scholars' meddling in ecclesiastical affairs, the fact is that both works dropped completely out of sight until they reappeared in the posthumous edition of 1577. Once again Ascham may have barely avoided disaster for speaking out on matters of religion. The first months of the protectorate were not a ripe occasion, regardless of the modifications that parliament was already introducing, for a humble fellow of St. John's to force his theological opinions on the practical ruler of church and state.

Ironically enough, in the spring of 1549 the king's commissioners visited Cambridge and heard licensed disputation concerning these very issues which not long before had been regarded as too explosive for open discussion. Madew, the regius professor of divinity who as vice-chancellor had interdicted the controversy in the schools, was now ordered to defend the two central propositions of Ascham's own *Apologia*, namely, that the doctrine of transubstantiation could not be proved by the words of scripture and that the Lord's Supper is but a memorial, in no way a re-enactment, of the sacrifice on Calvary.[39] What would have been dangerous presumption to maintain publicly a few months before was now the official position of the crown. Ascham, however, was not present to rejoice at this triumph for his views. A few months after the theological debates were banned, he had at last received a summons attractive enough to draw him away from troubled Cambridge to try his fortune in a different manner of living.

CHAPTER SIX

A Place So Slippery

IN JANUARY 1548, William Grindal died of the plague. The loss of this dearest friend, Ascham later confessed to Sturm, shocked him even more than the death of his parents. For seven years, starting with the younger man's matriculation at St. John's, they had studied Greek and Latin together in Ascham's chamber. Grindal had been his best pupil and had proved to be an outstanding tutor, under whose guidance Elizabeth had received such a foundation in languages that Ascham professed to be uncertain "whether to admire more the wit of her who learned, or the diligence of him who taught" (I, 272–73).

On January 22 he wrote to comfort the princess with the assurance that the new tutor who had been proposed for her, also named Grindal and a kinsman of the incomparable William, would make a worthy replacement.[1] For himself he requested only that she continue to hold the good opinion of him that Grindal had helped form in her mind. But Elizabeth had her own ideas about whom she wanted for an instructor. Ascham, whom she knew already from his occasional visits to Grindal, came to see her soon after sending his letter of condolence. Immediately she expressed her desire to be taught by him and by no other. He reported to Cheke that upon hearing the offer he at once began to depreciate his capacity for such employment. Through his apparent modesty, however, comes a tone of self-assurance and eagerness for the position. The princess and he had agreed that she ought to have the best person available; of course he could "say nothing of myself, yet am I brought to this hope, that although I am inept and of no account in almost all matters, still I can surely be of some use in teaching her the Greek and Latin tongues and in functioning as her secretary" (I, 161).

Although the implication of these words is obvious, Elizabeth's guardians, the queen dowager and her new husband, Lord Thomas Seymour, brother to the Protector, were of another mind. They did not regard Ascham favorably and preferred a man named Goldsmith. Ascham advised the princess to fall in with their wishes, at the same time recommending that she follow Cheke's judgment in the affair (I, 160, 162). She immediately went up to London to discuss the appointment with her stepparents, and whether by an assertion of the strong will for which she became known as queen, or through Cheke's growing influence with the privy council, she managed to get her way. Ascham immediately obtained leave from his college and entered her service at Chelsea Palace.

In joining this lively and soon to be notorious household, Ascham, though entering an unfamiliar world, was not completely among strangers. Grindal had introduced him not only to the princess, but to Lady Jane Grey, also in Seymour's keeping at the time; Ann Parr, younger sister to the queen and wife to the future Earl of Pembroke; John Whitney, a personable gentleman-in-waiting with a sister whose charms proved especially attractive to Ascham (I, 84); and Catherine Astley, Elizabeth's governess and sister-in-law to Richard Astley, one of the fellows of St. John's.

Encouraged by Grindal's recommendation to correspond with these new acquaintances, Ascham had already begun to render them small favors, to send them occasional gifts and words of advice. He urged Ann Parr, for example, to perfect her knowledge of Latin. In order to show that such learning was most admirable when joined to an upright life, he made her a present of a copy of the *De Officiis*. This book, he explains, is the most excellent of Cicero's writings. It contains so much human wisdom and such excellent examples of honorable conduct that whoever follows its teaching can scarcely fail to lead a worthy life. Ascham knows no other pagan book dealing with human conduct that excels this work in wisdom and distinction of language.

To John Astley, cousin to the princess through the Boleyns and husband to her governess, he writes in a similar vein. From Grindal he has heard so well of Astley that he sends him, too, a copy of the *De Officiis* (I, 92). In order that Astley and young John Whitney might not be deluded by their life at court into thinking that the world has any permanent good to offer, in 1547 he sent to each of them a series of pictures representing the dance of death, wherein he hoped that they would be able to "discern, as in a mirror, the decay of glory, the flesh, the world, lust, and all vanities" (I, 108). He urged Astley to progress in learning so that he might keep ahead of his diligent brother Richard and apace with those remarkable ladies, Queen Catherine and the princess. In this letter Ascham shows himself a true man of the Renaissance, for along with the *memento mori*, intended to keep Astley's mind on eternal things, he included another gift to encourage him to seek worldly fame through his learning, a catalogue of epistles to famous women compiled from the writings of St. Jerome and St. Augustine.

The brief note in English, the earliest extant in his native language, with which he opens his correspondence with Catherine Astley is the first evidence of his acquaintance with Elizabeth and influence upon her education. It contains, besides, an apt, if commonplace, metaphorical exposition of his belief in the importance of gentleness in teaching and of starting a child's education at an early age. "Good Mrs," runs his counsel, "I would have you in any case to labour, and not to give yourself to ease. I wish all increase of virtue and honour to that my good lady whose wit, good Mrs Astley, I beseech you, somewhat favour. The younger, the more tender; the quicker, the easier to break. Blunt edges be dull, and dure much pain to little profit; the free edge is soon turned if it be not handled thereafter. If you pour much drink at once into a goblet, the most part will dash out and run over; if you pour it softly you may fill it even to the top, and so her grace, I doubt not, by little and little, may be increased in learning, that at length greater cannot be required" (I, 86). He sends Mistress Astley a new silver pen and returns another that he has repaired for the princess. He also encloses a collection of prayers and an Italian book for Elizabeth.[2]

With such epistolary friendships already established, he seems to have made the transition from a Cambridge college to a royal household easily enough. The Astleys were cheerful company; with the husband Ascham in his free hours read the *Rhetoric* of Aristotle and a good portion of Livy and Cicero. They engaged also, as Astley reminded him later in looking back with nostalgia upon those days, "in free talk, mingled always with honest mirth," their conversations including "trim conferences" about notable contemporary events (III, 3). John Whitney shared a room with him, and Ascham taught him Latin. Their text was Cicero's *De Amicitia*, their method of study that of double translation—"out of Latin into English, and out of English into

Latin again"—which Ascham, following the teaching of Erasmus and Cheke, had adapted from Quintilian and later championed in *The Scholemaster*. Ascham boasted that his pupil, after a mere six months of daily exercise of this sort, could render English into Latin so perfectly "that some in seven years in grammar schools, yea, and some in the university too, cannot do half so well" (III, 172).

But the main source of his delight and admiration in this amiable company was the princess herself. Their studies together were to continue intermittently for another twenty years, but he never forgot his surprise and pleasure upon first encountering her zeal and capacity for learning. Though she was barely fifteen, he found her already an accomplished linguist, fluent in Italian, French, and Latin, and with some knowledge of Greek. In his opinion, she already manifested those gifts for which she was to become famous throughout Europe.

Much of his praise is no doubt conventional. Still, evidence from Elizabeth's later life does confirm what Ascham observed about her in her youth, and there is no reason to doubt his sincerity and the reasonable accuracy of his memory in describing her accomplishments. Every morning he studied Greek with her; in the afternoon they turned to Latin. Lessons began with a passage from the Greek New Testament, after which they read from the tragedies of Sophocles and selected orations of Isocrates and Demosthenes. To supplement her scriptural studies, Ascham gave her various works of St. Cyprian to read (probably among them the dull but suitable treatise *De disciplina virginum*), and also the *Loci communes rerum thelogicarum* of Philip Melanchthon. These two authors he found ideal for his purpose because their religious doctrine was sound and their language well-fitted to their subjects. After dinner the princess never failed to read something of Cicero, and in less than two years she got through a large part of Livy besides (I, 191–92). Such diligent application to classical studies foreshadowed the enthusiasm for Greek and Latin that continued well into her adult life. When she became queen and Ascham returned to her service as her Latin secretary, they regularly set aside time from state affairs to read their favorite authors together.

As he did with Whitney, Ascham taught languages to the princess by the method of double translation. He demanded of her no tedious drill in grammar, and although he admired Erasmus's various collections of model Latin sentences, he spared her drill in the same author's *Adagia*, the customary introduction to elegant style (III, 227). Because he preferred his pupils to go straight to the sources of eloquence, as soon as she had learned a few basic rules of declension and conjugation he immediately set before her the noblest ancient writers. Daily she rendered something of Demosthenes or Isocrates into English and back again into Greek; Latin she mastered by performing the same kind of exercise upon Cicero. The result, according to Ascham, was that within two years she had acquired a prodigious knowledge of both languages, had become an accurate judge of what constituted true eloquence, whether in Greek, Latin, or English, and had evolved an excellent prose style of her own (III, 180).

This account of Elizabeth's studies shows that Ascham was attempting to realize in a perfect subject the educational ideal that he had formed under Cheke's influence and practiced on his students at Cambridge. He sought to mold the mind and character of his apt pupil by combining the best learning contained in the classics with the saving doctrines of Christianity. This meant for him, as it did for Cheke in tutoring Edward VI, guiding her according to Aristotelian precepts of natural virtue, in order that she might achieve true *areté,* and at the same time inculcating Christian piety by having her read the Bible and selected patristic writings.

The emphasis on literary and rhetorical studies was an important factor in Ascham's theory of education. Like so many of his humanist contemporaries, he had little use for substance divorced from form; he believed that neglect of literary style infallibly signified the decay of thought in a civilization (III, 212). As proof of his contention, he observed that the best ideas of the ancients were those most nobly expressed; certainly no finer thought had survived than that of Homer, Plato, Sophocles, Demosthenes, and Cicero. Such authors provide not only admirable principles and lessons for human conduct, but also superb models for imitation in expressing one's own highest thought. Further, Greek and Latin were keys to the saving doctrine contained in the Scriptures and patristic writings. The end of education, the fashioning of a learned and pious adult suitably prepared to enact a destined role in the commonwealth, Ascham hoped to realize in Elizabeth by carefully blending these classical and Christian studies.

Although other evidence suggests that at times she could be a willful and recalcitrant charge, Ascham asserts that the princess lived up to his expectations in exemplary fashion. Even when copying out her lessons she did not, in her attentiveness to the substance of a passage, become careless of the manner in which she set it down on the page. For in addition to Greek and Latin, he taught her penmanship. When she wrote anything in either language, he boasted, there could be nothing more beautiful to view (I, 191). His testimony is supported by specimens of her writing that date from this time. Though as a busy and aging monarch she allowed her signature to degenerate into a scrawl, while under his supervision she did take care to write handsomely. He taught her the newly fashionable Italian script, which he practiced himself when composing official letters and which, mainly through his own, Cheke's, and Smith's efforts, was beginning to replace the old secretarial hand in English diplomatic and ceremonial correspondence.[3]

Ascham gave lessons in the new style of writing also to other young members of the royal household, and their accomplishment as a group must be largely credited to him. At court he met Henry and Charles Brandon, sons by a later wife to Henry VIII's brother-in-law, the Duke of Suffolk. Later both boys took instruction in writing from Ascham at Cambridge. There is a possibility, too, that Lady Jane Grey, while residing in the Lord Admiral's household, may have joined in Elizabeth's lessons. He also served intermittently as writing master to Edward VI. "Many times," he reminded Cecil in 1552, "by mine especial good, with Mr Cheke's means, I have been called to teach the king to write, in his privy-chamber" (I, 332). These lessons had begun even before he became Elizabeth's tutor. He speaks of having ridden to Hertford from the university "divers times" before 1548 for the purpose. He had been forced to do so at his own expense because Edward's attendants were indifferent to the drain on his meager income (I, 398). Partly as recompense for this unpaid instruction, he was designated royal librarian in 1550 and later nominated the king's Latin secretary, though Edward died before Ascham could begin to serve him in that office.

II

In spite of Elizabeth's aptness and the enjoyable company of his new surroundings, Ascham's months as a royal tutor were anything but tranquil ones. The household was merry enough, perhaps too merry in certain respects for even so tolerant and good-humored a man as he.

The disturbing and unwholesome feature of its domestic life was the conduct of the princess's guardians. While Ascham was teaching her Aristotelian ethics and Christian morality, the Lord Admiral was scandalizing the court by the unseemly familiarity with which he treated her and her young ladies-in-waiting. Sometimes alone and sometimes with the queen, he would enter Elizabeth's chamber to romp with her and tickle her as she lay in bed. On one occasion the queen even pinioned the girl while Seymour playfully cut away her gown and left her in her undergarments.[4]

Why Catherine Parr should have indulged these whims of her husband is inexplicable, for it was well known that immediately after Henry VIII's death he had made an unsuccessful attempt to secure permission from the council to marry Elizabeth. Even stranger is the fact that the young king and his advisers allowed the princess to remain with the queen after her clandestine marriage to Seymour less than four months after Henry was buried. Eventually Catherine did become jealous, particularly when she noticed that Seymour's behaviour was giving rise to gossip and that the young princess seemed to be responding to his familiarities in a manner no longer childlike. Despite the queen's tolerance, she could hardly be expected to put up with such a formidable rival in her own household. Around Whitsunday 1548, therefore, some four months after Ascham's arrival at Chelsea, Elizabeth and her servants were packed off to live with Sir Anthony Denny at Cheshunt in Hertfordshire.

Ascham, though he makes no explicit mention of it, appears from his letters to have been shaken by this scandal. The inexperienced scholar who had pontificated from Cambridge to Lord Mountjoy and had warned Astley and Whitney about the temptations and uncertainties of the court had now encountered the "slipperiness" of that way of life himself. Before he was well settled into his new quarters at Cheshunt, he wrote to William Ireland on July 8 that he hoped by Michaelmas to return to the university for good.[5] He had meant to come back for a visit earlier in the year, but the princess had forbidden it, either because a student in Ascham's college had just died of the plague, or simply "because she never willingly sends me away from her."

Probably both reasons applied. Having already lost one good tutor to the plague, Elizabeth would not have wanted to risk losing another. She had begun to suffer, besides, from a series of illnesses that kept her almost constantly indoors; in her restlessness at confinement she did

not want either her governess or her tutor out of her sight. The constant presence of Ascham, finally, may have given her some assurance,
in the midst of the moral chaos of her immediate surroundings, that
decency and stability still existed. As for Ascham, though he remained
fascinated by his brief experience of life in a royal household, he now
comprehended the reality of its dangers and the vanity of its allurements. He had recently been with the king and had observed a number of young noblemen, friends of Lord Robert Stafford, squandering
time in "talk about the most trivial matters." He contrasts their behavior with that of Stafford, who is occupying himself at St. John's in
profitable converse "with Cicero about weighty affairs such as are truly
fitting for a well-born man." Yet Ascham acknowledges that "many
men, once made courtiers, greatly praise the quiet of their former life,
but do not wish to give up the sumptuousness and display of this courtly
life." He wonders, sadly, whether he may not himself be such a willing
prisoner of his new environment. "About myself I cannot promise anything; still, I do reflect upon it somewhat" (I, 167). With these words he
first gives voice to a conflict that preoccupied him for the next several
years: whether he could return contentedly to the frugal and retired life
of a Cambridge scholar after having sampled the pleasures, vain and
delusive as he held them to be, of the court.

Events during the succeeding months tipped the scales temporarily
in favor of Cambridge. In August John Whitney suddenly died. Ascham
was deeply grieved by this loss, for Whitney had partly replaced Grindal
in his affections. He had also represented proof that a young man might
triumph over the corrupting influences of great households. "A court
full of such young gentlemen," Ascham declared afterwards in *The
Scholemaster*, "were rather a paradise than a court upon earth" (III,
172). He mourned Whitney in his longest effort in English verse, con-
soling himself with the conventional reflection that the good die young
and that he and Whitney would someday meet again in heaven. Though
the poem is totally undistinguished, Ascham's high hopes for Whitney
are reflected in two stanzas remarking his singular accomplishment in
living an upright Christian life in spite of the many allurements to vice
in his surroundings:

> Young years to yield such fruit in court,
> > Where seed of vice is sown,
> Is sometime read, in some place seen,
> > Among us seldom known.

His life he led, Christ's love to learn,
With will to work the same;
He read to know, and knew to live,
And liv'd to praise his name (III, 173).

It may have been at approximately the same time that Ascham composed another "rude little verse" expressing his disgust at the conduct
of the ambitious, as contrasted with that of such virtuous courtiers as
Whitney:

To laugh, to lie, to flatter, to face,
Four ways in court to win men grace.
If thou be thrall to none of these,
Away good Peckgoose, hence John Cheese.
Mark well my word, and mark their deed,
And think this verse part of thy creed (III, 127).

Whether or not he meant by this complaint that in order to survive in
high places he would have to practice the four-part creed, it is quite
clear that Ascham was beginning already to think that for him "hence"
and "away" might prove the wiser course.

For within a few weeks, in September, the death of Catherine Parr
in childbirth started a chain of events disconcerting to him and extremely dangerous to the princess. With his wife out of the way, Seymour again considered marrying Elizabeth. He intended to do so secretly in order to forestall the objections that would certainly arise. The
design was foolhardy, for Henry VIII's will had stipulated that neither of
his daughters should wed without the consent of the privy council. Seymour was aided in his plan by Elizabeth's steward, Thomas Parry, and
by her governess. Unfortunately Catherine Astley, though she had been
courageous enough to remonstrate against his earlier unseemly behavior, really liked Seymour and did all she could to further his interest
with the girl. Elizabeth was flattered, for she too was fascinated by
this dashing courtier. Yet since she already had the gift of circumspec-
tion that kept her out of damaging entanglements throughout her long
public life, she waited and committed herself to nothing.

The proposed clandestine marriage would have been risky enough,
since the Lord Admiral had already incensed the council by his hasty
wedding to Catherine Parr. His intriguing, however, was not confined
to matrimony. Vain, reckless, and insatiably ambitious, he resented his
elder brother's power and had already attempted to discredit him with
Edward VI. He now tried to win supporters within the council in hopes

of gaining custody of the king and, as his ambitions grew with his plotting, of supplanting Somerset as virtual ruler of England during his nephew's minority.

He had chosen an opportune time to bring his intrigue to a head. As has been seen in the account of the theological debates at Cambridge, many men were restive over the inchmeal progress of ecclesiastical reform under the protectorate. Then Somerset's recent campaign in Scotland, which had begun propitiously, was turning out to be militarily indecisive and unprofitable. Relying on the mounting discontent, the Admiral, a more popular man than his brother, began to rally support for himself in preparation for a coup. Mistress Astley was not the only person imprudent enough to be taken in by his personal charm. His brother-in-law, the Marquis of Northampton, secretly approved his plan. The Marquis of Dorset, Henry Grey, favored him and had been inveigled, partly by loans of money and partly by assurances that his daughter should marry the king, into permitting Lady Jane to remain in his household. To raise funds, Seymour corrupted the master of the mint at Bristol. To assure himself of military support, he curried favor in the west and augmented his naval forces by entering into an agreement with various freebooters of the English Channel, when his official duty was to rid the seas of them. Finally, to provide himself with armament, he had two cannon foundries producing at full speed.[6]

Matters were in this state when Ascham obtained leave from Hatfield House, to which Elizabeth had removed in the autumn, in order to spend Christmas with his friends at St. John's. He returned from this brief holiday just in time to witness the most dangerous crisis of his pupil's troubled girlhood. The privy council had long been disturbed about Seymour's actions and his insinuations against his brother. The ill-concealed, or deliberately open, measures he was taking to provide for himself could only be interpreted as conspiracy. Then rumors of his design to marry Elizabeth began to circulate openly. When added to the evidence of his other ominous preparations, this news was more than the councillors would stomach. Twice they called upon him to explain his behavior, but he refused on the grounds that he did not acknowledge the council's or his brother's authority over him. On January 17, 1549, he was committed to the Tower.

Immediately after his arrest, Sir Anthony Denny brought Parry and Mistress Astley to London for examination about their own and Elizabeth's part in Seymour's intrigues. The princess was questioned at Hatfield by the council's skilled and ruthless investigator, Sir Robert Tyrwhitt. Adept as he was at handling witnesses, Tyrwhitt could extract nothing from her. But at length Parry admitted his share in promoting the match, and upon hearing that he had broken down under questioning, Catherine Astley likewise confessed. Still Elizabeth would admit nothing; perhaps she was innocent and had nothing to admit.[7] Yet she was almost compromised by a last foolhardy gesture of Seymour's. Toward the end of February a bill of attainder was presented against him in parliament. On March 4, after all the evidence had been heard and the bill had passed Lords and Commons, he was told to prepare for his execution. Rashly he wrote to both Mary Tudor and Elizabeth urging them to plot against Somerset; when he went to the scaffold the letters were discovered and laid before the privy council.

Although Elizabeth managed herself remarkably well throughout this ordeal, she did not escape damage to her reputation. For nearly two years Edward did not receive her at court, and she remained in semi-official disgrace at Hatfield. Probably Ascham wrote little or nothing about these events; no letters from 1549 remain in his correspondence. In any case, his editor Grant would surely have deleted any allusion in the letters to this unfortunate episode of the reigning queen's stormy youth. Yet without question the months after Seymour's fall were exceedingly trying for Ascham as well as for the princess. Although he was not involved himself in the intriguing or in the subsequent inquisitions, his friends the Astleys had sailed close to disaster, and he had seen in Seymour's example a bitter confirmation of his view of the "tickle state" of the ambitious courtier's fortunes. The strain of the ordeal, moreover, had badly shaken Elizabeth and had nearly broken her health. In her nervous and dispirited state, she appears to have developed some coolness toward her tutor, while his relations with other members of the household seem also to have begun to deteriorate. Nothing further is heard of his life at Hatfield until January 28, 1550, when he wrote to Cheke from St. John's that he had been "shipwrecked" by a storm of "recent violence and injury at court." Without further elaboration, the letter reports that he has left, or has been dismissed from, the service of the princess (I, 174–76).

III

Although Ascham does not specify what the "tempest" was that sent him so abruptly back to Cambridge, it seems to have been a personal rather than a state matter. Certainly it occurred too late to have been connected directly with the fall of Thomas Seymour, nor is there any evidence that he had been implicated in the more recent embarrassment of the Duke of Somerset. He merely asserts that he had been "injured on all sides" and that perverse fortune rather than any fault on his part had caused him to leave Hatfield House. He denies that Elizabeth had suddenly turned against him, yet he says enigmatically that trouble had burst upon him from a source "whence I ought to have drawn the reward for my service rather than the fear of offence."[8] The one concrete fact revealed in his letter to Cheke is that he had been maligned by Elizabeth's *oeconomus*. If by the term he means her steward or cofferer, the person involved may have been the intriguer Parry. Possibly Ascham had rebuked this go-between for his activity in Seymour's behalf, and Elizabeth may have felt that the affair was none of Ascham's business. But this is only conjecture, since he gives no further clue to the identity of his adversary or the nature of the disturbance that led to his sudden departure.

To add to his chagrin, he had heard that certain persons were carrying false and spiteful tales about him to Cheke, apparently with the intention of discrediting him in the eyes of an old friend and benefactor. Ascham begs Cheke to hear his side of the story from two of their associates at St. John's who are coming to court, Henry Cumberford and Richard Wilkinson. When the true version is told, he hopes that the "good will, faithfulness, and works" that Cheke had formerly praised in him, might suffice to keep him in favor. Meanwhile, his career as Elizabeth's tutor having terminated so soon and so unprofitably, he sees before him two options, either to settle in again at the university, or, if Cheke is willing to help him, to go abroad for a couple of years of study.

Despite this talk of returning to scholarly pursuits, neither his disillusioning experiences among the mighty nor his dismissal from office seems really to have convinced him that his true place was in the university. Certainly his recent experiences should have made him wary of court intrigue. Upon what were, in his view, unjust and unfounded accusations he had lost his own position. He had seen from uncomfortably close range the fall of the Admiral and the embarrassment of Elizabeth and his friends the Astleys. Then, shortly before his return to St. John's, he had seen the Lord Protector lose his power. He had seen, too, the shifting fortunes of some of his closest Cambridge friends who had taken up public careers. In May 1549 Cheke had fallen into temporary disgrace and returned briefly to Cambridge. Upon his recall to court some months later, he was confronted with a new crisis, his wife having offended the Duchess of Somerset and he himself being accused of having betrayed the Protector.[9] In October of the same year Thomas Smith fell from favor. Loyal to Somerset to the end, he was deprived by the Protector's opponents of his secretarial post, his place on the council, and his regius professorship at Cambridge. For five months he was also imprisoned in the Tower and secured his release only upon acknowledgement of a fine of £3,000.[10] Even the circumspect Cecil apparently stumbled into trouble in 1550, since Ascham wrote to sympathize with him in his present distress (I, 177). Though all three men were to prosper during the second half of Edward's reign, their ups and downs, along with the dizzying rise and fall of various lords of the council, ought to have made Ascham content with his lot at Cambridge. But having enjoyed the delights as well as seen the perils of his enlarged world, he seems to have been more willing than ever before to surrender his academic quiet and security for a chance at adventure and an improvement in his career.

Sometime after his return to the university, he wrote to an unnamed friend that if any nobleman were to be made ambassador to the general council of the church at Trent, which was rumored to be reassembling, he would "be most willing to serve him on that journey" (I, 172). He was also beginning to think about marriage. Both Cheke and Smith had recently wed. Cecil, the one romantic episode in his life having ended with the early death of his first wife, Mary Cheke,[11] had taken as his second the bluestocking Mildred Cooke, a person whom Ascham ranked with Lady Jane Grey as one of the most learned women of the age.

Upon coming from cloistered Cambridge to a royal household, Ascham had not been immune to the charms of Elizabeth's gay ladies-in-waiting. He seems to have enjoyed their company and to have been capable of light banter with them. From Cheshunt he wrote to William Ireland that one Catherine R——, "a most excellent and honorable young woman," had come to visit him. Unfortunately he happened to be away at court on the day of her arrival; otherwise he would have presented her to the princess. "I said to her noble maidens," he confides, "that she both loved me alone, and would be my wife, which almost all of them readily believed" (I, 169). Though he seems here to have been teasing Elizabeth's attendants, some months later he was in earnest about wanting to marry a certain A—— B——, niece of the friend to whom he had expressed his desire to attend the Council of Trent. He had really composed that letter, in fact, to secure the uncle's approval of the match. Admitting his unworthiness and his present small income, he expressed hope that his friend's benevolence and his own prospects of future advancement would make him an acceptable suitor (I, 170–71). How the proposal was received is not recorded, but at the time no marriage took place.

Perhaps A—— B—— is the "Alice, my wife" to whom Ascham asks to be remembered in 1551 in a letter to Lady Jane Grey (I, 241). By the Latin term "uxor," however, he clearly does not refer to an actual wife, though he may mean by the word someone who had promised to marry him. A letter that he received from Thomas Lever late in the same year while he was away from his college shows that his plans for marriage were quite serious. Lever, who had recently succeeded William Bill as master of St. John's, acknowledges Ascham's request to be exempted from the statute of celibacy whenever he should return to read Greek in the society. The petition has been forwarded to Cheke, from whom a reply is expected soon. For his own part, Lever assures Ascham, he is "not unwilling that you should have and enjoy any privilege that may encourage you to better knowledge of the Greek tongue."[12]

Ascham, then, may have been secretly engaged at the time to his friend's niece. On the other hand, "Alice" may have been some other lady, and the words "my wife" simply a playful title conferred by him upon some attractive member of Lady Jane's household.

In still another letter he proposes marriage to a widow with a family of children, one Mistress N——. Again the woman's identity remains a mystery. It is possible that "A—— B——," "Alice, my wife," and "Mistress N——" are one person, for the initials supplied by copyists of the manuscript letters are simply indications that a name has been omitted. Whether the letters are addressed to one person or three, this correspondence establishes the seriousness of Ascham's intention to marry, even though he did not actually take a wife at the time.[13] It also underscores the return of the old unrest and indecision about where he should ultimately turn to seek a career.

Despite the attractions of fair ladies and the nearly irresistible call of foreign parts, he remained unwilling to resign his fellowship and other academic offices, and hence bided his time for some months at Cambridge. Besides writing letters as public orator and performing his other regular duties, he associated himself with Thomas Wilson, tutor to the Brandons, giving lessons in penmanship to both boys and to Charles also lessons in Greek (I, 222).

During this period of waiting for something to happen, he enjoyed a brief but significant friendship with Martin Bucer, the celebrated theologian and reformer from Strasbourg. Bucer, after much urging by Cranmer, had come to England in April 1549. For most of the year he remained with the archbishop. Then, after his companion Paul Fagius died in London in November, he accepted an offer to read divinity at Cambridge. On December 4, King Edward sent a letter to Haddon, now serving as vice-chancellor of the university, asking for confirmation of Bucer's appointment as a lecturer in theology. Early in 1550, following his incorporation, Bucer began to lecture in the schools.

Ascham had met Bucer at Lambeth Palace shortly after his arrival in England. During their acquaintance in London he spoke of his ill-treatment at Hatfield and asked Bucer, though evidently with no immediate result, to intercede on his behalf with the princess, who, he admitted, "was somewhat alienated from me" (I, 231). Now that both men were at the university, they frequently met and conversed. Ascham came to regard the theologian not only as an adornment to Cambridge, but also as his own spiritual father and teacher. Often their talk was about Bucer's close friend Johann Sturm (I, 183). Inspired by their conversations and encouraged by Bucer, Ascham wrote to Sturm for the first time on April 4, 1550, a date that marks the beginning of his most important epistolary friendship.

In this letter (I, 181–93), he commends himself to Sturm in his most polished Latin. Dispensing with the customary introduction, he opens directly by commenting on the value and interconnection of logic and rhetoric and on the primary importance of eloquence among the accomplishments of men. He rejoices in the achievements made in this art by the ancients and praises those who have excelled in it in contemporary Italy, France, and Germany. Above all he admires Sturm, of whose work he has read everything he could find in print or in manuscript. Now that he has mustered courage to take up his pen, he is emboldened to ask a favor, not for himself alone, but for all the world of learning. He begs Sturm to publish his long-expected commentary on Aristotle's *Rhetoric*, for, despite its excellent doctrine, the *Rhetoric* is hard going because Aristotle fails to provide cogent examples to illustrate his precepts. Ascham makes this request not out of laziness;

he has read diligently in both sacred scripture and humane letters, and (like Faustus) he has not scorned to glance into medicine and jurisprudence as well. Nor is he too ignorant to find for himself examples for comment and imitation; he knows that one may discover illustrations of every one of Aristotle's precepts in the writings of Plato. But so great is Sturm's skill in elucidating texts that mankind must no longer be deprived of the benefits of his eloquence and learning. Ascham does not believe the task will involve new and difficult labors but only the completing of old ones, since he and his friends at Cambridge have read much of what Sturm has already undertaken in explanation of the *Rhetoric.* Many scholars, he adds, would be happy to have Sturm provide commentaries, too, on Plato's *Phaedo* and Aristotle's *De Anima.*

In order to avoid giving an impression that he is rudely importunate, Ascham devotes the rest of the epistle to the state of learning among his countrymen and tries to show how England, Cambridge, and Roger Ascham are able to hold their own with Continental scholars in Greek and Latin studies. Cambridge (here he chooses to ignore the troublesome side of the past decade) has been flourishing, in divinity since the advent of Bucer, in the classical tongues since Cheke, Smith, and Haddon had inspired men to scholarship. If Cheke and Smith, now occupied with public affairs, were only able to devote all their time to study and writing, "not Sadoleto in Italy, nor Longueil in France, would excel them." He is not sure, on the other hand, about what is being read at Oxford. He can only state that when he was at court the conversation of "a certain man of that university" shocked his own more orthodox humanism and made him suspect that Oxonians were on the verge of decadence. They were, if one might credit what this person had told him, interested mainly in authors of the declining periods of Greek and Roman eloquence—Lucian, Plutarch, Herodian, Seneca, Aulus Gellius, and Apuleius. To Ascham such "corrupted" taste was a sure forewarning of the demise of true learning at the sister university.

Even more remarkable to him than the accomplishments of Cambridge scholars was the zeal for learning of the English aristocracy. Ascham singles out for praise the king, the Brandons, the daughters of Sir Thomas More, and, naturally, Elizabeth. If Sturm would write something to this accomplished princess, she would receive it graciously and read it through with sound critical perception. He has heard that Sturm may come to England. Whether the rumor is to be believed or not, he frequently prays that it may be true. He would like, meanwhile, to receive letters and sends Sturm as a memento a silver denarius of Caligula, with the assurance of further gifts of ancient coins should he wish to have them.

Ascham received no answer to this epistle until the end of the year. Sturm, a notoriously procrastinating correspondent, finally did write late in the summer and sent his long reply by means of Bucer's wife, who left Strasbourg in September to join her husband at Cambridge.[14] But she arrived too late to deliver the letter in person, for by that time Ascham was no longer in the university or even in England.

CHAPTER SEVEN

In High and Low Germany

DURING THE SUMMER of 1550, Ascham returned to Yorkshire for a visit with old friends. While there he received word from Cheke that he had been made secretary to Sir Richard Morison, the newly appointed ambassador to the Emperor Charles V. Here at last was the chance not only to travel and to visit famous Continental scholars, but, further-more, to reside in the most important court in Europe.

Since the privy council had specified Michaelmas as the date for Morison to take up his commission, Ascham set out from Yorkshire early in September.[1] Though eager to reach London in order to pre-pare for his voyage, he paused along the road for two memorable visits. Nearing Leicester, he turned aside to Bradgate Hall, home of the Marquis of Dorset. At once he was admitted to the chamber of Lady Jane Grey. Although everyone else was out hunting in the deer park, which lay immediately beneath her window, Ascham discovered Lady Jane "reading *Phaedo Platonis* in Greek, and that with as much delight as some gentlemen would read a merry tale in Boccace." To this thir-teen-year-old prodigy, learning was a greater pleasure than such aristo-cratic, but from her point of view frivolous, occupations as the chase. This opinion she had formed, not simply from bookish platitudes, but from her own experience. For, she told Ascham, whereas her strict and nagging parents would punish her for her mistakes "with pinches, nips, and bobs, and other ways," her gentle tutor, the future Bishop Aylmer, made her lessons so pleasant that "whatsoever I do else but learning, is full of grief, trouble, fear, and whole misliking unto me." This famous interview, the inspiration for a number of romanticized paintings and scenes in literature, was to be Ascham's last encounter with the un-fortunate girl whom he had first known at Chelsea.[2] Indeed, except for an elegant epistle he wrote to her from Augsburg (I, 239–41), it was the last exchange between them. By the time he returned from the Continent Lady Jane had already endured her unwanted nine days' reign and had been sent to the Tower by the rightful queen.

Somewhat farther along the road, though he approached the red-brick palace with some trepidation, he decided to stop at Hatfield. The interview with his former pupil proved far less painful than he had anticipated. Elizabeth "received me very kindly," he later wrote to Bucer, "and very gently reproved me, because I had been so minded to leave her, without having endeavored through any man to come again into her favor" (I, 231). Whether or not they completely patched up their former misunderstanding, at least pupil and tutor parted on terms that smoothed the way to a renewal of their old relationship upon his return from Germany.

Upon arriving in London, he wrote to Edward Raven on September 17 that he expected to set sail on the 19th. On the 20th, however, he was still in London and went to visit Cheke, who was convalescing from a fever. They chatted "about things pertaining to religion, the court, the commonwealth, the university" (I, 209). Cheke mentioned his approval of what he had been hearing about his old college, and Ascham took the occasion to commend several of the fellows to his notice.

At last, on the morning of Sunday the 21st, the ambassadorial party sailed from Billingsgate to Gravesend. The short trip downriver was smooth, and the travelers disembarked on the afternoon of the same day. On the 22d they took horse for Canterbury. That night John Hales, Edward VI's clerk of the hanaper, entertained them sumptuously; the next day they were greeted by Archbishop Cranmer, who accompanied them most of the way to Dover. On the 24th, after a rough Channel crossing during which everyone but the eager Ascham and a young gentleman from Lincoln became seasick, they arrived at Calais, where they rested until the morning of the 26th.

The six letters in which Ascham describes his journey from England to High Germany reveal some of the most engaging qualities of his character. The last of the six, which is the only one in English, is one of the finest specimens of realistic travel writing from the Tudor period. Ascham records accurately what he has seen and communicates his pleasure at encountering new peoples, places, and customs rather than trying to impress his friends at home with tales of foreign marvels.

When he does repeat fables and legends or records some nine days' wonder, he invariably does so in order to expose them as frauds or ridicule belief in such fantasies.

In their ability to communicate the sheer delight of traveling, the letters can compare even with Montaigne's celebrated journal. In them Ascham appears as indefatigable tourist and astute reporter, his mind and senses keenly alert for adventure as he strolls along the main streets or pries into the alleys and byways of each new stopping-place. Not once does he seem to have wasted an opportunity for exploration. As soon as he dismounted at Canterbury, though he had spent a tiring day slogging drearily along "a foul road" upon "a small and weary horse," he set out to tour the city. First he hastened to the cathedral, where he eagerly scrutinized every monument, noting particularly the inscriptions on the tombs of King Henry IV and that leader of brave archers, the Black Prince. He also paused at "the place where Becket was slain." Having satisfied his historical curiosity, he browsed among the bookstalls and goldsmiths' shops, then strolled among the citizens to observe their deportment, as if, good Yorkshireman that he was, he regarded these Englishmen from the far south as belonging to another race. The necessarily brief tour of Canterbury and the enthusiasm with which he describes it set the pattern for the remainder of his journey. Again at Calais, he left the others to recover from their tossing on the Channel and "at once walked entirely all around the town." Its situation, the disposition of the troops, the bustle of the port, the view of the outlying villages, his first panoramic survey of foreign, though English-held, soil, afforded him a picture that he believed would "never perish from my memory" (I, 210–11).

On the 26th, they rode by way of Gravelines to Dunkerque, whose buildings, though it was a mere fishing town, Ascham found comparable to those of any city in England. On the 28th they went on to Bruges, which "far surpasses London," and on the 30th reached Antwerp, to rest for two days in "the most splendid seat of trade not of Brabant alone, but of all the world" (I, 212). As he progressed eastward, amazement at the splendor of the cities and the density of the population grew upon the traveler from sparsely settled Yorkshire; to him there seemed to be as many people living between Bruges and Antwerp as there were in all of England.

Nothing, not even foul lodgings and miry roads, dulled his appetite for exploring, and he regrets only that no one else in the party was so eager as he. The young gentlemen were willing at first to start out on tours with him, but they quickly wearied of sight-seeing, so that "I stopped more by them than they provoked by me, left things I would gladly have seen" (I, 247). Even his manservant, Vaughan, seldom accompanied him, for he had been assigned by Morison to look after the baggage of the company. Ascham boasts, therefore, that unlike these indifferent youths and most other Englishmen who ventured abroad, he let nothing great or small escape his notice: the sight of famous men, the dress and behavior of young and old, the state of religion and learning in each locality, relics of the classical past, the plan and chief buildings of every city, even the kinds of crops growing in the fields along the way.

At Mechelen he saw the Protestant leader Philip, Landgrave of Hesse, who had been kept under arrest by Charles V since the imperial victory over the Schmalkaldic allies in 1547. At eight o'clock on the morning of October 4, Ascham watched the noted state prisoner performing his daily ritual of distributing alms to the poor. To make his verbal portrait of Philip come to life for Raven and the other "Johnians," Ascham likens him to a familiar person at home, a device that he frequently used in describing famous men whom he met on his travels. The Landgrave, he notes, "is lusty, well-favoured, something like Mr Hebilthwat [master of Sedbergh School] in the face: hasty, unconstant; and to get himself out of prison, would fight, if the Emperor would bid him, with Turk, French, England, God, and the Devil" (I, 244).

At Mechelen he also discovered a "convent," full "not of idle, but busy nuns," in all, sixteen hundred of them earning their keep by making linen garments. These "nuns" were free to leave and marry whenever they wished (I, 214). What a contrast their sober industry must have afforded to the mind of the Cambridge Protestant with the Breughel-like scene he encountered at Tirlemont three days later— nuns dancing lustily in the streets at a wedding! But what he had believed to be a convent was obviously a Béguinage, organized quite differently from a nunnery and, though common enough in the Low Countries, a strange institution to an inexperienced traveler from England. The most remarkable sight of all, however, was an exotic white bird that had formerly belonged to the Emperor Maximilian. This incredible creature was "well able to swallow, without grief or touch of breast, a white penny-loaf of England, except your bread be bigger than your bread-maker [MS. *bread-master*] of St. John's is wont willingly to make it" (I, 244). Thus, with a sly thrust at one of the college characters, Ascham describes for his friends his first sight of a pelican.

On the next day, since it was a Sunday, Morison decided to stop over in Brussels. Here Ascham shows to best advantage his real sense of color and love of spectacle. He went to mass at the ducal palace ("more to see than for devotion, some of you will think") and was in good luck for the "seeing" because the emperor's elder sister, Eleonore, widow of King Francis I, was there. Ascham's ear noted the fine Burgundian music, his eye took in every detail of the scene, and his wit played with the contrasts of color and of individual behavior at the service. The dowager queen was

clad very solemnly all in white cameric, a robe gathered in plaits wrought very fair as might be with needle white work, as white as a dove. A train of ladies followed her, as black and evil as she was white. Her mass was sung in prick-song by Frenchmen very cunningly, and a gentleman played at the organs excellently. A French whipit Sir John bestirred himself so at the altar as I wished Patrick by to have learned some of his knacks.[3] The mass was as hap was cut short; for the queen came late and was not disposed to tarry long. The queen sat in a closet above: her ladies kneeled all abroad in the chapel among us. The regent of Flanders had left at Brussels a sort of fair lusty young ladies; they came not out, but were kept in mew for fear of goshawks of Spain and France; yet they came to mass, and stood above in windows, as well content to show themselves, as we to see them.

They had on French gowns of black velvet, guarded down right from the collar with broad guards, one nigh another, some of cloth of gold, some of cloth of silver, great chains ornamented with precious jewels. On their heads they had glistering cauls of goldsmith work, and black velvet caps above, full of great agletts of gold, with white feathers round about the compass of their caps. They seemed boys rather than ladies, excellent to have played in tragedies. There was not one well-favoured amongst them, save one young lady, fair and well-favoured (I, 245–46).

While it thus delighted his eye, the spectacle undoubtedly served, besides, as amusing confirmation to Ascham of that decay of true worship under the "mass-priests" which he had deplored in his defense of the Lord's Supper.

After mass, his tourist's good fortune continued, for as a visitor from England he was admitted to the queen's chamber while she dined. But after noting the manner of service, the conduct of the attendants, and the quality of the first dishes brought in to her, he "was content to lose the second course, lest I should have lost my own dinner at home" (I, 246). In the afternoon he walked down through the park and toured the city. Toward evening he retraced his steps and, nearing the palace, entered the Carmelite house of which the theologian Eberhard Billicus (Steinberger), one of the most effective Catholic controversialists of the time, was warden. Since Billicus happened to be away at his native Cologne, Ascham missed a chance for conversation with this formidable antagonist of his beloved Bucer. He was hospitably entertained instead by another friar. This man was learned in Latin and Greek, and although he knew Ascham "to be a protestant, yet showed me all gentleness he could." They went through the house and the library, in which there stood "not one good book but [Nicholas of] Lyra," and they would have drunk something together "if the butler had been within" (I, 248).

His first direct experience of a Continental university came on the following day at Louvain. Although Morison tarried only from eleven until two, this time Ascham was willing to sacrifice his dinner in order "to feed mine eyes and ears." He did not find there either Christopherson, who had been in residence since 1547, or his old friend Brandisby. As he learned afterwards, Brandisby had ridden to Antwerp in hopes of meeting the English party, but had missed them somewhere along the road. Nor did Ascham, as he had hoped, arrive in time to hear the celebrated Peter Nannius (Nanninck) of Alkmaar lecture on Cicero. Nannius had already lectured earlier in the day and, as one of his English pupils impishly informed Ascham, was off somewhere drinking and making merry. He did, however, hear Theodoricus Laudius (Lange) expound twenty-one verses of *Oedipus Rex* above the clamor of eighty unruly auditors. He noted with satisfaction that Laudius pronounced Greek exactly as did Smith and Cheke. From the little he observed during this brief visit, he concluded that for scholarship Catholic Louvain could not compare with Protestant Cambridge. For an hour he sat listening to Laudius's exposition; then he had to gallop out of town because Morison and the others had already departed (I, 248–49).

At Tongeren on October 7 he enjoyed two gratifying sights and missed yet another. As the Englishmen came up to the town, they met the emperor's sister Mary, regent of Flanders, posting toward Brussels with some thirty attendants. This remarkable woman had completely exhausted her companions by covering the distance from Augsburg in thirteen days, seventeen being reckoned excellent time for the journey.

"She is a virago," writes Ascham admiringly; "she is never so well as when she is flinging on horseback, and hunting all the night long" (I, 249). In the fields close by he came upon one of the monuments of antiquity for which he was constantly on the alert, the walls of the ancient town mentioned in Julius Caesar's commentaries. But when he stopped later at Maastricht, where he was shown the first Roman coin that he saw in his travels, he learned to his regret that he might have had a "great sort" of them at Tongeren.

As he left the Low Countries, he compared their agriculture and economy with England's. Besides the cloth manufactured at Mechelen, he admired the water mills along the Meuse and wondered why the Thames had not been so efficiently exploited as a source of power. Although the meat and fowl, except for some delectable mutton and capons he had enjoyed at Bruges, were inferior to those at home, good husbandry and hard labor had made the region wonderfully productive of vegetables and grain. The well-cultivated gardens about the walls of every town suggested to him that Londoners might also make such good use of the "void places of the city." There would then be no hunger among the needy, and "all England should have victuals better cheap." He admired too the temperance of the people, for he remarks that "there is more wine indeed drunken in England, where none grows, than even there, from whence it cometh" (I, 250–51).

On Saturday the 11th, the travelers arrived at Cologne and rested again over Sunday before embarking on the Rhine for Mainz. The city was shrouded in a mist from the river, but Ascham could see well enough to admire its handsome parks; the buildings, however, struck him as inferior to those of the Flemish towns. Since they arrived early in the day, he was able to hear two lectures in the university. Justus Velsius, Strasbourg reformer and commentator on the works of Aristotle and Hippocrates, was just beginning the *Nicomachean Ethics* in Greek. He read in a monotone, without feeling; Ascham considered his performance sound but uninspired. He also heard Alexander Blanckaert, a Carmelite who had recently published a Dutch translation of the Bible (Cologne, 1548), expound the Acts of the Apostles. Ascham observed that "he read lustily with a plain pronunciation, good gesture, ready tongue"; his lecture-hall manner was commendable. Although he disapproved of the friar's effort to support the doctrine of the efficacy of prayers for the dead from an epistle of St. Cyprian, Ascham admitted that Blanckaert "made a goodly antithesis between active life and contemplative, preferring active" (I, 254). Billicus, whom he had missed at Louvain, was not lecturing that day. Ascham nevertheless tried to see him by pretending to be interested in certain manuscripts of St. Bernard which he allegedly possessed. A servant, however, put him off with the excuse that his master was busy. Ascham, considering that Billicus had cast him "off to another time, because he suspected me to be a protestant," accordingly dismissed from his mind this "proud popistant" and "went about to see the city" (I, 255).

He inspected several libraries without finding a single notable book, but he did enjoy himself thoroughly in St. Peter's Cathedral. There he viewed the magnificent shrine said to contain the remains of the three Magi, though he believed it not to be "so rich . . . as was [that of] the Lady of Walsingham" (I, 252). He also saw offerings being made to the legendary Reynaud of Montauban, who, according to the old romance of the *Four Sons of Aymon,* had been murdered by workmen for outstripping them all in helping to raise the fabric of this same cathedral. Finally, he looked upon the relics nearby of St. Ursula and the 11,000 martyred virgins. He asserts, lest his friends at home twit him for superstition, that he reports "what I hear and see, not what I believe and credit"; his readers may accept as much of it as they wish. If men would regard these shrines simply as monuments to virtue and "not as allurements of papistry," then he believes that he might have taken even greater pleasure in seeing them and describing them for others (I, 254).

On October 13 the travelers boarded a comfortable barge and began the voyage to Mainz. Ascham was impressed, like generations of visitors since, with the breadth and traffic of the river and with the spectacular scenery. His description of the trip has led a recent scholar to call him one of "the earliest of 'picturesque tourists' on the Rhine."[4] He marveled at the daring of men who built castles and cultivated grapes on the steep and rocky banks. For the entire seven days of the slow journey upstream the voyagers never lost sight of vineyards. Each day Ascham and several of his companions would leave the horse-drawn barge and walk for four or five miles along the towpath, admiring the scenery as they went, and "plucking grapes not with our hands but with our mouths if we list." This almost bacchanalian self-portrait of the respectable Cambridge don among the vine leaves lends Ascham an air of the *bon vivant* not encountered in his earlier writings. He supplies an additional touch later by alluding to the delight he took in his cups of Rhenish, and to his even greater taste for the wines of the Neckar. "I was afraid when I came out of England to miss beer," he confesses, "but I am more afraid when I shall come into England, that I cannot lack this wine" (I, 256). He even considered making arrangements to have a small annual supply shipped to him at Cambridge (I, 285–86).

At Bingen on October 17, he purchased two Roman coins, one of Diocletian, the other of Maximianus. The next day he thrilled at the sight of Drusus Germanicus's monument with its inscription, unusually simple for a Roman, "Memoria Drusi," and was reminded of the moving words in which Ovid had praised this noble son-in-law of Augustus.

Disembarking at Mainz, the company took horse for Worms, but finding that the plague was raging there, for once Ascham did not go exploring. He did remark, though, that the rounded spires of the cathedral made it appear "all the way like King's college cradle [*sic* Giles and MSS. for *chapel*]" (I, 258). When they arrived at Speyer on the 20th, he was hoping that they might go roundabout to Strasbourg for a visit with Sturm. Morison, who himself admired Sturm and had translated one of his works, was willing to go.[5] But Sir Philip Hoby, the incumbent ambassador, sent word from Augsburg that he was impatient for their arrival, and the visit had to be abandoned. Ascham contented himself with his first sight of Sturm's recent book, *De periodis unus* (Strasbourg, 1550). He also leafed through new editions of various works, including three Sophoclean tragedies and Paolo Giovio's *Historia sui temporis*. But the chief curiosity in the city was a ceremonial stone wine bowl in the market place, which every newly consecrated bishop filled with wine in order to bring prosperity to his diocese. The vessel reminded Ascham of the silver cup that Herodotus describes as being given by Croesus to the priests at Delphi. This episcopal tradition at Speyer he considered "both German-like and papistical-like, both for the drinking and diligent observing of pageants, rites, and ceremonies" (I, 259).

The next stopping place was Bretten, a future shrine of German Protestantism. Here he lodged with one of Philip Melanchthon's brothers-in-law, either Hawerer, the electoral secretary, or Peter Kecheln, and visited the house in which the reformer had been born. George Schwarzerd, Melanchthon's younger brother and mayor of the town, was still living in the tall, peak-roofed family home. He received Ascham graciously and made him a present of a letter written in his

distinguished brother's own hand. Ascham registers his disappointment, after so hospitable a reception by his family, that Melanchthon,
along with Joachim Camerarius, had urged his fellow Protestants to
accept the terms of Charles V's religious compromise, the Interim,
issued in 1548 in an effort to reconcile the Protestants with the church
(I, 219, 260). Later he took comfort from finding numerous devout
and unyielding Lutherans at Augsburg, even within the emperor's
court, where "the captain of his night guard" had defiantly married
according to "ceremonies forbidden by the interim" (I, 270). Yet
Ascham regretted, rather curiously for one who conformed at least outwardly to the different religious settlements of four Tudor monarchs,
that so many true believers were willing to compromise. Hence, he
observed disapprovingly, the day after leaving Bretten, that "a fair
church of the Protestants" at Vaihingen smelled "a little of the dregs
of interim" (I, 260).

At Esslingen he went to see a marvel, a young woman with an incredibly great belly that "tossed and heaved" alarmingly because, supposedly, it was full of serpents. Even the emperor and many of his
courtiers had visited her, and Charles had commanded his physician,
the celebrated anatomist Vesalius, to undertake her cure. But this the
woman would not allow because, according to Ascham, she believed
Vesalius "sought more his own experience than her health" (I, 262).
Some days afterwards Ascham learned that certain Spaniards had
proved the tremendous belly to be a hoax. Suddenly pulling off the
bedclothes, they discovered a huge oxhide containing a small boy who
threshed around and made a great stir whenever the woman prompted
him. So much for prodigies; in Ascham's view, the wonders of reality
were far more noteworthy.

Approaching Ulm on the 25th, he had his first glimpse of "the Alps
of Italy." In a state of high excitement, he hastened to the banks of
the Danube, the most thrilling sight of his entire journey. Eagerly he
drank of the water and washed his hands in it, remembering as he did
so "how Herodotus doth describe it, compare it, and prefer it to Nilus"
(III, 263). He was seized with a longing "to have a journey down
Danubius through almost all Europa." The buildings of Ulm, some of
them nine and ten stories high, aroused his admiration, as did the formidable defenses and provision against siege. He inspected the armory,
which, besides sixty-nine fieldpieces and thousands of pikes, hand guns,
and arquebuses, contained a "wonderful deal" of powder. The mu-

nicipal storehouse, whose stock of wheat was never allowed to fall below 48,000 quarters, also impressed Ascham. Another wonder was that the conduits that brought running water into every house within the walls were made not of lead, which was scarce, but of the plentiful fir.

On October 28, five and a half weeks after leaving London, Morison's company entered Augsburg. Hoby, who had been expecting them for nearly a month, and his half-brother, Thomas, recently a student at St. John's, were among those who rode out to meet them and conduct them to their place of residence (I, 265). Their entry into this dwelling, the Abbey of St. George, ended the first stage of Ascham's Continental travels and what had been for him, as his delightful letters reveal, the best journey in the world.

II

From Augsburg he continued to describe for his friends at home scenes and events that quickened his interest. Sometime before November 9, Morison was given a private audience with the emperor, who was ill with an attack of gout. Charles welcomed the new ambassador and gave Hoby, with thanks for his dutiful service, permission to return home.[6] Ascham described for Raven the unimperial appearance of his majesty. To him, the mightiest prince in Europe "looked somewhat like the parson of Epurstone. He had on a gown of black taffety, and only a furred night-cap on his head, Dutchlike, having a seam over the crown, like a great cod-piece" (I, 267). Three weeks later, Charles made a more impressive showing at a dinner for the Order of the Golden Fleece. Ascham, who "stood hard by" his table, noted the service carefully and concluded that although the emperor "fed well of a capon," he had enjoyed better fare himself in his own chamber at Cambridge. Awe-inspiring, however, was the imperial capacity for drink (small wonder that Charles was gouty!). He "drank the best that ever I saw; he had his head in the glass five times as long as any of us, and never drank less than a good quart at once of Rhenish wine" (I, 268).

Ascham was also impressed by the splendor of the city and the lavish display of wealth of such famous merchant families as the Schorers, Baumgartners, and Fuggers. His lodgings were opposite a Lutheran church, and he found his Protestant heart stirred by the num-

ber of communicants (fifteen hundred on Christmas day), their manifest devotion, and the fact that man, woman, child, and servant, in
contrast with the ill-instructed and indifferent congregations of England, all sang "perfectly and without book the whole psalter" (I, 270).
For three weeks in February there were jousts in the streets before the
Fuggers' princely house, where the emperor was lodging. Ascham
wryly observes that among the participants, Prince Philip of Spain
"justed gentilly; for he neither hurt himself, his horse, his spear, nor
him that he ran with" (I, 280). On "Shrove Thursday" the Catholics,
who according to Ascham could scarcely turn out a dozen persons for
mass throughout the rest of the year, held a nocturnal procession during
which "a wonderful sort of Spaniards did whip themselves naked
through the streets, deep with sorrow." Nor were these "penitentes" the
only contrite worshipers. He goes on to describe how the whole magnificent spectacle of penance struck him as an amusing paradox: "There
were many companies, and of the Emperor's house 113, which went at
nine of the clock at night, accompanied with 800 torches. No small fools
bare torches that night, but very many great lords, in gowns of crimosim
and purple velvet, full of agletts of gold. The prince of Piedmont, the
duke of Alva, one of the Emperor's council, bare torches that night; a
wonderful Ἐθελοθρήσκεια [will-worship] to live so abominable all the
year, and then will needs make amends with God whether he will
or not."[7]

During these first months at the imperial court Ascham made several
new friends. He quickly became acquainted with Christopher Mont,
English agent at Strasbourg, with whom he roasted chestnuts and discussed politics. Mont frequently served as bearer of letters and compli-
ments exchanged by Ascham and Sturm (I, 271; II, 123). Another of
his new associates was Vesalius, who though physician to an emperor,
willingly treated Ascham's servant Vaughan. Ascham reports with
amusement that the lazy rascal found Vesalius "the best physician in the
world, because he gave him pitcher-meat [drink] enough" (I, 287).
Other acquaintances were the philologist Vitus Polandus and Hieronymus Wolf, humanist, teacher, writer on education, and librarian to
the Fuggers. Twice Wolf came to dine at Morison's table, but in spite
of these overtures of friendship required some months of cultivation
before he would consent to show Ascham his master's noted library.
Once admitted, Ascham obtained an index of the Greek writers represented in the collection, and Jacob Fugger graciously offered him a

work of Aeschines with commentary. But Wolf, perhaps designedly, seemed unable to locate the volume. Although Ascham found the library truly impressive, he expressed annoyance with Fugger for locking so many important books "in perpetual shadows," out of the reach of scholars who would know how to use them. Somewhat scornfully he characterized the famous collector as being not a *philológos*, a lover of learning, but a *bibliótaphos*, a sepulchre for books (I, 289).

Despite so many new experiences, Ascham's first enchantment with Germany soon began to wear away. The wanderlust was evidently still strong upon him, for he was hardly settled at Augsburg before he began expressing the wish to be off on further travels and showing signs of his old discontent in several of his letters.

For one thing, none of the fellows of St. John's, Lever excepted, ever wrote to him, and he became starved for news of his friends. Then he learned that William Ireland and a companion, who had been on a journey to Venice, had returned home by way of France, without even bothering to try the route through Augsburg in order to pay him a visit. After November 18, 1551, he wrote to Ireland and Raven no more; his final attempt to draw a word from them was a threefold reminder that henceforth they might be fed only "with the hope of my next to come," that they might consider it fortunate if Vaughan would continue writing back to the college since Ascham would do so no longer, and that they might yet avoid such disaster by conveying letters to him through Morison's brother-in-law in London, Stephen Hales (I, 317–18).

He was also unhappy because for an entire year he found himself tied down to Augsburg. Once he complained to Cheke of being kept so busy with official correspondence that he seldom even went about the town. Nor could he find sufficient leisure to keep up his studies, especially in Italian and Latin (I, 236–37). Greek was the only tongue for which he could still find some time (I, 280). Further, the emperor, in spite of continuing rumors that he might remove to the Low Countries, to Italy, even to the Rhineland, or that he might proceed with his projected campaign against the Turks in Hungary, in fact moved nowhere. In the hopes of convening a Diet and settling the question of the imperial succession, Charles continued to hold court at Augsburg. Ascham's frustration is reflected in a letter to Raven: "We shall have hot war in Hungary; and would to God the Emperor would go thither" (I, 283). Only once did the chance for a little travel come his way. In July 1551 he accompanied Morison on an eight or nine days' trip to several cities north and east of Augsburg, among them Ingolstadt and Nürnberg. In Nürnberg, they marveled at the eighteen huge municipal storehouses in which grain had been preserved for generations, some of it having kept perfectly for as long as two hundred years.[8] But this interlude apart, his hopes of seeing more of Europe remained unrealized until the emperor decided, after war with France reopened in Piedmont, to remove his court to Innsbruck. When this news at last came, Ascham eagerly speculated that afterwards they might go on "to Milan, and so perhaps to Naples and Sicily, if the French do not trouble our journey" (I, 308). But by this time he had grown a bit testy and grumbled because the war had commenced so late in the year, "for now we must over the cold Alps, even now full of snow" (I, 312).

Even more dispiriting than boredom with confinement were his lack of funds and Morison's uneasy relations with the emperor. On the outward journey the ambassador had provided him with ample spending money, "which," says Ascham practically, "is the best comfort in a strange country" (I, 265). At Augsburg, however, such comfort was chronically missing. Within two weeks of his arrival, he informed Cheke that he was minded to seek the patronage of the dowager duchess and the young Duke of Suffolk, as well as the Marquesses of Dorset and Northampton. He was not really looking for "any pension, but a little ready money for this voyage" (I, 222). Prices had risen sharply, and Morison could not be generous, since his own income was suffering from the recent debasement of English currency. Then, shortly after arriving in Augsburg, Ascham lost the royal librarianship, a sinecure that Cheke had procured for him some months earlier; meanwhile he had been given no other benefice by which he might hope to replenish his slender purse (I, 237–38).

Ascham seems not to have been exaggerating his needs merely to secure additional sums for gratifying expensive new tastes. The ambassador was certainly in no position to help him. Morison, it is true, was a very rich man, for he had accumulated vast estates while in the service of Henry VIII. But his personal wealth was tied up in real property and could not always be converted into ready money. Furthermore, though the privy council had voted him £1,200 per year for maintenance while abroad, the amount was insufficient and the semi-annual payments invariably in arrears.[9] Like other English diplomats under the Tudors, he found himself considerably out of pocket for his service.

The fact that soon after their arrival Morison incurred the emperor's displeasure also daunted Ascham's spirits. After presenting his credentials, the ambassador did not again have audience until March 6, 1551. Then, acting upon instructions from the privy council, he asked to be heard on several issues. Chief among these were the impasse over Mary Tudor's right to practice the old religion, and Charles's refusal to allow Sir Thomas Chamberlain, Edward VI's ambassador at Brussels, to worship according to the reformed liturgy.[10]

Judging from the vivid account Charles sent to Jehan Scheyfve, his ambassador in England, his second encounter with Morison had been a highly dramatic one. After presenting various other complaints and requests of a routine sort, Morison came at length to the main issue. Since Scheyfve was permitted to hear mass in his lodgings in London, he argued that the English "might reasonably claim the same for the ambassadors of the King, their master, at our Court." Charles then reminded him that his own dear cousin Mary, despite an earlier promise that she would not be prevented from practicing her religion freely, had not in fact been allowed to do so. He also answered, in effect, that he could not permit heretics to worship contrary to the laws of his realm and the ancient and long-established practice of the Christian church. The response touched the zealous Morison to the quick, and he began to argue that the English were no heretics but that their belief "was founded on God's word." Then, warming to his subject, he began "preaching," to use the emperor's expression, that his "was the only true and old-established faith, and making comparisons with our own." Charles was even more offended by this sermon than he might otherwise have been because Morison enlarged upon the subject "in an unbecoming manner," and because he had already made himself a nuisance by discussing religion with other members of the court whenever an opportunity presented itself. He instructed Scheyfve to convey to King Edward the imperial displeasure at such undiplomatic conduct, adding that he was certain Morison had exceeded his instructions, since "we believe him to have been sent to us as an ambassador, and not as a preacher."[11]

When this news of the emperor's "preacher" reached the council, they decided at first to recall Morison and send another in his place. Upon further consideration, they wrote to him on April 6, reprimanding him in fairly mild terms for his blunder and informing him that Dr. Nicholas Wotton would be sent out as a special ambassador to inquire into the emperor's pleasure in the matter.[12] Wotton finally arrived on June 19 and had audience nine days later. Charles said that he was well enough content with Morison and would let King Edward decide whether he should stay or be removed. He added that his own temper had been shortened by reason of advancing years, his cruel affliction (gout), and an unpleasant memory of the similarly annoying zeal for Protestantism shown by the poet Sir Thomas Wyatt, when he had been Henry VIII's ambassador in Spain.[13] Although Wotton was a smoother diplomat than Morison and urged the request about Chamberlain's religious services in a more tactful manner, after his audience matters stood much as they had before. Morison reported to the council with undisguised satisfaction that in answer to his appeal "Mr. Wotton hath a more mannerly nay than I had, but even as flat a nay as mine was."[14] Some weeks later the emperor, having learned that Edward wished Morison to continue in office, kept his earlier promise and "acquiesced without further comment."

Morison's having been permitted to stay, however, could hardly be reckoned a personal triumph. He remained heavily in debt for lack of his "diets" from home, and his diplomatic work was hampered because in the minds of the imperials he was ever after considered a mischievous and untrustworthy person.[15] Whether or not Ascham was present at the nearly catastrophic interview, he did suffer emotionally with Morison through the months of tension and disfavor that ensued. As the letters to St. John's show, the ambassador's imprudence, added to his financial distress, had much to do with Ascham's growing disillusionment with the life of a courtier and his reiterated wish to be moving onward, almost anywhere, from Augsburg, the locus of their various misfortunes.

Yet if Morison's difficulties were a source of worry during this first year abroad, his company was Ascham's chief solace. He was kind, learned, witty, and companionable, a man also who did not lose his sense of humor for long even when beset by troubles. Though a few of his complaints about money were short-tempered, his natural gaiety soon returned; even in his dispatches to the council and to Cecil he could not repress his high spirits. Disregarding reminders that mirth had no place in diplomatic correspondence, he continued to enliven his letters with such amusing and facetious comments that his superiors soon dubbed him "the merry Morison."[16] After the period of uneasy relations with Charles began, Ascham defended this best of masters loyally, as the following passage from a letter to Raven shows: "My lord surely is a witty man, and serves his God, his king, and his country, noble here. If ye hear any thing to the contrary, be bold, Edward, of my word to reprove it" (I, 282–83). At the end of August 1551, he wrote again, with deep concern for Morison's reputation in England, that "my lord is merry, and one that doth God and his prince as good service as ever did ambassador. Mr. Wotton cometh home, and we tarry; and methinks I know what your Papists at home have talked of that matter" (I, 302). In return for this devotion and for his diligence as secretary, Morison in his letters to Cecil repeatedly sought Ascham's preferment.

In their free time the two Englishmen studied Greek together, sometimes as often as five days out of seven (I, 265). In six months Ascham read to Morison an astounding array of works: "whole Herodotus, five tragedies, three orations of Isocrates, and seventeen orations of Demosthenes" (I, 285). They had little time to spare for Latin, and Ascham was not quick to learn German; "surely," he admits in the same passage, "I drink Dutch better than I speak Dutch." In Italian, however, he did become proficient, through practice of conversation at court and lessons from Morison at home. The texts from which Morison taught the language to his household included the sermons of the Sienese reformer Bernardino Ochino and the writings of Machiavelli. Despite his protests to Cecil that he had turned to these particular books strictly "for the tongue," the ambassador's choice of reading matter apparently displeased the council. A disloyal servant had gossiped about the lessons around Augsburg; not only had unfavorable rumors spread to England, but the imperials were strengthened in their prejudice against Morison as "an apostle, a doctor, a preacher, and I know not what."[17]

III

At least one of Morison's pupils appreciated this exceptional introduction to Italian. Although Ascham never fully approved of Machiavelli's doctrines, the acute political analysis that he encountered in his works sharpened his own insight into the historical events that he witnessed himself from 1550 to 1553. For these were among the most dramatic and critical years in the life of Charles V and in the national history of Germany.

When the English ambassadorial party presented itself at Augsburg in the autumn of 1550, Charles's political position seemed more secure than at any other time during his long reign as emperor. Having defeated the two most troublesome of the Schmalkaldic leaders at Mühlberg in 1547, he now had both of them under arrest. Besides holding the Landgrave at Mechelen, he was keeping Luther's protector, John Frederick, Elector of Saxony, a virtual prisoner in the imperial court. On August 1 of the same year he had ratified a five years' truce with the Sultan, Soliman II. During 1548 peace was further secured by Soliman's preoccupation with the Persian wars, which diverted his attention from the west. Most important of all, Henry II, the new French monarch, had been neutralized by the temporary impotence of his Oriental ally. Meanwhile Pope Paul III had died, and his successor, Julius III, though his election had been supported by the French, seemed at first less hostile toward the imperial cause than his predecessor had been. Finally, in September 1550, Andrea Doria's capture of the key North African city of Mahdia gave the imperial forces an advantage over the Turk in the central Mediterranean. Some people even began to believe that the Council of Trent might at last be effectively organized. If so, Charles stood a chance of realizing his dearest hope, ecclesiastical reform and the return of Protestants to the mother church.

For observing the reversal of the emperor's good fortune, Ascham arrived at precisely the critical moment. At the end of 1550, Ottavio Farnese, son of the Duke of Piacenza, refused to accept a commission to hold Parma for the empire and called in French support to help him win the duchy for himself. This maneuver renewed the inveterate struggle for power in northern Italy among the empire, France, and the papacy. Next a fleet of Soliman's attacked Malta and then, turning aside, seized the vital port of Tripoli. At the same time another Turkish fleet was preparing for an attack on the Sicilies, a Turkish army was menacing Austria, and French naval forces were mustering at Marseilles. In the autumn of 1551, Henry II declared war on "Charles, King of Spain." He chose this formula to separate the quarrel from the empire, for he had begun to intrigue with two powerful and discontented German Protestants, Albert, Margrave of Brandenburg, and Maurice, Duke of Saxony.

In 1552 matters grew still worse. Having concluded a treaty of alliance with Maurice, the French occupied Lorraine and seized the bishoprics of Verdun, Toul, and Metz. In April, Prince Ferrante of Salerno, angered that Charles had ignored certain complaints of his against the cruel Viceroy of Naples, defected to the Turk. Then, apparently, though not in fact, without consulting the emperor, Pope Julius, a vacillating and weak ally, suddenly made peace with the French. In May the approach of Maurice's army frightened Charles out of Innsbruck, and his precipitous flight over the Alps in turn scattered the timorous delegates to the Council of Trent. Through negotiations with the emperor's brother Ferdinand, Maurice secured "everlasting recognition" of Protestantism in the empire. On August 15 Charles had to sign his consent to this agreement, the deathblow to any hope of reuniting the church. Last of all, his attempt to retake Metz by siege failed, and when the imperial court removed to Brussels early in 1553, he was both dangerously ill and, temporarily at least, in dire political straits.

Ascham's correspondence from Germany is filled with valuable first-hand information about many of these events, information that came readily to him as a visitor at Charles's court and as Morison's secretary. Not only did he transmit to the council the numerous letters composed by his master, but through his hands passed some of the "intelligences" sent by English agents in Italy, including the highly instructive dispatches of the English ambassador to Venice, Peter Vannes.[18] Finally, during the late spring of 1552, he began to keep a detailed journal of political developments in the empire, commencing with the unforgettable night of May 19, when Maurice's approach sent the imperial court flying out of Innsbruck and Ascham found himself swept into the midst of the wars of Germany.

In his personal letters home, he did not set down all that he knew, for, as he told Raven, his confidential position at court, which gave him opportunities to hear news, also made him responsible for keeping much of it close (I, 265–66). Still, he did write of such matters as the various efforts to get the Council of Trent successfully under way; the emperor's difficulties with Julius III; the maneuvers against Charles by the French in Italy and the Turks in Hungary. Nor did he merely report uncritically what he heard and observed. He tried to talk with everyone whose opinions might prove illuminating. From what he learned he began to form his own judgments of the emperor's political character and actions and to try to predict what course events might take.

Thus, in respect of the much-discussed Council of Trent, he speculated early in 1551 that neither the pope, nor the Protestants, nor Charles himself really wanted it to succeed. Julius might stand to "lose more than win thereby," and the Germans had become too constant in the reformed religion. As for the emperor, he was "too wise and forecasting a prince, either to fall out with Germany, or the Pope; for by a general council, he is likely to make either the Pope, of an uncertain friend, a stedfast enemy; or else the Germans, of secret repiners, open foes" (I, 279). Charles, with wars threatening from all sides, had "many irons in the fire, and every one able alone to keep him work enough"; it behooved him, therefore, to use his political wisdom everywhere to best advantage. Ascham enumerates the multitude of troubles from which the emperor would find himself hard put to escape. Recalling a striking parallel in Livy, he correctly predicts that the astute Charles would seek to be gentler with his former enemies in Germany and would now welcome the reconciliation with them that he had once adamantly refused (I, 313–14).

The court was filled, moreover, with agents from all over Europe, especially from the German states and the imperial cities of Italy; living in Morison's own household was the unreliable but very well-informed international spy Bernardine. With men of this sort, as well as others of more honorable standing, Ascham frequently discussed the affairs of the day. So eager was he to hear all sides of the various political issues that he asked Cecil whether he might "without shenting at home, sometime as occasion serveth talk with the Pope's Nuncio's men, as I do with other agents and Italians here." In the past, he claims, he has refrained from doing so because he does not know whether the council would approve. He promises, if permission is granted, to act discreetly, "so as neither any at home should have any cause to mistrust, nor those here occasion to hope that I thereby should become papistical" (I, 330–31). Following the lead of Morison, who had been instructed by the council to respond in kind to the courteous treatment offered him by Henry II's ambassador, Ascham kept on good terms with the French secretary, from whom he derived much intelligence about Duke Maurice's lackadaisical campaign for the emperor against the Magdeburg Protestants.

During his final year abroad, another important source of news, as well as of memorable talk about Italian humanism, was Marc Antonio Damula, the Venetian ambassador to Charles V. Damula promised to help him secure a diplomatic post that would take him to the eastern Mediterranean and gave him two copies of a fine map of Europe, northern Africa, and Asia Minor, one of which Ascham sent as a present to Cecil. This gesture pleased Cecil, as did Ascham's gifts of other maps, one of Mirandula and another of Germany.[19]

Ascham seems also to have read much history while abroad. In addition to Herodotus and Machiavelli, he had perused at least enough of Paolo Giovio's recent *Historia sui temporis* to form an unfavorable opinion of the work, and he mentions having glanced at a new edition of Polybius.[20] Through Polybius, and his modern disciple Machiavelli, Ascham became particularly interested in the "pragmatic," or political, branch of history. From the errors he perceived in Giovio's interpretation of current history he may have received the first inspiration to write a more objective study of the events through which he himself was living. In 1553, he began to compose an account and evaluation of what had taken place during his years at the imperial court. This work, which he apparently never completed and which survives only in a fragment published after his death, will be the subject of the following chapter.

IV

If the ambitious side of his nature looked toward a life at court in the midst of great events, Ascham was still primarily a scholar who continued to feel most at ease with other men of letters, especially if they shared his passion for Greek. As he confided to Sturm, "I value your most agreeable letters, replete with Sturmian substance, that is, with learning, eloquence, and humanity, far above all these Turkish, papistical, imperial, French affairs" (I, 274). His taking great pains, during his outward journey, to meet and hear noted lecturers, his quick befriending of Polandus, Vesalius, and Wolf at Augsburg have already been described. At Wolf's prompting, he wrote to Hieronymus Froben, the famous printer of Basel. He had hoped on coming abroad to visit that celebrated center of the book trade, but feared now that his official duties would prevent his ever doing so. The main purpose of his letter was to inform Froben that part of Erasmus's *Antibarbarorum...liber unus* (Basel, 1520) was still preserved in England. Someone had given Ascham the manuscript in 1549, and he had had it in his possession for several months. He was not sure whether his copy was the complete text or "some abridgement," or whether it was the same as the section that had been published but was now out of print. He had considered preparing it for press, but now, having learned of the close relationship between Froben's family and Erasmus, he meant to leave the decision to Froben. Should he wish to bring it out, Ascham offered to lend his help in recovering the manuscript. Nothing, however, seems to have developed from the proposal, since no further correspondence between the two men exists; the nature of the contents of the manuscript remains a mystery.

The rest of Ascham's epistles to Continental scholars are directed to three of the centers of learning that he visited during his stay abroad, Heidelberg, Strasbourg, and Louvain. During his last six months with the emperor, he received letters from Heidelberg from Hubert Leodius (Thomas), councillor and biographer of the Count Palatine, Frederick II, and from the noted jurist and historian Nicholas Cisner (Kistner). He heard, too, from Nannius and from his friends Brandisby and Christopherson in Louvain. Of the five men, Nannius was the only one with whom he was able to arrange a meeting. Brandisby was away at Mechelen and Christopherson at Antwerp when he revisited Louvain early in 1553, but this time Nannius was not off carousing. The encounter was a highly agreeable one, and Nannius, who prided himself on being a strict and impartial judge of character, confessed that through this single visit he had fallen in love with Ascham, both for his learning and for his other virtues (I, 377).

Nannius's enthusiasm, coupled with Ascham's letters, rekindled the affection of Christopherson, who diffidently sent to Ascham his recently completed translation of and commentary upon four books of Philo Judaeus.[21] Whether or not they were worthy to be rendered into Latin he left to the judgment of Ascham, whose candid opinion of the work he awaited eagerly (I, 356–57). Through Brandisby, who lamented having missed him for a second time, came word of further tribute from Nannius's lips. Nannius, something of a physiognomist, had read the civility, modesty, humanity, and kindness of Ascham's character not only from his letters but also from his countenance; even more flattering was what he had to say about Ascham's literary style. His letters were full of sound judgment, elegant language, and craftsmanship in composition. They displayed "nothing that is not choice, yet nothing affected, remarkable forcefulness without enormity, the utmost sweetness without slackness, brevity with vitality, on the other hand copiousness without luxuriance; [they were] well turned also and artistic, but without that unremittant coruscation for which the age of Pliny labored, eloquent without effeminate devices, their diction polished and pure, but without that scrupulous anxiety, through which the Ciceronians of our age wear

themselves away, as though they had loaded themselves with fetters."
Brandisby's only fear in reporting this tribute was that possibly the
increase of affection between Ascham and Nannius might leave less
room for himself in both their hearts (I, 359–60).

These letters from Louvain, however well they manifest the respect
that Ascham had gained among his peers, contain little matter beyond
exchange of compliment. The correspondence with Hubert and Cisner
at Heidelberg has more intellectual substance and includes a sprightly,
though inconclusive, debate over the pronunciation of Greek. Ascham
opened the argument with a letter from Brussels on March 6, 1553. Because the manner of sounding vowels and diphthongs introduced at
Cambridge by Smith and Cheke set England apart from almost all the
rest of the scholarly world, he wished to dispute the question frankly
with Cisner, Hubert, and their colleague Jacobus Micyllus (Moltzer),
the distinguished editor of Homer. The issue was whether England or
the Continent was being most faithful to the ancient pronunciation. If
the Continentals could prove that their way was the closer, Ascham was
prepared to submit. If, however, they were merely following the sounds
of modern Greek while the English proved to be nearer to the ancient
pronounciation, he could never admit the validity of Continental
practice.

For him, the criterion was not custom, as it was for his patron Gardiner in the dispute with Cheke, but correctness. Should his opponents,
therefore, attempt to defend themselves on the grounds that they were
observing what was traditional and accepted, he would remind them
how custom can often lead to grave error, as in the instance of the
Christian religion itself. Nor should one call in as authorities the modern
Greeks; the changes of time had made the ancient language no more
their private property than Latin was that of contemporary Italians.
Citing κυβέρνω (I steer) as his first example, he argues that on the
Continent three letters of this single word are mispronounced: χ as *ch*,
υ as *i* and β as *v*. An analogy with Latin *guberno* would show anyone
clearly what are the true values of the letters, allowing of course for the
change from χ to *g*. But in Germany he has heard nothing but "chi-
verno." Worse still, not only is β changed invariably to *v*, but υ, as well
as η and ε, is given the sound of *iota*. Yet this contradicts what Cicero
and St. Augustine say about these letters, and anyone can see, from
Eustathius's comment on Homer, what is the true pronunciation of βῆ,
the sound of a sheep. Pretending to be much amused at the thought,

he drives his point home: "I know that all English and German and Italian sheep make for us; but perhaps Greek sheep formerly did not *baa* [*non balabant*] but *vi'd* [*sed vilabant*]." Calling in sheep as witnesses, he grants, may seem ridiculous; yet nobody is ashamed to learn the pronunciation of the Greek letter *rho* from the growling of dogs. And, after all, the sound "bay" is from nature, an immutable and therefore infallible authority (I, 347–49).

The first of the Heidelbergers to reply was Cisner. He admits that all Continental scholars pronounce Greek in much the same manner, but denies that their reasons for doing so are necessarily the same. The German custom, he believes, has resulted from peculiarities in the German tongue itself. He grants that the practice of his countrymen may be wrong; if the English by sound scholarship succeed in truly reforming the pronunciation of Greek, both he and his associates will be highly gratified. Micyllus might explain the objections to some things in the Cambridge system better than he is able; he would not himself mind seeing certain undesirable features of the prevailing method reformed (I, 367–70).

Hubert's reply, which came a month after Cisner's, is more critical, though at the same time every bit as good-humored. He defends the Continental pronunciation of both β and η. Let Ascham cite the analogy between κυβέρνω and *guberno,* he knows himself an equally sound philological comparison to support his position. What can Ascham say after considering the two words for life, βίos in Greek and *vita* in Latin? As for the letter η, Hubert will never allow Ascham's contention that it represents a double *epsilon;* it is closer, in his opinion, to *iota.* The argument from the bleating of sheep is invalid because the spelling is but an imitation, not a perfect reproduction, of an actual sound, even as Ascham's own writing is the imitation, not the direct copying, of Cicero. He warns Ascham jocosely to avoid the long *e* and *o* sounds for which he is contending, lest "you seem to have a mouthful of mush, or to be an ostler" (I, 376).

Thus the brief and friendly sparring comes to an end. The three scholars had diverted themselves by the exchange, but neither side persuaded the other to alter its manner of pronouncing Greek, a difference between English and Continental scholars that has been preserved to this day.

The Strassburgers with whom Ascham established epistolary friendships were Johannes Sleidan (Phillipson), historian of the Reformation in Germany, Michael Toxites (Schütz), and of course Sturm. Shortly before leaving England, Ascham had commended Sleidan to Morison, and during the following year he frequently asked Mont and Sturm to convey his respects to the historian. At the close of 1551 and the beginning of 1552 he exchanged several letters with Sleidan, one of the few German Protestant delegates who cared or dared to attend the Council of Trent. Sleidan's letter of February 28, 1552, is full of comments on religious and political affairs, and is most interesting in its speculations about the probable effects on the church council of the war between the emperor and France. The epistle ranges over the various upheavals of the day; it touches on Pope Julius, Duke Maurice, Henry II, the Turk, and the Venetians; it calls to Ascham's notice Pietro Bembo's history of the Venetian Republic, as well as the fairly recent publication of Giovio's first volume, which Ascham had already seen and criticized. What news Ascham sent from the imperial court in return is not known, for none of his communications to Sleidan has been preserved. It would be interesting to see how much use they may have made of each other's letters and conversation on contemporary events when they sat down to write their respective histories of the times.

Through the agency of Sturm, Ascham had an opportunity to patronize scholarship in a modest way. In June 1551, Toxites, a Swiss scholar residing at Strasbourg, sent Ascham part of the revision he was making of Sturm's *Quinctiana Explicatio* (Strasbourg, 1538), a commentary on Cicero's oration *Pro P. Quintio*. Ascham was pleased with the offering, and out of his slender means, returned to the pleasantly surprised Toxites "not merely words for words, but rather gold" (I, 300). Immediately Toxites sent another book for Ascham to transmit to Princess Elizabeth. He would also have supplied the rest of the "Quinctianus," but unfortunately, when the printers were scarcely halfway through, one fell ill and his partner was forced to shut down the business for a long time. For Ascham, Toxites has the conventional, but still sweetest, words of praise a contemporary humanist could receive: "Not only are your epistles learned and delightful, but also pious and Christian: whence it appears, that you regard the true end of studies and pursue it, so that you combine virtue and piety with your learning" (I, 299). After visiting Sleidan and Toxites a year later, Ascham found himself able to pay this admirer a compliment in the same vein (I, 340–41).

By far his most prized correspondence was that with Sturm, whose first letter finally reached him at Augsburg in November 1550. Although both men were keenly interested in current affairs, they wrote little to each other about such matters. With Mont and, later, Ascham's host from Canterbury, John Hales, as their couriers, they could pass along news and opinions on politics more discreetly by word of mouth. Their chief topics were the interrelated arts of logic and rhetoric, about which they wrote enthusiastically, exhorting each other to keep on publishing, and discussing plans to collaborate on at least two works (I, 197). One of these, projected by Sturm in June 1551, was to be a preface and *vita* to accompany the *De regno Christi* of Bucer, who had died at Cambridge during the preceding winter. Ascham, though he encouraged Sturm to carry out the design, asked to be excused, since he had already contributed to a memorial volume of orations and epigrams.[22] The other proposed collaboration did come off. The zeal with which Ascham had extolled Princess Elizabeth and other royal and noble personages of England for their learning had drawn from Sturm in his first epistle a correspondingly enthusiastic response. Sturm immediately arranged to have these two letters printed as an inspiration to the nobility of Germany to become likewise learned, and Ascham took the opportunity to add a section praising Grindal for his excellent work as Elizabeth's tutor (I, 272–73). Under the title "Epistolae Duae de Nobilitate Anglicana," the letters appeared, along with Sturm's "De Educatione Principum," in Conrad Heresbach's *De laudibus Graecarum literarum oratio* (Strasbourg, 1551).[*]

As further evidence of his admiration for the splendid learning of the English, in contrast with the German nobility, Sturm sent a copy of his recently published *De periodis* to Elizabeth and, in his commentaries on the *Rhetoric* of Aristotle, "marked out a place" in which he meant to commend Edward VI (I, 223). Ascham rejoiced at this news and observed that divine providence must have had a hand in Sturm's timing, for the king was just finishing his study of the *Nicomachean Ethics* with Cheke and was about to take up the *Rhetoric* (I, 227). If the gesture could secure for his momentous scholarly project the support of such a royal patron, Sturm would be a fortunate man indeed.

The main request of Ascham's first letter had been that Sturm per-

---

[*] Besides this appearance and their inclusion in all editions of Ascham's *Epistolae* except the first, the letters were printed along with *Oratio Illustris & Generosi Domini Ioannis: Comitis ab Ostorog, etc.* (Strasbourg, 1581) and in *Epistolae Jo. Sturmii et ceterorum ad Rogerum Aschamum nec non alia Angliae lumina,* ed. J. H. Acker (Jena, 1712; Hannover, 1770).

fect this work, on the grounds that he possessed the necessary learning and ability and that no other scholar had as yet provided a satisfactory commentary. Sturm replied that he had in fact returned to the task during the preceding year and had even sent his copyist a portion of what he had completed. Since then, having no time to spare for the revision, he had changed his mind about publication, though he hoped to return to Aristotle during the following winter. Ascham continued his urging and offered to send along, though he was sure that the work was available at Strasbourg, a copy of Simon Grynaeus's commentary on the second book of the *Rhetoric* (I, 298). By March 1551, Sturm had progressed sufficiently to be confident of finishing before the end of the year (I, 281).

But the work crept along slowly. Not until November was the first book in final form; in December, a fair copy was ready for presentation to Cheke.[23] John Hales sent a portion to Ascham, who reported in a letter to St. John's that he "never saw any thing more to be compared with antiquity" (I, 316). Then, for nearly a year and a half, Sturm said little about further publication. Finally, in May 1553, he promised that Ascham would soon have "not only my second Aristotelian dialogue, but also the third." He intended, furthermore, to dedicate to Ascham the entire "dialogue concerning style and the kinds of speaking" (I, 358). By July, all three books were ready, but Sturm was unable to send them because he lacked a trustworthy scribe to copy them out (I, 371). For many years Ascham had no chance to peruse the dialogues. In 1561 he wrote to Sturm that he and Haddon had recently enjoyed going through the first and second of them (II, 65), parts of which he had seen earlier (I, 446). Then he heard through Hales that the commentaries had at last reached their final form. His joy at the news, however, was cut short when Toxites reported that two of Sturm's pupils, the brothers Werter, had taken the entire manuscript away with them, first on a journey into Italy (I, 444) and later into Thuringia (II, 64–65). Thus, although Sturm had promised to send him the third dialogue as well as the others, Ascham never did receive it.

The long-continuing exchange over the progress and scholarly significance of the commentaries led the two friends quite naturally to more general questions of rhetorical and educational theory. Several of the ideas that they discussed deserve special attention because Ascham was to treat them at greater length in *The Scholemaster* and to credit Sturm as their source. Among the many requests he made of Sturm was that he complete his promised book concerning the ideal method for learning how to speak and write Latin. Some years before, Sturm replied, he had undertaken to provide such a "ready way to the Latin tongue," but his duties as master of the Strasbourg gymnasium and his return to the Aristotelian commentaries had kept him away from that enterprise. Besides, as he had often told Bucer, he did not regard himself as capable of executing it satisfactorily. Consider, he writes, what a difficult task it would be: for after explaining the principles involved, one would then have to supply the means whereby the student might also learn to express in good Latin whatever his intellect was able to comprehend. It would be hard, moreover, to provide ready examples to show clearly which matters were to be furnished with the various kinds of sentences and rhetorical figures of words, as well as how to arrange all topics in speaking and writing, not in a confused heap, but distinctly treated and disposed in their proper places (I, 199). The implication is that even the ancients had not been able, or else had not taken the trouble, to do so.

Although he excused himself for the time being from assuming such a responsibility, his own comments regarding Latin style led him to the more general question of the relationship between matter and manner in education. "When I exhort my [pupils] to the cultivation of style," he writes, "I consider not only teaching the matter, but also its adornment and arrangement" (I, 200). Naturally, content is more important than the means of embellishing it, for no man who writes without an understanding of the substance of things can be regarded as eloquent. Whoever, indeed, borrows only the words and not the thought of the ancients is unworthy of praise. "It is plainly the duty of eloquent men, to undertake the care first of matter, afterwards of words. For it is vicious to say anything either trifling or stupid" (I, 202). Yet style is also important; the truth is that the two things are inseparable and that men distinguish between them simply for purposes of analysis and teaching. Therefore, he concludes, it is desirable to expose students first to those authors who best join eloquence to soundness of learning.

Both correspondents especially deplored the bad literary examples often set before the young in their time. "What benefits for the shaping and purity of his speech," Sturm asks, "will a boy get from the *Disticha Catonis*, Aquinas, Gerson, Cocca?" (I, 201). Ascham likewise regrets the tendency to ignore style when teaching subject matter, as happens all too frequently when Latin is taught by means of adages and other

snippets of the language. In tutoring Elizabeth he had gone directly
to the best authors, Cicero, Livy, Isocrates, the Greek Testament, in all
of which matter and manner were both excellent. "For I thought that
from those sources she might gain purity of style, and her mind derive
instruction that would be of value to her in meeting every contingency
of life." The happy result, he claims, is that the princess in reading

at once perceives any word that has a doubtful or curious meaning. She
cannot endure those foolish imitators of Erasmus, who have tied up the Latin
tongue in those wretched fetters of proverbs. She likes a style that grows out
of the subject; chaste because it is suitable, and beautiful because it is clear.
She very much admires modest metaphors, and comparisons of contrarieties
well put together and contrasting felicitously with one another. Her ears are
so well practiced in discriminating all these things, and her judgment is so
good, that in all Greek, Latin, and English composition, there is nothing so
loose on the one hand and so concise on the other, which she does not immediately attend to, and either reject with disgust or receive with pleasure,
as the case may be.[24]

Nor are the best examples there merely to be read; they should also
be imitated, "so that the course of studies may appear to be neither im-
peded by needless obscurity nor led away licentiously into error" (I,
187). Yet imitation is always to be of the spirit, not the letter, of one's
models. In his sources the imitator is expected to find matter for fashioning ideas anew for his own age and his own immediate purposes; he
will achieve nothing worthwhile if he simply reproduces the language
of his example. Thus Ascham undoubtedly felt complimented by
Brandisby's report that Nannius had likened his style to that of the
truly inventive, rather than the slavish, Ciceronians. Ascham would
have agreed too with Hubert's distinction between imitating and copying the Latin orator (I, 375). Sturm similarly recognized the difference; in Bembo's history he disapproves of the lament on the death
of the Duke of Urbino because it reproduces only the words, but none
of the sincere emotion, of Cicero's lament for Hortensius in the *Brutus*
(I, 372).

Ascham comments that he knows of one scholar at least who does
not share this enthusiasm for imitating the soundest ancient writers. In
his first letter to Sturm, he mentions a certain Cephas Chlononius, who
had insolently criticized the two chief adornments of Greek and Latin
learning. "Cephas Chlononius" is a play on the name Peter Ramus
(Pierre de la Ramée), originator of new systems of logic and rhetoric

that were just beginning to challenge the authority of Aristotle and Cicero.[25] Ramus, as Ascham himself admitted, was really attacking the late medieval and Renaissance Aristotelians rather than their master; his particular target was Joachim Perion, who had defended the two ancient philosophers by the curious exercise of trying to render the Greek of Aristotle into Ciceronian Latin. Ascham had likewise found certain of Perion's Ciceronianisms laughable, and he readily granted that Ramus was the better scholar (I, 318–19).

But Ramus had gone too far; a rumor had begun to circulate early in 1552 that the Frenchman had poked fun at some of the remarks on imitation, and the veneration of Aristotle and Cicero, to be found in Ascham and Sturm's *De Nobilitate Anglicana*. This report had come from some friends of Ascham at Cambridge; he suspected that Ramus had been instigated to criticism by English Catholics who had taken refuge at Paris. He also suggested to Sturm that part of the blame could be laid to Ramus's excessive contentiousness. "Ramus, I believe, will press you and rush upon you with the greater vehemence, because he knows in the first place that you regard as part of the art of rhetoric *inventio,* which he removes from the rhetorical school, and that with Aristotle you properly and learnedly consider *pronuntiatio,* which those little Ramists prize, as a matter of exercise rather than of learning. But I understand Ramus' stratagem; he does not wish to be μιμητής, lest he appear to ape Aristotle" (I, 320).

Though such an attack would have been in character, there is no evidence, beyond this rumor, that Ramus ever actually criticized the views of Ascham and Sturm. In later years he wrote a pleasant and gracious letter to Ascham that affords no hint of any former disagreement or antagonism (II, 96–97). The foregoing remarks are important, nonetheless, as the first recorded reaction of an English scholar of the traditional school to the doctrines of Ramism, which were soon to become a real threat to the Cambridge Aristotelians and Ciceronians. Its seriousness as a rival school seems to have been recognized by Ascham, for in *The Scholemaster* he did not let pass an opportunity to censure Ramus again for his unorthodox views on rhetoric (III, 176–77).

These early letters, then, contain ideas that Ascham was to develop in the last and best-known of his English works. The second half of *The Scholemaster* may be, in fact, an effort to provide in English that "ready way to the Latin tongue" which Sturm had always found himself too busy to write. The system of learning the language, not from handbooks or the various compilations of *flores* and *loci communes*, but rather from reading only the best authors for content and style, Ascham had already tried with success in tutoring Elizabeth, Whitney, and presumably his pupils at St. John's. The important question of rhetorical imitation as an effective means to learning and to cultivation of literary style, though only touched upon at this time, was to receive more detailed consideration in the later correspondence of the two friends and would lead to Ascham's long and famous discussion of the topic in *The Scholemaster.*

<h2 style="text-align:center">V</h2>

In contrast with the fairly uneventful twelve months in Augsburg, Ascham's last two years abroad provided him with as much excitement as anyone could have wished for. During the autumn of 1551, when the war with France had broken out again, the emperor found himself in a position in which he could neither depend upon the loyalty of the most powerful German princes, nor raise money to pay his troops and maintain his court in Augsburg. His sister, the regent of Flanders, advised him that Duke Maurice was not to be trusted and was in fact negotiating an alliance against him with Henry II. In view of the French threat and the uncertainty about the intentions of Maurice and his confederates, she recommended that Charles situate himself in Worms or Speyer, whence he could move conveniently against any attack on Lorraine, on the Low Countries, or from within the empire. Ascham hoped that Charles would follow this advice, for then at last he would be able to travel to Strasbourg and meet Sturm (I, 304). But the emperor elected instead to remove to his brother's city of Innsbruck. There he felt that he would be able to keep closer watch on the slowly reorganizing Council of Trent and on the progress of the war with France in northern Italy. He would also, as he supposed, be safe there until Ferdinand could supply him with sufficient money and troops to take the field against his enemies.

After several delays, the court finally began the southward journey, going by way of Munich. Morison wrote to the privy council on October 26 that he would wait until the emperor left Munich and then would overtake him by following the more direct route to the Tyrol that went up the valley of the river Lech. By November 17 he and Ascham had arrived at Innsbruck, for on that day he had audience with Charles and informed him of Somerset's recent arrest for stirring up "new troubles" at home.[26] On the same day Ascham wrote the last of his letters to Raven and Ireland. His main news is about Greek and Roman coins that he had seen and acquired before leaving Augsburg; this information he writes mainly for the pleasure it would give his old tutor Pember. He also describes a huge silver medal, worth at least £1,600, which the Tyrolese had cast to celebrate the return of Maximilian from Spain with his bride, the emperor's daughter Mary, and likens it to a familiar object at home. "It is very like a great Suffolk cheese," he observes, "as any cometh to Stridbridge [Stourbridge] fair, but somewhat thicker" (I, 316).

Life at Innsbruck proved no more satisfactory than it had at Augsburg. Morison and Ascham were as short of money as ever, and prices were high. Lady Morison, who was pregnant, had remained behind in Augsburg, and the ambassador now had to maintain two households on an allowance that was never sufficient for one and never came on time. Maximilian's arrival added to the Englishmen's troubles. On a cold December day they were turned out of their lodgings to make room for the Bishop of Cartagena. As a result of this "sudden, unseasonable, and unexpected move," Morison contracted a fever, which prevented him from being present with the other foreign ambassadors to welcome Maximilian. Instead, he moved to the nearby town of Hall and swore that he would "go no more amongst those of Innsbruck."[27] He sent a letter of greeting to Maximilian, begging forgiveness for his enforced absence.[28] The incident, however, turned out favorably in the end; for when the English party eventually returned to Innsbruck in mid-April, they were quartered with the burgomaster, whose residence was superior to the mere "artisan's house" they had originally occupied.[29]

They did not have the opportunity to enjoy these more satisfactory lodgings for long. Maurice had completed his arrangements with the French and insisted, among other demands he made for the Protestants, that the emperor release his troublesome father-in-law, Philip of Hesse. In order to force a response, on April 4, 1552, he took Augsburg and prepared his forces to move on to the Tyrol. Charles, cut off now from escape to the Low Countries, tried to bring him in for a conference. Although Maurice would not come in person, perhaps fearing treachery, he did agree to negotiate with Ferdinand at Linz, where they arranged for the historic meeting at Passau on May 26 that led to eventual recognition of Protestantism in the empire. The French, meanwhile, were busily capturing cities in Lorraine, and Maurice suddenly decided to move his troops southward in hopes of taking the emperor by surprise. On May 19 he overcame an imperial force at Reutte, and on the 23d he reached Innsbruck, only to find that Charles, left without adequate defenses, had craftily slipped out of town three nights earlier with a small escort, the entire court hastening after at his heels.

Curiously, Ascham nowhere gives a detailed account of his adventures on this precipitous flight. He is, indeed, heard from very little between the time of his first arrival in Innsbruck and the emperor's return to Germany during the following August. The only letters that have been preserved are one written from Hall to Sturm in January, and another to Cecil in July. Even in the latter he says nothing of the exciting weeks he has just been through; his doings, therefore, after the departure from Innsbruck must be pieced together from scattered bits of evidence. The southward flight over the snow-filled Brenner Pass must have been a trying one. According to Charles's biographer Alfonso Ulloa, it was pitiful to see the entire court scrambling out of the city in fear, leaving much of their baggage behind in their eagerness to escape Maurice's Lutheran soldiers. For want of horses, many of the courtiers were forced to toil on foot over the foul mountain roads.[30] By May 24 the fugitives had crossed the Brenner and reached Lienz in the valley of the upper Drau; on the 27th, they halted at Villach in Carinthia, where Charles remained until he was able to muster sufficient forces to return to Augsburg.

While the court resettled itself, Ascham obtained leave for a brief visit to Venice. Apparently he set out for Italy in June and returned by the 2d of July, ten days before he wrote the letter to Cecil that is so regrettably uncommunicative about his recent doings.[31] The only evidence concerning his Italian journey occurs in a letter written long afterwards and in the well-known passage in *The Scholemaster* in which he condemns at length the "Inglese italianato." "I was once," he writes in this passage, "in Italy myself; but I thank God my abode there was but nine days; and yet I saw in that little time, in one city, more liberty to sin, than ever I heard tell of in our noble city of London in nine year" (III, 163). The other reference to his brief stay in Venice is a mention of two English youths encountered there, or perhaps in Padua, with whom he seems to have corresponded until at least 1554 (I, 410–11). Possibly he did describe all these experiences in a lost document that he refers to as his *diarium*. Still, it is strange that so diligent a travel writer as he should have said so little about the visit and spent so short a time in the one country he had always been eager to see.

It may be, of course, that his voyage was cut short by a temporary upturn in the emperor's fortunes. Aside from one frightening day in midsummer, matters went well for Charles after his undignified retreat across the Alps. On July 2, as Ascham reported some months later in an epistle to Sturm, false rumors that the Turks were coming and that the Venetians might prove treacherous caused a panic that drove the terrified court briefly out of Villach. Ascham could afford, in retrospect, to be amused. "You would have laughed," he writes, "to hear me recite, how we were all stricken with even greater fear than at Innsbruck and, being scattered each his own way, were driven to flight" (I, 338). Quickly, however, everyone recovered from the scare to go on with preparations for the return to Germany. Further, a truce had been negotiated in Italy, and the emperor, assured of sufficient money from the Fuggers and other sources, went on raising and equipping an army. Ferdinand, meanwhile, was arranging for peace with the chief Protestant princes. Early in August Maurice, who had already renounced his alliance with the French, agreed to come to terms and went off to help Ferdinand in his war against the Turks. The emperor returned to Munich, where on August 15 he reluctantly signed the Treaty of Passau. He was free now to concentrate on putting down Albert of Brandenburg, who remained in the field against him, and on driving the French out of Lorraine. Soon he began to march westward, stopping for brief rests at Augsburg and Ulm along the way.

For Ascham, this campaign promised at last the fulfillment of his hope of seeing Sturm, since Charles intended to pass through Strasbourg and set up his headquarters nearby. From September 15 to 19 Ascham found himself in Strasbourg, where the simplicity and sobriety of the citizens' lives reminded him of the plain virtues of ancient Sparta (I, 340). Sleidan was at home to welcome him, and he also enjoyed a visit with Toxites.[32] Sturm, however, was away. Extremely disappointed at the news, Ascham nevertheless went round to his house, where the brothers Werter entertained him graciously and showed him some of Sturm's writings. Among these was a volume of great interest to him, *Aeschinis et Demosthenis orationes duae contrariae,* which Sturm had published in 1550 (I, 331). This was the only opportunity he ever had to visit Strasbourg, and though their epistolary friendship continued to the end of Ascham's life, he never met Sturm in person.

A similar disappointment occurred a short time later. From Strasbourg the emperor proceeded to Wissembourg; the English party went on to Speyer. Here Morison, falling ill, dispatched Ascham on two diplomatic errands. At the end of September, he sent him to Heidelberg with letters from King Edward to the Count Palatine (III, 29). Ascham was invited to dine with Frederick and afterwards toured the castle with Stephen Cirler (II, 166). This left him with no time to visit Hubert, Cisner, and Micyllus, for he still had his other mission to perform. Though he expected to come again to Heidelberg, perhaps to drink the fine Neckar wine that he liked so much and to argue with Hubert and Cisner over the pronunciation of Greek, the sudden withdrawal of the imperial court to Luxembourg in January prevented his return.

The emperor, meanwhile, began to make plans for retaking Metz, which, since its capture by the French, the Duke of Guise had turned into a fortress of exceptional strength. Charles's sister Mary wisely tried to dissuade him from attacking the city; instead, he followed the Duke of Alva's counsel that he woo Albert of Brandenburg away from the French alliance and commence the siege. As a security measure, once preparations were under way, he forbade all foreign ambassadors the imperial camp. Morison, finding that the restriction hindered his diplomatic work, sent Ascham to Bishop Granvelle at Landau to seek permission for him to attend upon the emperor there. Though Granvelle received Ascham with friendliness, he refused to make any exception to Charles's directive (I, 334–37).

Throughout the autumn, while Charles went on with his military plans, Ascham had little leisure to communicate with any of his friends, for Morison, as the ambassador himself reported, was giving him "his belly-ful of writings" in official correspondence.[33] When Ascham finally did write to Cecil on November 28, it proved to be another of those letters about dashed hopes and the disillusionment of one who had traded the scholar's for the courtier's way of life. Even as he was preparing to thank Cecil for having secured him the appointment as Latin Secretary to King Edward, he received news that his patent had been temporarily stayed. Yet by this time experience had taught him not to be surprised at the perversities of fortune, for, as he remarks stoically, "I that have seen in one half year two of the greatest princes subject to such tosses and toures of ups and downs, had learned very little, if two such great examples could teach me nothing" (I, 343).

Once more his immediate thought was to retreat to Cambridge, asking only for permission to concentrate his energies on teaching Greek and for exemption from certain of the statutes (probably those requiring fellows to be celibate). Some months later, he again expressed his wish, failing an appointment at court, to read Greek in the university, entreating Cecil to overlook his past "negligence in study" and supposed preoccupation with archery. Not that he was ashamed of the time he had formerly spent with longbow in hand. Following the same argument used in *Toxophilus,* he claimed that shooting had refreshed his mind rather than diverting him from study. He also argued persuasively that the disinterested scholarship of men of letters like himself should receive support: universities, he admits, are instituted for the sole purpose "that the realm may be served with preachers, lawyers, and physicians"; but when these enter the world, scholars are still needed in order to prepare the next generation of professional men and to preserve the heritage of learning. He could be content now to dedicate the remainder of his years to study, "for, as God be my judge," he writes, perhaps recalling the sermon he had preached in *Toxophilus* about proper self-estimation, "I had rather follow fitness in myself than search profit in any living" (I, 353–55).

While he was thus fretting about his own future, the emperor's affairs were turning out badly. The garrison of Metz, under the inspiring leadership of the Duke of Guise, withstood all imperial onslaughts, and a long stretch of damp and snowy weather disheartened Charles's soldiers, many of whom were Spaniards and Italians unused to the rigors of a northern winter. Early in January the siege was raised, most of the troops being left to shift for themselves while the emperor retired to nearby Thionville. The Englishmen followed him there and thence to Luxembourg, where Sir Andrew Dudley joined Morison as a fellow ambassador.[34]

Finally, on February 6, the court withdrew to Brussels. There, except for the brief trip to Louvain on which he was entertained by Nannius, Ascham spent the rest of his time abroad. In his free time he kept up his correspondence with Sturm, Hubert, and other Continental scholars, continued to petition Cheke and Cecil for preferment at home, and in all probability conversed about literature, travel, and current politics with young Thomas Hoby, whom he had once known as a student at St. John's. For Hoby, who had been working in Paris on his translation of Castiglione's *Courtier*, had come to Brussels when his half-brother, Sir Philip, rejoined the embassy in April.[35]

During these months Ascham also set about writing his little known but fascinating *Report of Germany*. If in the process he ever stopped to consider the import of his own experiences over the preceding three years, it must have struck him that, like his student days and his brief tenure as Elizabeth's tutor, this third significant period of his life had begun rich in expectation but was ending with his career apparently little advanced and his future as uncertain as ever.

CHAPTER EIGHT

A Report of Germany

IN A LETTER dated July 22, 1553, Sturm expressed his concurrence in an unfavorable judgment Ascham had passed on Cardinal Pietro Bembo's epistles and recent *Historiae Venetiae libri XII* (Venice, 1551). He follows this up with a suggestion: "Why don't you, Ascham, who understand so well the principles of historiography, produce a history . . . of those events that you have read about, heard reported, and observed in Germany. The feint of Maurice of Saxony at Innsbruck, the emperor's enforced flight, the subsequent peace and that now declined, and finally that cruel war, and the death of Maurice—if the things men say are true, are these matters not of great moment, and worthy of you?" (I, 372).

Sturm's prompting, however, was unnecessary, for on July 7 Ascham had already written to Cheke that he was occupying his time in "sketching out those true causes, for which Parma, Salerno, Brandenburg, and the Saxon have forsaken the emperor. I am also composing a narrative of what took place day by day in the court of the emperor, from the flight out of Innsbruck up to the abandoning of the siege of Metz: during which times there were great confusions of alliances, disagreements, plunderings, wars, fickle changes of fortune, and serious disruptions of affairs." He is setting down these things informally and artlessly "so that in one another's company we may beguile next winter's nights with pleasant conversation about and recollection of these events." And since he is merely recording the facts for his own and his friends' benefit, he is content to use plain English in his account rather than the more eloquent Latin (I, 365).

The original stimulus for the undertaking seems to have come from John Astley at Hatfield. Nine months earlier Astley had begged Ascham for news concerning the "great stirs" in Germany and the sudden, almost incredible, decline in the emperor's fortunes (III, 4). The work described in the letter to Cheke, begun as a direct response to Astley's request, is a slender volume published, apparently after Ascham's death, with the title *A Report and Discourse written by Roger Ascham, of the affaires and state of Germany and the Emperour Charles his court, duryng certaine yeares while the sayd Roger was there.* Of the original discourse, unfortunately, either a large portion was lost or destroyed, or else, as seems more likely, the work was never finished. For although Ascham offers Astley a narrative beginning with his own arrival in Augsburg and ending with the repair of the imperial court to Brussels in February 1553, he breaks off long before fulfilling his promise. According to a remark within the text, the existing portion seems to have been nearly completed by mid-July, when news of Edward VI's death reached the Low Countries and when Ascham may have broken off his discourse to turn his attention to the more immediately significant political troubles at home.[1]

Although the *Report* is, consequently, an unfinished and informal document, Ascham evidently intended to make it into something more than the trifling sketch he described to Cheke. The surviving fragment is really a prologue or opening book to an *historia sui temporis*, specifically, an eyewitness account and analysis of German political history from 1550 to 1553. In the final paragraph, he refers to what he has already composed as "this my former [i.e., first] book," and outlines for Astley the plan of the rest of the narrative. He has in mind at least two additional books, possibly several more. Having traced out the back-

---

* The single, undated edition of this work was printed at London by John Day (*STC* 830). The most reasonable date to which its publication may be assigned is 1570, for in that year Day brought out *The Scholemaster* and may have been trying to profit from simultaneous release of two titles by Ascham. It is unlikely that the *Report* was published, as some bibliographers surmise, in 1553, for its evaluation of Charles V's political behavior would scarcely have pleased Queen Mary Tudor, who was the emperor's cousin. Besides, in a letter to Bishop Gardiner written late in the same year, Ascham hints only indirectly at his having composed anything regarding the wars of Germany; certainly he would not have spoken so guardedly if the work were already in print or about to be printed (I, 383–84). Copies of a supposed edition dated 1570 (*STC* 831) have proved upon examination to be examples of *STC* 830; the "dated" edition is a ghost. A MS. copy prepared for Archbishop Matthew Parker, but of no especial textual significance, is preserved in the library of Corpus Christi College, Cambridge (MS. CX., Nos. 24–25). The *Report* has been reprinted in the editions of Bennet, Cochrane, Giles, and Wright, and Katterfeld translates large portions of it in his monograph.

ground and specified what he regards as the immediate causes of Charles's difficulties, he proposes next to follow the course of events from his own arrival at Augsburg until the siege of the city begun by Albert and Maurice on April 1, 1552. Thereafter, he promises, "my whole diarium shall at full instruct you" concerning developments from the time of the ignominious departure out of Innsbruck until the present sojourn of the court in Brussels.[2]

Had Ascham carried out his design, he would have left the world the earliest reasoned historical account of the various crises that eventually led to Charles's abdication in 1556. Even in its fragmentary state, the *Report* is valuable enough to deserve closer attention than it has yet received from students of English historiography.[3] Possibly its unpretentious title has contributed to its neglect, for, apart from translations of several perceptive treatises on French politics, most of the "Reports," "Discourses," and "Newes" printed in Elizabethan England were bare narrations of isolated events with little or no attempt at analysis of their causes. Such pamphlets as *A true discourse of the late bataill fought betweene our Englishmen and the Prince of Parma* (London, 1585) and Thomas Digges's *A briefe report of the militarie services done in the Low Countries by the Erle of Leicester* (London, 1587) are fairly representative. They and the rest of their kind remind one of the ephemeral dispatches of news correspondents, of which, indeed, they are remote but recognizable ancestors. Some of them, like Ascham's, assume the form of personal letters; unlike his, they are intended merely to describe, not to interpret, the events which they record.

Thus, modest as it is, Ascham's little book is a pioneer effort in English historiography, among the first in which the author conscientiously endeavors to sort out a complicated web of political events and determine their proximate causes from the evidence. The *Report* does not fully achieve this admirable aim, but considering the complexity of the affairs described and the rather primitive state of historical writing among Englishmen at the time, it deserves commendation for what it does accomplish. Ascham strives to provide a mirror for political conduct that goes far beyond the *de casibus* or providential explanations resorted to by most contemporary chroniclers and poets. He views character as a real cause in history and makes an honest, if not entirely successful, attempt at objective analysis of the motives underlying the political behavior of individual men. Working in the tradition of Polybius and Machiavelli, who provided him with ideas and served him as models, he may be credited with having introduced their kind of "pragmatism" into English historical writing. Finally, he sets forth and writes under a complete theory of historiography which, though indebted as much to treatises on rhetoric as to the statements and practices of actual historians, represents the first clear formulation of an historical method by a Renaissance Englishman.

The *Report*, brief and incomplete though it is, is a noteworthy accomplishment. It stands alone until the publication, twenty-five years later, of superior works by Bacon, William Camden, and Sir John Hayward, the recognized founders of modern historiography in England.[4] For in spite of their many protestations about the utility of histories and their genuine interest in national chronicles and firsthand reports of contemporary foreign affairs, sixteenth-century Englishmen had little skill as historians. Nor did their incapacity stem from lack of practice or of models from which they might have learned the craft. Most of the historians, both ancient and modern, were available to them, as were the raw materials provided by chroniclers and eyewitnesses of current events. As translators they were energetic enough, and from the middle of the Tudor period onward produced English versions of many important historians, starting with Herodotus and continuing down to the most accomplished and instructive of the moderns, Comines, Machiavelli, Guicciardini, and Sleidan. But in contrast with what happened in poetry and the drama, widespread translation and dissemination of foreign works had little effect on original historical writing.

Before Ascham, only Polydore Vergil in his *Anglica Historia* had tried to write what may be truly called political history, and his judgments on matters, though more objective than those of most Tudor historians, are nevertheless distinctly colored by his Lancastrian partisanship.[5] He wrote, moreover, not in English but in Latin. More's *Richard III* is also biased and prefers the providential interpretation of events to serious effort at analyzing Richard's behavior or searching after the immediate causes of his downfall. Edward Halle's *The union of the two noble and illustre famelies of Lancastre and York*, admirable in certain respects, stands mainly in the tradition of the London chronicle. The one other contemporary endeavor to study cause and effect in a political crisis was John Proctor's *The historie of Wyates rebellion* (London, 1554, 1555). Yet since this little-known and unambitious work could not have been written before April 1554 (the month in which the younger Sir Thomas Wyatt was executed for treason), Ascham's *Report*, though concerned with German rather than British affairs, remains the earliest essay at pragmatic political history by a Tudor Englishman.[6]

In several respects, he was well qualified for the undertaking, so that Sturm's promptings were not mere compliment or flattery. In addition to being familiar with all the better-known classical authorities, he knew and had commented perceptively on the writings of a number of contemporary historians, among them More, Comines, Sleidan, Bembo, Paolo Giovio, Halle, Avila y Zuñiga, Girolamo Falletti, and Machiavelli. Nor was his interest in the political branch of history a passing one. Years after his return from the Continent he corresponded with Sturm about the recent intrigues in France and on one occasion urged him to write a history of the Guisean conspiracy (II, 72). Toward the end of his life, he projected an account of the character and public acts of Queen Elizabeth during the first decade of her reign, though he seems never to have carried out his intention.[7]

Probably his main qualification for writing about German affairs was closeness to the events and source materials. If in nothing else, he regards himself as ideally suited to the task in this one respect, for during his years in the imperial court he had come to know several of the chief participants, had actually witnessed some of the most important crises, had heard and weighed the counsels and observations of ambassadors and agents of all sides, and had continuing access to diplomatic reports. "What better commodity to know the truth," he boasts, "any writer in Greek, Latin, or other tongue hath had, I cannot perceive, except only Xenophon, Caesar, and Philip Comines; which two first worthy writers wrote their own acts so wisely, and so without all suspicion of partiality, as no man hitherto, by my opinion, hath borne himself so uprightly in writing the histories of others; the third, having in a manner the like opportunity, hath not deserved like commendations, at least as I suppose" (III, 8).

Ascham, as his letters dating from this period demonstrate, was not likely to waste his opportunities for studying the characters of important men and watching their behavior in political crises. The keenness of observation and talent for description that he had exhibited in *Toxophilus* and the long letters to the fellows of St. John's did not fail him in the *Report*. The characterizations of the principal actors in this drama of German politics, though somewhat colored by rhetorical theories, and by his religious and ethical views, are convincing. The later German historians Georg Voigt and Leopold von Ranke admired especially his handling of Albert and Maurice and drew upon his observations, as the best by any contemporary, in their own accounts of these two personages.[8]

It is evident that Ascham recognized the emperor as the focus of contemporary history; if, therefore, the art of the historiographer had any lesson to offer, one might expect it to be an explanation of how the dominion of so powerful and fortunate a ruler could be violently shaken within so brief a span of time. Perhaps this particular story also afforded a lesson immediately applicable. Since the foreign relations of all the countries of Europe hinged upon the decisions and movements of this mighty prince, it behooved the head of every other state to watch closely and try to predict the course of his affairs. It is conceivable, then, that Ascham ultimately intended his work for the eyes of Edward VI's councillors. Contemporary monarchs and their advisers were becoming increasingly aware of the value of judicious "reports" and ambassadorial dispatches as sources of information upon which policy might be shaped. Presented not as the mere trifle he claimed it to be in his letter to Cheke, but as a considered evaluation of the current crisis in imperial affairs, his account might help the council to reshape England's foreign alliances.

At this very time Northumberland, who had displaced Somerset as Protector, and his advisers were considering a shift in England's commitments abroad. A body of correspondence exists on the subject between the privy council and the English ambassadors at Brussels. Many of the communications, dating from April and May 1553, are transcribed in Ascham's hand. On April 27 Morison proposed that the council allow him and his fellow emissaries Hoby and Bishop Thirlby to approach the emperor concerning the possibility of a new defensive alignment in Europe. The proposed league would include Charles, England, the German states, Sweden, Poland, and Denmark against— obviously—France and the Turk. Morison's reasoning was that Henry II would thus be neutralized, while the Turk would not dare attack either the empire or Italy in the absence of effective French support. On the next day the three ambassadors requested that they be permitted to sound out Charles on the advisability of forming such a league, but cautiously, so that if he were against the idea, England would not be compromised. Their principal worry was that the shrewd emperor would see in the proposal (quite rightly) the likelihood of a disconcerting alliance between England and the German Protestant states.

A week later, Hoby wrote on his own initiative to Northumberland that the emperor was dangerously ill and seemed likely to die. Therefore, rather than aligning England with the Spaniards, that is, with the future King Philip II, he suggested that the council negotiate "with Ferdinand, Maximilian, and the rest of the Empire" concerning a defensive agreement. A treaty with the Spaniards, especially since the German electors favored Ferdinand and Maximilian, might prove disadvantageous. Northumberland, like Somerset before him, had learned to play cautiously with Charles and Henry II, for he realized that a balance of the two powers was England's best security. Of late he had been carrying on tentative and secret negotiations with France, but he was interested in any means of keeping the two Continental rivals neutralized. During the preceding year he and the council had ignored Maurice's request for aid against the emperor out of fear that the result might be too great an advantage for the French. Now, with his own private plots spinning in his head, Northumberland wavered, uncertain which kind of alliance might best further his dynastic aims. Of one fact he could be certain: the emperor would never tolerate his design of preventing Mary Tudor's succession to the throne. If lining up with France were too dangerous, a German alliance might be the best solution. Whatever Northumberland's motives, on May 15 the council sent Hoby a letter approving his plan. In a return dispatch of the 26th, the ambassadors expressed various doubts about the projected alliance, but nevertheless recommended that, with certain modifications, the proposal be pursued. Charles, however, lived on, and instead it was the death of Edward VI a month and a half later that interrupted the negotiations.[9]

Now Ascham had begun his work about the time that Morison and his colleagues offered to the council their remedy for the tangled diplomatic situation. Even more relevant may be the fact that most of the *Report* was composed after the council had approved Hoby's plan. This historical study, therefore, which found the root of the troubles in a fundamental weakness of Charles's character, may have been conceived by its author as a warning to proceed cautiously and to avoid unprofitable commitments. At the same time, by showing the increasing strength of the Lutheran princes, it might suggest the emergence of a new Protestant power with which England could join in order to check the ambitions of both Hapsburgs and Orléans.

Naturally one must be cautious about ascribing such a motive to Ascham. He had insisted to Cheke, after all, that the work was meant solely for his friends, and it did remain in the form of a personal letter to Astley. Yet even if its striking connection with current diplomatic maneuvering does not prove that it was composed to be read by the king and his advisers, there can be no question that it is intended to afford an instructive lesson in political behavior. It is, above everything else, a humanist's mirror for princes, offering living models for imitation and avoidance in the conduct of public affairs.

II

Like other Renaissance historians, Ascham makes the conventional disavowal of fitness for the task he has undertaken (III, 5, 62). Yet his disclaimer may have been in part sincere, for he was presuming to fathom the causes of one of the most puzzling turns in the history of sixteenth-century Europe. To contemporary witnesses, the rapid political decline of the most powerful ruler in Christendom seemed incredible, an effect attributable only to the extreme caprice of fortune. So great and so sudden a falling off as Charles V had experienced in Germany after 1551 constituted a severe challenge to any attempt at causal explanation, particularly by a simple Cambridge don turned ambassador's secretary. Ascham knew that the enterprise was a risky one and consequently begins his communication to Astley with a rhetorically conventional, but none the less pertinent, summary of the principles of historiography by which he hoped to abide:

When you and I read Livy together, if you do remember, after some reasoning we concluded both what was in our opinion to be looked for at his hand that would well and advisedly write an history: First point was, to write nothing false: next, to be bold to say any truth; whereby is avoided two great faults, flattery and hatred: for which two points Caesar is read to his great praise, and Jovius [Giovio] the Italian to his just reproach. Then to mark diligently the causes, counsels, acts, and issues in all great attempts: and in causes, what is just or unjust; in counsels, what is proposed wisely or rashly; in acts, what is done courageously or faintly; and of every issue, to note some general lesson of wisdom and wariness, for like matters in time to come; wherein Polybius in Greek, and Philip Comines in French, have done the duties of wise and worthy writers. Diligence must also be used in keeping truly the order of time; and describing lively, both the site of places and nature of persons, not only for the outward shape of the body, but also for

the inward disposition of the mind, as Thucydides doth in many places very
trimly, and Homer every where, and that always most excellently, which
observation is chiefly to be marked in him; and our Chaucer doth the same,
very praise-worthily: mark him well, and confer him with any other that
writeth in our time in their proudest tongue whosoever list. The style must
be always plain and open, yet sometime higher and lower, as matters do rise
and fall: for if proper and natural words, in well-joined sentences, do lively
express the matter, be it troublesome, quiet, angry, or pleasant, a man shall
think not to be reading, but present in doing of the same. And herein Livy,
of all other in any tongue, by mine opinion, carrieth away the praise (III,
5–6).

Despite Ascham's assertion, the substance of this theory is scarcely
the result of discussions at Hatfield Palace. Rather, it is a direct para-
phrase, with supplemental details from other ancient sources such as
Lucian's *How to Write History,* of a speech assigned to Marcus Antonius
in Cicero's *De Oratore.* Antonius's speech, itself an epitome of classical
attitudes toward the historian's task as seen through the eyes of the
rhetorician, had been frequently echoed by humanist historians of the
Renaissance from Guarino onwards.[10]

Yet if his ideas come from such a source, one ought not to conclude
that Ascham is merely a Cicerolater viewing history as a handmaiden
to the rhetorician's art. His drawing upon the *De Oratore* for maxims
is no cause for doubting the sincerity of his effort as an historian; the
principles, besides, are perfectly sound, and Ascham conscientiously
tries to put them to work in his discourse.

Hence, his caution about "keeping truly the order of time" is not
mindless parroting of Antonius's words. While the injunction may
appear so obvious as to be hardly worth setting down, Ascham knew
that complex subject matter demanded more than merely chronological
arrangement. Near the close of the existing fragment he expresses his
awareness of the difficulty and justifies the manner of his own approach
to his materials: "Hitherto I have followed the order of persons, which
hath caused me somewhat to misorder both time and matter, yet where
divers great affairs come together, a man shall write confusedly for the
matter, and unpleasantly for the reader, if he use not such an apt kind
of partition as the matter will best afford, 'Which thing (Plato saith)
who cannot do, knoweth not how to write'" (III, 61). This conscious-
ness that historical narrative must be ordered according to the complexity and relative significance of the various causes and effects makes
the *Report* a far cry from the undiscriminating, unilinear annals and
"histories" typically produced by contemporary English chroniclers.

Likewise an echo of Cicero, as well as of a dictum of classical biographers, is the assertion about the necessity of portraying "the inward disposition of the mind." This is undoubtedly a reference to the conventional verbal portrait (*descriptio*) of classical history and biography, which was compounded of an *effictio* (delineation of the subject's physical attributes) and a *notatio* (comment on his moral qualities).[11] Although the idea and even its application to history are commonplace in ancient literature, with Ascham the principle is vital. Since he believes that the ethical character of the main actors has much to do with shaping the course of history, insight into their habits of thought and behavior is indispensable. His own portraits are an integral part of his attempt at fathoming the influence of individual character on the outcome of public affairs. For only by understanding the connection between events and the "inward disposition" of the participants does the historian, in Ascham's view, attain to the essence of his art, namely, careful analysis and clear exposition of "the causes, counsels, acts, and issues in all great attempts." Only if this rule is diligently observed, will the history provide worthwhile guidance to the reader for his own future political conduct.

No individual writer, of course, not even Livy or Ascham's own favorite, Herodotus, could be cited as having perfectly embodied all the virtues of the ideal historian. Among English works, none but More's *Richard III* manifested any real competence (III, 6). As examples, therefore, of effective historical writing, Ascham selected a number of different authors, concentrating his attention, however, on Polybius and Machiavelli. For those Renaissance humanists who became interested mainly in the political branch of history, Polybius had come to rival and then succeed Livy as the foremost classical model. It was felt that his analyses of character and motivation, and his concentration on political affairs, afforded invaluable lessons for practical conduct. Thus Ascham may extol Caesar and Livy as exemplary historians, but, as writers of instructive history, Polybius and Philippe de Comines bear away the palm (III, 6).

Polybius defines his aims in the preface to the ninth book of his *World History*. Here he declares his intention of restricting himself to "the doings of nations, cities, and monarchs," for not only does this "transactional" or "pragmatic" branch of history always contain new matter for fresh interpretation, but it offers a practical lesson, providing men "with a method for dealing with any contingency that may arise."[12] History is, in other words, "philosophy teaching by example."

The statements in this "Proem," however, are fairly generalized; even the prefaces to Renaissance chronicles and epitomes of world history read in similar fashion. The crucial passage in Polybius for Renaissance political historians is the following: "Now I maintain that it is most essential both for writers and for students to know the causes from which all events spring and grow. But most writers are guilty of confusion in this matter, owing to their not observing the difference between a pretext and a cause, and between the beginning of a war and the pretext for it."[13] An historical work is idle if its author simply describes battles; of what use are these if he shows the reader nothing "of the causes to which in each case success or failure was due? For the results of actions merely interest readers, but anticipation of what is to follow, when the inquiry is properly conducted, is of benefit to students. Most salutary of all to those who give due attention to it is an exposition of the detailed management of each particular question."[14]

For the humanist Ascham, who had renewed his acquaintance with Polybius in the edition he had found at Speyer in 1550 (I, 258), this was the kind of lesson to be derived from the theories and practice of the Greek historian. It had likewise been the principal lesson for "realists" like Niccolò Machiavelli. Both humanist and realist assumed that, human nature being in the main constant and unvarying from one generation to another, history is primarily a guide for the attentive reader to rational and successful political action. While their conceptions of the precise nature of this success may have differed, the goal in either case was prudent statecraft. Thus, two writers of such widely differing tempers as Ascham and Machiavelli could and did stand within the same Polybian tradition. Odd though it may seem to link the Florentine secretary and the moralistic Cambridge reformer, Roger Ascham was definitely Machiavelli's pupil and took instruction in the art of writing history from his books.[15]

Certainly he had not read Machiavelli simply "for the tongue" while he lived with Morison. Nor had he read only to disapprove. A casual reader of the *Report* may be misled by finding there what is apparently the first use of the word "Machiavels" in the unfavorable sense that it came soon to have among Ascham's fellow Englishmen. Because he employs it as a reproach to the politically unscrupulous, he did help to fix the term in the Elizabethan mind as one of opprobrium.[16] His work, on the other hand, shows a considerable positive debt to Machiavelli, for though repelled by some of the Florentine's moral standards, Ascham was yet attracted to his theories. Both ardently admired Livy and Polybius; Machiavelli's *Discourses* are essentially essays on government with examples taken from Ascham's favorite Roman historian and manifesting the influence of the political theories of Polybius. No other historian or writer on politics up to Ascham's time, including Comines and Guicciardini, had succeeded so well as Machiavelli in the study of proximate historical causes. Machiavelli, furthermore, in diagnosing complicated political situations, had emphasized the role of character in determining historical issues.

For Ascham's purposes no better teacher existed. At the same time, because his own outlook and intentions in writing differed so markedly, his attempt to apply Machiavellian principles to his analysis of recent German history did get him into at least one major difficulty in the *Report*. In trying to regard Maurice of Saxony's conduct "objectively" in a work whose historical lessons depended otherwise on a Christian humanist view of man's political nature, Ascham fell onto a dilemma from which he could not quite extricate himself. Though he disapproved of amorality in political action, through studying Machiavelli he had glimpsed that at times the bolder, rather than the more honest, venture may be necessary to secure victory for a worthy enterprise. This passage is worth looking at in a little more detail.

Maurice, by astute but ethically questionable maneuvering, had succeeded in attaining several of his political objectives, including the release of the Landgrave of Hesse and the religious compromise of Passau. In order to justify, or at least excuse, Maurice's actions, Ascham is forced to displace for the moment the clearly defined moral standards upon which he judges the conduct of princes earlier in the work and to stand upon Machiavelli's requisites for political success. Although he claims that he neither condones nor condemns Maurice's actions and disapproves of those who interpret his conduct with "Machiavel's heads," in effect he applies Machiavellian formulae himself in expressing admiration for the stratagems of the young Protestant leader: "First with close policy, after with open power, both wittily and stoutly, he achieved more by force than he required by suit" (III, 58). He commends Maurice, too, for having had the sense and skill to play off rivals against one another. The passage illustrates perfectly the ambivalent viewpoint into which Ascham is sometimes forced: "As he had wit to take money plenty of the French king, so he had wit also to furnish himself so from home as he durst first fall out with the French king, and durst also after to set upon the emperor, till he had brought his honest purpose to pass" (III, 56). In Frenchman or Spaniard such double-dealing would have been purely reprehensible. In Maurice, because his purpose was "honest," that is, good for the Reformation, it is commendable. Thus Ascham, though he protests more than once that he renders no judgment but only records the facts, cannot help admiring a statesman who knows so well how to play both the lion and the fox.

Another echo from Machiavelli occurs in a passage about Ferrante Gonzaga, governor of Milan and instigator of the assassination of the Duke of Piacenza. In recording that Gonzaga tried also to murder the Duke's son Ottavio, Ascham remarks: "Men never love when they have just cause to fear, but must needs still mistrust without all hope of reconciling whom they have before hurt beyond all remedy of amends" (III, 15). This recalls Machiavelli's warning in *The Prince*: "And whosoever thinks that in high personages new benefits cause old offenses to be forgotten, makes a great mistake."[17]

These are the obvious debts, indicating familiarity, and, wherever they help resolve a practical dilemma, agreement, with the rules of political conduct set forth in *The Prince*. But the *Report* appears also to owe much, though Ascham nowhere alludes directly to either work, to the *Discourses* and the *History of Florence*. Machiavelli had undertaken a labor similar to Ascham's, though a far more complicated and ambitious one, in setting out to write the story of his own city. His aim was to explore the immediate causes of foreign wars and internal disorders, the advantages and disadvantages of various treaties and alliances made over the centuries by the Florentines, and above all, the characters of the men whose counsel and actions had affected the course of civic history. He would describe all these issues with faithfulness to the truth, especially where the task is most difficult, in portraying the behavior and motivations of individuals. He intended to concern himself with the causes and consequences of civil discords rather than with external matters, for it was the former, he believed, that constituted the greatest threat to the unity and security of the commonwealth. He hoped that his fellow citizens, thus warned that the worst evils are brought on by internal strife, would learn how to manage their own political life more prudently than they had in the past.[18]

The *History of Florence* was therefore rich in principles and examples applicable to Ascham's task. Other possible sources do exist for most of these precepts, but that Ascham was consciously drawing upon his familiarity with Machiavelli's history is strongly suggested by a number of parallels between the two works.

First of all, both writers subscribe to the opinion that internal discord is the greatest source of injury to the state. Ascham, having lived through twenty stormy years in the miniature commonwealth of St. John's, understood this fact even before his experience of the courts and camps of kings. As in Machiavelli's view no combination of enemies could have effected so much harm to Florence as had her factious citizens, so in Ascham's the emperor might have withstood any combination of foreign enemies had he been able to retain the loyal backing of the quarrelsome German nobility.[19]

One striking feature of the Report is the amount of space given to descriptions of the main characters. The portraits, though recognizably exercises in descriptio in the manner of Livy, are used to excellent purpose. Ascham tries to show, by offering the characterization just before someone enters significantly into the action, how his ethical nature, along with the personal impression that he makes upon others, constitutes a moving force in history. Comines and Guicciardini had employed this device to good effect, but here again Machiavelli seems to have been the chief influence. Machiavelli's portraits are introduced for the identical reason, and he defends the practice, while presenting an extended characterization of Cosimo de' Medici, on the ground that doing so is as fitting for the historian, even the author of a "general history," as it is for the biographer.[20]

Further evidence of Machiavelli's influence on the Report is Ascham's adoption of the theory that the root of political disorder in Italy was the secular ambition of the papacy (a view to which he hardly needed converting). In the Discourses (I, xii) Machiavelli lays the entire blame for the partition of Italy to this cause, and in the first book of his history the main thesis is that the popes, sometimes for the benefit of the church but nearly always for their personal interests, brewed continual strife among the lay states of the peninsula. Then, whenever they had stirred up more trouble than they could handle, they would summon foreign princes to their aid, with the result that Italy became a spoil for Germans, Frenchmen, and Spaniards. In the Report, Ascham makes Julius III appear to follow exactly this kind of policy, first pitting the local rulers against one another in order to weaken princes with lands adjacent to his own, then playing Charles V off against Henry II in an effort to secure advantages for his family and the papal domains.

In structure, also, the two works are strikingly similar. Machiavelli begins by discussing the impact of foreign and papal politics upon the internal affairs of Florence before turning to the actual history of the city. Ascham, similarly, starts by pointing out how Charles's troubles in Italy and with the Turk, along with the intrigues of Pope Julius, impinged upon events within the German empire. Again, each of the eight books of the *History of Florence* opens with a generalization about what Machiavelli regards as the specific proximate cause of the events under consideration, usually an identifiable defect in the political character of the citizens or their leaders. The ensuing narrative presents the historical evidence upon which the generalization is based and from which a sound moral may be extracted for future political guidance. In the third book, for instance, enmity between the populace and the nobility is seen as the root of all civil discords; Machiavelli finds his evidence principally in the history of the city during the latter part of the fourteenth century. Book VIII begins with a disquisition on the nature and historical importance of conspiracies; Machiavelli cites as incontrovertible proof of their damaging effects the difficulties encountered by the Medici during the fifteenth century. Ascham's account runs a like course: first he states the cause, which he finds in a grave defect of character in the emperor; the narrative then attempts to demonstrate the evil produced by this single failing. The "spring of the matter from whence all these mischiefs did flow," he concludes, their "very seed," was Charles's "unkindness" (III, 9). In the Tudor mind, "unkindness," or ingratitude, was a particularly heinous vice because it was regarded as monstrous or unnatural, literally against nature or "kind."[21] In a monarch, it was especially offensive, since it was opposed to the "nature" of the ruler as embodied in the Aristotelian ideal of *magnanimity* (megalopsychía).

An historian who ascribes all of Charles V's troubles to this one flaw of character may seem to the modern mind incredibly naive.[22] Ascham does, in fact, acknowledge the existence of other factors such as the restless ambition of Duke Maurice. He was also aware that some men sought the heart of the matter in still other causes, for example, in "religion and liberty" (III, 9). Yet he refuses to qualify his contention and does bring forward some quite formidable evidence to maintain it. For a precedent he could again point to the fairly sophisticated Machiavelli. In describing the uprising in 1381 against the popular leader Michele Lando, Machiavelli declares that in spite of the immeasurable debt owed to this hero by the citizens, Florence was to him "poco grata" (unthankful), "an error often committed by princes and republics, and one which often causes those who are alarmed by such examples to injure their princes before they have experienced their ingratitude."[23]

The idea of ingratitude as the mainspring of political ill is, of course, a commonplace that Ascham could have found as readily in, say, Cicero's *Epistles to Atticus* as in the *History of Florence*.[24] But the practical application to an actual series of historical events is Machiavelli's. Ascham, moreover, seems to have taken from the *Discourses* the further hint that ingratitude is the cause of overweening ambition in an offending ruler's subjects.

III

What Ascham's "glass of government" tries to show, then, is that Charles's inability to maintain order in the vast domain committed to his care was directly dependent upon this one flaw of ingratitude. At the same time, Ascham felt obliged to demonstrate that the persons whom the emperor had treated "unkindly" were not previously inclined to sedition or rebellion, but had been trustworthy and devoted servants. The historical lesson was strengthened precisely because each of them was, in Ascham's eyes, a man who could have been driven to turn against his lawful ruler only by some extreme provocation. For this reason, the existing fragment is ordered so as to contrast the emperor's ungracious conduct with what Ascham sincerely believes to be the honorable character and behavior of the persons whom he has offended. Thus, like the Earl of Clarendon in the next century, Ascham viewed history largely as "character in action," a fact that helps explain his concentration on ethical portraiture and upon analysis of the motives of the principal actors.

Accordingly, to Ascham the immediate occasion, though not the cause, of Charles's difficulties was failure to keep his promise to return the North African city of Mahdia to Soliman II.[25] In retaliation, the Turks captured Tripoli and, disregarding a pledge they had made to the contrary, put most of the defenders to the sword. The Turkish excuse for such inhumanity serves to point up for Ascham the unnaturalness of Charles's supposed breaking of his word: because the Christian emperor did not keep faith with Moslems, the Turkish general explained, he felt no obligation himself to keep faith with Christians. Soon afterwards, hostilities were resumed in Hungary, with further examples of broken pledges and horrible cruelty on both sides. As Ascham believes, the most important effect of the new breach with the Turk was that Charles's subjects now became "bolder to put out their heads to seek some open remedy for their private injuries," especially since the King of France was constantly at hand to encourage "whosoever had cause to be aggrieved with the emperor."[26] Starting from this introduction, the *Report* discusses in turn the specific grievances against Charles that compelled four of his subjects, Duke Ottavio Farnese, Prince Ferrante of Salerno, Albert of Brandenburg, and Duke Maurice, to defect to the French or the Turks.

The unnaturalness of Charles's behavior is first stressed by a brief, contrasting character sketch of Soliman. The Turk, says Ascham, has been reported to him as "a good and merciful, just and liberal prince, wise in making and true in performing any covenant, and as sore a revenger of truth not kept."[27] Had the emperor treated his own subjects and allies with equal justice and liberality, Farnese and the others would not have been driven elsewhere to seek redress of their grievances, and Charles could have relied upon their loyalty and ability to provide substantial military aid. Within his own domains he would have been reasonably secure and hence able to concentrate on his wars with the French and Turks. Above all, Henry II would not have gained an advantage over him in Italy or had the opportunity to enter into the bargain with Albert and Maurice that led to his winning the imperial cities of Metz, Toul, and Verdun.

The earliest defection from the emperor, that by his own son-in-law, Ottavio Farnese, is explained by Ascham as follows. In 1547 Charles, who had helped to advance the Farnese family in the first place, apparently connived at the assassination of Ottavio's father, Pierluigi, Duke of Piacenza, by hirelings of the imperial governor of Milan, Ferrante Gonzaga.[28] Piacenza thereby was lost to the Farnese and came under Milanese domination. Ottavio, aggrieved at the emperor's failure to right this wrong done by one of his own officials, became disaffected. Unable to gain any assurance from Charles of either his right in Piacenza or his safety from Gonzaga's henchmen, he sought next the counsel of the pope, who advised him to call upon the King of France for protection from the Milanese.[29] Ascham claims that the pope's stratagem was to weaken the position of the emperor, whose possessions flanked the papal states on north and south. The upshot was the war in 1551 in the north of Italy, with Charles and a not too helpful Julius pitted against Ottavio and France. Early in 1552, seeing that the imperials were losing ground and that France in turn might become too strong a neighbor in Italy, the pope negotiated a peace with Henry II, which in turn enabled the French to concentrate on the more recently opened war in Picardy and Lorraine.

In all this maneuvering Ascham views Julius as a clever intriguer, alert to seize "a fit occasion to set the emperor and France together by the ears" (III, 17), and craftily diverting Henry II's attention to other fronts upon perceiving that the game was getting too hot in Italy. The truth is that the pope, though he did prove to Charles a vacillating and finally untrustworthy ally, was not the skillful politician that Ascham makes him out to be. It was his weakness and hesitation, rather than a propensity for troublemaking, that caused him to act as he did. In the beginning he had actually tried to dissuade Ottavio from going to the French for help, rightly judging that such a course would only add to the political confusion of Italy.[30]

It is not difficult to see why the Protestant Ascham should have misinterpreted Julius's behavior. Although the alleged cause of the war in the *Report* is Charles's "unkindness," Ascham can only feel sorry for "the emperor, good man," when he comes up against the even greater "unkindness," that is, the cunning and deceit, of the Roman pontiff (III, 22). He quotes with relish a witty saying about the pope by Charles's secretary, Pyramus, "which Pyramus is a papist for his life. And being asked how he could excuse the pope's unkindness against his master the emperor; he answered smiling, Julius Tertius is a knave; but the pope is an honest man; which saying is common in this court."[31] Of course Ascham's sources of information, being largely imperial, would scarcely have provided him with the papal or French side of the story. It seems likely, moreover, that in regarding Julius III as the mainspring of the action in Italy, he is viewing Italian politics through spectacles provided by his master, Machiavelli.

His characterization of Ottavio is likewise hampered both by insufficient knowledge of the total situation and by eagerness to support the theory about Charles's fatal flaw of character. As in the one-sentence ikon of Soliman, Ascham goes too far, in order to heighten the contrast between the emperor's "unkindness" and the good behavior of the person whom he has offended, in commending the character of the "victim." Modern biographers of Charles have regarded Ottavio and the rest of the Farnese as a breed of ambitious upstarts, quick to use the contention between Henry II and the emperor as a means of furthering their own ambitions in Lombardy.[32] Ascham, however, records nothing but good of Ottavio and insists that only as a last resort did he go to Julius for advice about how to avenge his wrongs. He was, asserts Ascham, "so far from seeking blood and revenge, and so given to pity and gentleness," that on one occasion he refused to execute some of Gonzaga's hirelings who were planning to poison him, preferring instead to grant them "life and liberty." Ascham's authority, he takes pains to point out, is an eyewitness, and one, moreover, who was "a gentleman of Milan, an agent in the court, a doer for Gonzaga, who the same time was prisoner in Parma" (III, 15–16).

Nor is Ottavio remiss in seeking justice first where he ought. Ascham stresses the frequency and warmness of his importunity to Charles, and the contrasting coolness with which his petitions were received. Hence his calling upon Henry II for aid is seen as partly excusable, if ever treason can be, because he had clearly exhausted the lawful means of securing redress. At length Ottavio, "compelled against his nature turned his hate due to Gonzaga to revenge this undeserved unkindness in the emperor" (III, 16). Ascham drives home the political lesson in good humanistic fashion by citing a parallel in Quintus Curtius, namely, the death of Philip of Macedon, who overcame all his external enemies only to be slain by Pausanius, a formerly loyal subject whom he had suffered to be outraged by another of his generals.

With the same intent but with better effect Ascham draws a purely favorable portrait of the Prince of Salerno. Again the emperor's ingratitude forces one of his subjects to react unnaturally. In this example, moreover, the "unkindness" is compounded, for despite the tyrannous government of Naples by the viceroy, Don Diego de Toledo, Charles refuses to remove the oppressor. Ascham catalogues the principal misdeeds by which Don Diego had made his rule infamous. He had relentlessly extorted money from the Neapolitans, he had conducted cruel and illegal inquisitions, punishing not only the acts but the very thoughts of men, and he had diverted civil suits "from common law to private will" (III, 23–24). Ascham points out the consequences of similar misgovernment in ancient times, how Julius Caesar was undone "for pulling down the laws" and Croesus for taking away men's property and so losing their hearts.

The Neapolitans, desperate under such tyranny, begged Prince Ferrante to intercede with the emperor. When he did so, Charles promised relief, yet took no action against the viceroy, who continued his cruelty and extortion. Hence, in April 1552, the prince, seeing the emperor beset by France, the Turk, Maurice, and Albert, took the opportunity to desert first to Henry II and then to Soliman. Even as Ascham was writing about him in the *Report*, he heard that Ferrante was "on the sea with sixty-three galleys of the Turk at his commandment."[33]

This man, writes Ascham, was everywhere loved and respected and had done "so good and faithful service" that many of Charles's most loyal defenders were willing to excuse his defection. Thus a second deserving person, "being so unjustly handled by his enemy, the viceroy of Naples, and so unkindly dealt withal by his master the emperor, was driven by necessity to seek an unlawful shift" (III, 23). The blame lies clearly, not on the viceroy, but on Charles. Don Diego had created the disorders, but Ascham wishes to affirm the inescapable obligation of the monarch to maintain the rule of law and provide for the welfare and harmony of the commonwealth. The Neapolitan incident points, as forcefully as any, the chief political lesson of the *Report*: unrest among a misgoverned populace can easily burst forth into open rebellion and give an advantage to foreign enemies. Fortunately, says Ascham, Don Diego died in 1553, so that the Neapolitans forgot their grievances, and their loyalty to the emperor was restored.

Once again Ascham stresses the fact that the authorities from whom he derives his information are not partisans of the deserter but "true servants of the emperor," men who have no cause to make light of defection from their master's service. This he does in order to establish his own objectivity; otherwise his recurring contrasts of character between emperor and subject might seem to parallel Giovio's twin errors of flattery and hatred. In spite of this device, the modern reader may be inclined to think him partial in his account. Charles was in truth much loved and respected by his subjects, and even during the dismal months of early 1553 enjoyed great prestige among them. Certainly he was a more admirable ruler than any of the French kings and most of the German princes against whom he struggled throughout his reign. Ascham does not deny these facts; in one place, as though he had momentarily forgotten the thesis of his little history, he even speaks of Charles's "great wisdom and natural clemency" (III, 42). Still, he recovers himself in time to present these good qualities as corroboration of the lesson to be derived from Charles's conduct. Even an otherwise admirable prince may come to grief if he behaves ungratefully toward subjects who have served him well.

Without question Ascham is willing to detect the emperor's main flaw wherever he can, but two facts remain to give him some standing as a responsible historian. First, when he has not actually observed an event himself, he never fails to give as his authority an eyewitness whom he trusts, though on at least one occasion he was misled by a supposedly reliable informant. Second, had he carried his narrative somewhat further along chronologically, he could have cited even more extreme examples of Charles's unnatural behavior. Not that one would expect him to mention these incidents out of their proper time sequence; but hindsight might have led him to paint an even blacker picture of Charles than in fact he did.

For as secretary to the English ambassadors, he certainly had the opportunity to collect further evidence of the emperor's misdeeds. On January 25, 1553, for instance, he transcribed a letter in which Morison and Dudley describe two such cases. According to this account, when Albert of Brandenburg, who had just returned to the emperor's service, was sent to Trier to levy reinforcements for the siege of Metz, Charles gave him permission to challenge an old personal debt of fifty thousand crowns from the bishop of the city. Of course Albert's loyalty, then a political necessity, had to be bought by such concessions, but the English diplomats regard it both as an ill deed and as a provocation to the bishop, who was "not greatly Imperial before," to go over to the French. The second case, even more deplorable, is that in retiring to Luxembourg and then to Brussels Charles "left behind him a certain number of Italians, Spaniards, and Dutchmen sick and needy whom Monsieur de Guise hath taken into Metz, and such as do recover he sendeth them through France with money and passports to their countries; and such as remain sick are in an hospital so provided, so far as they lack nothing that physicians can say is good for them. This practice of Monsieur de Guise shall win him much honor, and the Emperor some reproach when these soldiers not only in France but in their own countries also shall declare their entertainment of both sides."[34]

IV

Whatever the merits of Ascham's analysis of Charles's conduct, it did not serve him adequately in his attempt to get at the real causes of the political crisis in Italy from 1550 to 1552. Yet the weakness of this portion of his work is not due solely to his preoccupation with Charles's "unkindness." Except for his nine days' stay in Venice, he was unfamiliar with the country and had no direct knowledge of its political affairs. He admits, therefore, that the Italian and Turkish sections are but a prologue and that he passes over them rapidly "for the haste I have to come to the matters of Germany" (III, 23). In dealing with this latter material, though he comes far short of his own specifications for the ideal historian, he does fare considerably better.

Essentially this portion of the *Report* is an account of Charles's complicated relations with Albert and Maurice, whose rising against him in 1552 dealt the final blow to his hopes for a satisfactory political and religious settlement within the empire. By forcing him into the Treaty of Passau and losing him the city of Metz through their compact with Henry II, these two princes had nearly broken his will to rule in Germany. Ascham orders these materials much as he does his account of Turkish and Italian affairs, except that he expands the treatment and, in dealing with Duke Maurice, finds himself compelled by his interpretation of events to modify the pattern slightly. The character sketches of both German princes are more extended than those of Farnese and the Prince of Salerno, not only because of Ascham's greater knowledge of the two men, but also because the consequences of their breach with the emperor are the principal subject matter of the discourse. On both occasions when he was in their presence, Ascham had carefully noted the appearance and behavior of Albert and Maurice. As a follower of the imperial court, he was also able to gather considerable information about them in addition to what he had been able to "mark for myself." Maurice he could have encountered only in 1552 upon the emperor's removal from the Tyrol to the Rhine, but he did observe him closely enough to compare him in physique and countenance to one of King Edward's council, Sir Ralph Sadleir (III, 54). His opportunity for studying Albert had been better, for he had actually "dined in his company at the siege of Metz, in the County John of Nassau's tent" (III, 32).

In the portrait of Albert with which the German section of the *Report* begins, Ascham startles the reader by expressing unqualified admiration for this notorious historical personage. Although the margrave's personal and moral deficiencies and his questionable political motives and actions have seldom escaped some measure of disapproval from other historians, Ascham extols his virtues and asserts that his only fault lay in excess, rather than any deficiency, of what in moderation are good qualities.[35] The contrast, for example, between Albert's hot-headed refusal to accept "benevolences" from the emperor, and his promptness to better his fortunes by treasonous employment of his sword, Ascham cheerfully explains away as the "violence, which cometh somewhat of too stout a courage" (III, 35).

In his youth, according to the *Report*, Albert had been reckless in his spending and rough in his manners, showing little promise of becoming a person to reckon with in Germany. Ascham suggests that the roughness may have been due either to the lack of education common among German princes, or to bashfulness, "which property Xenophon wittily feigned to be in Cyrus at like years, judging bashfulness in youth to be a great token of virtue in age." The comparison of Albert to Xenophon's ideal prince prepares the way for an admiring *descriptio*, based in part on Ascham's own observation of the thirty-year-old margrave. He is, Ascham notes, of a proper height, strong-boned but not fleshy, handsome, "stern, and manly" in visage. He has a cheerful expression when he speaks, "and yet when he giveth ear to other, he keepeth a sad [serious] look without sign of suspicion, and also a well-set eye without token of malice" (III, 32).

Thus, already in the *effictio*, Ascham suggests that it is a man of obviously noble, frank, and trusting nature, not some restless "politician," who has suffered from the emperor's "unkindness." In the *notatio* of the portrait he sketches in additional details that make the margrave appear a most honorable prince and ideal military commander. He prefers listening to venting his own opinions. When he does talk, his strong voice commands respect, and "speaking and meaning seemeth to be always at one in him." Though he says only what he truly believes and does only what he says he will do, he is nevertheless wise enough to keep his own counsel and never betrays his designs to his foes. He is a born soldier. Son of the warrior Casimir, who was known for his prowess against the Turks as "Achilles Germanicus," it is small wonder that in warfare Albert is himself a "hot Pyrrhus."[36] He is "most courageous in hardest adventures, most cheerful in present jeopardy, and most painful in greatest labours, having no soldier under him that can better away with heat and cold, or longer suffer hunger and thirst than he himself." He dresses suitably for martial service; "his soldiers fear him for his stoutness, and love him for his liberality"; because of his manly appearance and character, he has obedient troops and enjoys the authority necessary to successful generalship. On one occasion, when some of his men began to mutiny because they lacked pay and provisions, he boldly hanged the most disorderly among them and yet generously supplied the wants of the most needy from his own private store (III, 32–34). As in his youth Albert resembled the fictionalized Cyrus, in the sketch of his soldierly qualities in his mature years he is like the Hannibal of Livy's well-known portrait, but without the Carthaginian's defects of cruelty and unfaithfulness.

To enforce once again the point about the "natural" goodness of the disaffected prince and the "unkindness" of the emperor and his advisers, Ascham balances against this portrait of Albert as a champion of Protestant and German right, unfavorable characterizations of a pair of imperial councillors, Lazarus von Schwendi and Dr. Heinrich Haase.

Schwendi, commissary for enforcing the Interim in Saxony and later Maximilian's commander-in-chief against the Turks, appears in the *Report* as a handsome man who had been educated under the reformer Oecolampadius at Basel, but who, making "more account of his tall stature than any beauty of the mind, began to be weary of learning, and became desirous to bear some brag in the world, and so made a soldier, marred a scholar."[37] Turning papist for personal gain, Schwendi had become a cruel persecutor of Protestants. Unlike Albert, he is represented by Ascham as a dissembler and a coward, afraid to speak out frankly what he is thinking. On one occasion, the margrave railed against the Interim and against the emperor for "striving with God, in defacing true religion, and tossing the world, in debarring all men's liberties . . . adding, that he was a prince unkind to every man, and kept touch with no man, that could forget all men's merits, and would deceive whomsoever he promised." Schwendi, cowed by the presence of this fearsome warrior, replied to the tirade "gently and quietly" (III, 38). Yet once he was safely away from Albert, he seems to have reported the incident to Charles, for shortly thereafter (February 25, 1551) Duke Maurice received a letter in which the emperor declared that he would pay no wages to the margrave, who had come to assist the imperial forces in the siege of Magdeburg. In abandoning the quest for learning and changing his religion for worldly ends, Schwendi has acted unnaturally, in sharp contrast with Albert, who both behaves as a man should in his proper calling in life, that of a soldier, and supports the evangelical faith against Romanist persecution.

Haase, who also played a significant role in carrying through the Interim and who was sent by the emperor to ferret out Albert's plans in

1552, had likewise apostasized from the reformed religion. Again it is obvious that Ascham considers it unnatural of Charles to employ an unscrupulous subordinate in furthering his end of rooting out evangelicalism. Haase had been "an earnest Protestant" and a privy councillor of the Palsgrave, "but, for hope to climb higher, he was very ready to be enticed by the emperor to forsake first his master and then God." Since in his former position he had often attended the councils of Protestant princes, Haase was especially useful to Charles, who supposed, says Ascham, that his knowledge might make it easier to "overthrow the Protestants, and with them, God and his word in all Germany" (III, 39–40).

The emperor's employment of such vile instruments serves to underscore Ascham's conviction that he treated his subjects with "unkindness." But in addition to the wrongs he suffered in common with his fellow Germans, Albert had, in Ascham's view, legitimate personal grievances against Charles. Upon his return from the court of France, he published his *Kriegsmanifest* (April 1, 1552), "wherein he declared the causes of his falling from the emperor" (III, 28). Besides deploring Charles's public misdeeds, he complained especially of an historical work bearing the imperial privilege in which he felt himself and other German princes to be maligned. In 1547 Luis de Avila y Zuñiga, a Spanish diplomat and soldier, had published his *Commentarios de la guerra de Alemaña, hecha de Carlos V en el año 1546 y 1547*.[38] During that campaign against the Schmalkaldic League, the margrave had lost Rochlitz for the emperor and had been imprisoned by John Frederick at Gotha. Avila, while admitting that opinions varied concerning the defensibility of Rochlitz, nevertheless attributed its capture to Albert's negligence. At Heidelberg, Ascham had also heard the Palsgrave of the Rhine complain about "a certain spiteful place in that book against him," and he believed that Avila had slighted the father of the Duke of Bavaria, to whom Charles ought to have shown exceptional gratitude. Not only had the old duke furnished him with men and supplies, but he had provided him with Bavaria as a base of operations for the war. Had Charles forbidden the appearance of the book, Ascham argues, he might have had more help from the Bavarians in the spring of 1552, and Maurice would never have been permitted to advance through their country toward Innsbruck.

The moral Ascham draws here is twofold: first, the emperor should never have permitted the slandering of loyal supporters by one of his courtiers; second, and even worse, Avila had violated a cardinal rule of historiography. Flattery and spite make a travesty of this noble art, and the consequence may be not merely bad history, but irreparable political damage. Though Ascham would not label the *Commentarios* "the chiefest cause of this stir in Germany," he did believe that the book, by grievously offending Albert and several other German princes, had helped to lose Charles their support when he most needed it.[39]

Whatever the justice of his various complaints, the important fact to Ascham is that Albert considered his treatment by the emperor to be "unkind." And, what is more, he was able to make his grievances public in his *Kriegsmanifest*, and to use them as a justification for having espoused the Protestant and national cause. In November, 1551, he appeared at the French court disguised as a *Lanzknecht* and remained there throughout the winter, negotiating an alliance and making preparations with Henry II for war against Charles. When hostilities began early in the following spring, he joined his forces with those of Maurice at the siege of Augsburg.

If Ascham falls shy of rendering justice to Albert's complex and unpredictable character, in Maurice he recognizes a personage whose behavior requires the most scrupulously objective evaluation. Albert he seems to regard purely as an ideal commander and a loyal follower of Charles who declares for his nation and his religion only when provoked beyond endurance by the emperor's ingratitude. Maurice, on the contrary, was a prince who had behaved unnaturally himself toward his people and toward Duke John Frederick, his cousin and greatest benefactor. Though he was the head of a predominantly Protestant state and had espoused the reformed religion himself, contrary to everyone's expectations Maurice had joined forces with Charles against his own kinsmen in the campaign of 1546–47.[40] He continued to fight for the emperor against rebellious Protestants until 1551, when he suggested to Albert that they seek French aid in pressing their demands for religious and political concessions, and for the freeing of the Landgrave and John Frederick. Maurice's transformation from a self-interested politician into the most effective military leader among the Protestants is, for Ascham, substantial proof that Charles's ungracious behavior was the main cause of the recent wars in Germany.

In spite of its apparent casualness, this final section is the most instructive and skillfully handled part of the *Report*. It begins, not with the usual portrait of the chief actor and the occasion of his quarrel with the emperor, but instead with an extended *descriptio* of John Frederick and a sketch of the reasons for his disaffection with Maurice. John Frederick, a huge man physically (as one may see in the magnificent portrait Titian painted of him in 1547), was, in Ascham's judgment, "a great deal bigger in all kind of virtues, in wisdom, justice, liberality, stoutness, temperancy in himself, and humanity towards others, in all affairs and either fortunes using a singular truth and steadfastness." Like Albert of Brandenburg, he spoke fearlessly whatever he thought, and carried through whatsoever he had promised. A discreet and generous man himself, he could abide all but two sorts of men, mockers and flatterers. A lover and patron of learning, his library was even larger, so Hieronymus Wolf had reported to Ascham, than that of the Fuggers at Augsburg. Nor was it a mere mausoleum for books; according to Sturm, he read and wrote more than Melanchthon and the physician Andreas Aurifaber (Goldschmidt), "the greatest readers and writers in all the University of Wittemberg" (III, 43).

Among the anecdotes Ascham relates of the elector, perhaps the most striking concerns his reaction to an imperial writ of execution, served upon him while he was playing chess with a fellow prisoner after his capture at Mühlberg. Although the writ specified that he was to be publicly executed the next morning in the presence of his entire family, John Frederick read it without changing countenance, laid it aside quietly, and returning to his game, gave his rival "a trim mate."[41] Charles, marveling at such fearlessness, rescinded the order and afterwards treated the elector with more honor and humanity, says Ascham, than ever prisoner before had received from any captor. Small wonder that with all his remarkable qualities, this model of a Christian prince should have been loved and respected by everyone at court, not excepting his Spanish enemies. Even the Catholic historian, Girolamo Falletti, and that "reviler" of the German nobles, Avila, "were so compelled by his worthiness to say the truth, as though their only purpose had been to write his praise."[42]

At first reading, one may wonder why Ascham interpolates this long eulogy of a man who was politically inactive during the years covered by the *Report*. Although he pretends that his admiration for the elector has caused him to stray "far from my matter," the portrait is by no means a digression, but functions vitally in the study of Maurice's character and actions. For in spite of the benevolence, the steadfastness in the reformed religion, the model princely behavior of this elder cousin, Maurice did not scruple to turn against him and his own father-in-law, Philip, Landgrave of Hesse, in order to fight at the emperor's side. He did so, moreover, even though he owed his duchy and his rearing to the elector. For when Maurice's grandfather, Duke George, had disinherited his son for adopting Protestantism, John Frederick "by force of arms, set and kept his cousin Duke Henry [Maurice's father] in his right" (III, 45). Such ingratitude as Maurice showed toward John Frederick could scarcely, in Ascham's view, have arisen from any natural cause, nor would anyone have risked the attendant infamy unless driven by some overpowering motive. This motive, says Ascham, and even men who were "well willing on Duke Maurice's side" confirmed his opinion, was "the foul vice of ambition," the *radix malorum* in the book of Tudor politics (III, 47).

Ascham dutifully reports, as an impartial historian should, what he has heard from Franz Kramm, Maurice's agent at the imperial court, concerning certain grievances of his master against John Frederick. He dismisses the allegations, however, if not as false, at least as insufficient to have caused Maurice to forsake his benefactor so shamefully. Ambition, on the other hand, is an understandable motive, proved to be so by many historical instances. Through this one vice men worthy in all other respects have forgotten their natural ties and loyalties and in attempting to vault into power, have usually come to miserable ends. Ascham digresses for a moment to lament the ills brought on by rivalry within families in contemporary England, and no doubt he had in mind the Seymours, whose fortunes his own career had brushed slightly. But instead of naming any modern examples he cites Polyneices, slain by his own brother, and Julius Caesar, struck down by Brutus, his supposed natural son.[43] Ambitious men never pay heed to good counsel, but listen only to the fair promises of flatterers. Thus Maurice, seeing that all Saxony might be his if John Frederick were defeated and proscribed by the emperor, submitted to the overwhelming temptation. Then the worldly-wise Charles, eager also to have the Landgrave in safe keeping, made a "trim prey" of the inexperienced Maurice "with fair new promises sounding altogether to honour and profit," and the ambitious young duke unintentionally betrayed his father-in-law into the emperor's power (II, 50).

The characterization of John Frederick as the ideal prince, behaving always according to the laws of God and nature, is thus used to set off the unnaturalness of Maurice's conduct during the early years of his

career. It serves further as a political lesson on the great evils into
which ambition may lead the unwary. And it is introduced for still
another purpose: it emphasizes the remarkable nature of Maurice's
"conversion" from such an ill beginning to his championing of the German and Protestant causes.

By imprisoning the Landgrave, Charles had overplayed his hand.
Ascham declares that Maurice and Joachim, Elector of Brandenburg,
had arranged for Philip to come before the emperor at Halle upon
assurance that he would not be imprisoned. The unscrupulous Duke
of Alva, however, after entertaining the three German princes at a supper, placed the Landgrave under arrest. Maurice and Joachim protested
that the emperor had broken his faith; Alva replied that Philip had been
assured only that he would not be imprisoned for life. The misunderstanding, claims the *Report,* was due to a clever play upon German
orthography. As John Frederick's chaplain showed Ascham at Villach
five years after the event, Maurice had understood the pledge to read
"nicht in einig gefengknes"— not in any prison. The imperials, on the
contrary, said that it was written "nicht in ewig gefengknes"—not in
perpetual imprisonment. "And," confides Ascham, "how soon *einig*
may be turned into *ewig,* not with scrape of knife, but with the least
dash of a pen, so that it shall never be perceived, a man that will prove
may easily see" (III, 52). Although this version of the incident is
dramatically impressive and Ascham was undoubtedly sincere in credit-
ing it, it is, according to responsible later historians, probably apocry-
phal.[44] As in his conception of Julius III's character, Ascham seems
once again, for all his honest intentions, to have been the unwary victim
of his relish for witty anecdote.

In any event, the imprisonment of his father-in-law caused Maurice
to think himself "most unkindly handled" after having helped the emperor to an overwhelming victory. He had won the goal of his private
ambition, for Charles did create him Elector of Saxony, but he began
to perceive that in exchange for what he had gained he "must now be
rewarded with shame in all Germany, and be called a traitor to God,
and his country, his father, and his friend" (III, 52). Though he did not
plunge rashly into open rebellion, this was the cause of Maurice's
eventual rising against Charles. Craftily he bided his time until he had
acquired sufficient strength and, meanwhile, tried by lawful means to
secure the Landgrave's release. Ascham is careful to cite all the diplomatic efforts of Maurice to accomplish his purpose. He wishes again to

show, of course, that the injured person is not by nature wantonly rebellious, but rather negotiates, so long as hope remains, according to
the accepted law of nations. Maurice makes four attempts to win over
the emperor by appeal—first by private suit, and then through the intercession of the Diet, of Prince Philip of Spain, and, finally, of ambassadors from all the German and several other central European states.
Charles, however, remains adamant, thus leaving Maurice no recourse
but arms. Ascham stresses these efforts at negotiation to counter the
opinion of many of his contemporaries that Maurice was a downright
traitor and a Machiavellian. The last few pages of the *Report* are taken
up with a creditable effort, somewhat impaired by the ambidextrous
behavior of Maurice, at modifying this unfavorable opinion.

Ascham purposely delays the *descriptio* of Maurice until he is ready
to discuss the occasion of his breach with the emperor. Still adhering
to his thesis that character is a most significant proximate cause in history, he describes the change wrought in Maurice by his conversion
from selfish opportunism to a nobler ideal. Formerly a heavy drinker,
he becomes an abstinent man. "Small diet and little sleep in these last
years" have made him so bold and cunning that "he never took enterprise in hand wherein he put not his adversary always to the worse" (III,
54). Within the brief space of eight months he stoutly declared himself
enemy to four mighty powers and succeeded in achieving his ends
against all of them. By describing Maurice's accomplishments against
each of these—the Turk, the pope, the emperor, the French king—
Ascham deftly brings all the parts of his *Report* to focus on this one key
adversary of Charles V.

His remarkable achievements emphasize how greatly the emperor
was made to suffer for his ingratitude toward so courageous and enter-
prising an ally and friend. For in the final year of his short life Maurice
helped Ferdinand drive back the Turk in Hungary, dispersed the Council of Trent by the feint against Innsbruck, forced Charles to the compromise with Protestantism at Passau, and after enlisting the aid of
Henry II in his designs, dared to fall out with him, as Ascham boasts
with some inaccuracy, "before he achieved anything against the emperor" (III, 56). This last he ventured even though he knew that he
must succeed or die, for he had gone beyond the point at which he could
ever make sufficient amends for the offense he had given to Charles.
Yet Ascham does not condemn these actions as rash, for Maurice did
succeed. Further, if he had lived, he might well have rid Germany of

the Spaniards, "for he had joined unto him such strength, and there was in him such policy, as they durst never have come upon him with power, nor never should have gone beyond him with wit" (III, 53).

Because he not only admired, but also approved, Maurice's accomplishment, Ascham encounters considerable difficulty in appraising his conduct. Up to this point in the *Report* he has been able to draw from the deeds of the chief personages lessons that in no way conflict with the moral standards to which he is committed by his training and view of human nature. In his own eyes, if not always in reality, he has managed to do so without betraying his responsibility as a truthful and unprejudiced historian. But here the facts offer difficulties. He approves Maurice's managing to win the release of his father-in-law ("bringing his honest purpose to pass"), and his gaining recognition for Protestantism and the restoration of the German princes' rights. He sees Maurice, correctly, as a key figure in Charles's decline and also regards him as the savior of the empire from its external enemies. Yet he cannot deny that Maurice had succeeded by questionable, even immoral, means. Spurred on at first by personal ambition, he is guilty of ingratitude and treason against kin. Toward the end of his life, though for unselfish reasons, he betrays his lawful monarch and illegally bargains away from the empire the important city of Metz, which controlled the vital line of imperial communications between north and south. Having done all this, he suddenly deceives his new ally, the King of France.

In approving what Maurice had done, Ascham would seem bound to invalidate the political lesson taught in all the foregoing part of his discourse. If he abandons morality as a basis for judgment, he weakens his initial humanist's view that true political success is inseparable from proper ethical conduct. Yet if he should reject Maurice as a moral failure, he must deny him credit, in contradiction of the historical facts, as an agent of political good. Ascham decides finally to present the facts as sees them, describe the practical results of Maurice's actions, and take his chances with the reader's judgment.

Admitting that Maurice's earlier actions will hardly bear excuse, Ascham offers only to "report on him as his doings since my coming to this court have deserved" (III, 52). Confronted nevertheless with the fact that the duke had gained his ends by questionable means, he argues, with some support from followers of Charles, that these means were no more politically cunning than necessity required. Ascham's fascination with certain of Machiavelli's theories did not lead him to accept wholesale the Machiavellian doctrine. To prove, therefore, that Maurice went no further than his own security and "honest purpose" demanded, Ascham records disapprovingly the comment of "a lusty Italian priest," an imperial sympathizer who thought Maurice unwise for having allowed Charles to escape to Carinthia. "Lo such be these Machiavel's heads," Ascham writes, "who think no man [to] have so much wit as he should, except he do more mischief than he need" (III, 59). Again in his final summing up, he asserts that "if Duke Maurice had had a Machiavel's head or a coward's heart, he would have worn a bloodier sword than he did."[45]

Ascham thus manages to bring off this account to his own satisfaction by recognizing the truth of Machiavelli's assertion that necessity often dictates choice in political action. At the same time, he salvages morality by insisting that Maurice behaved with honor and restraint whenever he could. Attracted though he was to Machiavelli as political realist and accurate historian, Ascham was at the same time repelled by the amorality to which undiscerning acceptance of his theories led. The compromise, if not wholly satisfactory, helped him at least partially to solve his problem and made these final pages the first really promising effort by a Tudor historian at appraising the causes that underlie political failure or success.

V

The task remains of evaluating Ascham's achievement in this fragment of a history and of determining how well he succeeded in applying his classically derived set of principles for historiography; that is, how effective he really was at ordering his matter, maintaining a "plain and open" style, describing in a "lively" manner not only the physical but also the significant psychological characteristics of the persons involved, adhering to the truth and avoiding partiality, and finally, discovering the main causes of the historical events treated in his work.

Although only the introductory portion of the Report has survived, its final paragraph clearly indicates Ascham's plan for ordering his material. Having discussed the background, the causes, and the chief personages of the action, in the next part he meant to go back to the autumn of 1550 and trace developments down to the commencement of the siege of Augsburg in 1552. He planned to "use a gross and homely kind of talk" and proceed "apace" (write, as the rhetorical manuals specified, a plain and swiftly moving narrative), since his introduction had already touched upon many of the most important issues and incidents. In the last section, bringing the story up to the spring of 1553, he hoped to be able to render a fuller account because he had been a direct observer and because matters had then become most open to view. He grants that by arranging his material acording to persons rather than time he has tended "somewhat to misorder my matter," but he justifies his design on the grounds that it has enabled him to make the complex interrelationships among scattered events more intelligible to the reader. In this respect, Ascham was well ahead of contemporary historians, on the Continent as well as in England, most of whom were still following the purely chronological order. He had, however, the precedent of Appian, who had arranged events in his *Roman History* by nations, rather than according to strict considerations of time.[46] By using this more subtle arrangement, Ascham succeeds in explaining to Astley and the rest of the world what they had been most curious to know: by what steps the emperor had been brought into such overwhelming difficulties.

When Ascham speaks of a "plain and open" style he means, not a spare and unadorned kind of writing, suitable only for direct teaching; he has in mind rather Antonius's observation in the *De Oratore* that the language and style of history, though not fixed by rule, should be in the main "free and flowing."[47] His own style is just this: for the most part, even and fluent, but with some of his starkest prose appearing here and there, and, at the other extreme, passages in which the expression rises to fit the occasion.

The heightening of the language is achieved through rhetorical devices that he had already practiced effectively in *Toxophilus* and would use even more extensively in *The Scholemaster*. He uses these rhetorical figures either to heighten the emotion of a passage, or to drive home the point of one of his amplifications or moral digressions. In describing the cruel torture of a Christian captive whom the Turks carved up alive and fed to their dogs, he introduces alliteration and sharp antithesis in order to impress upon his reader's mind the horror of the scene: "Thus the poor gentleman suffered grief, great for the pain, but greater for the spight; not so tormented in feeling his flesh mangled by knives, as seeing himself piece-meal devoured by dogs" (III, 13). He uses *parison* (careful syntactical paralleling of grammatical members in successive phrases) to heighten the eulogy of Albert of Brandenburg, who is "most courageous in hardy adventures, most cheerful in present jeopardy, and most painful in greatest labours" (III, 33). John Frederick's good nature shows in his manner of speech, because "he talketh without taunting, and is merry without scoffing, deluding no man for sport, nor nipping no man for spite" (III, 43). Again, a *sententia* on the greed of the Viceroy of Naples is rendered pithier by this same figure: "For a prince that will take men's goods when he listeth without order, shall want men's hearts when he needeth without pity" (III, 25). In no passage, however, is Ascham carried away by his ornamentation from what is evidently a solid and fluent literary style. The *Report,* despite the alleged and real deficiencies of early Tudor prose, is lucidly written in simple, yet not arid, language, and comes very near to fulfilling Lucian's requirement for style in historiography, that it be "such as ordinary people may understand and the learned praise."[48]

Because of his emphasis on the vital role of character in history, Ascham naturally concentrates on his descriptions of the principals involved in the action. It has already been admitted that he borrows this device from classical biographers and historians, who used it to subserve rhetorical ends; yet he is exceptionally effective in making it point up the conflict between the emperor and the various princes to whom he has given offense. An evident disadvantage of the device is that the portraits are somewhat overdrawn. Still, allowing for the inescapable exaggeration, the sketches of John Frederick, Albert, Maurice, and the others, particularly those with whom Ascham was personally acquainted, are definitely real and not simply the conventional portraits that fill the pages of so many histories from classical times to the end of the Renaissance. In writing from his own observation Ascham makes the portraits come alive for his friends, while his descriptions and anecdotes have become valuable documentary sources for later historians.

The apparent one-sidedness of some of the characterizations does bring up the question of Ascham's objectivity, whether he really managed, as he hoped, to remain impartial, avoiding both "flattery and hatred." As an Englishman he had little use for the ambitious Henry II of France, and religion somewhat obscures his vision when he comes to such figures as Julius III, of whom he is willing to believe too much that is bad, and Albert, in whom he discerns too much that is good. It is also true that in marking "just and unjust" causes he too readily assumes injustice on the imperial side, and equity in nearly all the claims of the German Protestants. Yet to some extent the dangers of these prejudices are offset by another assumption, his belief in the God-given right of the emperor to his subjects' loyalty and in the loathsomeness of rebellion. Thus, while his sympathies with the Lutherans are manifest, he displays no rancor toward Charles and surprisingly little toward the imperials in general, except for the apostate councillors Haase and Schwendi. If hindsight proves that Ascham may not always have written the whole truth, in general he seems to have presented the facts as honestly as he could. There is no passage in the *Report* in which he can be accused of writing out of mere flattery or spite.

Although he shows awareness of their existence, Ascham makes little account of religion, nationalism, the ambitions of other rulers, and the new social and economic developments of the Renaissance that later historians have considered major causes of change within sixteenth-century Germany. Still, while it is improper to reduce so involved an historical situation as that treated in the *Report* to a single cause, one must remember that the many forces at work in the age are more clearly discernible today than they could possibly have been in 1553. As for nationalism and religion—one may fairly ask what form of nation or religion were destined to emerge triumphant from the complex of events? How many different conceptions were there and have there been since of the meaning of the terms *Italia* and *Germania?* How could a clear issue, especially in the political sense, be seen between Protestantism and Catholicism, when the Turk was allied with "the most Catholic" monarch of France, when the pope himself tried to stall the reformation from within the church that Charles was urging, when Catholic princes of Germany withheld their aid from the emperor, and when men like Maurice and Albert were for years among the ablest generals he had in his wars against the Protestants? As for the new social forces of the Renaissance, the sort of history that deals with such matters had not yet been invented, and even from the distance of four hundred years scholars find it hard to determine what these forces were.

One may inquire, still, why Ascham in this age of vaulting national, dynastic, and private ambitions did not make more of ambition as a cause, especially since he recognized its presence in the behavior of Duke Maurice. Guicciardini had given to this political vice the same prominence that Ascham reserves for "unkindness."[49] Certainly it would have provided an equally plausible explanation and acceptable moral. Henry II, the Turk, the popes, various German and Italian princes, all entertained ambitions that conflicted with Charles's own dynastic interests and are now recognized as having contributed to the outbreak of the various wars in question.

There is much to be said, nevertheless, for Ascham's point of view. Like Machiavelli in the *Discourses,* he sees ambition in subjects as contingent upon the behavior of their ruler. If the prince shows weakness (which Charles does not) or ingratitude (which he clearly does), subjects will dare to conspire against him and will rebel as soon as a fit opportunity presents itself. If he displays neither flaw, his state will remain secure.[50] So long as his internal affairs stood in good order, Charles could have coped with his enemies from without; Ascham finds this fact illustrated in his extraordinary prosperity from 1547 to 1550. The French and the Turks were no less ambitious during those years, and regardless of the truce, as ready as ever to pounce upon him, but at the time he enjoyed his greatest strength within the empire. When, however, his "unkind" or, if one prefers, injudicious treatment of certain of his followers gave rise to internal conspiracies, his foes seized upon these new troubles as a means to furthering their own interests. To Ascham, then, in this instance ambition was simply an outgrowth or function of ingratitude. Charles could have averted most of his difficulties had he comported himself like a "natural" and Christian prince.

Such an analysis, it is true, is oversimplified, and ethical considerations, along with the rhetorical bent of the classical and humanistic traditions of historiography in which he had been reared, finally did come into conflict with his desire to be an objective, "pragmatic" historian. The *Report* is scarcely a neglected masterpiece, nor is its author by any means a rival of Comines, of Guicciardini, or, despite the lessons he had gleaned from his works, of the shrewdest of his teachers, Machiavelli. And though Ascham had been with Charles V for nearly three years, he never became, as Comines had become through long service under Louis XI, thoroughly familiar with the affairs and character of his subject. Nor was he writing, as Guicciardini and Machiavelli had written, about his own people. Further, he arrived too soon to profit from the additional lessons for historiographers to be found in the writings of d'Aubigné and de Thou. Yet whatever his shortcomings, for his time and nationality Ascham shows himself a skilled historian, and it is well to remember that the cause and effect relationships in this complicated period of German history have not always been better worked out by more recent authors.

The chief matter for regret is that a complete, or at least a more extensive, version of the *Report* has never turned up. From the existing fragment, nevertheless, certain conclusions about Ascham's achievement may be drawn. The work has proved useful to at least some later historians as a firsthand account of the final crisis in the long and troubled reign of Charles V. It is the earliest genuine attempt in English to write the newer kind of political history with which Italian humanists and "pragmatists" of the age had become concerned; it is the earliest, moreover, to show familiarity with the theories and historical practice of such writers as Comines and Machiavelli. It is the first sustained effort by an Englishman, and a not badly managed one, to produce an historical work in accordance with a coherent theory. Reasonably objective in its viewpoint and apparently free of any deliberate flattery or spite, it stands in these respects against the unfortunate tendency toward partisanship of much Renaissance historiography. In organization it returns to the principles and example of Appian and Lucian, of Polybius and Thucydides, and breaks with the chroniclers' undiscriminating arrangement of events in mere order of time.

If the *Report* had been widely read by Tudor historians with an aptitude for perceiving its values as a model, England might not have had to wait an entire generation for works even of the quality of Camden's, Hayward's, and Bacon's. Unfortunately, there is not the least sign that it influenced the practice or theories of Ascham's immediate successors, perhaps because of its slightness and because it dealt with foreign matters that were no longer of vital concern by the time it appeared in print. Possibly its author lost interest in it himself during the unsettled summer of 1553. Only once in later years did he advert to the work in writing. For the time being, he had to turn his attention to the more pressing task of assuring his own future under the new regime at home.

CHAPTER NINE

⁂

To Be a Courtier

In the days following the death of King Edward, Ascham had little to occupy his time. He apparently set aside the *Report of Germany*, and the ambassadors seldom called upon him to transcribe communications to the privy council.[1] Yet it was perhaps best that he remained idle in Brussels until the struggle for power ended at home with Northumberland's execution for his abortive attempt to set up his son Guildford and Lady Jane Grey as puppet monarchs. For as Ascham prepared to return to England at the end of August 1553, quiet was returning to the country, and Mary was enjoying a brief honeymoon with her surprisingly loyal subjects. Though there had been some disruption at the university and at court and all patents issued during the preceding reign had been temporarily suspended, he had no particular reason to be gloomy about his future prospects or to fear that his name would be deleted from the pension lists when the routine examination of the rolls should take place. He had served honorably at the imperial court, and he was apparently not included in the new queen's distrust of Morison.

Further, with the single exception of Cheke, who had cast his lot with Northumberland, the councillors who had done most for him in the past had weathered the summer's political tempests and, now that the air had cleared, found themselves once more in control of the government. Bishop Gardiner, after five years of political eclipse, was again Chancellor of Cambridge University, and was now Lord Chancellor of England as well. Paget, too, had been restored to his former dignities. Cecil, temporarily out of office, was nevertheless in good position to speak for his friends. For at some risk to his own safety, he had worked behind Northumberland's back to help bring about Mary's succession and thus stood high in the queen's regard.[2]

Meanwhile, Ascham's distinguished acquaintances on the Continent, Nannius and Sturm, had written to ask Paget to take care of him upon his return (I, 377–81). But if even under their prompting the queen should fail to confirm the pension for *Toxophilus* and his appointment as Latin secretary, voided by Edward VI's death, he could always return to his meager, but assured, living at Cambridge. There, since he had been permitted to retain both positions *in absentia,* he was still public orator and Greek reader in his own college.[3] He may also have entertained hopes, as he began his journey homeward, that in the reshuffling of professorships and other university offices he might benefit from Gardiner's patronage.

According to Thomas Hoby's diary, the recalled English ambassadors left Brussels on August 26, after the regent of Flanders, that indomitable princess whose energy had amazed Ascham on the outward journey, had entertained them sumptuously at a farewell banquet.[4] On Sunday, September 3, the travelers arrived at Richmond, where Mary was holding court. Hoby reports that his brother and Morison, despite the queen's intense dislike of the latter, were rewarded for their service with gold chains worth "one thousand crowns the piece." Whether Ascham accompanied the others to this royal interview he does not say, nor does he mention whether he remained for a while in London or went immediately to Cambridge. By the beginning of the Michaelmas term he was definitely back in his college, at least for a brief stay, for on September 28, when his old friend Thomas Watson was installed *in absentia* as eighth master of St. John's, Ascham officiated in his capacity as president of the society of fellows.[5]

His presence at this induction is, however, the only record of his appearance in Cambridge at any time after 1550. Nor is there any evidence that he resumed his public duties at the commencement of this academic term. It is likely that he soon grew disillusioned with what he found upon his return. The college halls for which he had longed in nostalgic letters from Germany may now have seemed dull and confining after three years in an imperial court. For abroad he had experienced, as his correspondence shows, a certain awakening from his earlier Cambridge provincialism. His insatiable curiosity about men and great events, his bonhomie and love of good living had had a real chance to develop. And after witnessing political maneuvering and shifts of fortune on a grander scale and becoming something of a man of affairs with many international friendships and associations, he must have found the little world of the university with its petty academic gossip and college bickering, with its reliance on bookish authority to provide explanations for all human occasions, a somewhat duller and tamer place than he had remembered.

He may have felt, too, that during his absence the university had failed to keep pace in scholarship and in attracting endowments to support its increasing needs. Further, the old dissension between Catholics and Protestants was threatening to break out again, with the latter once more at a disadvantage after their brief interlude of domination. The heads of most colleges were being replaced by more orthodox successors, Lever, for example, having been forced to step aside for Watson at St. John's. Years later, in *The Scholemaster,* Ascham spoke of the months that followed his return as a time "when Aper de Silva had passed the seas" and all but destroyed the two seats of learning and religious reformation in England.[6] One wonders, of course, how the university could have become much worse off than he had made it out to be in the supposedly dismal period of the 1540's. Perhaps Ascham also forgot how he had written to Cecil from Brussels that "the goodly crop of Mr Cheke is almost clean carried from thence, and I in a manner alone of that time left a standing straggler" (I, 351). But unquestionably the nub of the matter for him was that in Marian Cambridge the power had shifted back to the conservatives, whose policies and intellectual attitudes were not at all to his liking.

Inflation of the currency, besides, had made his stipends, which had never been handsome, inadequate for his simplest needs. Morison, though temporarily hard-pinched himself, had generously given him a sum of money upon their homecoming, but soon even this small help was gone (I, 397). Ascham may also have acquired somewhat more expensive habits during his travels, for he began imprudently to borrow on his expectations. "At my coming home," he confesses, "I having more credit than money crept without care into debt, [by] the hope which I had both to be rewarded for my service, and also to receive my pension due by patent at Michaelmas last" (I, 397). On October 8, he did write to Gardiner that although he would not mind becoming Latin secretary or going abroad again with some ambassador, he would rather have an income sufficient to keep him at his books (I, 383). But this seems merely to have been a last unconvincing gesture toward attempting to re-establish himself in the university. For despite Grant's assertion that he went away from Cambridge reluctantly (III, 334), bitter words in another letter of Ascham's to Gardiner show that he was now determined to leave forever. "No," he writes, "I will never so return thither again, to spend my age there in need and care, where I led my youth in plenty and hope, but will follow rather Isocrates' counsel, to get me thither where I am less known, there to live, if not with less care, at least with less shame" (I, 399). If he could find neither content nor comfort in the scholar's life, better to try his fortune, however uncertain and "slipper," at court. Besides, Gardiner, who now held the key to advancement in both places, made it explicit that he wished his protégé to enter the royal service (I, 408). "I shape myself to be a courtier," Ascham therefore wrote on Christmas day to Sir William Petre, one of the secretaries of state, and for the remainder of his life a courtier he became (I, 396).

Throughout the autumn and winter he spent most of his time in London. He had not yet resigned his academic offices, but he quickly discovered the meager income they provided to be insufficient for living in a great city. Where he resided is not known. Possibly he became associated with the Inns of Court and lodged in the Middle Temple, for at a meeting of that body held a year later, one "Roger Askam" was among the members fined for having missed the autumn vacation.[7]

During these months he deluged Petre, Gardiner, and Paget with petitions, flattering them with large praise and with small, but significantly chosen, gifts as he begged repeatedly for both his pension and confirmation of his new office. The Latin secretaryship was worth forty marks annually, and Petre had promised to secure it immediately for him with half the stipend in ready cash (I, 389). In an effort to speed up matters, in November Ascham forwarded to Paget a copy of the treatise *De Gloria* (Florence, 1552) of Jeronimo Osorio da Fonseca, the renowned Portuguese churchman and Latin prose stylist. He regarded this book, which he esteemed for its Ciceronian wisdom and eloquence (I, 444), as particularly suitable for Paget, who fulfilled in his own person Osorio's requirements for true glory; namely, humanity and benevolence toward other men rather than the borrowed and accidental prestige of ancient blood and dignity (I, 390). With the Christmas letter to Petre he offered his "dearest jewel," a small clock that Sturm had sent to him during the emperor's campaign against Metz (I, 394). His meaning was to put the secretary of state "in remembrance of time," for he had grown weary of begging and of his continuing poverty. His New Year's gift to Gardiner was accompanied by the most flattering compliment of all. It was a gold coin of the empress Helena, which he had received at Trier from the bishop's secretary. He cherished the coin because of its association with the discoverer of the cross and with the ancient city on the Mosel in which she had once dwelt. At first he had considered presenting it to the queen, who had brought true religion and political safety to England even as Helena had once brought these precious blessings to Rome. But since he was too timid to make such an offering, he had decided to send the coin to Gardiner, the minister who was helping her majesty most in her worthy enterprises (I, 400–402).

By this time Gardiner had secured reconfirmation of the pension for *Toxophilus* and, moreover, had managed to have it improved. In Edward VI's time the renewal, as Grant notes, had contained the disturbing proviso "during the king's pleasure" (III, 331). The patent issued by Queen Mary on December 1, 1553, conferred the grant for life and doubled the amount.[8] The increase was due to a little joke that Ascham shared with Gardiner, who had regarded the pension from the first as inadequate. Probably because no one could do the job with a neater hand, the bishop instructed Ascham to draw up the necessary form himself. In doing so, "by chance" he made the blank space for the sum too large for the small word *decem*. It was really great enough to accommodate "*viginti* or *triginta*, yea, with the help of a little dash *quadriginta* would serve best of all" (I, 412). As Ascham recounted the incident several years later to Queen Elizabeth, Gardiner, when the beneficiary slily observed that it would be tedious and costly to draft the document again, "fell into a laughter and forthwith went to Queen Mary and told what I had said, who, without any more speaking, before I had done her any service, of her own bountifull goodness made my patent twenty pounds by year during my life, for her and her successors" (II, 154–55).

Confirmation of an augmented pension was something, but it did not mean an end to financial difficulties. The grant was retroactive to the preceding Easter, but in Mary's reign, as in Edward's, payment on the rolls was usually long deferred. Ascham doubted, besides, that he would be able to sustain the expense of living in London even with the additional salary of a royal secretary. In mid-January he warned Gardiner that unless his warrant of appointment were issued soon, he would be forced, against all his inclinations, to return to Cambridge and somehow make shift there. In less than five months since his arrival in

England he had gone through forty pounds, "and yet I have been as ware in expences and as bare in apparel, as any man could be" (I, 406). The paradox of greater poverty in his supposedly grander new status made him observe wryly that whereas in the university he had been shamed by his inability to maintain a servant, now in his present position as a courtier he could not even provide for himself.

In order to supplement his income, he offered his services as a tutor to Petre (I, 394) and to Margaret Roper's daughter Mary, now Lady Clarke and a lady-in-waiting to the queen (I, 403–5). Apparently failing to get a response from this woman whom he had refused to teach in her childhood, he begged Petre, if other employment were not to be had, at least to find him a situation in the house of some prelate. He would have been quite content to live with Bishop Bonner or with one of the deans, Weston of Westminster or Feckenham of St. Paul's, "till God and your goodness shall help me to maintain some little house of my own" (I, 395). Petre, not yet fully adjusted to the changed religious atmosphere, suggested as an immediate solution a prebend in some cathedral chapter. But Ascham was astute enough to foresee the dangers in accepting that kind of office. He replied that as a layman he could not in conscience accept an ecclesiastical benefice. The purity of his motives in this refusal is questionable; yet he may be credited with prudence in declining a temporary convenience that might eventually have embarrassed him with the Marian hierarchy. For two years later Convocation declared itself firmly against the corrupt practice of appointing absentee and unqualified persons to prebends and canonries.[9]

The anxious waiting in the antechambers of privy councillors must have seemed interminable to Ascham, for his patent as secretary was not sealed until May 7, 1554. Meanwhile, he had wasted a full half-year after hastily leaving the university on the assumption of immediate preferment. Some of the reasons for the long delay are given in his own correspondence. Two were important technicalities. Petre's draft of the appointment had not specified that it was to be for life. Gardiner, according to Ascham, was dissatisfied with the oversight, and some time was spent in gaining consent for the stipulation. Another difficulty lay in the wording of the renewed pension grant. The document contained the reservation that upon his promotion "to any other living of the yearly value of 20*l.* or more," Ascham should lose the award for *Toxophilus*. Since the Latin secretaryship was worth forty marks, or something just over £26, he would stand to profit little by exchanging a free gift for the slightly better revenue of a burdensome office.

A more serious obstruction was the disapproval of certain members of the Catholic party at court. The most strenuous objections were raised by Sir Francis Englefield, returned from a brief Edwardian exile at Louvain. Englefield wished to have Ascham closely examined concerning his writings and religious opinions. Fortunately, a number of the councillors, Paget among them, were quite indifferent about religion, and Paget, next to Gardiner, was the strongest man in the government. Gardiner for his part refused to have his candidate either cited before the council or "touched elsewhere" for his beliefs. "There were not wanting those," Ascham wrote to Sturm shortly after the events took place, "who tried to stand in the way of the course of his benevolence to me, but these accomplished nothing" (I, 445). This kind of favor, he remarked to the Earl of Leicester a dozen years later, he enjoyed throughout Mary's reign, from bishops like Gardiner, Nicholas Heath, and Reginald Pole, "although they knew perfectly that in religion, by open writing and privy talk, I was contrary unto them" (II, 129).

Although he speaks here of "open writing," he may have been fortunate that only *De nobilitate Anglicana* and *Toxophilus* were readily available for scrutiny. His theological exercises, in which he had directly attacked Pole, and the *Apologia pro caena dominica* lay hidden somewhere in manuscript. His sometimes outspoken letters from the Continent were in safe hands, and he had set aside the possibly compromising *Report of Germany*.[10] The unpublished translations from Oecumenius, harmless enough even though one of them had given offense to Archbishop Lee, had long since been forgotten. *Toxophilus* did contain some trifling matter that might have offended a zealous Catholic. The epigraph, which may actually be the composition of another, included the pope among the four great enemies of "trothe" and England whom Henry VIII had overcome, the others being "the Scot, the Frenchman, . . . and heresy."[11] The dialogue also included some slighting references, as in the digression on union with Scotland, to friars and "the dregs of our English Papistry" (II, 76). Yet Gardiner and the lords of the council could, or would, detect nothing objectionable in his writings. They still had not officially recognized the papal authority, and for the time being only a bold man would have questioned the orthodoxy of Henry VIII's religious settlement. Some of the bishops, Gardiner in particular, seem actually to have been working toward restoration of that settlement rather than reunion with Rome.[12] Had the majority of the council really been worried about Ascham's opinions, they could easily have chosen another man. But in view of his qualifications and the power of his sponsors, they were in the main willing to accept Gardiner's nominee. His fine italic hand and distinguished epistolary style would enhance state correspondence regardless of his questionable religious views. In spite of this brief flare-up of opposition, therefore, he received his appointment and remained undisturbed for religion throughout Queen Mary's reign. Petre, moreover, reworded the grant satisfactorily. Ascham was made secretary for life and allowed to "have this without impediment to an annuity of 20*l*. which he has by another patent from the queen."[13]

II

The eagerness with which he sought to have his patents confirmed was probably intensified by a new interest in Ascham's life. Among the various requests in the urgent Christmas appeal to Petre was "that when I shall purpose to marry, I may have your Mastership's letters, or by your means, the Queen's Majesty's," apparently for some additional source of income (I, 396). In writing to Gardiner a few weeks afterwards he uses much the same phrasing, except that the word "when" is replaced by the more conditional "if" (I, 408). The change of wording, however, did not imply a change of plan, for on June 1, 1554, he married Margaret Howe (or How), of a good, though not wealthy, county family from South Ockenden in Essex.[14] Margaret's mother was one of the daughters of Sir Clement Harleston, also of South Ockenden.[15] Another of Sir Clement's daughters, Elizabeth, was the wife of Sir John Walop, onetime ambassador for Henry VIII at Paris and in 1541 a commander of English troops in northern France.

On June 24 Sturm, having learned of the marriage from some source other than the bridegroom, sent congratulations but chided Ascham for not having written the good news himself. "I hear," he says, "that your spouse has for a maternal aunt the wife of Master Walop, commander at Guisnes when I was at Calais some time ago." Do let me know, he continues, whether the bride is truly the niece of that "beautiful and charming woman" (III, 333). Ascham delayed more than a year before satisfying his friend's curiosity. "Concerning the wife about whom you wish to know," he then wrote, "in her countenance she does resemble very much her maternal aunt, the wife of Sir R. [sic] Walop. And I have such a wife as John Sturm would gladly wish for Roger Ascham."[16]

Although the record of the courtship is scant, enough remains in

Ascham's own words to show that its early course ran anything but smooth. He was now about thirty-eight, and Margaret Howe apparently no more than half as old.[17] For years now he had suffered from ill-health. By Tudor standards he was already past his prime and started into his declining age. Further, though he had spent five of the preceding six years in noble houses and royal courts, part of them among the gay young ladies attendant upon Princess Elizabeth and Catherine Parr, he had small experience *in re uxoria*. His betrothed, on the other hand, was not only young, but apparently attractive and highly impressionable, for at least one other wooer thought her so and proceeded to take advantage of her youth and inexperience.

Both Margaret's parents and her guardians (possibly the Walops) approved of Ascham as a suitor and had agreed to the marriage. But before the final ceremony could take place, the impetuous rival decided to circumvent the girl's elders and the husband of their choice. According to Ascham, this man, one "J.B.," was well schooled in the ways of women, or at least "in the practice of depriving others of their justly contracted wives." J.B.'s plan for winning Margaret was simple and direct. He surrounded himself with what Ascham indignantly calls "a throng, I do not say of profligate prodigals, though certainly of insolent youths," and "undertook to carry away the maiden by a most shameful kidnapping, from her obedience to and the affection of her parents, from the authority and dwelling-place of her guardian: which outrage is grosser, than any rightly constituted commonwealth can bear." Nor was this the first time that J.B. had made an attempt of this kind. "Not long before, he had set about the same purpose, in the same house, in a very similar fashion, and I believe with a like event." Now J.B. was alleging that Margaret had plighted troth with him before two witnesses.

The friend to whom this account of the abduction or elopement is addressed was one of the judges assigned to arbitrate the case. Even though he knew himself wronged, Ascham offered to drop his suit gladly "if those two main props of [J.B. and his accomplices], the confession of the girl, and the concurrence of the two witnesses at the event, were not discovered to be concocted and false." Only compare, pleads Ascham, with all the epistolary eloquence he can muster, the manner of my wooing with that of my rival and then decide which of us had the honorable intention of marrying. Consider also "the sorrowful parents, who have come here with great journeyings and expenses to see their beloved first-born daughter joined in a marriage of her own free choice: consider the solicitude of those, into whose keeping this maiden had been entrusted, consider the cares and anxieties of [all] those, both parents and guardians, if in this manner worthy young ladies should be given up to anyone for the sake of his fancy." Consider above all else, he begs, "the equity and honorableness of our cause," for by rendering this one just decision the judge will "securely join me to a wife, a daughter to her parents, and all of us to you forever" (I, 392–93).

The dénouement is reported in the letter to Sturm. With forgivable relish Ascham explains that in spite of his "turbulent" rival's fierce opposition to the nuptials, "by the decree of justice and the equity of my cause this man has been overcome" (I, 444). To a romantically disposed reader, it might not seem true that justice had been done in the affair, but rather that an unloved and aging suitor, with the consent of her insensitive parents and the connivance of powerful friends at court, had come between a distressed maiden and her handsome cavalier. Had this proved a genuine and successful elopement, an unsympathetic eye might easily write off Ascham as Pantaloon hoodwinked by the young lovers in the comedy. There is no evidence, however, to justify such an interpretation. Nor can one determine whether Margaret acquiesced or not in the intrigue. Possibly she was in love with her abductor or at least carried away by his dashing spirit. It may be significant that Ascham nowhere mentions her among those who felt outraged at the rude seizure of her person. It is just as likely, on the other hand, that she had given no encouragement to J.B., and may have been as startled and humiliated by his behavior as were her parents, her guardian, and her future husband. For while his choice of confederates suggests youth and impetuosity, there is no hint that he had any other qualities to recommend him as a lover. The sole version of the incident being the aggrieved Ascham's, it may not be an entirely reliable one. Yet in it J.B. reminds one no more of Lochinvar than he does of Don Juan with a dash of Roister Doister.

Whatever Margaret's role in the contretemps, she returned dutifully and, as far as can be determined, willingly to her promised spouse. Thus ended what was perhaps the most uncomfortably thrilling episode in Roger Ascham's life. If romance would wish to see the issue reversed or, failing that, would picture Margaret as dragging herself on leaden feet down the aisle of the church to the miseries of enforced marriage, the truth is that the sequel was far from unhappy. Throughout the fourteen years of their wedded life, Ascham proved himself in both words and deeds a loving and considerate husband.

A moving bit of evidence of the affection and religious piety that existed between them is a letter of consolation that he addressed to her, probably during the earlier years of their marriage, upon the death of an infant son.[18] In purely worldly reflections upon their sudden loss, he found for himself and his "sweet Mag," as he addressed her in the letter, "nothing but sorrows and cares." But when he considered God's will in the matter, he discovered cause for rejoicing rather than mourning. This discovery he wished to communicate to her, since in marriage they were meant to be not only "the one comfort to the other in sorrow but also full partakers together in any joy." Nor would he offer her the true, but stark, consolation that "God knoweth by his wisdom what is best." He could show her, rather, how their bereavement was indeed a cause for rejoicing, an especial favor from heaven and a manifestation of divine good order.

"You well remember," he writes, "our continual desire and wish, our nightly prayer together, that God would vouchsafe by us to increase the number of this world; we wished that nature should beautifully perform her work by us; we had care to provide for it so as honest fortune should favor and follow it." Now if by the child's death, all their prayers seem to have been in vain, Ascham means to prove to his young wife that each hope has actually been fulfilled in the highest degree.[19] For their first prayer, he continues, has been answered more generously than they could have hoped in that they have helped to increase not merely the world, but heaven itself. "Secondly, when nature had performed what she could, grace steps forth and took our child from nature, as where it could not creep on earth by nature, it was made straightway able to go to heaven by grace." If Margaret should object that their son might have grown up to be a joy to them, a faithful servant to England, and, then, after a useful earthly life, a saint in heaven, he would reply that many children prove "rather a care than a comfort to their parents" and that "the number are fewest that grow to goodness" in this uncertain world. God, on the other hand, "hath given to our child already the sure and certain hope of virtue, and hath not left him to the danger of losing such a benefit." Finally, their son enjoys a lasting prosperity such as he could never have possessed on earth. For in this life it is difficult to live continually in that "honesty and good order" in which true good fortune consists. As for riches, they commonly do so much harm to their possessors that they should be called not the goods, but "the ills of the world."

The skeptical reader may find in this letter not a tender and sincere message of consolation to a grieving mother, but instead an artificial exercise in persuasion. He may even wonder why Ascham wrote to his wife at all, when he could have comforted her directly with the same thoughts. To this objection one may reply that he was sometimes away from home for extended periods when the court removed from London to, say, Windsor. It is therefore quite possible that he wrote the letter because the death of the son occurred while he was away, or because the comforting thoughts which he expresses came to him at such a time. Admittedly, he carefully blocks out his thoughts into the recommended pattern for a certain type of consolatory epistle that is intended to persuade its reader to take comfort where none is at first discernible. He invents and duly confirms four acceptable topics and in turn refutes objections that might be raised against them. Yet to grant that Ascham, who thought habitually in terms of recognized epistolary and rhetorical structures, did not forget his art in composing this letter is not to prove him insincere. By following a prescribed formula, he manages to keep the thought and emotion clear and controlled, but they are none the less genuine for being kept within the bounds of severe artistic discipline.

III

During the summer following his marriage, Ascham settled quickly into his round of duties at court. His new position was far from being a sinecure. The queen was preparing to marry her somewhat reluctant cousin Philip of Spain, and the correspondence in anticipation of the prince's coming and the announcements and petitions that followed his arrival kept Ascham busy for months. After lengthy negotiations and delays—the *cosas de España* so exasperating to northern Europeans— Philip and his entourage sailed for England in July. On the 25th the marriage was solemnized, and the royal couple commenced their brief joint rule. Ascham proved his diligence as a secretary at this time, according to Grant, by drafting "in only three days forty-seven different epistles, to various princes of whom the very least were cardinals." Grant finds the proof, "if this seems astounding, or if anyone thinks that I am making it up," in words of Ascham's own to Edward Raven. This was an amazing performance, especially since he not only composed the letters but also transcribed every one of them in his neat and careful hand.[20]

Nor were his labors in this kind restricted to drafting state correspondence for Philip and Mary. Paget (I, 428–29), Sir John Bourne (I, 454–56), Lord Lumley, and other noblemen and privy councillors (I, 449–51) employed his talents for private and semi-official letters of their own. Men and women with suits to present at court also called upon him, or were perhaps advised by Lord Chancellor Gardiner, to have him draw up their petitions. Among these are pleas from various unfortunate debtors (I, 414–16, 420–21); from a supporter of the traitor Sir Thomas Wyatt the younger, who was seeking remission of the balance of his fine (I, 424–25); from a gentleman who had neither received his pension for three years nor been reimbursed for expenses incurred in raising troops to fight against the Kentish rebels (I, 422–23); and from Lady Ro[gers?], whose husband Sir Ed[ward?] had almost "wasted away through illness during his long incarceration."[21]

Most significant historically and perhaps personally are two letters that Ascham composed for the wife of Lord Ambrose Dudley. Within a year of the beheading of their father, all of Northumberland's surviving sons, Ambrose excepted, had been paroled. In November 1554, Lady Dudley, the former Elizabeth Talboys, asked for Ambrose's release (I, 419–21). Upon the granting of this petition, she had Ascham draft a second in February 1555 or 1556, asking for return of estates held in her own right that had been confiscated with her husband's upon his arrest.[22] Lord Ambrose thereafter redeemed himself in Mary Tudor's eyes by fighting in Philip's French wars; in the next reign he succeeded to his father's title as Earl of Warwick and became a power in the council. Ascham's later good relations with the Dudleys, especially with Queen Elizabeth's favorite, Robert, were probably due in some measure to his having rendered this small but important scribal service.

For some of these petitions, Ascham no doubt realized a modest present or fee. It is even likely that Gardiner, through whom as Lord Chancellor most petitions to the crown were channeled, steered some of this work his way to help fatten his never-bulging purse. Tudor officials, like their counterparts in other ages, expected tangible evidence of gratitude for favors performed. Ascham's own frequent gifts to patrons out of his slender store are evidence enough of the prevailing custom.

Without question he needed extra money. By marrying, he had for-
feited his college readership in Greek and his public oratorship in the
university, though the queen and Gardiner did permit him to retain
both offices for some time after he moved to London. He resigned both
places, according to Grant, shortly before the feast of St. John (June
24), in 1554 (III, 332). The loss of even these small sources of revenue
must have hurt, for his annual income at the time could not have been
much over £40, more than he had ever received as a celibate scholar
but scarcely a handsome amount for a married man serving at court.
Margaret, though she had brought him connections with a good family,
had not brought with her a large dowry; he had definitely not made the
match for profit. His new family ties, in fact, were soon to involve him
in burdensome additional expenses.[23]

Some months after his marriage, he described his poverty in a letter
to "Sir W.P.," most likely Petre.[24] Worse, in Ascham's opinion, than
the "grief in having an ill" wife is "the care in having a good," for it is
harder to bear one's inability to provide adequately for a worthy
woman than to put up with the waywardness of a bad one. In his own
bride, he claims to have found a rare jewel, for "the less she seeth I do
for her, the more loving in all causes she is to me, when again I have
rather wished her well than done her good, and therefore the more
glad she is to bear my fortune with me, the more sorry am I that hitherto
she hath found rather a loving than a lucky husband unto her." Then
come the words showing that he had married Margaret for herself, not
for her dowry: "I did choose her to live withal, not hers to live upon,
and if my choice were to choose again, I would even do as I did, so
that the comfort I take because I have so good a wife is the only cause
of my care, because she hath so poor a husband."

In this complaint, though he was reluctant to beg for anything
specific before he had proved his worth to the queen, he implies that
he would welcome some further beneficence. While he had to make
shift for quite a time with what he had received already, at length
Mary did give him assistance. On January 22, 1557, she granted him
the reversion to the lease of a manor known as Salisbury Hall, in
Walthamstow parish, Essex. He was to enter upon this holding no later
than March 25, 1564, to enjoy it for forty years, and to pay the crown
an annual rent of £22 12s. 6d. The manor was a substantial property,
consisting of nearly two hundred acres of pastures, meadows, and arable
lands, as well as a fishery and the profits from all osiers gathered along

an adjacent stretch of the River Lea.[25] Although for the present he held only the reversion, for Ascham the prospect of realizing the income from this estate must have been pleasant. The manor, furthermore, had important associations with the family of his newest patron, the papal legate and Archbishop of Canterbury, Cardinal Reginald Pole. It had once been owned by Pole's mother, Margaret, Countess of Salisbury, niece of Edward IV, and had been confiscated when she was sent to the block by Henry VIII because of the strength of her hereditary claim to the throne.

Whether or not Pole himself had anything to do with the grant of Salisbury Hall to Ascham, the two men had been on excellent terms from the time of the cardinal's triumphant return. Pole had landed at Dover in November 1554, after an absence of more than twenty years. Although he had been commissioned papal legate immediately upon Mary's accession, his return to England had been postponed, since the queen, realizing that parliament was not yet prepared to submit without qualification to Rome, wanted him to come merely as an ambassador, rather than with legatine authority. She was abetted in this policy of procrastination by Charles V, who had reasons of his own for wanting Pole's homeward journey delayed. Mary's impending marriage to his son was not popular in England, and the cardinal, descended from the Plantagenets, had once been proposed as a suitable royal consort. Although he had declined the honor, Charles wanted no mischance to prevent a union by which he hoped to bind the English, after their recent wavering, to their old alliance with him against the French. Not until the wedding of Mary and Philip had taken place was Pole allowed to cross the Channel. As he stepped ashore he was still legally a traitor, but before he arrived in London parliament repealed the bill of attainder that had been standing against him since 1539. On November 24 he sailed up the Thames, to be welcomed by the king and queen on the steps of Whitehall. On the 27th, he stood before the Lords and Commons and delivered an address in which he urged them to undo those acts of recent years that had separated England from the one Christian fold.

On the following day parliament, speaking through Lord Chancellor Gardiner, submitted a plea for forgiveness to Philip and Mary, vowing to do whatever it could to abrogate statutes that were prejudicial to the Apostolic See. Pole then ordered his commission to be read, gave general absolution, and though Thomas Cranmer was still Archbishop of Canterbury, assumed practical leadership of the church in England.[26]

It was in connection with the address to parliament that Ascham first came to Pole's attention. After the oration had been read, it was put into his hands to be rendered into eloquent Latin for transmission to Pope Julius III. This he was asked to do, boasts Grant, who possessed a copy of the translation, even though Pole was famed himself as a Latin stylist. Ascham's performance in no way fell short of the tribute to his competence. His effort pleased the cardinal, who had it sent on to Rome and thenceforth, "contrary to the general haughtiness and arrogance of proud cardinals," treated him in very friendly fashion (III, 335). Ascham's own testimony to Sturm bears out Grant's assertion. "The most reverend Cardinal Pole," he writes, "is very humane, and I do not know whether any Italian can be compared with him for eloquence. He uses me very kindly" (I, 445).

In Pole he seems to have found an agreeable companion. Though he formed no such lively intellectual partnership at Mary's court as he had done with "merry Morison" at Augsburg, in the cardinal Ascham did have someone who shared many of his scholarly enthusiasms and was eager and competent to discuss them. In April 1555, he gave Pole a copy of Osorio's *De Nobilitate Civili Libri II. Eiusdem de Nobilitate Christiana Libri III* (Florence, 1552). As usual, the gift and the recipient were made to seem an inevitable combination, even though, following his economical practice of re-using material from his copybooks as appropriate occasions arose, Ascham had previously sent copies of the same book and almost identical letters to Petre and Bishop Tunstall.[27] Osorio's object in these discourses was to establish that true secular nobility cannot exist apart from a virtuous Christian life. Ascham takes care, consequently, to insist that while Pole is noble by reason of his royal blood, he is also by fortune and merit a prince of the Christian church in whose virtuous behavior others may discern an example of the true nobility described by Osorio. As a student of Latin eloquence, moreover, Pole will undoubtedly appreciate the style of Osorio, a Ciceronian of commanding reputation throughout all Europe. Ascham can recall few authors who have used the language with greater purity or distinction since the Augustan age. He manifests, indeed, all the excellences of a copious and fluent Latinity without any sign of bombast or excess. Thus, "neither Italy in its Sadoleto, nor France in its Longueil, nor Germany in its Sturm ought to take greater pride now than Hispania in its Osorio." If one may judge from the rather florid character of Pole's own Latin, he probably did find Osorio's style as congenial as Ascham believed he would. In later years, Ascham became somewhat more critical of Osorio's Latinity and even cited him in *The Scholemaster* as one whose over-full writing might well be amended by rigorous exercise in epitome.[28] In 1555, however, he seems really to have considered Osorio a nearly flawless stylist. A copy of this letter to Pole eventually reached Osorio himself and helped establish an epistolary friendship between him and Ascham.[29]

From this letter of Ascham's to Sturm, one may gather the general tenor of some of his conversations with the cardinal about writing and scholarship. While they were dining together on one occasion during the summer of 1555, Pole began to speak of certain learned contemporaries and, among them, mentioned the name of Sturm with respect. Warmed by the praise of his friend, Ascham described the long-awaited commentary on Aristotle's *Rhetoric*. He also expounded Sturm's views on composition, citing especially his preference for arrangement of matter in its "natural" order rather than according to some predetermined artificial scheme. The cardinal approved of this view and "averred plainly and frankly," Ascham reported, "that in you there was, not only great learning and rare eloquence, but also moderation and the faculty of discernment." With the cardinal Ascham conversed too, as he had once corresponded with his friend at Strasbourg, about Cicero's still undiscovered treatise *De republica*. Pole had once spent 2,000 gold pieces in an attempt to have the lost work traced in Poland. Now he wanted Ascham to inquire whether Sturm had any further news of its whereabouts. Such devotion to the greatest of the Romans greatly increased Ascham's good opinion of the cardinal (I, 445–46).

On another occasion Pole showed him the new edition of his own *Pro Ecclesiasticae Unitatis Defensione, libri quatuor* ([Strasbourg], 1555). This treatise, which had led to his attainder when it first appeared in 1536, aroused Ascham's curiosity for a special reason. Among the legatine party was Alvise Priuli, Pole's close friend and executor, and a kinsman to the Doge of Venice. Priuli had wanted to know whether the preface to the cardinal's book, signed with the pseudonym "Vergerius," might not be the work of Sturm. Well-disposed as Ascham was toward Pole, he knew that Sturm would scarcely relish having their names associated. Without hesitating, therefore, he had replied "not only that the style differed greatly from your writing, but also that what was done was quite inconsistent with your belief and opinion."[30] And, he might properly have added if he had dared, in matters of religion it was inconsistent with his own.

IV

That Ascham enjoyed the favor of a monarch and two prelates whose names are infamous to English Protestants embarrassed his earlier biographers. Even Grant reluctantly admits that certain persons had resented the immunity secured for him by Pole and Gardiner: "Some men do say that he served the time, and accommodated himself to the change of circumstances." Yet, Grant protests, he remained "ever the same in religion, the same in honesty, the same in faithfulness to his friends, the same in piety, the same toward the two queens in constancy, industry, diligence" (III, 234–35). Unfortunately the last phrase, suggesting impartially zealous service to both Mary and Elizabeth, rather weakens the apology. Taken with the fact that Cheke was singled out for humiliation and that a number of his other close friends spent the Marian years abroad or in retirement, it does make Ascham appear willing to sacrifice his loyalties and beliefs wherever his own advancement and safety were concerned. Consequently, the eighteenth-century Cambridge antiquarian, William Cole, assumed that he had never been a convinced Protestant, but was rather "a complier with the Religion that was in Fashion, tho' a most furious and bigoted Fanatic in the next Reign."[31] Cole, who was flirting with Catholicism at the time he set down this observation, was obviously only too happy to make such a conjecture about a celebrated early Protestant. More sympathetic writers, on the other hand, among them Dr. Johnson and Hartley Coleridge, seem merely disappointed at his failure to champion the reformed religion.[32]

To infer, however, that outward compliance means absence of religious conviction would be unjust to Ascham. Granted that the sole unequivocal testimony of faith is willingness to die rather than abjure, and that martyrdom was the ultimate proof of the sincerity of his venerated contemporaries More and Fisher, Latimer and Ridley, there remain other, though less certain, means of determining the genuineness of a man's beliefs. The letter to his wife on the death of their child, together with other examples of his later correspondence, demonstrates that the author was a man of deep religious feelings.[33] There also exists one fairly reliable bit of evidence, unknown to his earlier biographers, that during this period of restored Catholicism Ascham remained inwardly convinced of the truth of the basic tenets of the reformed religion. Few books have survived from his rather extensive personal library, but in recent years the Bodleian has acquired his copy of St. Ambrose's treatise on election and justification, *De Vocatione Omnium Gentium Libri Duo* (Geneva, 1541). Along with his initials, Ascham has placed on the title page a notice that he had this book with him "at Wicheford, 22° Ianuarii 1555 [i.e., 1556]."

The place mentioned is evidently Whittlesford (or Wicklyford), a town about seven miles south of Cambridge, where his wife's parents held the lease of the rectory. Presumably Ascham, and Margaret with him, went to visit them at the beginning of 1556. While there, he seems to have found leisure to read and annotate heavily the first, though not the second, book of St. Ambrose's treatise. Many of the marginal jottings are simply of the kind often made by readers to help them find their way about the long paragraphs of Renaissance books. Several of them, on the other hand, afford some clue to Ascham's stand on certain essentials of Christian doctrine. One must always be cautious in offering a unique document of this sort as confirming evidence. Yet precisely because the annotations and underscorings were written in private for his own convenience and as an expression of his spontaneous reaction to what he was reading, they quite probably reveal Ascham's real convictions about such matters as the effects of original sin, imputed merit, justification by faith, and special election.

In this particular work, St. Ambrose treats the proposition that God wills all men to be saved, even though not all men are chosen for salvation. He endeavors to explain some of the paradoxes inherent in this doctrine: how all men may be said to be called by God even though He rejects some at the judgment; how man can be said to have free will and therefore to be culpable when he sins, yet unable to avoid sin without the free gift of divine grace; how human nature, being much wounded though not totally depraved by original sin, can be regenerated not by one's own merits and good works, but only through grace and faith in the redemption by Christ; how, since the fall of Adam has set the desires of man's sensual will against those of the spiritual will, no natural good performed outside the state of grace has any bearing on salvation.

These are among the most pressing of theological issues, and St. Ambrose's interpretations are ground upon which Catholic, Anglican, and Calvinist alike might take their respective stands, depending upon the relative emphasis each would give to the various arguments. Through a consideration, then, of what his annotations center upon, one may fairly conclude that certainly at this date Ascham had none of the Calvinistic leanings sometimes attributed to him. The injuctions against evil pastimes and travel to Italy in his own treatises have been seized upon as signs of Puritanism in his moral code and hence, because of his formerly close association with Marian exiles who were exposed to the influences of Zürich and Geneva, in his religious beliefs. But the Ascham who deplored the spread of Calvinistic doctrines concerning predestination among the younger men in the university had not changed his views in the ensuing decade. He notes with approval, to cite but one instance, St. Ambrose's assertion that in the fall of man free will was not lost absolutely, and that in his regeneration, in "putting on the new man," no new nature is supplied but rather the much impaired one is restored. At the top of the page on which this matter is expounded Ascham writes in Latin, "a new will is not created but instead a weaker one repaired" (p. 15). As a Christian humanist he might well be expected to approve a doctrine which, though it denied the spiritual efficacy of good performed by the infected will without divine assistance, yet acknowledged the fundamental inclination to good in the human soul and its capability of repair through grace and good education. Ascham does not imply, on the contrary, that any amount of purely natural good can merit spiritual regeneration for man. He holds with St. Ambrose that, without grace, even the noblest human acts are but as evil in the sight of God (p. 12).

This denial of the efficacy of human efforts toward salvation is, of course, a reply to the Pelagian insistence that man is saved by his own works. Thus St. Ambrose interprets the parable of the laborers in the vineyard as signifying that divine grace is a free and unmerited gift, not a reward for one's efforts. Although Catholics likewise regard this as an essential belief, Ascham places himself on the side of the Reformation by the degree to which the doctrine attracts him in the treatise. Wherever he encounters arguments that grace is God's free gift and that faith is the essential element in salvation, he underscores and annotates the text with evident approval. "Fides" is literally writ large (sometimes actually in capital letters) in the margins, and in one place Ascham concludes that "to merit is to profit to eternal life through faith, as I have inferred from these passages."[34]

Certain other facts about his annotations in this volume are worth remarking. He notes well several of St. Ambrose's comments on lapses of the Jews from the true faith as recorded in the Old Testament; possibly he does so with the recent defection of his own country from the reformed faith in mind (pp. 11, 28, 34). Wherever he finds mention of the failure of the chosen people to hold fast to the truth, as well as of the inability of pagans, lacking revelation, to accomplish spiritual good, he makes notes in the margins. His numerous comments suggest that he was deeply concerned at this time about the difficulty of living in conformity with what he believed to be God's will, especially as a public servant in Marian England. Yet he seems to be looking for comfort in the thought that if a man can but keep faith within the spirit, this, rather than his outward works, is the true sign that his salvation has been sealed.

The very fact that he made these notes also speaks in his behalf. At least he cared enough about religion to examine this theological treatise, and perhaps others as well, in an effort to find patristic support for the beliefs about which he was required to remain silent. Hero or martyr he was not, yet he ought not to be classed with that merely opportunistic group of Tudor courtiers and politicians, among them Paget and the Marquis of Winchester, who served their own interests at any cost and remained indifferent, even cynical, toward changes in religion.

It should also be kept in mind that lifelong dependence for all he possessed upon the good will of others, early reproofs for speaking out on controversial matters, the almost obsessive need for security exhibited throughout his correspondence, combined to make Ascham walk circumspectly through these dangerous times. Perhaps he did attend mass at Court and conform outwardly in other ways to the re-established Catholic religion. Yet men and women from whom far greater courage might reasonably have been expected, acted likewise out of regard for their personal safety. Even the recalcitrant Elizabeth, having acquired superb schooling over the years in the art of survival, finally consented to hear mass as the Smithfield fires grew hotter.

One might wish that Ascham had been made of sterner stuff. Yet the cautious person is not, *ipso facto*, a coward, for men often display the courage of their convictions only when forcibly thrust into a trial of their spiritual strength. Like the majority of his contemporaries, including several other anti-Romanists maintained in the queen's service, Ascham was never put to the test. In fact, although the number of his acquaintances who went over to the Continent at the time is considerable, the majority of them, at least the laymen, might well have remained undisturbed in England by the wave of religious persecution. Among those who chose to live abroad were Thomas Wilson, Laurence Humfrey, Alexander Nowell, Edward Whitechurch, printer of *Toxophilus*, John Astley, Sir Philip and Thomas Hoby, William Ireland (who had once been a Benedictine) and several other fellows of St. John's, including James and Leonard Pilkington and the three Lever brothers, and, finally, Sir John Cheke and Sir Richard Morison.[35]

Most of these friends of Ascham survived their Marian exile and prospered upon the accession of Elizabeth. Not so fortunate were the two whose personal influence upon him had been the strongest. Morison, believing himself compromised by a letter to the privy council in 1553 in which he had made the mistake of alluding to Guildford Dudley as king, soon grew uneasy at home. In 1554, abandoning a long-cherished project of completing his beautiful house at Cashobery in Hertfordshire, he withdraw to Italy and later to Strasbourg, where he joined Cheke and Sir Anthony Cooke. There he resumed the scholarship that had first brought him to the notice of Henry VIII and had made him so enjoyable a companion for Ascham in Germany. For some months he studied with the theologian Peter Martyr Vermigli, who in Edward VI's time had been to Oxford what Bucer was to Cambridge. On March 17, 1556, the "merry Morison" died at Strasbourg.

Cheke's decline is an unhappier story, perhaps the unhappiest of the time. After a year's imprisonment in the Tower, he was pardoned for his complicity in Northumberland's dynastic schemes and was permitted to go abroad. At first he maintained himself by lecturing at Strasbourg, where he supervised the publication of his and Smith's controversy with Gardiner over the pronunciation of Greek. Moving on to Padua, a center, like Zürich, Strasbourg, and Frankfurt, of English refugees, he read Demosthenes to a group of his countrymen and, though he was in fact abroad with royal permission, settled into the life of a virtual exile. In May 1556, Paget and Sir John Mason invited him to come to Brussels. Although he should have been wary, he may have welcomed the invitation because his wife was then in the Low Countries. Consulting his horoscope and foreseeing no danger, he set out on the long journey. In spite of the astrological reassurance, the summons had been treacherous. On May 15, by order of Philip II, he and Sir Peter Carew, who had been implicated in Wyatt's plot against the queen, were seized by the Spanish provost marshal and shipped off to London. Upon arrival, Cheke was returned to the Tower, the charge being that he had overstayed his license to travel.

The true reason for his arrest was evidently neither the one alleged nor his having supported the cause of Lady Jane Grey. It was rather that he had been the leader of the new humanism at Cambridge and was looked to by Protestants everywhere as the glory of English learning. If the government could secure a recantation from this internationally famous scholar, it would have won a symbolic triumph over academic heresy that might be broadcast to all Europe. In an attempt to convert him to Catholicism, two of Mary's chaplains and the kindly Abbot Feckenham, who had failed in his spiritual struggle with Jane Grey, visited him in the Tower. Cheke had no courage to match that of the girl whom he had helped to set briefly upon the throne of England. He gave in with surprising alacrity, begging only that he might recant privately before Cardinal Pole in order to avoid the shame of a public confession. Naturally, owing to the importance of the victory, the privy council denied his request. On July 15, he submitted formally to Pole, and on October 4, did so again before the queen and the entire court. The end for which he had been lured home having been obtained, he was released from custody and received new lands from the crown in exchange for his old ones. Within a year, however, he was dead; the usual explanation given for his rapid decline is that betraying his friends and the reformed religion had broken his heart.[36]

It seems unlikely, though he nowhere mentions having been present, that Ascham was spared the scene of Cheke's public humiliation at court. Certainly it must have grieved him deeply that the finest product of early Tudor Cambridge had deserted the cause of which he had once been so conspicuous a leader. And now, in September of 1557, this intellectual begetter of "the goodly crop" that had made the university famous, this man in whose footsteps Ascham had dreamed of following, this "dearest friend, and teacher of all the little poor learning" he would ever own (III, 240), had apostasized and departed under a cloud of shame.

V

Another sorrow for Ascham was the queen's and Gardiner's treatment of Princess Elizabeth. So long as Mary Tudor failed to produce an heir, her half-sister continued to be the hope of the Reformation party. Both Simon Renard, the imperial ambassador, and the Lord Chancellor were convinced that she was the center of much treasonous plotting. They hoped, therefore, to have her married off to some minor Continental prince or, better, to prove that she had become involved in some conspiracy so that she might be got out of the way. But disposing of Elizabeth was no easy matter, for she cannily managed to keep herself dissociated from all plots and compromising situations. Besides, she enjoyed great popular and parliamentary support as well as the protection of several influential noblemen, among them the new admiral, Lord William Howard of Effingham. She thus remained a source of displeasure to the queen, who except on rare occasions kept her away from London.

During the five years of Mary's reign, Ascham had few opportunities to see his former pupil. Toward the end of August 1555, she was released from a year's confinement at Woodstock and recalled to court. During this time, she and Ascham resumed the studies that had been interrupted by his sudden departure from her service almost six years before. On September 14, he wrote to Sturm that he was finding more leisure to read now than he had ever known in the university. He and Elizabeth were comparing the opposing "orations of Aeschines and Demosthenes περὶ Στεφάνου" (respectively, "Against Ctesiphon" and "On the Crown"). The temperamental fifteen-year-old prodigy had grown into a mature and perceptive young woman. Ascham, burdened no longer with responsibility as her official tutor, was able to study with her for the pure joy of learning. This time he was impressed not only by her gift for languages but also by the maturity of her political understanding. She outstripped him, he declared, in comprehending the text and grasped immediately not only the intentions and the propriety of language of either orator, but also the issues at stake and the character and behavior of the Athenian auditors. Sturm would be amazed if he could only be present to witness her precocity (I, 447).

This happy interlude, however, was short-lived. Elizabeth was allowed to stay at Greenwich for less than two months before being sent away again. Parliament was scheduled to convene on October 21, and the council decided that it would be prudent to get her "out of sight and out of the reach of intrigue."[37] Only once more was she permitted to return to London, when in the summer of 1557 Mary and she exchanged brief complimentary visits. Nor would the queen allow Ascham to travel very often to Hatfield; on the rare occasions when he did get leave, he and Elizabeth would spend at least part of their time in study. Their reading and conversation confirmed what he had already written to Sturm. Although he had spent the past half-dozen years in the courts of an emperor and a queen whereas the princess had passed the same interval in virtual seclusion, she had grown far beyond him in political wisdom and maturity, in knowledge and judgment of the world.[38] She was ready now to rule a kingdom, and in his opinion there could be no better evidence of this capacity than her refined taste in classical literature. After her coronation, it must have gratified him deeply that the works she preferred to read during their hours of leisure were these same paired orations of Aeschines and Demosthenes (II, 63).

Meanwhile, until the day of her accession should come, he could only wait and keep himself occupied with his secretarial duties and the responsibilities of family life. His own good treatment at court and happy marriage made the years tolerable in spite of the uneasiness of the times and continuing attacks of the quartan fever (I, 448). There were, moreover, increasingly hopeful signs for English Protestants as misfortune began to dog the queen and Cardinal Pole. Although Ascham probably served them dutifully and had little, if anything, to complain of in his own treatment, he could scarcely have regretted the eventual failure of his patrons to assure a Catholic future for England.

As Latin secretary he was closely associated with them in their greatest disappointments. In May 1555, the queen, mistakenly convinced that she had become pregnant early in her marriage, began to prepare for her confinement. Ascham was set to work at Hampton Court drafting announcements to be released upon the birth of the royal heir. He made copies, several of them still extant, of a form letter, with spaces left for the date of birth and sex of the child, to be sent to Pope Paul IV, the Doge of Venice, and the heads of various other states.[39] Unhappily for Mary, the symptoms resembling those of pregnancy were signs of a fatal malignancy. She learned now that she would never bear children to succeed her and to keep her heretic half-sister from the throne. Except for a few months in 1557, she would not even have the comfort of her husband's presence. For Philip, glad of an excuse to part from a spouse he had never wanted, crossed over to the Continent at the end of the summer to help in his father's wars. As for Ascham, whatever the measure of his loyalty to the queen, he must have been gladdened by the thought that her inability to have children left Elizabeth the unquestioned heir presumptive to the throne.

In 1557, the hopes of Reginald Pole were also broken when Paul IV, his inveterate personal enemy, revoked his legatine commission. The pope alleged that Pole's orthodoxy was doubtful and his management of religious affairs in England unsatisfactory. Apparently the motives for the revocation were partly political, for Philip of Spain was preparing to renew the French war, and Paul IV was committed to an alliance with Henry II. Mary, shocked at this high-handedness and the absurdity of the allegations, on May 21 caused Ascham to draft a protest. The cardinal, the letter insisted, had diligently led the country back from schism to the true faith, had revived and strengthened the church in England, and was now administering its affairs effectively. The suspension of his legatine powers was disheartening, not only because these were necessary for the secure re-establishment of Catholicism, but also because such powers had always been assumed to go automatically with appointment to the see of Canterbury (I, 452–53). Paul, however, remained adamant. The consequence was that Pole, who was making his name a byword among English Protestants for his persecution of heresy, ironically found his own orthodoxy impugned during the last year and a half of his life.

Remembering his informative accounts of life at Cambridge in Henry VIII's time and of Germany during King Edward's, one could wish for some of Ascham's personal reactions to the events of Mary's reign. But nothing has been preserved to show how he felt about such matters as the queen's disillusionment, the fall of Cardinal Pole, the recantation and unhappy end of Cheke, the deaths of other friends abroad and at home, the decline in his nation's prestige, or the surrender in 1558 of Calais, which his cherished longbow had helped to defend against French assaults and sieges for more than two centuries. To some of his former correspondents—the exiles Astley, Ireland, and Lever, as well as Thomas Smith and the Princess Elizabeth at home—he possibly did not write at all through fear of royal displeasure. And if ever he did express his opinions and feelings about the times in any epistle, it seems more than likely that he would have asked the recipient to destroy it.

Almost as disappointing is the surviving record of his reading and other intellectual interests between 1554 and 1558. From every other period of his adult life, ample evidence remains concerning the books that he had acquired or examined, the ideas and scholarly activities that were engaging his attention, his personal or epistolary relationships with other learned men. The scattered correspondence from these years, by way of contrast, tells little about such matters. Beyond allusions to recently published books that he had sent to his patrons, the conversations with Pole, the brief interlude of reading Greek with Elizabeth, his letters remain curiously silent about any intellectual interests he may have had.

The one surviving epistle to Sturm (perhaps the only one he sent to Strasbourg during all these years) gives the most detail about his personal life at the time. In it he not only mentions his marriage, his friendship with Pole, his reading with the princess, but also shows that he is still interested in the doings of various scholars. He asks to be remembered to Sleidan, Valentine Erythraeus, and "my most sweet Michael Toxites." He has met the papal nuncio to England, Antonio Agostino, and with him the famous scholar Johannes Metellus, with whom he has become friends. He believes that Sturm will recall how Osorio honored these two men by making them interlocutors in his dialogue *De Gloria*. Metellus intends to stop over in Strasbourg on his homeward journey. Ascham inquires about the progress of Sturm's Aristotelian commentary, for thus far he has seen only drafts of the first and second dialogues. He expresses some concern that so precious a manuscript should be in the keeping of those untrustworthy Werters.[40] He also remembers Sturm's intention of immortalizing their own friendship by including him among the speakers in the final dialogue. He wonders, since he has never received this portion of the work, whether the design has been carried out. He also expresses curiosity about the nature of the digressions Sturm will incorporate in the third book; in the first two, he had found these the outstanding parts. He would like, since the dialogue would memorialize his own three-day stay in Strasbourg, to find in it such topics as he and Sturm might actually have discussed had they ever met: the intrigues at the emperor's court, current affairs of both war and peace, and the best method of acquiring true learning.

Although silence is no authority, one may infer from the absence of other letters to Sturm, and from the survival of only two epistles to other scholars, both of which are merely complimentary (I, 431–35), that Ascham, if he did make some effort to keep up with the world of learning while serving as Queen Mary's secretary, did so less consistently than in his younger days and in the more congenial decade that was to follow.

≈⊱ ⊰≈

CHAPTER TEN

Secretary to Two Queens

MARY TUDOR and Cardinal Pole both died on November 17, 1558, and Elizabeth ascended the throne amid general rejoicing. Immediately, she called several members of the former Cambridge group to serve her. Among those whom she summoned first were Cecil and Haddon. Cecil, on hand for a second time to smooth the rightful monarch's way to the throne, carried out secretly prearranged instructions for ensuring her own and the nation's safety. Appointed principal secretary of state, on November 20 he assumed the practical leadership of the council that he was to exercise for nearly forty years. Haddon, in part for his knowledge of the civil law and perhaps in part for having consoled Elizabeth in Latin verse during the past difficult years,[1] was rewarded with a mastership in the Court of Requests and a place on her first ecclesiastical commission. Matthew Parker and Thomas Smith came out of retirement. Parker was consecrated Archbishop of Canterbury, while Smith served first on a commission to revise the Book of Common Prayer, and then as ambassador to the court of France. The queen retained Ascham, who may have expected some greater preferment upon her accession, in his post of Latin secretary.

From the Continent Ascham's expatriated friends now began to stream homeward, most of them to prosper once again. Thomas Wilson, after escaping from a prison of the Inquisition in Rome, stayed in Italy long enough to take the degree of doctor of laws at Ferrara and returned to London in 1560.[2] Thomas Hoby came back and in 1561 published his translation of *The Courtier*, which Ascham enthusiastically recommended in *The Scholemaster* (III, 141). In 1566 Hoby was knighted and named ambassador to Paris. John Astley became master of the royal jewel house; Alexander Nowell, Dean of St. Paul's. James Pilkington, immediately upon his return, assumed the mastership of St. John's College and the regius professorship of divinity. He also served on a commission appointed to visit and reform the university; one of his partners on the commission was William Bill, now occupying the post of queen's almoner. In 1561, Pilkington was consecrated Bishop of Durham; his brother Leonard succeeded him as master of the college and later became Dean of Durham Cathedral. Lever, who had picked up a tinge of Calvinism abroad, passed up several opportunities for ecclesiastical preferment and chose, instead, to minister to a strongly Protestant congregation in Coventry. Ireland became a lesser functionary in the ecclesiastical courts and a rector of country parishes in Essex and Hertfordshire. He was possibly the William Ireland who later administered an oath taken by Margaret Ascham concerning Roger's will. Cheke and Morison were gone, as was Ascham's beloved Edward Raven, who had died shortly before Elizabeth came to the throne. In his will, proved on November 15, 1558, he memorialized the old three-way friendship at St. John's by providing a legacy for "his brother Ireland" and leaving Ascham an appropriate gift of books: "Demosthenes in Greek, *Orationes Ciceronis,* 3: vol:. and Nizolius, acknowledging no debt to be betwixt Mr. A. and him, saving only of friendship."[3]

While the new regime brought good fortune to most of these old acquaintances, to a few of Ascham's Catholic friends it meant disaster. By their outspoken disapproval of any change in religion, Christopherson and Watson, who had become Marian bishops, quickly incurred the new queen's displeasure. Ten days after her accession, Christopherson preached a sermon at Paul's Cross in which he defended the ancient faith and attacked as novel and heretical the doctrines of the Reformation. For his presumption he was committed to the Tower, where he died within a month. In the following year Watson, who had been persecuted and imprisoned for his religious views in Edward VI's time, was deprived of his see and sent to the Tower once more for refusing to compromise with a new religious settlement. For the remaining twenty-five years of his life he was shunted in and out of prison, and from the custody of one bishop to another, until he died at Wisbech Castle, Cambridgeshire, in 1584. John Seton, who had returned from Louvain to become a canon of Westminster, was officially labeled a "rank papist" and forbidden to travel more than twenty miles from London. Later he was imprisoned for his "obduracy" in religion, but eventually contrived to escape and make his way to Rome, where he died in 1567. Thus the old company of Cambridge friends, twice before separated by religious change and exile, was finally divided sharply along the lines of the Elizabethan settlement.

Upon resuming his secretarial duties in Elizabeth's court, Ascham found himself working with a privy council quite differently constituted from that of Mary's last years. So far as he was personally concerned, its recomposition meant that he must seek new patrons. Two of his chief benefactors, Pole and Gardiner, were dead, and the wily Paget, though he had managed to hold office in all three preceding reigns, was not invited to serve in a fourth. Sir William Petre and the indestructible Marquis of Winchester were still respectively secretary of state and lord treasurer, but effective power was now in the hands of another group of men, chief among whom were the Marquis of Northampton; Thomas Radcliffe, Earl of Sussex; Lord William Howard; Sir Francis Knollys; Cecil; and Sir Ambrose Dudley and his younger brother Robert, future Earl of Leicester.

Still, the need to find new supporters presented Ascham with no major problems. Except for Gardiner, it is doubtful that he had been deeply attached to anybody, even Cardinal Pole, at Mary's court. As a known Protestant, though protected first by Gardiner and, after Gardiner's death, by Pole, he could scarcely have felt comfortable with the other Marian bishops and with courtiers like his enemy Sir Francis Englefield. One of the special compensations of the new era must have been the absence from the council table of Englefield, who had discreetly slipped off to Spain. Ascham's last connection with this would-be persecutor dates from March 1568. Englefield's estates having been confiscated after his unlicensed departure, Philip II sought to have Elizabeth restore them. Unless his charity was more than human, Ascham must have derived great satisfaction from transcribing the queen's reply, a flat refusal.[4]

Among the men close to Elizabeth, the two with the most influence were Robert Dudley and Cecil, both of whom Ascham claimed to be his "greatest and best friends" among the mighty. Although the association with Dudley, the queen's favorite, seems to have brought Ascham few benefits, the patronage of Cecil held considerable meaning for him and for his family. Cecil, working closely with Cheke, had already looked after his interests while he was in Germany, and his later benefactions, especially to Ascham's heirs, were to be substantial.

So highly did Ascham esteem Cecil that on one occasion he ventured to praise him at Dudley's expense, though he could hardly have been unaware of the keen rivalry between the two men. About 1564, to the neglect of an apparent earlier interest in rhetoric, Dudley, now Earl of Leicester, had suddenly developed an enthusiasm for geometry. Ascham, no lover of mathematical studies although he had once lectured in the subject, disapproved strenuously. He feared that Leicester had done himself "injury in changing Tully's wisdom with Euclid's pricks and lines," in exchanging the almost divine art of eloquence for a kind of knowledge in which the very beasts frequently excelled men. To emphasize his belief that rhetoric is the proper art for a nobleman and statesman, Ascham concludes that he himself "had rather write and speak English, as Mr Cecil doth, or Latin, as Mr Haddon doth, or both, as our most noble mistress doth, than be a pretender to them and ignorant" (II, 103–4). The effect on Leicester of the scarcely welcome compliment to Cecil may have been softened by the even greater praise of the queen; yet the tribute indicates that Ascham was willing to risk offending one patron in order to render due credit to so true and generous a friend as the other.

The compliment also points to the renewal of Ascham's studies with Elizabeth during these early years of her reign. In spite of the difficulties and overwhelming responsibilities facing her, she found time, Ascham reports, "daily, orderly, and constantly," to withdraw with him after dinner to read some work in Latin or Greek. Only illness or a royal progress could interfere with this practice. Their long-standing admiration for the famous exchanges between Demosthenes and Aeschines continued; Ascham recalled that they had been reading one of these orations on the occasion when he formed his design of writing *The Scholemaster* (III, 81). To Sturm he reported, in words very similar to those he had used in 1555, that the queen's feeling for the language and comprehension of the issues in these orations still amazed him (II, 63). Not only he, his letter goes on, but "all her own household, and many foreigners, are witnesses to what and how much she is capable of in other tongues." For besides her mastery of written texts, she could converse fluently in several languages. Other observers have remarked on Elizabeth's competence as a linguist, describing how she would translate for foreign visitors the lines of plays being performed in her presence. To this evidence, Ascham adds a much-cited anecdote of his own: "On a certain day I was present, when at one time she replied to three ambassadors, the emperor's, the French, and the Swedish,

in three languages, to the one in Italian, to the second in French, in
Latin to the third, not haltingly, promptly, without discomposure, to
various matters as they uttered them in their discourse."

In his judgment, moreover, it would have been impossible to find
four men in all England who were more proficient than the queen in
Greek. Adding to this praise of her zeal for learning and great capacity
in languages, he later wrote in *The Scholemaster* that she devoted more
time to study than any six of the "best given gentlemen" one might pick
out at court. "Yea, I believe," he adds, "that beside her perfect readiness in Latin, Italian, French, and Spanish, she readeth here now at
Windsor more Greek every day, than some prebendary of this church
doth read Latin in a whole week. And that which is most praiseworthy
of all, within the walls of her privy chamber, she hath obtained that
excellency of learning to understand, speak, and write both wittily with
head, and fair with hand, as scarce one or two rare wits in both the
universities have in many years reached unto" (III, 143).

It may be that Ascham exaggerated Elizabeth's scholarly and linguistic attainments. She was, after all, a queen who fed upon flattery.
It was under his direction, besides, that she had acquired much of the
skill attributed to her in Greek and Latin, and in penmanship as well;
upon the tutor of so accomplished a pupil a certain amount of reflected
glory was bound to shine. Yet because his statements are corroborated
by the testimony of foreign ambassadors and other disinterested witnesses, there is no reason to doubt Ascham's essential sincerity. When
he counts it his chief blessing, next to the gift of the Christian faith, to
have been "one poor minister in setting forward these excellent gifts of
learning in this most excellent prince" (III, 143), the claim is probably
not so extravagant as it may sound in a modern ear. As the writer of one
of the fairest hands in England and a zealous promoter of the study of
languages, as a follower of Cicero who regarded eloquence as the most
godlike quality in man's nature, Ascham could not help being gratified
by Elizabeth's aptitude and unwearying interest in these arts. In a
broader sense, too, as a ruler who in his view put her learning to the
service of religion and her people, Elizabeth was the perfect embodi-
ment of all his educational ideals.

In almost every respect the young queen was living up to his earlier
expectations. In 1562, though she had been ruling for less than four
years, he proudly outlined for Sturm her impressive record as a monarch. First of all, he writes, she has cleansed the polluted religion of her

country with such moderation and tolerance "that the papists themselves are not minded to say that they have been harshly treated." Having discharged this primary duty as God's vice-gerent, she has also
brought about peace between her nation and all others, whereas upon
her accession she found herself at war with both France and Scotland.
By frustrating the effort of the Guises to seize control in Scotland, she
has made friends of her northern neighbors who had been inveterate
foes. Nor in her attention to external policy has she neglected internal
reforms. She has restored the coinage, for a number of years much de-
based with copper, to its original sterling purity, "a difficult and truly
princely work, which not Edward, not Henry himself, had ever ventured
to undertake." By other prudent fiscal measures, she has likewise benefited her realm, above all by not coveting the riches and lands of her
subjects. She has spent her own revenues "sparingly and thriftily on
every personal pleasure, but regally and bounteously" for the public
welfare and "domesticae magnificentiae splendorem." England's military and especially its naval might, greatly decayed under Edward and
Mary, are once again to be reckoned with, for the queen is diligently
restocking the arsenals and building a superb new fleet of which any
nation in Europe might be proud. Finally, she has established a reign
of law, not of bribery or favor, for though she is forgiving of personal
injury, she will allow nobody, however highly placed, to commit a
crime in her realm with impunity. Nothing is left for her subjects to
desire but that she marry; then there would remain no room for her
higher praise.[5]

II

As secretary in almost daily attendance upon this paragon of rulers,
Ascham was certainly in a position to describe for Sturm the early years
of Elizabeth's reign. His own role in the government was minor, and
many of the letters that he composed or transcribed involved only the
most routine business of state. His principal function was to note down
the instructions of the queen or her councillors, or sometimes to take in
hand Cecil's English draft and convert it into Latin.[6] Yet his office was
by no means that of a mere clerk. Though he may have had little to do
with determining policy, he was close witness to its daily shaping, as
well as to the significant historical developments of Elizabeth's first
decade of rule. He was not to see her most triumphant days. Nor
would he live to learn that she would never marry and that his hope,

so fervently expressed in *Toxophilus,* for the rule of one prince over both England and Scotland would be one of the consequences of her celibacy. He would not see the inevitable war with Spain break out at last, or the domination of the seas by English ships and English seamen. But he did live to witness the first stirrings behind the later, more glorious events.[7]

Although the old enmity of Scot for Englishman continued, with protests from both sides over acts of piracy against one another's shipping (II, 49–50, 55–58), a few of the official letters in Ascham's hand record the beginning of a shift from ancient hostility toward the eventual linking of the two nations (II, 25–27). After Lord Darnley's murder, and the arrival of Mary Stuart as a refugee at Bolton Castle, where his own father had been steward, it was Ascham who composed the first of Elizabeth's unsuccessful requests to the King of Denmark for extradition of the Earl of Bothwell to answer for the crime.[8] A number of his official letters also reflect the expansion of English commerce and of the horizons of Elizabethan adventurers. Some tell of the maritime rivalry with Spain and Portugal that helped bring on the struggle in the last years of the century for command of the sea.[9] Others record the extension of trade routes into the Baltic, to Russia, and beyond.[10]

Two letters regarding commercial relations with the Russians are especially noteworthy. One has a strangely modern ring. The Muscovites having encroached on the eastern borders of the German Empire, Elizabeth is prompt to assure Ferdinand and other central and northern European monarchs that she has forbidden her subjects to export supplies of war into the Czar's territories.[11] The other has to do with the attempt of Anthony Jenkinson of the Muscovy Company to open up commercial relations with Persia after returning from his celebrated journey into central Asia. Elizabeth dispatches Jenkinson with letters to the Czar and the Shah, asking that he be permitted to trade in the lands which he has been the first Englishman of his time to visit.[12] Ascham's thoughts as he neatly inscribed these requests for the merchant's safe-conduct would be worth knowing, for Jenkinson was journeying to the antique world that he himself once dreamed of visiting. Unfortunately he comments nowhere on any of the enviable voyages of English adventurers, his only comment on travel being the strange diatribe in *The Scholemaster* against youthful visits to Italy.

Most extensive is the correspondence about the formation of a Protestant alliance to offset the power of both France and Spain. Until she passed the age of childbearing, English diplomatic maneuvering was complicated by various offers of matrimony to the queen. In 1559 the proposal of Charles, Archduke of Austria, is put off with a "not just now" while Elizabeth sounds out the signatories of the Augsburg Confession about a prospective league "against all enemies of Christ's doctrine" (II, 9, 87). Thus, she must continue to humor her Lutheran suitor, Eric of Sweden, yet cannot risk completely dashing the hopes of Charles, who is the Emperor Ferdinand's son (II, 36). Among those to whom she directs Ascham to write concerning this possible alliance of Protestant states are three princes whose names no doubt stirred his memories of the days when he followed the armies of Charles V. Writing to Duke John Frederick II of Saxony, Frederick III, Count Palatine of the Rhine, and the old foe of the emperor, Philip of Hesse,[13] must have called to his mind the admirable John Frederick I; the energetic and dangerous Philip quietly distributing alms during his confinement at Mechelen; a dinner with the Count Palatine's predecessor and a tour of the palace at Heidelberg (II, 166).

This state correspondence sometimes was a link with other acquaintances from his years abroad. Vitus Polandus, replying for the Count Palatine about the suggested Protestant league, asks to be remembered to his "old friend Ascham," whom he had known at Charles V's court.[14] Johannes Spithovius (Spithove) of Münster, writing in behalf of the King of Denmark concerning an altercation between English and Scottish fishermen near Iceland, begs Ascham to "keep our mutual friendship warm and firm" by sending letters whenever he can (II, 57–58). Christopher Mont, still English agent at Strasbourg, writes nostalgically of their having roasted chestnuts together at Morison's fireplace in Augsburg; he sends verses urging Ascham to procure some relief for the family of a deceased member of Sturm's faculty, the Dutch scholar Gerhard Sevenus, or Finck (II, 123–24, 168). Stephen Cirler, recalling Ascham's visit to Heidelberg, expects to find letters from him in Immanuel Tremellius's wallet when the distinguished Hebraist returns from England (II, 166). An anonymous informant of Cecil's about the Guisean intrigues in France remembers a happy meeting with Ascham in Germany.[15] Ascham, if he ever saw the letter, would have welcomed the intelligence it contained, for at the time he was jubilant over the discomfiture of the Guises in Scotland and had been urging Sturm to compose a history of their conspiracy to seize all power in France (II, 71–72).

In addition to these connections abroad, Ascham's association with

Leicester and Cecil and his daily waiting upon the queen gave him the reputation of being a person whose opinions carried some weight. His value as a sounding board to Leicester's views is at least once on record, in the case of a certain Francis Newdigate, suspected of complicity in the clandestine, and therefore treasonous, marriage of the heir apparent, Lady Catherine Grey, to Somerset's son, the Earl of Hertford. Newdigate, having heard Ascham express the opinion that Leicester's support might be won, offered this information as sufficient reason for requesting an interview with Cecil in order to exonerate himself.[16]

Further evidence that Ascham's views were respected occurs in connection with Charles of Hapsburg's proposal of marriage to the queen. In reporting the reactions of the English court, Baron Caspar Breuner, the emissary charged with presenting the archduke's suit, links the name of Ascham, as though he were a personage of consequence, with that of Cecil. These two, Breuner writes, are the only "councillors" who favor a Swedish bridegroom; the rest of the court look for a Scottish or Imperial match.[17] To this extent, at least, were the opinions of Ascham weighed among those of more powerful courtiers during the years in which he served as Elizabeth's secretary. Thus, though he never became a privy councillor, or received a knighthood or an ambassadorship like his friends Smith and Hoby, he had nonetheless earned a place in which he might have found reasonable content, if only he had also enjoyed moderate prosperity and good health.

III

The story of his last ten years, however, is largely one of chronic illness and financial predicaments. Early in Elizabeth's reign he began to suffer increasingly frequent and violent attacks of ague; in 1562 he offered its debilitating effects as an excuse for not having written to Sturm in three years (II, 60). Nor was the apology specious; in 1559 he had described his illness to another friend as being "dangerous for my life" (II, 21). For half a year, moreover, during the summer and autumn of 1560, he was so incapacitated that Cecil, despite the enormous burden of his own responsibilities, assumed his secretarial duties, not only composing Elizabeth's Latin correspondence but thoughtfully transcribing it himself in Ascham's official copybook.[18] Poor health may explain Ascham's failure to gain further advancement at court or to extend his public service beyond the routine duties of a Latin secretary. The only other office that he held was his but briefly. In the parliament convened in 1563, he represented the borough of Preston, in Lancashire, but before the session was dissolved his seat had been assigned to a son of the mayor of the town.[19]

Besides the nagging misery of illness, Ascham felt genuinely incapacitated by his comparative poverty. His biographers, puzzled that a queen's secretary and apparent favorite should have fared no better, have ventured various explanations of his seemingly unrelieved shortage of money. Some have speculated that he may have disenchanted patrons by too great importunity; others, that he was less demanding than he ought to have been in seeking relief. A number have accepted the legend that he consumed much of his income and property by gambling. This charge was first made by the antiquarian William Camden, who remarked of Ascham in his *Annales* that "since he was overmuch addicted to dice-play and cockfighting, he lived and died in straitened circumstances."[20] Because such spicy tidbits are the delight of popular biographers, the legend of Ascham the inveterate gambler has thriven. When the chatty Thomas Fuller and David Lloyd picked it up and passed it along, it became a persistent feature in accounts of Ascham's life.[21]

But though it is true that Ascham displays a certain interest in cockfighting, the allegation is unsupported by convincing evidence. Camden, who bore no ill will toward Ascham and even prefixed a rather lengthy commendatory poem to the first edition of his *Epistolae* (I, cv-cvii), had served as an usher at Westminster under Edward Grant before he became headmaster himself. He may have had his story from Grant or even from Ascham's son Giles, who was a pupil in the school in his time. He may have got the notion, on the other hand, from various allusions to gambling in Ascham's writings. Toxophilus, after all, had amused Philologus with his suspiciously authoritative knowledge of the sleights of cony-catchers and the hair-raising blasphemies of dice-players. In *The Scholemaster*, Ascham speaks of having completed or projected a "book of the Cockpit," and calls himself "a looker-on in this cockpit of learning these many years."[22] On his voyage up the Rhine in 1550 the round building near Oberwesel used for coronation of the King of the Romans had struck him immediately as resembling "a great cock pit" (I, 257). Finally, an admonition against gambling that he sent to his brother-in-law might seem to be the voice of sad experience;

"Use not dicing nor carding; the more you use them the less you will be esteemed; the cunninger you be at them, the worse man you will be counted" (II, 29–30).

Such passages may appear to reflect a certain preoccupation with games of chance. Yet if Camden's story has any basis in fact, its importance should not be exaggerated. It implies, unjustly in view of other evidence, that Ascham wagered away substantial goods, leaving his wife and children inadequately supported both before and after his death. The truth is that even if he had been inclined to do so, he never had in hand very much money to squander. Apart from Camden, moreover, no contemporary ever accused him of such a failing.

That he suffered from his shortcomings as a petitioner, on the side either of diffidence or of excessive importunity, is also doubtful. Because of his many earlier pleas for assistance, one might at first tend to believe that he simply wore out the patience of benefactors by persistent supplication. Even the sympathetic Dr. Giles, though he cannot decide "whether Ascham was poor by his own fault or the fault of others," disapproves "the numerous and clamorous letters" with which he sought to better his fortunes after Elizabeth's accession (I, xcix, lxxxix). He wonders, too, whether the queen may have been reluctant to advance someone "who had left her service so hastily ten years ago, and whom she might still suspect of serving her rather from interest than affection" (I, xc). Yet if Ascham perhaps overexerted himself in seeking promotion in his earlier years, attentive reading of his personal correspondence after he became Latin secretary turns up, in spite of Giles's remark, surprisingly infrequent requests for new favors. From the period between 1558 and 1568 there are extant only five petitions in all, two to Cecil, two to Leicester, and only one, not written until 1567, to the queen herself. Further, though he complained freely about his poverty, he seldom asked for additional means to relieve it, and then he did so reluctantly, as when he inquired whether Cecil might help him to redeem a worrisome bond by securing him "a licence for some quantity of bear [MS. *beer*], or some number of unwrought clothes, or some lease of farm, some forfeit, or some other thing, which may by your judgment seem less to trouble any stablished good order" (II, 48–49).

No one would deny that Ascham knew how to flatter his superiors "by the book" in order to gain their good will. But there is something to consider in Grant's insistence that during his years at court he was no beggar and never asked anything of the queen (III, 336–37). In his one surviving request to Elizabeth he protests, in a sentence that incidentally reminds one of his conviviality and love of "pastime with good company," that "I never opened my mouth to utter any suit to make myself rich, except it were for venison to make my friend merry" (II, 155). There is evidence from the queen herself to support this claim. In 1566, she mentions having given Ascham a certain sinecure some years previously "without any his suit or knowledge thereof."[23] Grant also supplies an anecdote that makes Ascham appear singularly high-minded in an age when courtiers had developed begging into a fine art. On one occasion, he was taken to task for his diffidence by the Marquis of Winchester. Winchester, who had been born when a Plantagenet was on the throne, had excelled all other Tudor statesmen at weathering political and religious change. As one monarch succeeded another, he continued to acquire new titles and estates until, by Elizabeth's time, he had made himself one of the richest men in England. He is reputed to have summed up in a cynical motto his remarkable capacity for survival: "Ortus sum e salice non ex quercu—I was sprung of the willow, not the oak."[24] To Ascham he observed, "It behooves you to execute your office less zealously, and more boldly to seek from the queen." To this and similar well-intentioned advice, says Grant, Ascham's reply was ever that he "would rather be well thought of by my prince for diligence and zeal, than be undeservingly provided with magnificent rewards" (III, 337).

The foregoing evidence comes, of course, from Ascham himself, his panegyrist, and a monarch who is perhaps trying to convey the impression that she has provided a servant with a handsome living out of pure benevolence. It must be weighed, therefore, against the many petitions for advancement of his younger days and against one contradictory admission about his character in Grant's oration. For Grant, though he insists that in general Ascham bore all his difficulties and disappointments with equanimity, concedes that at times he would become exceedingly vexed at what he considered to be his ill recompense and unkind treatment (III, 338). If he expressed his annoyance openly, it may be that he did in fact alienate potential patrons by complaints and importunity.

In all, however, there is not sufficient evidence to enable one to attribute his poverty to either diffidence or importunity, or to overfondness for dice and fighting cocks. Nor can the oft-alleged parsimony of Elizabeth, though she did procrastinate more than once before coming to his assistance when he was in need, be given as the cause. For here the ground is too uncertain. Some historians describe her avarice and caution in money matters, inherited from her grandfather; others criticize her for injudicious spending, niggardliness toward deserving courtiers and capricious lavishness toward her favorites. But whereas she did give too much to Leicester and perhaps too little to the diligent Sir Henry Sidney, it is also true that to others like Cecil she meted out due and handsome rewards. Her apparent neglect of Ascham should be considered against more surely demonstrable reasons for his perennial want.

Though all of the alleged causes may have contributed, the really important ones seem to have been the rapid growth of his family, legal impediments and suits that prevented his enjoying the income from various crown grants, and, much to the credit of his good nature if not to his good husbandry, an impulsive generosity toward others in need, in particular his wife's relations.

In abandoning the celibate life of the Cambridge scholar, he had indeed given many hostages to fortune. From about 1560 onward, his wife bore him a number of children. How many is not certain, but references in his own writings and in contemporary legal documents fix the minimum at seven, or possibly eight. Only four are mentioned by name—Giles, Sturm, Dudley, and Thomas. Giles was the eldest surviving son, though presumably he was younger than the infant whose death is commemorated in Ascham's famous letter to his wife. He was probably born in 1560 or 1561, for he is evidently the child mentioned in the preface to *The Scholemaster* as being nearly of an age with Robert Sackville, second Earl of Dorset, whose birth occurred in 1561 (III, 82). The next boy, Sturm, godson to the humanist in whose honor he was named, was born on October 13, 1562, and died before his fifth birthday (II, 174, 176). On October 10, 1567, Ascham wrote to the queen that he was the father of "many fair children," but of only two surviving sons, Giles and Dudley (II, 156–57). For some reason he does not mention his daughters' names.

Of both Giles and Dudley, the later record is fairly substantial; the circumstances attending the latter's birth and christening deserve brief attention here. In August 1564, the queen went on progress to Cambridge, a visit to his old surroundings that Ascham was most "desirous" to share. But on the 5th he wrote to Leicester, pleading his wife's con-

finement as an excuse for missing the progress and asking his lordship
to stand godfather through a proxy to the expected child (II, 101–2).
Leicester must have consented, for not only was the infant christened
with his surname, but two years later Ascham referred to him in another
letter to the earl as "Dudley, your son" (II, 131).

After Dudley, there were apparently two or three more children. In
April 1566, Ascham wrote to Leicester again that he could not appear
at court because young Dudley was "perilously sick"; his wife, moreover, was pregnant, and both her own life and that of the child she was
carrying were in danger. Margaret is so wasted with care and illness,
he laments, that she is "ready to lie down, weak, sick, and sorrowful
. . . not worth the ground she goeth on."[25] Again, in the letter to
Elizabeth, he describes his children as "all within the years of innocence,
so not able to speak, not able to go, and one (though shortly) not yet
born" (II, 156). Whether these two expected children survived infancy
is not known. Of the last boy, Thomas, more is on record, for his name,
seal, and signature appear on various documents concerning later disposition of the family property. Evidently he was born in 1569, after
his father's death, since in his last epistle to Sturm, completed late in
1568, Ascham mentions Giles and Dudley as his only living sons and
says nothing of the imminent birth of another child.[26]

Within five years of his marriage, Ascham had also assumed responsibility for helping out his mother-in-law and her younger children.
During Lent 1559 Margaret's father died, leaving Mistress Howe, as
Ascham movingly describes her situation, "in that dead time of the
year an house without money, barns without corn, fields unsown, rents
to pay, wages to answer, children to find, sore wages, and small relief,
rich in [MS. *with*] present care, and hope only of next year's store, and
that as yet not growing on the fields" (II, 46).

Immediately he obtained leave from court, and with ready cash
from Cecil in his purse, hastened to assist her. The amount Cecil had
given him turned out to be insufficient for any but the most immediate
needs of the family. So, despite his own small income and smaller
estate, in order to procure additional money Ascham generously "became also surety by my own hand, for all her former debts, that any
auditors could ask, without requiring of her script or scroll, hand-surety
or bond, to answer me or mine again." As security he soon afterwards
mortgaged his one hope of future competence, the reversion to the
lease of Salisbury Hall. For, as he explains his admirable, but im-

prudent gesture, "finding my mother-in-law in such a case, and thinking that I might get again such a lease, but never again such a mother, whose virtue, womanhood and wisdom was such, as I loved her as much by judgment as ever I did my own mother by nature, I laid my said lease to gage to Antony Hussey, for a hundred pounds to be paid at the font in Poule's [St. Paul's] on Christmas Eve, 1561, or else to forfeit it forever."[27]

Nor was this all he did for Mistress Howe and her children. Though he could not always supply them with ready money, he did manage to help them in other ways. He seems to have placed one of the boys in the school of the well-known master Ralph Radcliffe; in exchange for this tutoring he taught penmanship to Radcliffe's son.[28] For his brother-in-law Christopher he found a position in the household of the Earl of Warwick; this place he may have been able to secure because of the petitions he had once composed for the countess when Lord Ambrose was in the Tower. But if he was able to find service for the youth and to offer him a letter of conventionally pious advice, Ascham had to confess his embarrassment at being unable to provide him with a suitable wardrobe for his new station in life.[29]

IV

The need to mortgage his interest in Salisbury Manor was only the first of many difficulties for Ascham in his effort to build up a modest estate. In all, he managed to secure four promising grants, two from the crown, one from his old college, and the last from his mother-in-law's will. But none of these was to bring him either financial competence or assurance of his heirs' future well-being.

On October 6, 1561, less than three months before the bond for Salisbury Manor was due to expire, he wrote in desperation to Cecil for some means to avoid forfeiting the lease. This was the extremity that had driven him to ask for a monopoly, much as he was opposed in principle to "private licences granted against public statutes." Rightly, he felt that Cecil was his best hope and likened his own obligations toward this friend and benefactor to Oedipus's debt to Theseus: "I have that I have only by you and by no mo."[30] Although he received no license or privilege, the request served its purpose, for the queen herself immediately advanced him the money to redeem the bond.

Cecil's most recent good office, before presenting the matter of the bond to Elizabeth, had been to have Ascham nominated to the "canonry and prebend of Wetwang in York Cathedral," the patent for which is dated November 1559.[31] Ascham's readiness to accept this appointment, when he had refused another like it six years earlier, may be explained by the changed ecclesiastical climate and the responsibilities of marriage and parenthood. Wetwang was a tempting sinecure worth more than £24 annually.[32] Had the see of York been in a settled condition at the time, he might have begun to enjoy the revenue without hindrance. For months, however, administration of the diocese was badly disorganized while the council deliberated about deposing Archbishop Nicholas Heath, one of Ascham's patrons in Queen Mary's time and Gardiner's successor as Lord Chancellor. To complicate matters, after Heath's deprivation, the archbishop-elect, Dr. William May, died before he could succeed. Not until 1561, with the choice of a Marian exile, Thomas Young, was the diocese finally occupied. In such an extended crisis, no one thought of pressing the cathedral chapter for installation of a mere prebendary; to his credit, Ascham refrained throughout from protesting the delay.

But instead of ending his anxious wait, Young's election only prolonged it. The new archbishop, either deliberately ignoring Ascham's nomination, or else unaware of any prior claim to the prebend, bestowed it privately on another candidate, referred to as Dudley, who belonged to Leicester's household (II, 131). For nearly five more years the title stood contested, and the consequent litigation almost ruined Ascham by causing him to go heavily into debt, and even to sell "away my plate, and that which grieveth me much, my wife's poor jewels" (II, 127). Though he obstinately refused to trouble the queen about the matter, he did take other steps to secure his right. He may even have traveled to Yorkshire to plead his case personally, since on October 3, 1563, the archbishop sent letters back to Cecil by "this convenient messenger, Master Askam."[33] If he did make the journey, it was without profit, for nearly two years afterwards Haddon wrote to Sir Thomas Smith that the issue was still in doubt.[34]

Apparently emboldened by long waiting, on April 14, 1566, Ascham finally got up courage to beg Leicester himself to intervene, since it was his servant, or perhaps kinsman, whose nomination constituted the sole obstacle. With unwonted temerity, he places the burden squarely upon Leicester. Not even the proudest churchman in Queen Mary's and Gardiner's days, he protests, would have been allowed to treat him as

Archbishop Young has done. But then, he goes on, with no attempt to conceal which patron's conduct appears the shabbier by contrast, Gardiner's "good will stood not in speaking fair and wishing well, but he did indeed that for me whereby my wife and children shall live the better when I am gone." Someday his widow and orphans will have to acknowledge that their sustenance is due entirely to the Bishop of Winchester, since they will "have not one penny to live upon gotten by my Lord of Leicester in Queen Elizabeth's time" (II, 129). Even worse, they will remember that Leicester, though influential enough to secure some other good place for his servant Dudley if he should perform this favor for his godson Dudley, refused to do so and hence took away the one living provided for Ascham by the queen. Two weeks later he wrote again to remind Leicester of his obligation to his godson, in the previously cited letter in which he describes his wife and young Dudley as being "perilously sick."

Ironically, on another occasion Leicester had willingly helped, at least with letters, to get Ascham out of a financial predicament into which he had been driven by litigation over this prebend (II, 150). Whether he now responded by offering to withdraw his candidate is not known, but within a few months the contest over Wetwang came to an abrupt end. On June 20 the queen sent a mandate to Young, scolding him for frustrating her intentions and specifying that he ratify Ascham's appointment under a long-term lease "for the present maintenance of his service, and comfort hereafter of his wife and children" (II, 135). Four months later Ascham thanked Elizabeth for delivering him at last "out of trouble and care" with, as usual, a fitting gift, the Old Testament books of Kings with commentaries by Peter Martyr Vermigli.[35]

Why the queen delayed so long, especially when her prerogative was being openly flouted by Young, remains one of the many mysteries of her subtle character. Instead of asserting her will much earlier, she long affected ignorance of the affair even though Ascham was in her company almost daily. Either he and the rest of her court had kept an incredible five years' silence about the disputed appointment, or else she took pleasure in rescuing him like some *dea ex machina* just when his cause appeared most hopeless. Or possibly, as her long delay in relieving still another of his economic worries suggests, it really did pain her to sign away lands and livings.

For, as has been mentioned, the litigation over Wetwang almost caused Ascham to lose his only other substantial property interests, the leases of Salisbury Hall and Whittlesford Rectory, against which he borrowed money from the crown in addition to the sum required to redeem his bond at Christmas 1561. Although the queen had not demanded security, his total debt to the crown exceeded £200, and Ascham, as he informed Cecil in 1567, delivered up the reversion to Salisbury as evidence of his intention "speedily to repay it" (II, 149). Instead of asking to have the debt remitted, he began negotiating to sell his lease for Whittlesford. When she heard that this modest living was about to change hands, Elizabeth's sense of the sanctity of property was stirred. "Ah, fool, fool," she protested, though smilingly, to Ascham, "I did not let you have that money to take it again: keep your living still, sell it not, for livings be not easy to come by. I will take order with Sackvile for it" (II, 150).

Sir Richard Sackville, who was her chancellor of the Court of Augmentations, had in fact often urged the queen to sign a deed remitting the loan, but she (so Ascham excuses her procrastination) "being weary, and loth to sign many things at once, hath ever deferred it to another time." The delay, though there is no hint of bitterness toward Elizabeth in his correspondence, must have been exasperating to a man seriously in debt. The original patent had specified that he take over Salisbury Hall in March 1564; now, more than three years later, he had not yet realized a penny from the estate because it remained in mortgage. Again the appeal to the watchful and persuasive Cecil, a masterpiece of the epistolary petition, seems to have brought results, for Ascham never again mentioned the bond that had caused him so much distress. Yet if in these last months of his life his immediate fortunes began to mend, he had not freed himself from his greatest care, how to assure the future maintenance of his wife and children. His salary and pension would terminate with his life; Salisbury, Wetwang, and Whittlesford were all merely "lent" to him. Similarly undevisable was the one other parcel of land in which he held an interest.

This was a sizable farm near Windsor Castle known as Broomhall Manor. While residing at Windsor during the plague that had driven the court from the city in the winter of 1563–64, Ascham apparently remembered that Broomhall belonged to St. John's College. Perhaps he rode over to inspect it, or having ridden past frequently enough to note its extent and the condition of its buildings, had decided that, though sadly run down, it might provide a suitable dwelling for his family whenever the court removed to Windsor. On January 18 he wrote to ask the master and fellows of the college for the lease, offering his services as "steward" of this farm on whatever terms they cared to propose (II, 74). On November 7, 1565, the society granted him the reversion to the lease, "for 40 years from Michaelmas, 1574, at a rent of £7. 6s. 8d."[36] But since the award did not include his successors, it proved no more to his purpose than his other promises and holdings; soon after his death the reversion was assigned to another family.[37]

In the autumn of 1567, therefore, he decided to try at least once a direct appeal to the queen. If his slightly earlier petition to Cecil is masterly, this last bid for help far exceeded it in skillful composition and accurate judgment of the recipient's character.[38] The letter, though written in English like that to Cecil, observes scrupulously yet ingeniously the formal principles set forth for its kind in the Latin epistolaries. Since its end was to move the reader to decisive beneficiary action, the rules for it were similar to those for the deliberative oration. The main parts, in addition to the salutation and valediction, were typically an introduction, a statement of facts, the petition itself, and finally a peroration, preceded according to some handbooks by a confirmation and refutation.[39] Ascham includes all these and manages the appropriate topics under each heading with great finesse, the whole being grounded, as Renaissance authors believed an effective composition must be, in a "fine invention." As the likeliest way to make his petition striking in its appeal to Elizabeth, Ascham conceives of her as two distinct persons. She is at once her "highness," alone capable of satisfying his request but too awesomely majestic to be addressed directly by so humble a suitor, and her "goodness," a friend of many years who has her "highness'" ear and whose intercession he may ask without embarrassment. Thus, after greeting her as "Most excellent prince, my best lady and mistress," he goes on to say that "as I daily wish and pray that you may long and long remain both highest sovereign and greatest friend unto me, so for this time of reading this letter, I humbly beseech your majesty to imagine that your highness were absent in some withdrawing-chamber, and your goodness only present to read the same; for I write not now as to the queen to make any suit, but as to my dearest friend to ask some counsel in a suit I would fain make to the queen."

Throughout the letter he carefully maintains this fiction. In the introduction, the function of which is to win a hearing by demonstrating that the favor asked is necessary, just, and reasonable, as well as being easy for the one addressed to perform, he stresses that his plea "shall neither be unreasonable for your goodness to ask, nor great for her highness to grant, nor intolerable to any other person; it shall not be to enrich myself now, but only to leave some comfort to my good wife and children hereafter." The statement of facts, through which he shows further the reasonableness and justice of his petition, retells the history of his pension for *Toxophilus* and his long years of service to the crown. Simply by pointing out that her three predecessors "did always better one another" in goodness toward him, he offers a clever bait for the queen. These other monarchs had granted him favors when, excepting Edward for a little instruction in penmanship, they owed him nothing. It would thus appear anticlimactic and ungracious if the sovereign whom he has served longest should prove least beneficent. Ascham speaks of "friends" who have argued that if he would only get up courage to lay his request before her "goodness," he would soon realize the full extent of her "highness'" benevolence toward him.

As if this were not encouragement enough, the substance and phrasing of the petition proper show how well Ascham understood Elizabeth's character. He attempts to move her by appealing to her womanly sentiments, her pride as a monarch in being thought munificent, her inclination, all the same, to parsimony; he also knew how to play upon the conflict in her spirit between the last two qualities. He pretends, therefore, that one of his anonymous, or fictitious, friends has suggested how he might best provide for "my careful wife, sitting now at home weeping and praying for the good success of this my suit, and make happy my poor children for their good bringing up in virtue and learning, thereby to serve the better, God, their prince, and their country another day." The friend's plan is to surrender the income from his pension and office in exchange for grants of Salisbury Manor to one son, of Whittlesford Rectory to the other. Such an arrangement will put an end to his worries and will cost the queen nothing. She will have, in truth, the better of the exchange, "yea, five-pence for a groat," since Ascham's income was somewhat over £46, whereas the two properties brought only about £40 annually into the royal treasury. The "friend," besides, is certain that the queen's "goodness will grant more than you require," that she will agree to the exchange without requiring her faithful secretary, for the few years of life remaining to him, to forfeit his small income.

Whether the "friend" is real or fictitious, his proposal serves as the confirmation and refutation of the letter, showing clearly how just and reasonable it is that a man of Ascham's good character be granted his request. In this part he manages to insinuate that he is not inclined to beg and even now is doing so only for his sons, and that he would never suffer the queen to be held responsible for his poverty simply because he had never asked anything of her. No strong arguments can be offered against a man who seeks "nothing for himself, but something for his children," who would be perfectly content with the proposed settlement, though it is "a small portion as ever secretary to a prince did leave behind him." Even if the petition should not be granted, at least he can leave his sons a copy to prove that their father has not died without trying "to do them good as much as lay [in] his power and learning to do."

Probably this careful working within the prescribed formula, the highly balanced, alliterative style resembling that of *The Scholemaster*, and the sustained conceit of "highness–goodness" appear too deliberately contrived according to later standards for epistolary prose. The elaborate artfulness, or "artificiality" in the sixteenth-century usage of the term, may have been one reason that some earlier critics censured Ascham for too great adeptness at importunity. But he must be judged by what his contemporaries would have expected in this kind. An appeal that could be woven into intricate, yet deftly controlled, language proved the merit of its author and was regarded by that very fact as worthier of consideration. To say that deliberate cleverness in supplication necessarily precludes sincerity is not to understand the workings of the Elizabethan, and especially of Elizabeth's, mind. The letter, though actual confirmation did not come until after his death, accomplished exactly what Ascham had hoped for. As he had anticipated, the queen did not take seriously the offer to "chop and change lands with him" for his salary and pension. On the contrary, she not only assured to his sons the income from Salisbury Manor and Whittlesford Rectory, but even divided among them his former stipend of forty marks as Latin secretary.

V

In spite of ill health and financial burdens, Ascham seems to have revived during these years his zeal for humanistic studies and to have maintained his zest for convivial gatherings with other scholars. Besides his already mentioned daily reading with the queen, he made new friends among the learned and was surrounded with old ones from the golden days at Cambridge. Among those who came to dine with him, perhaps upon some of the venison he mentions having begged from the queen "to make my friend merry," were the Scottish humanist George Buchanan and Sir George Bromley, elder brother to the future lord chancellor and himself a celebrated jurist.[40] What they discussed none of the three reports. One likely topic was the drama, for Ascham considered Buchanan's *Jephtha* one of the two modern tragedies that could "abide the true touch of Aristotle's precepts and Euripides' examples" (III, 241). He also presented a book to Buchanan, for which he received as thanks a pledge of friendship in Latin elegiac verses.[41] A younger scholar who may also have graced his table was Bartholomew Dodington, the new regius professor of Greek at Cambridge, for in 1566 he gave to Dodington his personal copy of Carlo Sigone's *De Rep. Atheniensium libri IIII* (Venice, 1565).

Further stimulation of his intellectual interests came through association at court with various members of the former Cambridge circle. Although their leader, Cheke, was gone, there remained in Elizabeth's service Cecil, Haddon, Wilson, Smith, William Bill, and Archbishop Parker. Bill and the archbishop do not figure significantly in Ascham's later life except for Parker's apparent interest in the *Report of Germany*. His close relationships with the others, however, are well-documented. Cecil, of course, had become his new idol, not only as a statesman and patron but also as a scholar. In the preface to *The Scholemaster* Ascham proudly reports "Mr. Secretary's" custom of laying aside "weighty affairs of the realm" while dining in order to converse "pleasantly of other matters, but most gladly of some matter of learning, wherein he will courteously hear the mind of the meanest at his table" (III, 79). Another member of the group was Haddon, whom Ascham and all the others regarded, though he was unfortunately deficient in Greek, as the best "Latin man in England."[42] With this fellow Ciceronian Ascham appears to have shared a passing interest in alchemy, though probably not in hopes that it might afford a means of overcoming his financial distress. In *The Scholemaster* he praises Thomas Norton of Bristol, fifteenth-century author of *The Ordinal of Alchymy* (III, 250), and he seems to have thought sufficiently well of the poem to have had it copied in the same manuscript as the first draft of his own treatise.[43]

Haddon and he also enjoyed close friendship with Smith, who was abroad much of the time and depended upon them for chatty news from home. None of Ascham's epistles to Smith from this period has been preserved, and only one of Smith's to him. Yet from this single letter, along with an exchange of correspondence between Smith and Haddon, their intimacy, as well as Ascham's growing deficiency as a correspondent, is evident. In 1565, during his ambassadorship to France, Smith complains to Haddon that Ascham has not written to him in over two years. If Ascham really expects news of France, which he has never visited himself, he must in turn keep Smith posted about what is going on in England. Or, asks Smith punningly, is he so charmed by his fighting cocks (*gallos*) that he is no longer concerned about his friends or about the political affairs of Frenchmen (*Galli*)?[44] Haddon, at the time in Bruges on a special mission for the queen, replies that he has himself had no letter from Ascham during this brief absence.[45]

Late in 1568, after Smith had returned to settle down at Hill Hall in Essex, Ascham sent him an astrological chart made by some unnamed friend. Ascham seems not to have shared his and Cheke's enthusiasm for astrology, possibly because of his aversion to mathematical studies; he rather approved St. Ambrose's condemnation of soothsayers and astrologers for attributing the dispensations of God's providence to the fates or the stars.[46] Yet for some reason he wanted to have Smith's opinion of this particular chart; Smith judges it to be learnedly compiled, though not quite conformable to the newer astrological tables. He comments also on the recent publication of Haddon's epistles (1567) and reports that he has finished some little book of his own which Ascham has asked to see, and is now having it copied (II, 192).

From *The Scholemaster* and Ascham's scattered, but informative, letters to Sturm, the nature and scope of his studies in these later years can be determined. As might be expected of a man who long had felt death at hand, and whose humanism accordingly assumed an increasingly religious character, he seems to have read more extensively than ever before in the scriptures. He also turned to *The Imitation of Christ*, though characteristically not in Thomas à Kempis's medieval Latin, but in the more "proper and eloquent" version published by Sebastien Castalion in 1563 (III, 182). In part his purpose was to find examples and arguments for his *Scholemaster*. But his frequent references to the psalter and to the Pauline epistles imply a quest for solace and comforting doctrine as his health declined. Parnassus and Helicon are not to be scorned, he wrote in 1562, in commending Sturm for his treatise on the Lord's Supper; yet Jerusalem is better, and there is more eloquence in "David, Isaiah, John, and Paul, than in all of Pindar, Plato, Demosthenes, and Cicero" (II, 66–67).

His secular reading, nevertheless, proves to have been quite varied, extensive, and up to date; many of the works to which he alludes are recent publications. He ranged over the new books, from the lyrics of Wyatt and Surrey (III, 250), which he apparently read in one of the early editions of *Tottel's Miscellany,* to various commentaries on Platonic philosophy (III, 243) and Aristotelian logic (III, 231). Perhaps with his projected essay on Elizabeth in mind, he purchased several political and historical commentaries, among them the treatise of Sigone that he later gave to Dodington, and Claude de Seyssel's *De Republica Galliae* in Sleidan's Latin version (Strasbourg, 1562), his personal copy of which is still in the British Museum.

But he continued to prefer those classical authors who had formed his tastes and ideas since his youth. He maintained his enthusiasm for the great Athenians; all the extant ones, he boasted, were represented in his own "poor library."[47] He refers most often to Cicero and Horace, to Plato, Aristotle, Homer, Euripides, and Xenophon. Besides studying them in the original, he looked curiously and even approvingly into such recent vernacular translations as the Ovid of Arthur Golding (1561) and that of George Turbervile (1567), Thomas Phaer's *Aeneid* (1558, 1562), and the versions of Seneca's tragedies issued from 1559 to 1566 by Jasper Heywood "and other gentlemen" (III, 25). To Thomas Blundeville's partial rendering of Plutarch's *Moralia* he contributed eulogistic verses.[48] Arthur Hall, the first Englishman to undertake a version of the *Iliad,* credited Ascham with having encouraged him in 1562 (or 1563) "to go forward with my begun enterprise."[49]

Not all the new translations met with his approval. Italian *novelle* were just beginning to appear in English dress, and these he viewed with alarm. He is obviously thinking of such volumes as William Painter's *The Palace of Pleasure* (1566) and Geoffrey Fenton's *Certaine Tragicall Discourses* (1567), harmless enough though these may now appear to be, when he condemns the "bawdy" and "merry books of Italy" that "corrupt honest living" and "subdue true religion"; he suspects them of being a device of "subtle and secret papists at home" to subvert the youth of England (III, 158–59). Boccaccio he also mistrusts, and he disapproves the "reverence" accorded by his "Italianated" young countrymen to Petrarch's *Triumphs,* Englished about 1565 by Lord Henry Parker (III, 161). Even the *Morte d'Arthur,* he complains, which consists of "open manslaughter and bold bawdry," does not cause one-hundredth "so much harm, as one of these books made in Italy and translated in England." But if young men would read instead Sir Thomas Hoby's version of *The Courtier,* they would discover in this one worthy book how to avoid the lures of frivolous works and "to join learning with comely exercises" (III, 141).

Most of his reading bears upon topics that he takes up in *The Schole-master,* and especially upon the one which dominates the second half of that work, literary and rhetorical imitation. His preoccupation with this subject is, in fact, one reason for the many allusions in his correspondence to the two pairs of opposing orations of Aeschines and Demosthenes. In 1550 he had urged Cheke to translate into Latin the earlier pair, *On the False Embassy,* evidently with the idea that they should be used as models for teaching Latin through the practice of double translation and imitation (I, 220). In 1561 he also asked Osorio for his version, undoubtedly so that he might have the speeches in another eloquent Latin rendering. Sturm had already provided a commentary on the later pair, *On the Crown,* and *Against Ctesiphon.*[51]

Ascham's last communication to Sturm, almost a "little book" he calls it, is an epistle devoted mainly to this same topic of imitation. In July 1568, Sturm had offered to send him, after all the years of discussing the question in their letters, as much as he had already written on the subject (II, 169). Ascham, who was busy reading everything about it that he could come by, replied that he wanted nothing so much as to see his friend's work. For he too was putting together "something on the same subject," though it was "still unfinished, and for unskilled boys" to study, whereas Sturm's must already be "perfect, and for learned men" to read.[52]

His unfinished work, he goes on, is a pamphlet which he calls his *Praeceptor (Scholemaster).* This humble teacher speaks rudely in the vernacular, rather than eloquently in Latin, because he is "not imported from Greece or Italy, but born in this barbarous isle, . . . not a Canta-brigian, but a Windsorian; a courtier, not an academician." He might speak better, even in English, if he had the tongue of a Cheke, a Smith, or a Haddon. Whatever good is in him comes from the stock of ideas given to his creator by Sturm. Yet he will suffice, if he can but show Ascham's sons the right path to learning. The *Praeceptor* is in two books; the first is concerned mainly with the characters of the tutor and his scholar, the second with the method of instruction. In this letter, Ascham says no more concerning the first part, which he has already finished; he discusses at length the contents of the second, which he was still endeavoring to complete (II, 176–77).

The first sure step to learning, in his opinion, is to exercise oneself in double translation "by regular practice and sedulous writing, always joined with a fitting and not an inappropriate style." By turning passages from Greek into Latin and then back into Greek again, the pupil will soon acquire a marvelous understanding, as has Queen Elizabeth under Ascham's tuition, of both languages. Of the remaining steps, "Paraphrasis, Metaphrasis, Epitome, Imitatio, Commentatio, Scriptio, et Declamatio," the indispensable one is imitation of the choicest models. The section on this topic in the *Praeceptor* will therefore be somewhat longer than the others, and it has given Ascham much difficulty. For though he has "eagerly read almost all the ancients and moderns who have written concerning imitation, he can approve many, but admire none, save Sturm alone." If Sturm would only provide what is yet missing, a supply of examples of successful imitation to accompany the perfect set of precepts in his *Nobilitas literata* and *De amissa dicendi ratione*, Ascham would require nothing more to help him finish his task (II, 178). But because Sturm, even as he had long been remiss about getting out his commentaries on Aristotle's *Rhetoric*, was so exasperatingly slow about completing his work *De imitatione oratoria* (not published until 1574), Ascham had been forced to search everywhere for illustrative examples. In both this letter and in *The Scholemaster* itself he cites numerous works dealing with imitation, not only as practiced by poets, dramatists, and orators, but by historians and philosophers as well. The letter is particularly instructive because in it is described the full plan for the second half of *The Scholemaster*, on which he had been working intermittently for nearly five years.

VI

The long epistle to Sturm was not quite Ascham's final literary endeavor. Throughout most of December he concentrated on finishing, as a New Year's gift for the queen, a Latin poem of thanksgiving for the blessings enjoyed by England during the first decade of her reign (III, 288–93). Artistically the work is of little consequence, for it is undistinguished in either conception or execution. One may take it, indeed, as the ultimate confirmation of its author's own admission that he "had never poetical head to make any verse in any tongue" (III, 172). Still, it deserves some notice because it expresses the almost religious devotion that Englishmen were beginning to feel toward the queen.[53]

Ascham addresses Elizabeth as "dea magna Britannis," great goddess to the British people, for whom she is both "the sole support of Christ's true doctrine" and "the chaste pattern of the virtuous life." In words that echo what he had written to Sturm in 1562, he rejoices in her truly regal accomplishments. Because hers is a reign of law, "everywhere wise counsel, not force; reason, not blind will, have dominion." She administers justice with proper measure; her sword causes no fear to the upright, but only to the iniquitous. She does not "goad on her subjects with hatred, but rather leads them with love," so that their fear is the less, their reverence the greater. Her virtue is so remarkable that all men deem her worthy of "the government of the vast world and the direction of all its affairs" (III, 288–89).

As justification for this hyperbole, Ascham offers what he believes to be the chief blessing Englishmen have enjoyed under this paragon among princes. In other nations, the king is a Mars; his rule, as any of England's neighbors can testify, brings only the law of force along with interminable wars that consume his people. Perhaps recalling what he had witnessed while following Charles V's campaigns (I, 365), Ascham lists the ill effects of "masculine sway" as "exiles, plundering, and sad confusion of things: cruelty, the sword, devouring flame, hunger, blood, sanguine massacres, and a prolonged succession of internal evils." Englishmen, on the contrary, are governed by a second Minerva. Under her aegis, war has been kept far away and blessed peace fostered; the golden age has finally returned. Ringing harmonies upon the words *virgo* and *virginea*, Ascham stresses the benefits of feminine guardianship as contrasted with masculine tyranny. Elizabeth's people thrive and learn virtue, experiencing such safety and bounty as England cannot remember in nearly two thousand years of rule by kings. This queen excels all other monarchs "as far as the sun overmatches the other lights, or as you, O moon, surpass the lesser heavenly bodies" (III, 290). The comparison, making Elizabeth at once the sun and the moon, appears clumsy; yet with it and the praise of her virgin powers

Ascham anticipates the host of later poets to whom she did become a Diana, a Cynthia, a "goddess excellently bright."

The climax of the poem is an attack on the meretricious papacy, and an exhortation to Elizabeth to be the salvation, as she is the hope, of the countries suffering from Rome's "Babylonian frenzy." Perhaps with the memories of Smithfield still upon him, he wonders how Englishmen can stand by unmoved while their neighbors are being burned at the stake for their convictions: "What if we who watch now as idle spectators, may be actors ourselves in time to come?" In the most unrestrained language that he has left on record, he laments the fierce persecution of evangelical believers wherever the pope bears sway. All human kindness, all laws of nature, are forgotten by the raging minions of the Bishop of Rome. Nothing may be kept inviolate from the pollution of the beast with "a thousand hands, a thousand feet, and a thousand stratagems for inflicting injury" (III, 292). This monster's most deadly weapon is gold, with which, in a corrupt age, it seems able to buy almost everyone and everything. Yet not quite everyone, for in England gold neither rules nor deceives; it is spent rather for humane purposes by the gracious queen. His muse has not raised this clamor, says Ascham, merely to move Elizabeth to sorrow. But he would have her win lasting fame either by stilling the papists' wrath through arbitration and stern warning, or in extremity, by breaking their power with her own sword of righteousness.

Though perhaps expressed overvehemently for her taste, the sentiments in Ascham's verses could scarcely have displeased the queen. She too viewed Rome and the pope's supporters as the greatest threat to her realm. For although she had avoided wars and dangerous alliances, in seeking England's safety she had made gestures that had raised Protestants' hopes elsewhere and had come to be regarded as the champion of their cause. She had maneuvered the Guises out of Scotland and had granted unofficial aid to the Huguenots in France. Haunted by the fear of Spanish invasion, she was learning how to keep Philip II from disturbing the balance of power by denying him undisputed control of the dangerously near Low Countries.

The poem would thus have made an acceptable New Year's offering. But Ascham never brought it to completion. Grant asserts that the effort to have it ready in time, coupled with an excessive application to official correspondence, proved too much for him. He became so weakened from lack of sleep, that when an ague struck him on December 23, he fell mortally ill. The account of his last days, while it smacks of the conventional pious ending of commemorative oratory, sounds authentic from the unusual character of several of its details (III, 340–41). As his discomfort grew worse, Ascham could neither sleep nor lie quietly in his bed, and his servants made futile, but touching, efforts to bring him some repose. Sometimes they would lift his small and wasted body in their arms and carry him up and down the chamber. In hopes of lulling him at least to moments of rest, they even prepared an oversized cradle and rocked him in it like a baby.

During this final week of his life, he was frequently visited by his friend Dean Nowell and by William Gravet, vicar of the parish church that he attended, St. Sepulchre's, outside Newgate. Nowell was a particular comfort to him; as Ascham remarked after one of his visits, the gentle dean "nourished his soul with imperishable food." For his part, Nowell remarked that he could not remember having ever witnessed a more Christian ending. In spite of his persistent ill health, Ascham had apparently never thought to draw up a will. Instead, at some time between eight and nine o'clock on the evening of December 30, four witnesses being in the room, he made a simple oral disposition of his property. According to Grant, "he committed all that was his unto his wife, above all his beloved children; he asked that she manage everything according to her own best judgment, that she look with a truly maternal spirit after their education, that she see to their instruction in virtue, piety, learning, and good manners."[54]

Having thus disposed of his earthly obligations, he addressed himself to Gravet, who had arrived in the meantime to offer some final comfort. "I am afflicted," lamented Ascham, "with a great sadness; I am oppressed with a great illness: this is my confession, faith, prayer; this is my sole desire: *I want to die and be with Christ.*" After repeating these words of St. Paul once again, he spoke no more, and toward ten in the evening he died. On January 4, he was buried in St. Stephen's Chapel on the north side of St. Sepulchre's.[55] The ceremony was simple, with a moving sermon preached by Nowell. Though Grant does not tell who else attended the rites, he speaks of the great distress at court at the news and quotes the statement attributed to Elizabeth concerning the magnitude of her loss. He mentions also the deep sorrow expressed by Sturm and other scholars over their "gentle Master Ascham," though they heard of his death by "cold report" long after it

happened. For this friend who had won the affections of many, who
had diligently served, though without much reward, two reigning monarchs of England, and who had devoted his life to classical learning,
George Buchanan composed verses that would have served fitly as an
epitaph:

> Aschamum extinctum patriae, Graiaeque Camoenae,
>   Et Latiae vera cum pietate dolent.
> Principibus vixit carus, jucundus amicis,
>   Re modica, in mores dicere fama nequit.[56]

CHAPTER ELEVEN

The Scholemaster

FROM THE STANDPOINT of literary history, the most important step taken by Ascham's widow to provide for her orphaned children was to arrange for publication of *The Scholemaster*. Within a year of her husband's death she sent the manuscript to the printer accompanied by a dedicatory epistle to Cecil as the truest past, and hopefully also future, benefactor of her family (III, 76–77). In 1570 the printer, John Day, published the work under the long, self-descriptive title *The Scholemaster, Or plaine and perfite way of teachyng children, to understand, write and speake, the Latine tong, but specially purposed for the private bryngyng up of youth in Ientlemen and Noble mens houses, and commodious also for all such, as have forgot the Latin tonge, and would, by themselves, without à Scholemaster, in short tyme, and with small paines, recover à sufficient habilitie, to understand, write, and speake Latin.**

---

* Day paid the Company of Stationers 4*d*. sometime between July 22, 1569, and July 22, 1570, for entering "the scholemaster of Wynsore made by master ASKE-CHAM . . ." (*A Transcript of the Registers of the Company of Stationers of London, 1554–1640 A.D.*, ed. Edward Arber, Birmingham, 1894, I, 410). The treatise proved an immediate success; within the next twenty years it went through four more editions. Besides the first (*STC* 832), Day brought out others in 1571 (*STC* 834), 1573 (colophon; title page still reading 1571; *STC* 835), and 1579 (not in *STC*; Bishop, *Checklist* 835+). In 1589, Abel Jeffes published the final sixteenth-century edition (*STC* 836). There has been some confusion over the number and dates of the early editions. Besides those already cited, various biographers and bibliographers have reported printings in 1569, 1572, and 1583, but no specimen to prove the existence of any of these remains. The supposed edition dated 1570 (1571) (*STC* 833), thought to be represented by a unique copy in the Pierpont Morgan Library, is probably a "ghost." Examination proves that it lacks fol. T$_{1v}$, which would have borne the supposed 1570 colophon. In all respects it appears to be identical with the edition of 1571 (*STC* 834). Since the eighteenth century, the work has been reprinted a number of times, both separately and in all collections

Although it offers nothing wholly original in educational theory and is not even the earliest exposition in Renaissance England of most of the ideas that it contains, ever since its appearance Ascham's treatise has been widely discussed, quoted, and imitated. It shares with *The Governour*, to which it is much indebted, the honor of being the most influential of Tudor treatises on education. Historians of pedagogy almost invariably turn to *The Scholemaster* for illustrations of the Elizabethan attitude on education: the care to be exercised by parents in rearing their children, incitement to study by praise rather than punishment, adjusting the pedagogical system to the individual child rather than the child to the system, teaching by cogent example and practical exercise rather than rote memorization, the preferability of learning to raw, untutored experience, and the dangerous allurements that lie in wait for the unwary youthful traveler, particularly the impressionable English voyager to Italy.

Nor has the influence of the work been limited to its educational theories alone. Ascham's opinions on classical and native literature were adopted, sometimes quite uncritically, by many of his contemporaries. His views on imitation of the ancients and the use of classical meters in vernacular poetry exerted a perceptible, if not in all ways salutary and lasting, influence on Elizabethan prosody and literary criticism. Also, like *Toxophilus* before it, *The Scholemaster* is credited with marking a new stage in the rise of English formal prose. But above all, it has appealed to successive generations of readers because of the lively contemporary anecdotes and the flavor of his own personality that Ascham provides while treating what are largely commonplaces of humanistic ethical and educational theory.

According to the preface, the treatise sprang from a dinnertime conversation at Windsor Castle on December 10, 1563, when the court had withdrawn from London to escape a "great plague" that was raging in the city. Although written long afterwards and somewhat embellished

---

of Ascham's writings. The first new edition was that of James Upton (London, 1711), "revised and improved" (London, 1743). The standard edition, copiously annotated, is that by John E. B. Mayor (London, 1863; reprinted 1884, 1892). Edward Arber issued *The Scholemaster* in his English Reprint Series in 1870 and 1895; it appears also in Cassell's National Library (London, 1900; New York, 1902). More recently it has been edited by D. C. Whimster (London, [1934]). During the decade following the appearance of *The Scholemaster*, every one of Ascham's works, certain of his letters excepted, was either first published or reprinted, perhaps in an effort by his widow and others to gain patronage for his family.

to make the alleged origin and the contents of the work fit more neatly together, this introductory account gives a sprightly picture of one side of life at the English court during the earlier years of Elizabeth's reign. Gathered to dine with Cecil in his chamber were Ascham; Petre, the secretary of state; Sir John Mason, diplomat and chancellor of the University of Oxford; Dr. Nicholas Wotton, who had hastened to Augsburg in 1551 to patch up Morison's differences with the emperor; Sir Richard Sackville; Sir Walter Mildmay, future chancellor of the Exchequer and founder of Emmanuel College, Cambridge; Walter Haddon; John Astley; Bernard Hampton, clerk of the privy council; and Nicasius Yetswaert, apparently an agent for the queen in Flemish affairs.[1]

Upon sitting down at table, Cecil introduced a bit of news that immediately provoked a spirited discussion among this generally learned company. He had just been informed that "divers scholars of Eton be run away from the school for fear of beating" (III, 79). The incident made him wish that masters would use more discretion in whipping, lest promising students should come to "hate learning before they know what learning meaneth." With this sentiment Petre, a man "somewhat severe of nature," disagreed; he favored beating as a means of keeping "the school in obedience, and the scholar in good order." Wotton, "a man mild of nature, with soft voice and few words," took Cecil's part, but Haddon, perhaps to Ascham's surprise, agreed with Petre "and said, That the best schoolmaster of our time was the greatest beater, and named the person." Ascham politely suggested that although it had been that particular master's "good fortune to send from his school unto the University one of the best scholars indeed of all our time," it was not the punishment but rather the capacity of the scholar that had brought about this happy event.[2] Under Cecil's prompting, he then went on to explain at some length why he believed that "young children were sooner allured by love than driven by beating, to attain good learning" (III, 81).

When Ascham had departed to his customary afternoon reading of Greek with the queen, Sackville also came to her chamber and drew him aside "to a window," perhaps one looking across the Thames to the college from which the unhappy schoolboys had just fled. Sackville remarked that in his youth a foolish master had frightened all love of scholarship out of him with the threat of the rod. Such a misfortune he wished to spare his little grandson Robert, future Earl of Dorset. Could Ascham but find a capable and gentle tutor for the boy, Sackville was willing to pay for the instruction of his son Giles under the same man. "We had then," Ascham continues, "farther talk together of bringing up of children, of the nature of quick and hard wits, of the right choice of a good wit, of fear and love in teaching children. We passed from children to young men, namely, gentlemen: we talked of their too much liberty to live as they lust; of their letting loose too soon to overmuch experience of ill, contrary to the good order of many good old common-wealths of the Persians and Greeks; of wit gathered, and good fortune gotten by some, only by experience without learning. And lastly, he required of me very earnestly to show what I thought of the common going of Englishmen into Italy" (III, 82–83).

With these words Ascham in effect outlines the chief topics of the first book of *The Scholemaster*. Sackville had asked him, at the end of their conversation, to write down for his benefit the main points they had touched upon. The next day, after a sleepless night spent in think-ing about this request, Ascham began to work out his ideas on paper, hoping to have a brief pamphlet ready for his friend by New Year's Day. But as he wrote, the treatise expanded, and he continued to work at it throughout 1564 and perhaps during much of the following year. By early 1566, he had finished a preliminary draft of the first book, a copy of which is preserved in the British Museum.[3] He then set the manu-script aside for some time because the death of Sackville in April 1566 made him lose all heart to get on with the work and probably, too, be-cause this was the period when his financial difficulties became most complicated. "Almost two years together," he says in the preface, "this book lay scattered and neglected, and had been quite given over of me, if the goodness of one had not given me some life and spirit again" (III, 85). The "one" to whom he refers is Cecil; the "goodness" was apparently favorable action upon his request in June 1567 for the queen to remit the mortgage on Salisbury Manor (II, 148–52). By October of the same year Ascham had either produced a rough version of the whole treatise or revised the already drafted first part sufficiently to permit the manuscript to circulate among his friends (II, 158). Finally, though the printed text is incomplete, he may actually have finished the entire *Scholemaster*, at least in a preliminary draft, by the autumn of 1568. The preface, in all likelihood composed shortly before his death, announces that the hope given by Cecil's benefaction "hath helped me to end this book." The final letter to Sturm, evidently written slightly earlier, suggests, moreover, that the "as yet not concluded" manuscript lacked only certain details and was rapidly nearing completion.[4]

II

As Ascham had informed Sturm, *The Scholemaster* divides into two sections of nearly equal length, the first "ethical for the greater part, the second concerned with method" (II, 176). Book One, as in *Toxophilus*, is a search for general principles; Book Two is mainly a discussion of the best approach to mastering the art under consideration. The running titles make the distinction clear. The first book is devoted to "Teaching the Bringing up of Youth"; the second, to "Teaching the Ready Way to the Latin Tongue."

Both in the British Museum manuscript and in the printed version, Book One, after a brief exposition of a few guiding principles for the earliest stages of grammatical instruction, conforms point by point to the outline given in the reported conversation with Sackville. The child should not be set immediately to translating English sentences into Latin, a manner of learning characteristic of the common schools and exemplified by the "beggarly gatherings" of exercises in the widely used *Vulgaria* of William Horman and Robert Whittinton (III, 88, 200). Nor should he be encouraged to speak Latin too soon, for both too early speaking and "making of Latins" give rise to faults that may never afterward be eradicated.[5] Not that Ascham objects to conversation in the language, but he would avoid early beginnings since the master is all too frequently "as ignorant as the child, what to say properly and fitly to the matter" (III, 89).

The pupil should learn instead by double translation, an exercise recommended by Cicero and Pliny, and far more certain, as the splendid example of Queen Elizabeth has shown, to produce correct and eloquent expression.[6] Having learned his parts of speech and a few rules of syntax, the child should be troubled with little more formal grammar. The master should give him instead one of Sturm's selections from Cicero's letters to translate into his copybook.[7] Then after "an hour, at the least," has elapsed, he should be required to take a second copybook and retranslate his English into Latin without consulting the original. In order to gather a "supply of language," he should also keep a third notebook for examples of proper Latin expression, particularly the "most notable *phrases,* in all his lecture [reading]" (III, 95). Throughout the exercise, the master should criticize the child's efforts gently, not chiding or punishing him for errors if he has done his best, but rather commending him wherever he has done well. "For I assure you, there is no such whetstone to sharpen a good wit, and encourage a will to learning, as is praise" (III, 90).

This abrupt beginning is by design far more than a summary of elementary pedagogical method. Again as in *Toxophilus*, the opening paragraphs subtly introduce the ideals which the author means to champion. Insistence upon example rather than prescript as the finest instrument of teaching had always been a leading principle with Ascham.[8] Not only does the recommended system prepare for the later extended defense of double translation and imitation; it also implies, as Ascham intends that it should, that all the future depends on the nature of the beginnings. He believes that by loving mastery of Latin, the key that unlocks the treasury containing the wisdom of both the philosophers and the fathers of the church, the apt child will come to delight in all good learning and moral discipline. But if he should be made to hate Latin by dull instruction and harsh punishments, he may in after years abandon study altogether. For this reason Ascham already indicates in the opening passage that gentle treatment is mandatory for sound education; from his wish for a "gentle nature" in the schoolmaster the quest for general educational and ethical principles develops quite naturally.

Up to approximately the middle of Book One, the concern is primarily with the qualities desired in the pupil and the means for alluring him to study; the remainder is devoted to the moral discipline of young gentlemen during the dangerous years from seventeen to twenty-seven. Unfortunately, Ascham writes, Englishmen tend to mishandle the education of their children right from the cradle. Often neither tutors nor parents know how to recognize true "wit," that is, real intelligence and aptness for learning. Too many masters favor the quick-witted prodigy and chastise as indolent the child who learns slowly; "even the wisest of your great beaters, do as oft punish nature as they do correct faults" (III, 97). Yet "hard wits," those who are less pliable and less ready to jump at new suggestions and yet are not "over dull" or "lumpish," often prove the best scholars in the long run.

In comparing these two kinds of intellectual capacity in children, the master should be discreet enough "not so much to weigh what either of them is able to do now, as what either of them is likely to do hereafter." For the chief fault of "quick wits" is flightiness; they are "apt to take, unapt to keep; soon hot, and desirous of this and that; as cold, and soon weary of the same again; more quick to enter speedily, than able to pierce far; even like over-sharp tools, whose edges be very soon turned" (III, 98). Though eager for light studies, they are neither deep in judgment nor diligent in "high and hard sciences"; they are likely, asserts Ascham, expressing the values of his own rather than more recent times, to "prove the best poets, but not the wisest orators." Some people, moreover, whose wits are "moderate enough by nature," become spoiled by too zealous pursuit of mathematics and music, arts which Ascham had ever suspected of diverting men from worthier endeavors.[9] "Quick wits," too, are often undependable in their behavior, "very ready of disposition to be carried over quickly, by any light company, to any riot and unthriftiness when they be young; and therefore seldom either honest of life, or rich in living when they be old." Their usual fate is to "live obscurely, men know not how, or die obscurely, men mark not when."[10]

"Hard wits," on the contrary, if properly handled from infancy, usually prove best in the long run, even as "in wood and stone, not the softest, but hardest, be always aptest for portraiture, both fairest for pleasure, and most durable for profit" (III, 101). Although "hard wits" may require longer to grasp an idea, they retain it longer; they are also more constant morally and "deeper in judgment" than their more flighty rivals.[11]

Ascham holds no quarrel with ready intelligence, but he means here to emphasize the folly of masters and parents who are dazzled by superficial brilliance into misjudging the capacities of children. He complains, as he had in *Toxophilus*, that fond elders jeopardize the common good by sending the wrong youths to the universities to become "our divines, lawyers, and physicians." Often parents exert greater care in choosing a trainer for their horses than a tutor for their sons and daughters. In order to help others to distinguish real from false intellectual promise, Ascham presents seven "true notes," adapted from Plato's dialogues, by which one may detect a "good wit." The promising youth should be *euphuès*, well endowed with all good qualities of mind and body that serve learning; *mnémon*, retentive; *philomathès*, predisposed to love learning; *philóponos*, willing to work and take pains; *philékoos*, glad to learn from others; *zetetikòs*, diligent to investigate every aspect of a subject until he is perfectly taught; and *philépainos*, eager to be praised for doing well.[12]

All these qualities, granted that some are gifts of nature, may be fostered by proper handling and marred by mistreatment of the child. Learning should be inspired, not "by compulsion and fear, but by playing and pleasure." The only reason young gentlemen prefer horsemanship (in itself recommended by Ascham as the most suitable exercise for noblemen) to studies is that "fond schoolmasters, by fear, do beat them into the hatred of learning; and wise riders, by gentle allurements, do breed up in them the love of riding" (III, 112–13). What a boy will grow up to desire depends upon his experiences during childhood. If the schoolroom were made "a sanctuary against fear," as John Aylmer had made it for Lady Jane Grey, all the best hopes of good parents for the education of their children might be realized. Or, as Ascham puts it in one crucial sentence that epitomizes all the Christian humanist doctrine of the treatise, "if to the goodness of nature be joined the wisdom of the teacher, in leading young wits into a right and plain way of learning; surely children, kept up in God's fear, and governed by his grace, may most easily be brought well to serve God and their country, both by virtue and wisdom" (III, 116).

How to keep the young "in God's fear" so that they may serve him and the commonwealth fittingly is the concern of the rest of Book One. Significantly, Ascham devotes more space to this topic than to intelligence and learning. In the humanist view of education, moral excellence outranked intellectual achievement; "of all earthly learning," wrote Sir Philip Sidney in *The Defence of Poesy*, "the ending end" is "virtuous action."[13] Even the tutor is to be chosen principally for his goodness of character and then, as Elyot had said, "if he be also learned, he is the more commendable."[14] Yet English parents, according to Ascham, are even more neglectful, if that be possible, of the moral supervision of their offspring than of their intellectual training. The children of gentlefolk are brought up with too much indulgence and "cockering"; lawlessness consequently prevails throughout the country, and all true sense of moderation has been taken away. Even girls are given so much freedom (perhaps his memory was pricked here by the troubles preceding his own marriage) that they wed where and as they please "in spite of father, mother, God, good order, and all" (III, 122).

Ascham, finding the root of these faults, as he had those of Charles V and the young Duke Maurice in *A Report of Germany*, in unnatural conduct, believes that "all these misorders be God's just plagues, by his sufferance brought justly upon us for our sins, which be infinite in number, and horrible in deed; but namely for the great abominable sin of unkindness" (III, 128). His countrymen have been indifferent to the precious light of "the candle of God's word" and are risking by "unthankfulness in doctrine and sinful life, to leese again light, candle, candlestick and all" (III, 129). As an instance of this monstrousness in behavior he offers the following anecdote:

This last summer I was in a gentleman's house, where a young child, somewhat past four year old, could in no wise frame his tongue to say a little short grace; and yet he could roundly rap out so many ugly oaths, and those of the newest fashion, as some good man of fourscore year old hath never heard named before. And that which was most detestable of all, his father and mother would laugh at it. I much doubt what comfort another day this child shall bring unto them (III, 131).

Besides deploring such indifference to profitable studies and sound morality, Ascham decries the rash assumption of many parents that experience is after all the best teacher. To him it is a costly rather than a good teacher, "the common schoolhouse," as Erasmus had called it, "of fools and ill men" (III, 137). But learning "teacheth more in one year than experience in twenty." When joined with honest exercises and pastimes, it gives a complete education and a standard for judging all experiences, good and ill, that are encountered in later life.

Yet Ascham does not want the child always to be "poring on a book." He favors honest and cheerful recreation, for "beside natural disposition, in judgment also I was never either stoic in doctrine or anabaptist in religion, to mislike a merry, pleasant, and playful nature, if no outrage be committed against law, measure, and good order" (III, 138). He would have the youth, like Castiglione's ideal courtier, engage in "all pastimes generally, which be joined with labour, used in open place, and on the day-light, containing either some fit exercise for war, or some pleasant pastime for peace," all such as are "not only comely and decent, but also very necessary for a courtly gentleman to use" (III, 139–40). If all English noblemen would take heed of their responsibility to strive after perfection within their state in life and would follow the example set by their accomplished and learned queen, the rest of society would follow suit and good order might everywhere be restored.[15] Then those born to govern would once again fill the leading offices in the realm, now usurped by "meaner men's" more virtuous and deserving sons, and "how great soever they be now by blood and other men's means, they shall become a great deal greater hereafter by learning, virtue, and their own deserts; 'which is true praise, right worthiness, and very nobility indeed'" (III, 147).

To be avoided above all if a young man wishes to achieve true nobility is the morally hazardous voyage into Italy. Although some may withstand the "Siren songs" of this now corrupted land, Ascham has known others, "some sometime my dear friends," who have been transformed by living there as though they had been at Circe's own court. So depraved do many become that their evil behavior has produced a byword among Italians: *Inglese italianato è un diabolo incarnato.*[16]

Why Ascham, who had once longed to see all the wonders of Italy, and who never ceased to praise the Italian language for its beauty (III, 148), should have turned upon this land so vehemently in *The Scholemaster* is not fully clear. The attack, though in much curtailed form, appears, too, in the earlier manuscript version, which he had composed before the great flood of translations of "fond" and "merry books of Italy" had appeared to corrupt English morals. The Marian years, it is true, had led many of his countrymen to identify Italy with papistry and persecution; added to this, the misconduct of his "dear friends" and others with whom he was acquainted may have increased the tendency to priggishness from which he had never been wholly free. Whatever his reasons, his condemnation of Italy was unqualified: "A young gentleman, thus bred up in this goodly school, to learn the next and ready way to sin, to have a busy head, a factious heart, a talkative tongue, fed with discoursing of factions, led to contemn God and his religion, shall come home into England but very ill taught, either to be an honest man himself, a quiet subject to his prince, or willing to serve God, under the obedience of true doctrine, or within the order of honest living."[17] In these words sounds that deep mistrust of the effects of ill-chaperoned travel to Italy that lingers among Anglo-Saxon peoples even to the present day.

III

Sources for every one of these opinions may be found readily among classical and contemporary writers on the bringing up of children. For Ascham's program is fundamentally that of the ancients, adapted to current conditions by the humanist educators of fifteenth- and sixteenth-century Italy, and further modified in the direction of Christian piety and patriotism by the writers of the northern Renaissance. As a lifelong popularizer of traditional ideas rather than a creative thinker, Ascham cheerfully acknowledged his role as transmitter and his almost total dependence upon the prior wisdom of others. Completion of his little English "school-house," despite its rude and unpretentious fabric, lay beyond his unassisted intellectual means: "Yet, nevertheless, I myself spending gladly that little, that I got at home by good Sir John Cheke, and that I borrowed abroad of my friend Sturmius, beside somewhat that was left me in reversion by my old masters Plato, Aristotle, and Cicero, I have at last patched it up, as I could and as you see" (III, 84).

Undeniably he owed much to Cheke and Sturm, and of his classical triumvirate, Plato contributed most to the first book of *The Schole-master*, and Cicero to the second. Plato, besides supplying the key-notes of a "good wit," provides such ideas as that proper rearing of its children is the highest trust committed to a society, that education begins not in the school but in the nursery, that learning ought always to be pleasant business but that the merely pleasurable ought to be mistrusted because it is often an enticement to evil conduct, and that too much moral freedom and license to travel may corrupt impressionable youth. Sometimes Ascham borrowed these opinions directly from *The Republic* and the *Crito*; sometimes he had them indirectly from the various other authorities, both ancient and modern, who had a hand in formulating humanistic doctrine.

In addition to these acknowledged sources, Ascham draws upon a vast number of other ancient and modern writers in shaping his own treatise.[18] Though not all of them can or need be mentioned, his obligations to a certain few are worth remarking. Of the ancients, apart from Plato, he most admires Xenophon, whose views on moral discipline in the *Cyropaedia* he cites with unqualified approval. Also important are the counsels of Isocrates to the tyrant Nicocles. Isocrates also, as will be shown later, strongly influenced the literary style of *The Schole-master*, an element in the treatise and in Ascham's total educational perspective that was as significant to him as the content itself. From the author of the essay "On the Education of Children" that appears among Plutarch's *Moralia* came several notions about moral discipline and gentleness in education. Since, however, the principles set forth in this essay were almost universally approved, Ascham could have had them from contemporary adapters, for example from Elyot, who had incorporated several ideas from this work in *The Governour* and had also translated it into English.[19]

But most significant in shaping the distinctive character of Ascham's treatise were the acknowledged contributions of Sturm and the unacknowledged, though equally evident, contributions of Elyot and Quintilian. That these three authors, in addition to Plato and Cicero, should have had a marked influence upon *The Scholemaster* is not surprising. Quintilian has more to say on education than any other classical writer, and the discovery of his entire *Institutio Oratoria* by Poggio early in the fifteenth century inspired much of the theory and practice of the great humanist teachers of Italy. As his ideas came down to the sixteenth century by way of Vittorino, Vergerio, Guarino, and Patrizzi, among those who assimilated them wholly to his own thinking was Elyot, and the first sixteen chapters of *The Governour* embody many opinions and recommendations derived from Quintilian.

Although Ascham does not mention Elyot as one of his sources, he derives much of his inspiration from him, both in *Toxophilus* and in *The Scholemaster*. A strong kinship in ideals existed between the two men, who stand together at the entrance to a new period in humanist educational theory. The combined "ethic and politic consideration" of the fifteenth-century Italians and of Castiglione continued to prevail, but already in the northern countries the emphasis had begun to shift. For although the Italians had never denied the indispensability of the Christian faith in the formation of the ideal nobleman, they tended to concentrate on the natural virtues and graces. In the north, particularly after the Reformation but already in the circle of More with such a treatise as Erasmus's *Education of a Christian Prince*, there is a noticeable stress on piety and the role of divine grace in the educational process. Mankind is still regarded as naturally inclined to the good, but this belief is held with somewhat less optimism. The end of learning becomes, as Sidney defines it for his time and place, "to lead and draw us to as high a perfection as our degenerate souls, made worse by their clay lodgings, can be capable of."[20]

Even the rage for Greek studies among English humanists led as frequently to the Fathers as to the ancients and had as its aim learning informed with Christian piety. The best of the classics could help men to wisdom and goodness, if read, as Ascham made clear in describing to Grindal how he tutored Raven and Ireland and to Sturm how he instructed Elizabeth, within a Christian frame of reference (I, 74, 192).

Taken in themselves, even Plato, Aristotle, and Cicero may prove
treacherous rather than salutary guides to wisdom and right conduct.
"I never knew yet scholar," Ascham writes, "that gave himself to like
and love and follow chiefly those three authors, but he proved both
learned, wise, and also an honest man; if he joined withal the true
doctrine of God's holy Bible, without the which, the other three be but
fine edge tools in a fool's or madman's hand" (III, 213).

Along with the circle of More and Erasmus, then, Elyot and Ascham
stood for an ideal of "education in virtue and piety for the service of
the commonweal."[21] But unlike the more democratic More and his
friends, the two younger humanists concerned themselves with fashioning a program of education that might regenerate the decadent aristocracy of England. They hoped to realize in the gently born that
Boethian "verray gentillesse" consisting of "virtue and wisdom," without
which noble ancestry alone "is blood indeed, but blood truly without
bones and sinews; and so of itself, without the other, very weak to bear
the burthen of weighty affairs" (III, 123). Neither man approved the
change then taking place whereby commoners of outstanding talent
and character were succeeding to public offices that traditionally had
belonged to men of noble birth and ancient wealth.[22] The stress of both
authors on preparing young men for service to England, and in
Ascham's case for service to the religion of England as well, thus gives
a distinctly national cast to their humanism.

That both, and especially Ascham, drew so heavily on the *Institutio
Oratoria* is due to more than the pervasive influence of Quintilian's
work on Renaissance humanism. Although Ascham twice disparages
certain of his views on rhetorical imitation (III, 176, 221), it is clear
that in general the theories of the Roman rhetorician are particularly
to his own taste. Comparison of the opening pages of their treatises
demonstrates that Ascham, the eclectic who can condemn one part of a
predecessor's thought while blandly appropriating another, deliberately
and almost topic by topic, echoes the views expressed in Book One of
the *Institutio Oratoria*. One evident reason is that, even more emphatically than Cicero, Quintilian insists that real eloquence involves not
merely persuasiveness in speaking but also wisdom and goodness, the
very belief that is at the heart of *The Scholemaster*. It is likewise the
informing principle of Sturm's program of grammatical and rhetorical
education, upon which Ascham claims to have modeled the structure of
his own "poor school-house."

Quintilian's aim, to fashion the "good man skilled in speaking" (*vir bonus dicendi peritus*), is the same, allowing for the change of times and the added element of Christianity, as that espoused by Sturm and Ascham, and attributed to Sir John Cheke by his disciples. The insistence in the *Institutio Oratoria* that only the learned and good man can be called eloquent is echoed in the goal of "wise and eloquent piety" (*sapientem atque eloquentem pietatem*) upon which Sturm elaborated the curriculum of his gymnasium and Ascham the method of instruction outlined in *The Scholemaster* and practiced on his pupils both at Cambridge and at court.[23] Further, though Sturm and Ascham profess ultimate concern with that piety by which one is fashioned to serve God and prince just as Quintilian had maintained that his end was to prepare the ideal Roman statesman, once they have laid down their basic principles, all three turn with obvious relish to discussing practical methods for acquiring an effective manner of speaking. Thus, while he disagrees in part with Quintilian's *ratio* for perfecting oneself as an orator, Ascham finds his general theories of education and his stress on its earlier grammatical and rhetorical stages wholly consonant with his own viewpoint and aims.

How closely akin their works are may be seen in a brief summary of the chief points in the opening book of the *Institutio Oratoria*. In his preface Quintilian too justifies his especial attention to elementary pedagogical and moral considerations. Unlike those before him who had done no more than outline a method for putting the finishing touches on the orator's training, he will omit no detail in the preparation of the aspiring statesman, for the eloquently wise man must be properly reared from his infancy (Proem, 4–5). Since first impressions, moreover, are the most important of all, and since bad ones are almost indelible, the infant should be entrusted only to a nurse who speaks correctly and is of good character (i, 4–5). The same must be true later of his *paedogogus*, for the society of bad slaves has pernicious effects on children (i, 8). If possible, both parents, the mother as well as the father, should be learned and should speak good Latin; the example cited, and repeated by Ascham, to prove the value of maternal learning and eloquence, is Cornelia, mother of the Gracchi (i, 6). And like Ascham after him, Quintilian disapproves of allowing a child to speak extempore too early (iv, 15–17).

The child's lessons ought to be made pleasurable, a game (i, 20). Though he should not be permitted to move ahead without having mastered the rudiments of grammar (iv, 22), he must not be stupefied by too much rote learning (i, 25). He should be inspired to study by gentle encouragements and rewards (i, 20), never by flogging, which is fit only for slaves and produces insensitivity (iii, 13–14). All too frequently vicious masters indulge in beating simply to gratify their own perverse natures (iii, 17). Great care, therefore, must be taken to choose a teacher of the best character, particularly for the all-important early years. Fathers should look to the good example of Philip of Macedon, who would have no less a master than Aristotle for his son (i, 21–23).

The right sort of teacher will pay attention to individual differences among his students (ii, 4), and he will especially attend to the child who is eager to succeed and anxious to be praised for learning (iii, 7). He will understand, too, that "the precocious kind of wit never brings forth good fruit readily."[24] The flashy accomplishments of prodigies have no lasting value and are remarkable only in consideration of the children's extreme youth; their real achievement is trifling and they seldom excel in later years (iii, 5). The master should also see that his pupils are well instructed in all the arts that help to fashion the perfect orator (iv, 4; x, 6), but he should not allow overindulgence in any one art lest the student be diverted from the true end of education (xii, 14). Finally, the good master will understand the need for recreation from studies (iii, 9–13) and will see to the physical training of the boys placed in his charge; for love of play in children is a sign of a lively temperament (xi, 15).

Of equal importance with schoolroom studies is the future orator's ethical training. From his earliest years he should read works that are morally excellent as well as eloquent; licentious and erotic poetry, if not absolutely proscribed, ought to be kept from him until he reaches the age of discretion (viii, 4–6). Parents should diligently supervise the conduct of their children instead of criticizing the schools for corrupting them, since it is often lack of discipline at home that causes their ruin (ii, 6). Good can scarcely be expected of the young when parents live indulgently themselves and applaud innocent children for speaking indecencies or aping their elders' effeminate manners. "We rejoice if they say anything licentious: words not permitted even to Alexandrian minions we receive with laughter and a kiss. We have no reason to wonder; we have taught them, and they have given ear to us" (ii, 7).

Thus closely do Ascham's and Quintilian's first books run parallel. The only differences are that Quintilian is better disposed toward music and favors sending boys to schools, as does Sturm, over "the private bringing up of youth in gentlemen and noblemen's houses." Yet even these small points of disagreement are more apparent than real. Quintilian also warns against giving too much attention to music, especially the worthless modern melodies played on viols and psalteries, instruments unbecoming to any honest person, even to young maidens (x, 31). Nor may one really judge whether they disagree over which is the better place to learn, the home or the schoolroom. Ascham had begun writing, after all, at the request of Sackville, who was seeking out a tutor, not a school, for his grandson.

Close as Ascham is in ideals, therefore, to contemporaries like Erasmus, Vives, and Elyot, he tends with Sturm to stand apart from these earlier humanists through his emphasis on form rather than content. Elyot, for instance, deals at far greater length than Ascham with the substance of the texts upon which he bases his recommended curriculum. Ascham, though he condemns contemporary Italian books and medieval romances (III, 159), would allow reading of Plautus and Terence, despite their "base stuff," because of their excellent language (III, 245–48). While Sturm and Ascham would never have admitted to the charge that they were primarily interested in the arts leading to *eloquentia* rather than those containing *sapientia*, and would, moreover, have denied the validity of such a distinction, their main efforts toward realizing the aim of *pietas litterata* went into developing a sound *ratio* for acquiring a commendable Latin style.[25] The titles and contents of the works of Sturm from which Ascham claims to have derived his own basic ideas clearly indicate the focus of their mutual interest. These are *De educatione principum, Nobilitas literata, De litterarum ludis recte aperiendis liber,* and *De amissa dicendi ratione.*

Although the notion that learning is indispensable to a prince or gentleman was commonplace by his time, Ascham's exceptional stress on the necessity for eloquence in the wise and pious statesman was strongly influenced, as his correspondence with Sturm shows, by the first two works. In his first letter to Ascham, Sturm had commended Edward VI and Elizabeth as much for their elegance of written expression as for their substantial learning and zeal for the Christian religion, and he had dwelt at length on the inseparability of *eloquentia* and *doctrina* (I, 202–4). Ascham in his turn praised *Nobilitas literata* because it recommended the study of eloquence to the German aristocracy, and he admired the zeal of Sturm's wellborn pupils, the brothers Werter, for Christian doctrine and elegant Latin expression (I, 322).

In the second two treatises by Sturm he found what appeared to be the one proper *ratio* of study for the young. This method, meant to instill a love for the eloquent wisdom of the ancients and to produce a fine Latin style in him who follows it, consists of reading in the best classical authors, much practice in translation, and diligent imitation of Cicero.[26] Sturm would have reading and translating begin almost immediately; the good master will not bind his pupils for long to the grammar rules of Priscian and Donatus. He will teach them, in addition to writing, how to speak Latin properly, not in the prevalent disorderly and barbarous manner of the typical school.[27] Above all, he will banish from the classroom all those ill-ordered collections of snippets from ancient authors, for though many of the excerpts are admirably chosen, "this type of book destroys the force of memory, takes the edge away from one's style and often causes many things to be introduced inappropriately into one's writings."[28] Instead, Sturm would have the master present to the students carefully selected works of Plautus, Livy, Terence, Cicero, and Caesar; in his judgment, and Ascham echoes his opinion, the last three authors mentioned are the wellsprings of all good Latin.[29]

In only a few details do Ascham and Sturm differ over theory and method, and in the main their differences, like those between Ascham and Quintilian, arise from Sturm's having in mind the needs of his own gymnasium, whereas *The Scholemaster* is "a courtier, not an academician." Sturm is more willing to let his pupils speak Latin early, provided the masters guide their conversation with proper care. He has greater respect for arithmetic and astronomy, since, as rector of a boys' school, he must consider the practical requirements of his pupils, who are destined not exclusively for the court but for a variety of occupations. And since he is dealing with crowded classrooms rather than the chambers of the privileged few, he does not stress so much, though he also approves, continual exercise in double translation. In the grammar school there are simply too many boys, at too many different stages of learning, for this commendable method of instruction to be practicable.[30]

Otherwise, Sturm and Ascham are as close in their aims and theories as they were in their epistolary friendship; both emphasize *bene dicere* equally with, and in effect more strenuously than, *bene vivere*. This preoccupation with eloquence characterizes the writing of no earlier English humanist. For Ascham's adoption of Sturm's viewpoint is complete: that knowledge without eloquence is of no value, and that wherever there is indifference to manner of expression, sound doctrine tends to be displaced by frivolity, captiousness, and heresy.[31] Thus the writings of the two friends, less broadly philosophical and more concerned with method than the educational treatises of other well-known humanists, have sometimes been criticized for unduly stressing the value of acquiring a Latinity cut from the Ciceronian pattern. Yet if their vision appears constricted by such close attention to the practical, their influence on pedagogical thinking proved to be the greater, for good as well as bad, precisely because they did condescend to grapple with specific questions of method.

IV

The principal topic of the second book of *The Scholemaster*, as Ascham had reported in his final letter to Sturm, is the doctrine of imitation. As Ascham turns from the more general psychological and ethical concerns of Book One to his method of teaching Latin, he lists "six ways appointed by the best learned men, for the learning of tongues and increase of eloquence," namely, *translatio linguarum, paraphrasis, metaphrasis, epitome, imitatio,* and *declamatio*.[32] Although he undertakes to evaluate all of these except *declamatio*, he agrees with Cicero that the two best are the closely related exercises of *translatio linguarum* for the younger pupils and *imitatio* for more advanced students.[33] The other steps, he believes, are "fitter for the master than the scholar" (III, 174), and when they do profit one's style, they do so precisely when they most closely resemble the exercise of imitation. *Paraphrasis* becomes nothing other than imitation whenever the scholar alters "the composition, form, and order" of the original (III, 183), for imitation is never mere copying but rather similar treatment of dissimilar material or dissimilar treatment of similar material (III, 214). *Metaphrasis,* turning verse into prose or prose into verse, tends to become imitation when it is done with imagination, as in Plato's rendering of Chryses' oration at the opening of the *Iliad* into prose in the third book of the *Republic* (III, 193–95). Further, in suggesting that his friend Osorio might profitably discipline his own exuberant style by epitomizing passages of Demosthenes in "strait, fast, and temperate" Latin, Ascham again is recommending something that resembles imitation (III, 204). Even double translation necessarily involves imitation, since the works of Cicero provide the standards of correct expression.

Once the student, therefore, has attained some proficiency through much *translatio linguarum*, imitation is the means to "bring forth more learning and breed up truer judgment, than any other exercise that can be used" (III, 216). Ascham defines imitation as "a faculty to express lively and perfectly that example which ye go about to follow. And of itself it is large and wide; for all the works of nature, in a manner, be examples for art to follow" (III, 210). He is careful to distinguish the kind of rhetorical imitation with which he is concerned from the *mimésis* of the dramatic poet; the latter he calls a "fair lively painted picture of the life of every degree of man," an art that "doth not much belong at this time to our purpose." He is concerned rather with imitation in the sense of following "for learning of tongues and sciences, the best authors" and, having "determined whether you will follow one or more, to know perfectly, and which way, to follow that one; in what place, by what mean and order; by what tools and instruments ye shall do it; by what skill and judgment ye shall truly discern whether ye follow rightly or no" (III, 213–14).

Although *The Scholemaster* breaks off in the middle of the discussion, it is not difficult to determine where Ascham stands on the issue of following one or more models. There can be no question that in doctrine, though not necessarily in his own vernacular or even his own Latin practice, he inclines toward a rather strict Ciceronianism. Nannius, it is true, had commended him for avoiding in his letters the "scrupulous anxiety" to be purely Ciceronian that had attenuated the style of so many of their contemporaries (I, 360). Again, Ascham's analyses of the styles of Terence and Plautus, Varro, Sallust, and Caesar, as well as the apparent effort to keep his definitions neutral, might seem to place him among the compromisers, or even the "liberals" in the Renaissance controversy over the imitation of Cicero: "Here riseth amongst proud and envious wits a great controversy: whether one, or many, are to be followed; and if one, who is that one; Seneca, Cicero, Sallust, or Caesar, and so forth, in Greek and Latin."[34]

In the very next sentence, however, he betrays his own preference. Once it has been "determined whether you will follow one or more," the question is "which way to follow that one." The slip places Ascham

undoubtedly among those who would recommend a single model—
Cicero. Hence, as he weighs the merits and deficiencies of style in
Cicero's contemporaries, he does so mainly in order to win the reader
over to the viewpoint that only one complete pattern of excellence has
been left from the best age of Latin prose. He grants that Varro and
Sallust are admirable in some, and Caesar in all, respects. Unfortunately, they have survived only in fragments; their remains are "like
broken jewels" or beautiful but detached limbs of eloquence. But of
Cicero's work, posterity has inherited a corpus with "a perfect head, a
whole body, forward and backward, arms, and legs, and all" (III, 274).
If the scholar, moreover, were to combine with the exercise of imitating
his writings diligent inquiry into Cicero's own manner of following his
favorite Greek models, "what perfect knowledge of both the tongues,
what ready and pithy utterance in all matters, what right and deep
judgment in all kind of learning would follow, is scarce credible to be
believed" (III, 227). Thus it behooves everyone to regard Cicero as the
principal, if not indeed the sole, pattern of all true eloquence.

One may also note that among the numerous authors to whom he
had turned in the course of writing this portion of *The Scholemaster*,
Ascham cites with most evident approval those controversialists and
writers on imitation who advocate a pure, some even a rather servile,
type of Ciceronianism. He is excessively annoyed at Quintilian for suggesting that there are authors who have excelled Cicero in some
things. He sides with Paolo Cortesi, a strict though by no means foolish
Ciceronian, against the more liberal views of Angelo Poliziano; with
Pietro Bembo against Gianfrancesco Pico's insistence that good writing
is to be imitated wherever it may be found. He implies that Guillaume
Budé's rough and obscure style may have stemmed from "over-much
misliking the imitation of Tully."

With none of the authors whom he cites was the issue ever whether
one should imitate Cicero; it was simply whether he alone among the
Romans was worthy to be followed. That is why Ascham, and most
contemporary humanists would have responded in the same manner,
found Peter Ramus's iconoclasm in regard to Cicero almost beyond
belief. On the other hand, Ascham seems well aware that he greatly
exaggerates the "anti-Ciceronian" sentiments of some of the people
with whom he disagrees; he tries, by way of compensation, to gloss
over the very real differences in the views of Erasmus and Christophe
de Longueil, represented in Erasmus's dialogue *Ciceronianus* (1528),

watershed of the long-protracted controversy. According to Ascham, the only difference between these two men, the most notoriously slavish and the most independent in spirit of sixteenth-century Ciceronians, is that Longueil "seemeth to give over-much, the other over-little, to him whom they both best loved, and chiefly allowed of all others."

Everywhere the emotion of Ascham's language gives him away. The writers on the question with whom he is most sympathetic are Melanchthon, Camerarius, and Sturm, all three of whom agreed in principle with Erasmus's judgments against the uncritical "servilists" and yet by their own teaching and example showed that they were in favor of a stricter Ciceronianism. He praises Melanchthon for handling imitation "learnedly and truly"; Camerarius, though "somewhat confusedly, and with over rough a style," had written of it "largely with a learned judgment"; and Sturm had treated it "far best of all, in mine opinion, that ever took this matter in hand." Sturm alone "hath most learnedly declared, who is to be followed, what is to be followed; and the best point of all, by what way and order true imitation is rightly to be exercised."[35] Cicero, indeed, is diligently studied in judicious selections by boys of every age in his Strasbourg gymnasium; yet even Sturm, regrettably, has published far too little on this subject. In the absence of his long-awaited *De Imitatione Oratoria*, Ascham has been compelled to search everywhere for examples to illustrate Sturm's doctrines, since everyone knows how precepts "without applying unto them the imitation of examples, be hard, dry and cold, and therefore barren, unfruitful, and unpleasant" (III, 231). So urgently needed is a treasury of good examples of imitation that Ascham has even thought of compiling one himself, "if God do lend me life, with health, free leisure and liberty," to accomplish the task (III, 230). This wish, of course, God did not grant, and Sturm's work did not appear for another six years.

If the second part of *The Scholemaster* contained merely this long and ardent plea for double translation and imitation as the royal road to Latin eloquence, one might, recalling Bacon's scorn for the "infinite and curious pains" expended by Ascham and Sturm upon "that delicate and polished kind of learning," dismiss it as a curiosity in the history of pedagogical theorizing.[36] For in effect the emphasis on grammatical techniques, though justified by Ascham's preoccupation with the elementary stages of education, does obscure the avowed end of the process, preparing the pupil for those serious university studies that lead to learned piety and thence to worthy service of God and one's prince

(III, 167). Yet scattered among the pages of Book Two are incidental comments on literature that give Ascham a place in the earlier history of English literary criticism and prompted Spingarn to call him "not only the first English man of letters, but also the first English classicist."[37]

Everything that Ascham has to say about literature, however, grows directly out of his abiding concern with imitation. For the Renaissance, the doctrine was all-inclusive; it was the means by which man acquired every art and science. Thus, in his extensive search for notable examples of the practice Ascham did not confine himself to the poets and orators, but turned also to the writings of historians (III, 229) and philosophers (III, 231). Like most of his contemporaries, moreover, he did not clearly differentiate poetics from grammar and rhetoric so that, in approaching literary works, he is interested primarily in their formal and rhetorical aspects: diction, phrasing, metrics, and, above all, style and decorum.

The Scholemaster embodies, therefore, a number of neoclassical opinions that Ascham must be credited with disseminating, though in some instances ineffectually and even wrong-headedly, among his countrymen. In the drama, for example, he finds that "the Grecians, Sophocles and Euripides, far overmatch our Seneca in Latin, namely in Οἰκονομία et *Decoro*: although Seneca's elocution and verse be very commendable for his time."[38] In part this judgment, sound as it is, simply reflects the contemporary snobbishness among the initiated about things Greek. Yet it also represents, as the expression "our Seneca" reveals, an effort to suggest better models than the main classical source to which native tragedians were looking for inspiration. The real touchstone for tragedy, as Ascham, Cheke, and Watson had long since decided in their conversations at St. John's, remains "Aristotle's precepts and Euripides' examples" (III, 241).

Although Ascham does not himself get at the essence of Aristotle's criticism, he is noteworthy as the first English writer to mention the *Poetics.* In at least two respects, moreover, he follows Aristotle against the main current of Renaissance literary opinion. He regards Euripides, rather than the more formally perfect Sophocles, as the most tragic of the dramatists,[39] and he considers tragedy, though for didactic rather than artistic reasons, superior to the epic as a literary form.[40] Yet when he tries to formulate his own definition of *mimésis,* he apparently confuses the Platonic and Aristotelian conceptions of the term. Thus, if the discussions at St. John's mark the first sign of interest in the *Poetics* in England, it remained for Sidney, profiting from the earlier tentative explorations in *The Scholemaster*, to provide a clearer understanding and application of Aristotelian principles to the task of criticism.

Even in the passage on the deficiencies of contemporary drama it is manifest that Ascham's standards for poetic excellence are primarily metrical and linguistic. Although as a humanist he always takes into account the moral value of literary works, more immediately important to him than the matter of an author is his manner. One of his main objections to a play by a certain anonymous fellow Cantabrigian is that the writer "began the *Protasis* with *trochaeis octonariis*; which kind of verse, as it is but seldom and rare in tragedies, so is it never used, save only in *Epitasi*; when the tragedy is highest and hottest, and full of greatest troubles" (III, 241). Watson, by way of contrast, showed himself to be more scrupulous about adhering to strict formal principles, and "would never suffer yet his Absalon to go abroad, and that only, because *in locis paribus, Anapaestus* is twice or thrice used instead of *Iambus*." When he turns to Plautus and Terence, Ascham finds the verse "very mean" because "of the time wherein they wrote" (III, 248), and the matter "base stuff for that scholar that should become hereafter either a good minister in religion, or a civil gentleman in service of his prince and country" (III, 247). Yet having registered these objections, he would still have selections from these two comic dramatists read for the excellence of their language (III, 246). The nondramatic poets he approaches from much the same standpoint. Pindar and Horace are worthy of study, but mainly because they can be set together to illustrate the principles of successful imitation. Catullus receives a nod of approval, again not for his matter (III, 223), but as "deserving well of the Latin tongue" (III, 259).

This preoccupation with the poets as texts for the study of language typifies vernacular literary criticism in Ascham's time. For although they did reflect upon the metaphysical assumptions underlying the art of poetry and upon its value as an instrument of ethical instruction and persuasion, Renaissance critics, searching for suitable language and forms to express the self-confident new spirit of their age, were interested mainly in such questions as the functions and proprieties of the genres and, above all, in prosody and language. One need only cite the program of the Pléiade, as epitomized in DuBellay's *Défense et illustration de la langue française*, to demonstrate the importance of these issues. In Elizabethan England, nearly every treatise on the art of poetry centers upon, or at least eventually comes around to, discussion of metrics, the genres, and the suitability of the vernacular for great literary expression. This generalization is as true for Sidney's more largely philosophical *Defence* as it is for Gascoigne's rather technical *Certain Notes of Instruction* or Puttenham's *The Art of English Poesy*. Hence, the second book of *The Scholemaster* points the direction to be taken by an entire generation of English literary critics.

Ascham's discussion of the meters of Plautus and Terence leads to his most famous, if not necessarily most salutary, contribution to Elizabethan literary theory and practice. In meter and verse, he warns, the two Roman dramatists are not to be followed because they lived before Virgil and Horace, "by right imitation of the perfect Grecians, had brought poetry to perfectness also in the Latin tongue" (III, 248–49). He had often discussed this subject with Watson and Cheke; they had agreed that contemporary English versifiers, like the wisest Roman poets, should "follow the best examples" rather than that "rude beggarly rhyming, brought first into Italy by Goths and Huns." Though otherwise commendable, the poetry of Chaucer, Thomas Norton of Bristol, Wyatt, and Surrey was marred by their having "been carried by time and custom to content themselves with that barbarous and rude rhyming" (III, 250). Surrey, it is true, had wisely avoided rhyme in his partial translation of the *Aeneid*, as had King Philip II's secretary, Gonsalvo Perez, in his Spanish version of the *Odyssey* (Antwerp, 1553). Yet neither poet, in Ascham's view, wrote true meters. Surrey's blank verse did have "just number, and even feet," but Ascham, failing to recognize that stress was the principle, objected to such verse as having "feet without joints; that is to say, not distinct by true quantity of syllables" (III, 254).

This argument that vernacular poetry should be written, after the custom of the ancients, in quantitative measures, led to considerable speculation and experiment until the turn of the century, when the Campion–Daniel "debate" over rhyme marked its end as a living issue. Nor was the controversy, in spite of the many prosodic horrors it produced in the interest of the antirhyming party, the purely academic curiosity that some literary historians have taken it to be.[41] The theorizing and experimentation did lead to deeper understanding of the principles governing English versification and to intelligent substitution of fit native equivalents for standard Greek and Roman metrical forms. Jonson's truncated tetrameter couplets constitute, in the best sense of the word, effective imitation of Catullus's hendecasyllabics, whose grace and lightness can scarcely be rendered otherwise, certainly not in an eleven-syllable English line. And in the apology for the most familiar example of substitution of all, Milton's use of blank verse for an heroic poem in *Paradise Lost*, the influence of Ascham's original observations may be clearly discerned.

Ascham was not, of course, so perceptive in the matter as were the great poets who came after him, and one must admit that in part his championing of classical meters merely reflects the humanistic preference for things ancient over what were believed to be the "gross inventions of a monkish and barbarous age." Still, it should be remembered that in 1568 he could have found precious little in the native tradition of verse that he might fairly have adjudged "smooth and pure." The principles of Chaucer's versification had been lost, while even today Wyatt's are not fully understood, and "there was," as one modern critic has noted, "no general understanding of the structure of English verse which would enable a humanist to formulate clearly the essential difference in mechanism between the native verse he despised and that which he wished to supersede it."[42] In all the extant English criticism of the period, moreover, with the exception of Puttenham and Campion and an obscure passage in Gascoigne, practically no reference occurs, not even in Daniel's *Defence of Ryme* or in the apology prefixed to *Paradise Lost*, to *accent* in the modern technical sense and as the native equivalent to classical quantity.[43]

Although his own scattered efforts at making English quantitative verses are undistinguished, Ascham is by no means slavishly uncritical in his proposal to acclimatize classical meters. He is actually, as the Spenser–Harvey correspondence shows, less dogmatic and uncompromising than Spenser at least seems to be; oddly enough, it is the academic dons Ascham and Harvey who exhibit the greater moderation in the matter.[44] Ascham shows his awareness, too, of the differences between English and Greek that render certain meters more appropriate to one tongue than the other. Dactyllic hexameter, for instance, "doth rather trot and hobble, than run smoothly in our English tongue; yet I am sure our English tongue will receive *carmen iambicum* as naturally as either Greek or Latin" (III, 251).

The specimens of English quantitative verse sprinkled throughout the pages of *Toxophilus* and *The Scholemaster* prove sufficiently the astuteness of his observation. In *Toxophilus,* turning a pentameter line into a limping English hexameter, he renders Propertius's "anseris et tutum voce fuisse Iovem" (*Elegies*, III, iii, 12) as follows:

Thieves on a | night had | stolen Jupi | ter, had a | goose not a | kekede

(II, 125).

In this line, and in others where he tries to produce hexameters that ignore accent in favor of supposed quantities, the verse indeed hobbles:

What thing | wants quiet | and merry | rest, en | dures but a | small while

(II, 15).

The English language simply does not allow such ignoring of accent.[45]

Although he would not have recognized the fact, when accent and quantity coincide, Ascham's experimental verses come off somewhat better:

Twang quoth the | bow, and | twang quoth the | string, out | quickly the | shaft flew.[46]

This is even more apparent in his iambic lines, in which, though he still does not prove himself a poet, he does find it easier to achieve a certain smoothness. The most creditable example is perhaps a couplet on the herb *moly*, given to Odysseus by Athena to protect him from the enchantments of Circe:

No mor | tal man, | with sweat | of brow | or toil | of mind,

But on | ly God, | who can | do all, | that herb | doth find.[47]

Ascham's comparative moderation as a proponent of classical measures may be concluded from two characteristics of these lines. He prefers, because of what he has said about the different genius of each language, to convert the original dactyllic hexameters of the *Odyssey* into iambic meter, and rather inconsistently with his strong protestations, does not even eschew rhyme. This effort, along with a few others in *The Scholemaster*, suggests that he would not necessarily proscribe rhyme if English poets would also endeavor to observe the principles of quantitative measure.

It may seem incredible that such limping hexameters and crawling *senarii* could be taken seriously by his contemporaries as specimens of "true versifying." In 1577, however, Timothy Kendall printed ten of these choice bits from *Toxophilus* and *The Scholemaster* in his *Flowers of Epigrams*, a fairly important anthology of translations of classical and Neo-Latin verse. Poor as Ascham's illustrations are, they mark the beginnings of an Elizabethan eagerness to experiment with all kinds of classical verse forms that reaches its climax with the so-called Areopagi of Sidney, Spenser, and Sir Edward Dyer, and especially in the complex meters employed in several songs of the *Arcadia*. Ascham's lead was also followed in the translations of Virgil made by Abraham Fleming, Abraham Fraunce, William Webbe, and Richard Stanyhurst.[48] Within a few years of his death, English verse was to evolve its own distinct formal principles. But his raising of the issues, though only in a digression from his concern with imitation as a pedagogical device, helped to introduce one more element of neoclassicism into Elizabethan literary theory and poetic practice.

Of perhaps greater immediate significance is his recommended procedure for analyzing literary passages and the consequent implications, as he tests classical authors by means of it, for the stylistic development of English prose. This method he derives, as he does most of his critical standards and opinions, from Sturm and Cheke.[49] Pointing out that "it is no low point of learning and judgment" to be capable of distinguishing various kinds of skillful imitation from inept counterfeits, he guarantees the effectiveness of the method when one applies it to parallel passages from, say, Virgil and Homer, or Cicero and Demosthenes:

1. Tully retaineth thus much of the matter, these sentences, these words.
2. This and that he leaveth out; which he doth wittily to this end and purpose.
3. This he addeth here.
4. This he diminisheth here.
5. This he ordereth thus, with placing that here, not there.
6. This he altereth and changeth, either in property of words, in form of sentence, in substance of the matter, or in one or other convenient circumstance of the author's present purpose (III, 215).

Close examination of these criteria, and of Ascham's application of them to those Latin authors whose style he criticizes in the last pages of *The Scholemaster*, reveals that he is no mere source-hunter or mouther of ready-made critical tags. It is true that he does repeat a number of stock opinions, derived from Camerarius and others, on the prose of Varro and Caesar. But he is also concerned, as the last five points suggest, with determining exactly what constitutes intelligent imitation rather than slavish following of one's model in a given instance. He is impatient with mere citation of literary parallels unaccompanied by judicious scrutiny of the "ends or purposes" for which an imitator alters the materials he adopts from his sources. Thus, although he expresses gratitude to Bartolomeo Ricci for the wealth of examples of imitation gathered in his *De imitatione libri tres* (Venice, 1545), he blames him for not applying such a critical procedure to the texts that he provides (III, 223–25).

As Ascham goes about measuring writers in various genres with this method of Sturm and Cheke, he makes apparent that he means by eloquence a true "Athenian" sense of the right way to express every kind of matter, neither exceeding nor falling short of a just measure. This skill, however, is beyond the capacity of the beginner, and even the master will find it difficult "always learnedly and perfectly" to form a correct judgment of the fittest kind of style, or to imitate it effectively. Yet if he wants to be eloquent himself, or to be capable of judging eloquence, the scholar must learn "how to alter what is inappropriate; change what is awry; fill in what is wanting; remove that which impedes; blot out whatever is inane . . . prune the turgid; elevate what is low; repress the exuberant; arrange what is disorderly."[50] He must recognize also that each genre has its own peculiar structural and stylistic qualities "in framing of sentences, handling of arguments, and use of right form, figure, and number, proper and fit for every matter." Whoever has learned to note "diligently" the differences among classical authors and genres in these respects "shall easily perceive what is fit, and *decorum* in every one, to the true use of perfect Imitation" (III, 240).

Since what would have been the climax of the discussion, an examination of Cicero's style, is lacking, one cannot say what might have resulted from Ascham's applying Cheke's method of analysis to this most venerated of models. Possibly idolatry and the overwhelming weight of earlier critical authority would have led him to quite value-less repetition of commonplace judgments. One must turn, therefore, to the passage on Sallust as the best illustration of how the method worked and of the standards Ascham proposed for excellence in literary prose.

The matter of the passage is entirely Cheke's, or so, by reproducing a supposed earlier conversation with his old friend and mentor, Ascham wishes to suggest; if this is the case, it provides a fine illustration of how

Cheke actually applied the theories about language that he mentions in his famous letter to Hoby, and it shows him to be a fairly ingenious and perceptive critic of classical literary styles. It also gives a clue to Ascham's own ideals for English prose as they had evolved from Cheke's and from the earlier example of his own *Toxophilus*. Sallust, according to Cheke, was "a wise and worthy writer," but, as comparing his works with Cicero's will show, "not very fit for young men to learn out of him the purity of the Latin tongue; because he was not the purest in propriety of words, nor choicest in aptness of phrases, nor the best in framing of sentences; and therefore is his writing . . . neither plain for the matter, nor sensible for men's understanding" (III, 264). He does not, in other words, meet the criterion for "plain and sensible utterance" upheld by Ascham throughout *The Scholemaster*. His vocabulary and manner of phrasing are marred by a certain outlandishness, a smell of the inkhorn, and "an uncontented care to write better than he could." Not satisfied with the everyday language of men, he hunts curiously after neologisms and archaisms and hence expresses his matter "artificially after too learned a sort, as Thucydides doth in his orations."[51]

The many obscure passages in Thucydides and Sallust, according to Cheke, came about because both men wrote after long terms abroad that caused them to lose touch with the common speech of their native lands. Sallust, besides, used poor judgment in choosing models and was further handicapped by immuring himself in his study rather than exercising his speech in the forum. Thus, even when his vocabulary is free of deliberate affectations, it betrays an unidiomatic, Grecian manner of phrasing (III, 268–71).

Here is the argument for pure, native speech reflected back upon the classical tongues from which Cheke and his disciples had in the first place derived it. In Latin as in the vernacular, the exotic and the erudite are to be avoided. An eloquent style is to be reached not by the high and adventurous Asiatic road but by the clean and measured path of Attic expression. George Saintsbury, regarding the attitude of Cheke and Ascham as salutary for Elizabethan prose in its early, inchoate stage, looked upon this particular passage, though he recognized in it certain deficiencies of taste, as an important step toward maturity in English literary criticism. In it he discerned a perceptiveness and skill in precise critical analysis that was "advanced, in some directions, beyond anything that classical or medieval times can show."[52] Even more than in his comments on poetry and drama, it is here in the criteria for prose—correctness, propriety, polish, clarity, and careful imitation of the finest models—that Ascham demonstrates why he has been adjudged one of the earliest English neoclassicists.[53]

V

In the prose of his own treatise, he tries to measure up to the ideal of "plain and sensible utterance." This phrase should not be taken as implying that Ascham had finally adopted Cheke's standards without modification or that he was simply concerned, as he had been in *Toxophilus*, with making a rude and barbarous tongue fit at least for workmanlike and comprehensible, if inelegant, writing. In the twenty years since *Toxophilus*, his hopes and ambitions for his native language had risen, and he could now assert to Sturm that whatever crudities existed in *The Scholemaster* were due to his own incapacity rather than to any inherent deficiencies in English. "Nor yet am I myself so ill-disposed towards our language," he writes, "that I will not believe it to be fully capable of all the rhetorical adornments of both diction and thought; or this subject so dry and insignificant that it could not have been treated in far more eloquent English, if it had occurred to some artist such as was Cheke, or as are Smith and Haddon, who are still among us" (II, 176). Even though he could think of no worthy native precedents and consequently did admit the necessity of falling back for the present on Latin and Greek models, he had become convinced that eloquence was now within the reach of the vernacular author.[54]

He had not altogether neglected stylistic ornament in his two earlier English works, but believing native prose at the time to be in but a rudimentary stage of evolution, he had concentrated in them on proper ordering and clear expression of his matter. He had demonstrated in *Toxophilus* that his mother tongue was adequate in vocabulary and in grammatical and logical structure for effective prose discourse. In *The Scholemaster*, assured now of his control over diction and arrangement, he gave more attention to finding ways of "exornating" his periods. For the sentence, besides being the single "mindfull" that the senses can readily admit, is also the unit with which the rhetorician deals under the heading of *elocutio*, or stylistic adornment. On the whole, because *The Scholemaster* is designed primarily to set forth the guiding principles and method of an art, the prose remains workmanlike and unpretentious. But a considerable amount of ornament does occur, especially in passages in which Ascham evidently regarded heightening the style as necessary to persuade the reader on some important issue or to impress some ethical principle upon his memory. In effect, this is what he means by "plain and sensible utterance"—a forthright, everyday manner of speaking that nevertheless makes use of sharp visual imagery and harmonies of sound to strike forcefully through the eyes and ears upon what Sidney was later aptly to call "the sight of the soul."[55]

Ascham's imagery, therefore, since its function is both to instruct and to move, not merely to dazzle the senses as do the far-fetched images of the euphuists, is taken from daily experience. "Every man seeth," he says, for example, in speaking of childhood as the best time for learning, ". . . new wax is best for printing, new clay fittest for working, new-shorn wool aptest for soon and surest dyeing, new-fresh flesh for good and durable salting."[56] Again, in deploring the "ill choice of wits for learning" by English parents, he observes that "young scholars be chosen commonly, as young apples be chosen by children in a fair garden about St. James's tide: a child will choose a sweeting, because it is presently fair and pleasant, and refuse a runnet, because it is then green, hard, and sour; when the one, if it be eaten, doth breed both worms and ill humours; the other, if it stand his time, be ordered and kept as it should, is wholesome of itself, and helpeth to the good digestion of other meats" (III, 102–3). In each quotation the neatly schematic phrasing obviously adds to the force and memorableness of the image; as the image is intended to strike the mind's eye, so the figured arrangements of words are designed to strike through the ear upon the memory. In succeeding phrases, therefore, element is balanced against element, somewhat more flexibly in the second example cited, in more exact parallel in the first. Each phrase is carefully placed, out of regard for function as well as harmony, in order to define unmistakably the relationships of ideas within the sentence.

Unfortunately, he does not always show such discretion in his use of figures of speech. From the kinds of schemes and tropes he favors, it is clear that Ascham was an admirer, despite Plato's warnings against their pitfalls, of the so-called "Gorgianic figures," and that his main classical model was not Cicero but rather the Athenian orator and rhetorician Isocrates. Again and again in *The Scholemaster* the reader encounters such artificially designed antitheses and parallels as "not hasty in making, but constant in keeping" (III, 101) and "great love to learning, good lust to labour" (III, 110), or such elaborately schematized characterizations as that of "quick wits," who are "in desire, new-fangled; in purpose unconstant; light to promise anything, ready to forget everything, both benefit and injury; and thereby neither fast to friend, nor fearful to foe: inquisitive of every trifle, not secret in the greatest affairs; bold with any person; busy in every matter; soothing such as be present, nipping any that is absent" (III, 98). In passages like these, one may recognize all the schemes usually associated with the name of the rhetorician Gorgias: *isocolon* (equal or nearly equal numbers of syllables in corresponding members of a sentence); *parison* (exact balance, word for word, of syntax within corresponding phrases); and *paramoion* (resemblance in sound, through such devices as alliteration and similar endings, of corresponding words within sentence elements). These figures, which occur in varying degree in nearly all classical writers of prose, Ascham had inherited both in fee-simple from the ancients and by entail through the works of the church fathers and the pulpit oratory of medieval and Tudor preachers.[57]

Why Ascham, who was certainly aware of the moderation with which the best classical authors had used these figures and who had used them with moderation himself in his earlier Latin and English works, should have introduced them so extensively into *The Scholemaster* is not fully clear. Besides Plato, contemporary humanists like Erasmus and Wilson had objected to excessive dependence on the schemes. "Overmuch," says Wilson with reference to frequent recurrence in prose of similar sounding members, "(as all men know) was never good yet."[58] The only reasonable explanation is that however well Ascham knew the threat to real eloquence in their immoderate use, he sincerely believed that these Gorgianic figures might serve to adorn his style and might also render his utterances more vivid to the senses and hence to the memory of his reader. Quite often, it must be granted, the resulting harmonies strike delightfully upon the ear, but sometimes the verbal display is painful rather than pleasant. Then one may regret that Ascham and his immediate contemporaries were inclined to see reality in terms of such sharply defined antitheses and correspondences, and one may long for some of the qualification, asymmetry, and suspension of thought that characterize the prose of the period of Donne and Sir Thomas Browne.

At one time scholars were inclined to attribute the Elizabethan admiration for the tricksy phrase to Ascham's influence, alleging that he had passed on his Isocratean manner of expression to his literary stepchildren, John Lyly and the other euphuists. A number of critical studies, however, have since shown that Lyly and his imitators, though obviously somewhat indebted to Ascham, derived their stylistic peculiarities from other sources and that the characteristics of euphuism differ markedly from the features of Isocrates' prose that were imitated by Elyot and Ascham.[59] The testimony of Gabriel Harvey, in many ways an astute judge of contemporary prose, lends considerable authority to this view. To Ascham, whom he regarded for his Latin style as the best English Ciceronian of his time, Harvey also applied the epithet "noster Isocrates."[60] And in his pamphlet controversy with Thomas Nashe, he declares that "Sir John Cheke's style was the honey-bee of Plato, and Mr. Ascham's period the siren of Isocrates. His, and his breath, the balm and spikenard of the delightfullest Tempe."[61] One sentence of Ascham's, therefore, is worth "the tricksiest page in Euphues or Pap-Hatchet."[62] Nashe has no comparable artistic restraint; "It is for Cheke or Ascham to stand leveling of colons, or squaring of periods, by measure and number: his [Nashe's] pen is like a spigot, and the winepress a dullard to his inkpress."[63]

The mention of "leveling of colons, or squaring of periods, by measure and number," in other words, a style characterized by carefully wrought sentence patterns, shows why Harvey regards Ascham, but not Lyly or Nashe, as a literary descendant of Isocrates. For the Isocratean sentence is never loose or ill-planned. Its phrases and clauses (*cola*) are neatly articulated, and their relationships are always kept clear through balance and antithesis of thought and language, the result being a symmetrical whole. Isocrates pays close attention to rhythm, especially through *isocolon*, but otherwise uses Gorgianic figures quite sparingly. His unerring propriety of diction (hence Harvey's taunting reference to the exuberant Nashe's "inkpress"), by which everyday language is arranged into graceful phrases and sentences, achieves an "agreeable smoothness" of style, or as Ascham labels it, *suavitatem* (III, 227).

Thanks to Cheke, Ascham had long been an admirer of Isocrates' orations (I, 24) and had used them to exercise the young Elizabeth in double translation (I, 192; III, 180). During his years at court, moreover, he had read through Jovita Rapicio's *De Numero Oratorio*, which contains an extensive discussion of how Isocrates handles the rhetorical schemes and the harmonies of language.[64] Cicero himself had credited Isocrates with writing the first artistic prose in Greek, an aim that Ascham was now setting for himself in English. Finally, Sir Thomas Elyot had observed in the preface to his English version of Isocrates' *Ad Nicoclem* "that the form of speaking, used of the Greeks, called in Greek, and also in Latin, *Phrasis*, much nearer approacheth to that, which at this day we use, than the order of the Latin tongue: I mean in the sentences, and not in the words: which I doubt not shall be affirmed by them, who, sufficiently instructed in all the said three tongues, shall with a good judgment read this work."[65]

What Ascham derived stylistically from Isocrates may be illustrated by his epitome of a passage in Isocrates' *Areopagiticus* (37–49) concerning the education of young men in Athens:

The city was not more careful to see their children well taught, than to see their young men well governed; which they brought to pass, not so much by common law, as by private discipline. For they had more regard that their youth by good order should not offend, than how by law they might be punished; and if offence were committed, there was neither way to hide it, nor hope of pardon for it. Good natures were not so much openly praised, as they were secretly marked and watchfully regarded, lest they should leese the goodness they had. Therefore in schools of singing and dancing, and other honest exercises, governors were appointed more diligent to oversee their good manners, than their masters were to teach them any learning. It was some shame to a young man to be seen in the open market; and if for business he passed through it, he did it with a marvellous modesty and bashful fashion. To eat or drink in a tavern was not only a shame, but also punishable in a young man. To contrary, or to stand in terms with an old man, was more heinous than in some place to rebuke and scold with his own father (III, 131–32).

In its total effect Ascham's summary faithfully renders the spirit of Isocrates and, insofar as English can substitute for Greek, his rhythms, his fondness for *isocolon*, his balanced and antithetical manner of thought and phrasing. Most significantly, it lacks the other elaborate figures of sound with which *The Scholemaster* abounds elsewhere and which one usually associates with Elizabethan prose before Sidney.

Ascham's contribution to prose style, then, was to point out and illustrate various means of molding the sentence into a more harmonious and orderly unit of artistic expression. His attempt to render the vernacular eloquent was not entirely successful because he does tend to overwork the Gorgianic figures in the most obvious situations.

As a consequence, although one may no longer call him without qualification an immediate begetter of euphuism, the force of his example
undoubtedly lent authority to stylistic experimentation and may even
have led to some of the schematic, though certainly not the metaphorical, excesses of Lyly and his followers. At the same time Ascham,
for those who knew how to profit from his example, pointed the way to
a firmer and more graceful manner of expression. Saintsbury observes
that his contribution lay not so much in supplying ornate patterns of
phrasing as in regularizing the plain vernacular style, giving it "good
working and fair ornamental qualities," and providing the foundation
for, though not a remarkable demonstration of, the rhythmical possibilities inherent in the language.[66] Saintsbury also believes that the verbal
experimentation in *The Scholemaster*, despite its obvious imperfections,
tended "to establish a chastened, moderately classical, pattern of writing," not without significant effect on the prose of Richard Hooker and
even Ben Jonson.[67]

Recognition of Ascham's accomplishment came quickly.[68] Harvey
could think of no finer compliment for a discourse of Buchanan's than
to remark that "for elegant style" it approached the writing of "our
Ascham."[69] Even Nashe consented in one pamphlet, albeit somewhat
facetiously, to curb his galloping pen "and expostulate the matter more
tamely" out of respect for his fellow-Johnian Ascham.[70] The anonymous
author of the Parnassus plays ranked him with those "sweet birds" of
rhetoric whose words "to good ears make tuneful melody."[71] In his
Directions for Speech and Style, John Hoskyns asserted that his own
mastery of the principles of writing owed much to Ascham's example.[72]
And long afterwards, Samuel Johnson not only praised his "knowledge and eloquence frequently" but, according to his friend Sir John
Hawkins, "formed his style through study of Ascham and others."[73]

Among Ascham's immediate successors, the one who seems to have
benefited most from both his critical views and his stylistic experimentation is Sidney.[74] Although his general debt to Ascham has usually been
admitted, little has been made of the specific relationship between *The
Defence of Poesy* and *The Scholemaster*. The affinity between the two
authors was recognized by Harvey, who, in dissociating Ascham from
the euphuists, constantly associates him with Sidney. He writes about
"Sweet Mr. Ascham, that was a flowing spring of humanity, and worthy
Sir Philip Sidney, that was a flourishing spring of nobility," and parallels
the "art" of Cheke and Ascham with the "wit" of Spenser and Sidney.[75]

Whereas Ascham hinted at the latent eloquence of English, Sidney first realized it in his *Defence of Poesy*. Their ideals for vernacular discourse are identical, but Sidney finds the truer harmonies of the English sentence, for he is a master craftsman, while Ascham is but a competent journeyman in prose. Both, as has already been suggested, stand in the main for "plain and sensible utterance." Thus Sidney defines literature as a teaching instrument because it can uniquely "possess the sight of the soul." Both men regard *elocutio* as subservient to this end. Both will have only clear and apt examples and metaphors; Sidney derides the extravagant figures of the euphuists for "rather overswaying the memory from the purpose whereto they were applied, than any while informing the judgment, already either satisfied, or by similitudes not to be satisfied."[76] The patterns and rhythms of Sidney's sentences show a debt to Ascham, but with a notable advance in restraint and subtlety. An example of the skill with which Sidney handles clauses of equal measure is his description of poetasters, who scribble "as if all the Muses were got with child to bring forth bastard poets, without any commission they do post over the banks of Helicon, until they make their readers more weary than post-horses."[77] Even more skillful is his account of the virtues of the poet, a passage which Sidney particularly wishes to impress upon the reader and in which he employs the schemes with a freedom and telling effect not matched by his predecessors. The poet "goeth hand in hand with Nature, not enclosed within the narrow warrant of her gifts, but freely ranging within the zodiac of his own wit." He makes it possible for men to comprehend the ideal in a way that nature itself cannot, "since our erected wit maketh us to know what perfection is and yet our infected will keepeth us from reaching unto it." Poetry is an art not "of lies, but of true doctrine; not of effeminateness, but of notable stirring of courage, not of abusing man's wit, but of strengthening man's wit, not banished, but honored by Plato."[78]

It seems clear from still further evidence that Ascham was a major influence upon Sidney and not simply another author in the general tradition out of which he came. The careful attention of both to proper ordering of their matter, making all topics, even digressions, contribute to the unity of the design, their provision of frequent summary and transitional passages, are exceptional in an age preoccupied with devices of ornament and not strong on organization.[79] Again, the fine anecdotal openings of both treatises, drawing the reader artfully and yet, as it were, offhandedly into the body of the discourse, suggest a similar capacity in their authors to "invent" new matter in the examples that they are imitating. Finally, Sidney's "characters" of the moral philosophers ("angry with any man in whom they see the foul fault of anger") and the historian (that "tyrant in table-talk") call to mind Ascham's earlier sketches of "antic" archers in *Toxophilus* or, more pertinently, that in *The Scholemaster* of the "graceless" courtier (III, 126–27).

These resemblances might seem to be merely the result of a common literary heritage were it not that several ideas expressed by Ascham reappear, in slightly modified form, in the *Defence*. The basis for Sidney's apology for literature on rhetorical grounds, that *oratio* is "next to *ratio*" among the gifts of men, reiterates a view tenaciously maintained by both Ascham and Sturm. Sidney shares Ascham's opinion that Buchanan is the best of contemporary tragedians, and likewise applies classical standards of decorum in his famous passage on the deficiencies of current English drama. He agrees that English verse, though he finds rhyme completely acceptable, may be written effectively in classical meters and exemplifies the principles in the *Arcadia*. Like Ascham, he recommends learning to write by "attentive translation" of whole passages and orations of Cicero and Demosthenes, rather than by keeping "paperbooks of their figures and phrases." Finally, he would have men master the whole art of eloquence by diligent imitation of the best models, rather than develop only the partial skill of verbal "exornation."[80]

If by later standards Ascham seems to be a long way from possessing artistic ease and assurance in his vernacular writings, one need only recall the primitive state of English prose in his time to understand why his work excited his contemporaries. He had already shown them in *Toxophilus* the economy of organizing the whole discourse; they were soon to learn from Lyly and Sidney how to compose the paragraph. In *The Scholemaster* Ascham called attention, as no one had before, to the artistic possibilities of the English sentence. Some Elizabethans ignored the lesson and others learned it badly, but he taught those who were alert how to achieve distinction in language by means of palpable imagery and pleasing arrangement of simple, current words. If not himself a classic author, Ascham proved nonetheless to be an influential schoolmaster not only to later educational theorists and practitioners but also to the oncoming generation of writers of English prose.

❧❧

CHAPTER TWELVE

Afterword

THE FORTUNES of Ascham's family after his death can be traced in some detail through legal documents and the extant correspondence of his eldest son Giles. On September 28, 1569, Margaret Ascham and Thomas Rampston, a gentleman whose father held the manor immediately to the north of the Aschams' Salisbury Hall, applied for a license to marry.[1] Rampston, a quarrelsome and litigious man, may have sought Margaret's hand partly for reasons of property, for he had often tried to extend the acreage of his own farm by encroachment upon Salisbury lands.[2] Marriage brought the territorial dispute to an end, with Rampston not only enjoying possession of Salisbury for the rest of his lifetime but also seeing it assured to his descendants through a daughter born of his union with Ascham's widow.[3]

Of Margaret little more is known. She bore Rampston at least two daughters and presumably devoted her energies to rearing her children and assuring future means of living for her large family by both marriages. In 1582 she secured for Giles, then a student at Cambridge, an annual pension of £18 16s. 2d. from the crown rent of Whittlesford Rectory, her lease having been renewed three years previously.[4] Her petition to Queen Elizabeth, asking that the grant be made for twenty-one years, specifies that she and Rampston had seven other children to provide for, of whom as many as six may have been hers by Ascham.[5] The precise date of her death is unknown. Probably it occurred after July 30, 1590, when her name appears in another document concerning Whittlesford.[6] Certainly it was before June 26, 1592, when she is mentioned in the records of the Prerogative Court of Canterbury as "now deceased."[7]

For each of Ascham's three sons, Giles, Dudley, and the posthumously born Thomas, the queen, perhaps with some feeling of remorse for not having looked after their father better, supplied pensions or other sources of income. From the correspondence of Giles it is evident that in prompting her to see to their needs Cecil continued to take the initiative. Giles, indeed, was especially well cared for. In 1573, Cecil recommended him for admission to Westminster School, where he came under the tuition of Grant, recently appointed headmaster (III, 294–95). The most significant result of their relationship was Grant's *vita* of Ascham and his edition of the Latin epistles, but an additional benefit for Giles was that in 1578 Grant and Cecil prompted the queen to provide him with a scholarship to Trinity College, Cambridge (I, cxi; III, 299). During the academic year 1582–83 he took his bachelor's degree and shortly thereafter was mandated to a fellowship.

Insight into Giles's character as well as information about his career may be gained from seven letters that he wrote to Cecil.[8] Like his father before him, he seems at times to have been forced to wait before enjoying what was rightfully his. In the first letter, written in February 1582, he begs for an overdue installment on his pension from Whittlesford. One may easily pity the orphaned student over the dilatoriness of the clerks of the Exchequer in making payments on the rolls. Subsequent petitions, however, tend to lessen one's sympathy. In 1583, when the queen ordered the fellows of Trinity to elect him to membership, they proved recalcitrant. Giles accordingly wrote twice to Cecil, begging him as chancellor of the university and as his father's dearest friend, to see that the royal mandate was carried out (III, 357–59). These letters reveal a disposition in Giles to trade to the utmost on his father's reputation and on Cecil's sense of obligation to the family. Never does he try to justify any request except in "the name of my father," and in one instance he gratuitously reminds Cecil how Roger, with his dying breath, had commended the family unto his care (III, 363).

Although Giles has left no evidence of his own deserving, each of his petitions was granted, so that if he seems to have been relatively poor during his earlier years at Cambridge, as time went by he prospered in pensions and ecclesiastical livings. On October 10, 1583, his election to a fellowship in Trinity took place; on November 12 he thanked Cecil effusively for having brought it about. In 1586 he incepted as master of arts and was also incorporated with the same degree at Oxford. In July 1593 he was incorporated again at Oxford, apparently, though listed with the masters, as a bachelor of divinity since he received that degree at Cambridge during the same year.[9] In 1585 he complained to Cecil that as yet he possessed no settled estate and, in order that he might continue his studies, would like to have his father's pension for *Toxophilus* for the next seven years (III, 361–62). Since no immediate action was taken on this request, he wrote again to Cecil on September 1, 1587; on the 28th Elizabeth granted to him and his brother Dudley the stipend of forty marks that Roger Ascham had earned as Latin secretary. They were to share this income for life, with the provision that the "longer liver of the two" have the entire annuity upon the decease of the other.[10] After his mother died, Giles shared with his youngest brother, Thomas, an annual rent of £90 from the leasing out of Whittlesford Rectory.[11]

Besides these sources of income, Giles gained several livings in the church. In 1591 Trinity College made him vicar of the parish church of Sts. Mary and Michael, in nearby Trumpington; almost immediately, however, he resigned, apparently because of a dispute with the master and fellows over some further request of the crown in his behalf (III, 364–65). Next he was appointed rector of Stoke Fleming, Devon, but may have held this post *in absentia,* since in 1595 he became rector of St. Peter's church in Duxford, a village eight miles south of Cambridge. Little more is heard of him after this date. He seems never to have married, for in 1599 he was still listed as one of the senior fellows of Trinity.[12] In November of the same year he signed away his share in Whittlesford for the sum of £120.[13] He is last mentioned in a bill of the Court of Exchequer as having died "about April last." The bill is undated, but comes unquestionably from the years 1599–1600.[14] On September 26, 1600, the queen assigned all of the Whittlesford property to Thomas Ascham and his sons.[15] The combined evidence of these two documents, along with the succession of one Thomas Tilney to Duxford rectory in 1601, fixes the time of Giles's death as in or about April 1600.

The careers of Dudley and Thomas Ascham are more obscure; the sole records, except the grant to Dudley of a portion of his father's salary, are documents relating to Whittlesford. They seem not to have attended the university, nor is the occupation, if any, of either known. Dudley moves like a phantom, leaving behind no personal statement or signature to record his existence, through patents and indentures for the rectory from 1590 until the reign of Charles I. His name does not appear on the patent rolls until 1587, nor did he share directly in the reversion to his mother's lease of Whittlesford. In 1590, he was granted Giles's expired pension from the crown rent of the rectory.[16] Nothing else is known of him except that in succeeding patents and leases his right to an annuity of £18 16s. 2d. from the land is always entered as a reservation. He is last mentioned in 1633 in a document which implies that he may have died in 1603, before he was thirty years of age.[17]

The Whittlesford documents tell somewhat, but not a great deal, more about Thomas and his offspring, and about the tangled relationships between him and his stepsister Ann's father-in-law over the estate. Like his father, Thomas seems to have had no great success at managing his financial affairs or building up a patrimony for his sons. He is first mentioned in the 1579 grant of the rectory; at the time he would have been about ten years old. In 1590 his name appears on the patent for Dudley's pension. Then, from 1594 onward, his and Giles's interests become complicated with those of Ann Rampston's husband and father-in-law, both named Robert Symons. These two men leased Whittlesford from the Aschams for an annual rent of £90 and bought out Giles's share shortly before his death. This transaction brought them into conflict with Thomas, who was still living at Walthamstow, possibly at Salisbury Manor even though the Symonses had also recently purchased the reversion to that property. According to the terms of the 1579 grant of Whittlesford, upon Giles's death the entire income should have passed to Thomas, but Giles, whether legally or not, had signed away his portion. In a petition to the lords of the Exchequer, Thomas complained that the Symonses, "being very rich and of a contentious disposition, well knowing your orator's weak estate," were claiming the right to Giles's part in Whittlesford but had refused to show him the indenture. Consequently, he could not determine the "quality" of the bond or the boundaries of the share they claimed. Since he had scarcely money to pay his own rent and certainly not enough to defend his title in court, he asked that the Symonses be forced to show clearly what title they had in Whittlesford lands.[18]

The petition was acted upon quickly. On September 26, 1600, the crown set aside the Symons's indenture with Giles and assigned all of Whittlesford to Thomas and, in reversion, to his sons, Roger and John, both of whom had been born within the past three years.[19] Still, the new grant did not put the Symonses out of Whittlesford forever. Apparently they had a flair for charming property out of the hands of the Aschams, for on May 20, 1601, Thomas leased Whittlesford to Symons

Junior, having already moved away from Walthamstow, conceivably to allow Symons to occupy Salisbury Hall.[20] On October 22, 1608, Thomas, now residing at Framlingham, Suffolk, and evidently once again in need of ready money, promised to grant all of his family's interest in Whittlesford to Symons and another purchaser. The amount agreed upon was £1,020, of which £570 was to be paid to him immediately and £450 to be divided between his sons as soon as they should become of age. The transaction was completed on November 15 for £200 in cash, with the reservation for the sons to be held in surety until they should become old enough to sign away their interests.[21] No more is heard of Thomas after he affixed his seal and signature to this document. In due course, the sons completed the transaction, John on December 22, 1619, and Roger on March 3, 1621. At the time, John was a grocer, residing in Cheapside; Roger is described in the document simply as "of the City of London . . . gentleman."[22]

With this transaction, the record of Ascham's family seems to come to an end, for if these two grandsons left any descendants, their names are unknown. In 1603 one John Ascham, possibly a nephew, certainly no closer kinsman of Roger's, wrote an unpublished "Discourse against the peace with Spain."[23] Early in the 1620's a certain Mary, widow to "Ascam" and now the wife of Peter Langman, sailed to Virginia with her new husband and her two children by a previous marriage.[24] Besides various persons of the name in both universities, there was also that unfortunate Antony Ascham, tutor to the future King James II, who went as ambassador to Spain for the parliamentary government in 1650, only to be assassinated upon his arrival in Madrid.

None of these people, however, can be definitely established as relations of Roger Ascham. He survives instead in the offspring of his pen, which time has treated as justly and kindly as they have deserved. Quite properly, his mediocre verse and theological writings were quickly forgotten. *A Report of Germany*, though doubtless worthy of closer attention than it has received, survives after all in a fragment too slight to attract the notice of any but the most assiduous student of English historiography. *Toxophilus* is still read with affection by archers and lovers of "merry England," and is valuable both as a document of Tudor humanism and as a pioneering effort in the development of English literary prose. Ascham's letters served as models to be imitated until

the eighteenth century and have been admired by successive generations since.[25] As for *The Scholemaster*, its contributions to English prose
style and literary criticism were substantial, and its content of humanistic thought, though entirely derivative in nature, influenced the educational treatises of Englishmen from Mulcaster to Locke.

In the ranks of Tudor scholar-courtiers, Ascham stands closest to
his model Elyot, for both men strove to realize the same goals: to
fashion English prose into an apt instrument for serious discourse, and
to fashion Englishmen into pious and patriotic servants to God and
prince. Yet the lively personal note in Ascham, a note that is missing in
Elyot, looks ahead to their abler successor Sidney, and in turn to Sidney's more talented successors. Though not the rival of More or even
Elyot as a humanist or of Sidney as an author, Roger Ascham was
nevertheless the indispensable link between the earlier Tudor and the
great Elizabethan and Jacobean writers of English prose.

NOTES

Notes

1. "Ferunt Divam Elizabetham tum dixisse, se malle decem librarum millia in mare projecisse, quam suum Aschamum amisisse" (Edward Grant, "De Vita et Obitu Rogeri Aschami, ac Eius Scriptionis Laudibus," reprinted in *The Whole Works of Roger Ascham*, ed. Dr. J. A. Giles, 3 vols. in 4, London, 1864–65, III, 342; cited hereafter by volume and page number only). Grant's "Vita" is not in the strictest sense a biography. It is, rather, a demonstrative oration appended to his edition of Ascham's *Epistolae* (London, [1576]), and meant through its delineation of the inspiring life of its subject to enkindle zeal for learning in the pupils of Westminster School. Still, as the earliest authoritative account of Ascham's life, it forms, along with the letters with which it was printed, the basis for all later studies.

2. See *The Ascham Society. Two Hundredth Meeting. College Hall, June 3, 1901*, ed. F. Warre Cornish (Eton, 1901).

3. Harvey, *Foure Letters, and certaine Sonnets, etc.* (London, 1592), p. 64; Nashe, "To the Gentlemen Students of both Universities," preface to Robert Greene, *Menaphon* (London, 1589), fol. [**4r]; *The Pilgrimage to Parnassus with the Two Parts of the Return from Parnassus*, ed. W. D. Macray (Oxford, 1886), p. 10. Bacon's attack occurs in *Works*, ed. James Spedding *et al.*, new edition (London, 1883–92), III, 284.

CHAPTER TWO

1. The date of Ascham's birth cannot be fixed with absolute certainty. It is usually given, upon the authority of Grant's oration, as 1515 (III, 307). Yet Grant, after specifying this year, makes several statements, supported by official records of the University of Cambridge, which seem to rule out a birth date earlier than July, or later than December, 1516. He reports, for instance, that Ascham proceeded bachelor of arts on February 18, 1533/34, "being then in the eighteenth year of his age," and that he became master of arts on July 3, 1537, "being then in his twenty-first year" (III, 312–13). He gives the

date of Ascham's death as December 30, 1568, "in his fifty-third year" (III, 342). Katterfeld argues on the basis of the foregoing evidence for the autumn of 1516 as the date of Ascham's birth (*Roger Ascham: Sein Leben und seine Werke*, Strasbourg, 1879, pp. 349–51).

Grant's inconsistency is the more puzzling because he did nothing to correct it in subsequent editions of the *Epistolae*. Possibly 1515 is a printer's error that he never picked up, but it is equally possible that it is the correct date, given him by Ascham's son Giles, at the time his pupil in Westminster School, and that in the course of the oration his arithmetical calculation went astray. One might speculate further that Ascham was born between January and March, 1516, and on some occasion may have given the date (old style, 1515) to his son. If that were true, he would still have been in his fifty-third year when he died. An objection to such a theory, however, is that Ascham did not employ old-style dating exclusively in his own correspondence. Until more definite evidence turns up, one must bear with the uncertainty produced by Grant's oversight, since he remains the sole authority on this point.

2. At the beginning of the eighteenth century, William Elstob, editor of Ascham's epistles, mentioned that he could find no trace of the family in the vicinity of Kirby Wiske (Preface to his edition of the *Epistolae*, London, 1703, reprinted in Giles, I, cxi).

3. G. E. C. and Geoffrey H. White, *The Complete Peerage* (London, 1949), XI, 546.

4. See I, 34, 286, where he refers, respectively, to "our Thomas Conyers" and "my good cousin Coniers." This is almost certainly Thomas Conyers of Marske, who matriculated at St. John's about 1535 and later became vicar of a country parish in Suffolk (John Venn and J. A. Venn, *Alumni Cantabrigienses*, Cambridge, 1922–27, Part I: i, 382). If Ascham's mother did belong to this family, then it is also possible that she was distantly related through marriage to the Scropes. According to the *Dictionary of National Biography* (LI, 141), Mary le Scrope, daughter of the fifth Baron Scrope of Bolton, was the wife of Sir William Conyers of Hornby. Such a connection, if it did exist, would help to account for John Ascham's position in the Scrope household.

5. I, 29. The unnamed kinsman may have been Cuthbert Tunstall, respected humanist and Bishop of Durham, who was related to the Conyers and hence, possibly, to Ascham (see Hatch, "The Ascham Letters: An Annotated Translation of the Latin Correspondence," p. 61n, for tentative identification of the correspondent as Tunstall).

6. Thomas Dunham Whitaker, *An History of Richmondshire* (London, 1823), I, 264; *Testamenta Eboracensia* (Surtees Society; London, 1869), LIII, 271.

7. Venn, Part I: i, 43; Thomas Baker, *History of the College of St. John the Evangelist, Cambridge*, ed. John E. B. Mayor (Cambridge, 1869), p. 282.

8. *Grace Book Γ, Containing the Records for the University of Cambridge for the Years 1501–1542*, ed. William George Searle (Cambridge, 1908), p. 343; *Grace Book B, Containing the Accounts of the Proctors of the University of Cambridge, 1511–1544*, ed. Mary Bateson (Cambridge, 1905), Part II, 229.

9. *Cal. Pat. Rolls.* Edward VI, 1550–53 (London, 1926), p. 321; Venn, Part I: i, 43.

10. Anthony was still alive, but perhaps in his last illness, earlier in the year, when he was reported absent in the Royal Visitation of the Northern (York) Province (Henry Gee, *The Elizabethan Clergy and the Settlement of Religion, 1558–1564*, Oxford, 1898, p. 83). On December 29, however, he was listed as deceased, and a successor was appointed to the living of Burneston (*Cal. Pat. Rolls.* Elizabeth, 1558–60, London, 1939, p. 255).

11. *The Visitation of Yorkshire, Made in the Years 1584/5, etc.*, ed. Joseph Foster (London, 1875), p. 268.

12. Since no other person of that surname is known to have been in residence at Cambridge in the 1550's and since the astrologer Anthony Ascham had not yet been appointed to the living of Burneston, it seems almost certain that he was Roger's brother. Katterfeld attributes Roger Ascham's silence concerning his brother to what he imagines to be the astrologer's zealous Catholicism (p. 2). Yet the preferment of a "zealous Catholic" to two ecclesiastical livings during the reign of Edward VI, while not impossible, seems rather unlikely. The brothers may actually have been on the best of terms, and a lack of surviving correspondence may signify no more than the perishability of intimate family letters. The sole remaining communication of Ascham with any member of his family is a letter written to his wife upon the death of one of their sons; it appears to have been preserved mainly because it is an excellent model of a consolatory epistle written in English (II, 170–73).

13. *Some Records of the Wingfield Family*, ed. John M. Wingfield (London, 1925), p. 228; W. A. Copinger, *The Manors of Suffolk* (Manchester, 1905–11), I, 339.

14. Copinger, I, 168.

15. *Ibid.*, VI, 23–24. Although no documentary evidence survives to support the claim of one manor over the other as the place of Ascham's youthful education, local tradition holds that in the 1520's Brantham Hall was Sir Humphrey's principal residence. Bridge Place has disappeared, but Brantham Hall, though much altered in the eighteenth century, is still standing.

16. Pearl Hogrefe, *The Sir Thomas More Circle* (Chicago, 1959), p. 197.

17. Venn, Part I: i, 177.

18. *Letters and Papers, Foreign and Domestic. Henry VIII* (London, 1880), V, 528 (#1207.11). For much of the foregoing information about Bond, the Wingfields, and the Scropes, I am deeply indebted to Professor George B. Parks of Queens College, who has given me invaluable manuscript notes on their connections with Ascham.

19. I, 252. Caxton first published *The Foure Sonnes of Aymon* in 1489, and Wynken de Worde printed it again in 1504. Ascham probably read it in one of these editions.

20. *Early Cambridge University and College Statutes in the English Language*, collected by James Heywood (London, 1855), Part I, 235–36.

21. *Grace Book B*, Part I, xiii.

22. *Grace Book A, Containing the Accounts of the Proctors of the Uni-*

versity of Cambridge, 1454–1488, ed. Stanley M. Leathes (Cambridge, 1897), p. xvi.

23. James Bass Mullinger, *The University of Cambridge from the Earliest Times to the Royal Injunctions of 1535* (Cambridge, 1873), pp. 492–93 (referred to hereafter as Mullinger, I).

24. *Ibid.,* p. 459.

25. Rede's foundation was reaffirmed by his executors during the academic year 1523–24 (*Grace Book* B, Part II, 114).

26. Baker, p. 100.

27. Mullinger, I, 573. In a letter to Sir William Cecil (January 1548), Ascham himself uses the term "Germanos," though without any sense of disparagement, for Lutheran theologians (I, 156).

28. The foregoing information about the establishment of the college is derived from Baker, pp. 55–98.

29. *The History of the University of Cambridge, and of Waltham Abbey,* ed. James Nichols (London, 1840), p. 131. It is worth noting that Fuller, who was well acquainted with Ascham's works, mentions his first tutor, Bond, as an ideal schoolmaster, and takes Metcalfe as the model for his character of an ideal master of a college (*The Holy State and the Profane State,* ed. James Nichols, Cambridge, 1841, pp. 102, 96–98).

30. I, 52. According to the accounts of the university proctors, the first payment to Ascham for copying was made in 1534–35. Before that date he may have rendered the service infrequently and without compensation, but thereafter he often received fees for transcribing documents (*Grace Book* B, Part II, 193, 202, 212, 215, etc.).

31. II, *Toxophilus,* 68; compare Plato, *Republic,* IX, 590D.

32. Nothing further is known of this project of Ascham's. Cheke's Latin version of the two homilies was published at London, along with the Greek texts, in 1543 (A. W. Pollard and G. R. Redgrave, *A Short-Title Catalogue . . . 1475–1640,* London, 1950, No. 14634). Ascham, who cites Chrysostom frequently, more than once commended Cheke's translations (I, 35, 74).

33. Richard Mulcaster is the authority for this fact about Cheke's eagerness to promote study of Xenophon (*Positions,* ed. Robert Herbert Quick, London, 1888, p. 241).

34. The preceding account of the curriculum in Ascham's time is taken from H. C. Porter, *Reformation and Reaction in Tudor Cambridge* (Cambridge, 1958), p. 4, and from Mullinger, I, 342–58, 459–60.

35. Mark H. Curtis, *Oxford and Cambridge in Transition 1558–1642* (Oxford, 1959), p. 59.

CHAPTER THREE

1. *Grace Book* Γ, p. 280; *Grace Book* B, Part II, p. 186.

2. Baker, p. 109.

3. *Ibid.,* p. 283.

4. Mullinger, I, 630.

5. Grant, in III, 313; *Grace Book* B, Part II, p. 202; *Grace Book* Γ, p. 315. Grant gives the day as "the Tuesday after the feast of Sts. Peter and Paul." In 1537, that Tuesday fell on July 3.

6. Mullinger, *The University of Cambridge from the Royal Injunctions of 1535 to the Accession of Charles I* (Cambridge, 1884), p. 50 (referred to hereafter as Mullinger, II). Because this shortage of qualified masters of arts continued for many years, the statutory term for regents was increased in Edward VI's reign to three years, and in Elizabeth I's to five, even though the increased proportion of collegiate instruction rendered much of the regent lecturing in the schools superfluous (see Curtis, pp. 101–2, 125).

7. *De recta & emendata linguae Graecae pronuntiatione, etc.* (Paris, 1568), fol. 42.

8. I, 33–34. This latter work is unidentified. If it was simply a book owned by the brother of Ascham's friend, it could have been any one of several editions or recent commentaries on either the *Ars Rhetorica* or the *Progymnasmata*. No contemporary of Ascham's at Cambridge had published a work of this kind. From a statement by Ascham that he would like in some manner to help the Bishop of Chichester complete the *Ordo Psalmorum* begun by Edward Fox, Bishop of Hereford (d. 1538), Giles places the letter in 1543. His assumption is that Ascham is speaking of his fellow collegian George Day, who was raised to the see of Chichester in that year. The reference, however, is to Day's predecessor, Richard Sampson, whose *In priores quinquaginta psalmos Daviticos, familiaris explanatio* was published in 1539 (*STC* 21679).

9. *Grace Book* Δ, *Containing the Records of the University of Cambridge for the Years 1542–1589*, ed. John Venn (Cambridge, 1910), p. 571; *Grace Book* Γ, pp. 341–42.

10. "Item Magistro Aschamo pro lectura Mathematica xxvj[s] viij[d]," *Grace Book* B, Part II, pp. 226–27. At first glance it may appear that the "Master Ascham" to whom the sums were paid was Anthony, since Roger's assurance for the latter's request to be excused from "cursory" (roughly, apprentice) lecturing is recorded on p. 229 of this same volume. It is quite clear, however, that Anthony did not read in the schools, as was normally expected of recipients of the baccalaureate in medicine, for an entry some pages further along records that in 1540–41 Roger had still not paid the twenty shillings assured to the proctors for Anthony's exemption from lecturing (p. 235).

11. For an analysis of Seton's treatise, in the widely used revision by Peter Carter, see Wilbur Samuel Howell, *Logic and Rhetoric in England, 1500–1700* (Princeton, 1956), pp. 49–56. The first three books of the *Dialectica*, reversing the usual order of treatment, deal with *arrangement*, and only the fourth and final book with *invention*, which had received the major share of attention from Agricola and earlier authors.

12. III, 241. Watson's tragedy has been edited and translated from the holograph (B. M. MS. Stowe 957) by John Hazel Smith ("Thomas Watson's *Absalom*, an Edition, Translation, and Critical Study," unpub. diss., Illinois, 1958). Frederick S. Boas analyzes and praises the play in the Stowe MS.,

though he hesitates to identify it as Watson's (*University Drama in the Tudor Age*, Oxford, 1914, pp. 62–65, 352–65).

13. G. C. Moore Smith, "Plays Performed in Cambridge Colleges before 1585," *Fasciculus Ioanni Willis Clark dicatus* (Cambridge, 1909), p. 268.

14. Christopherson's tragedy is preserved in a manuscript in the library of Trinity College, Cambridge. Apparently there was also a Latin version which is now lost (Boas, *University Drama*, p. 45, n. 1). It seems odd that Ascham, who regarded Watson's *Absalom* and Buchanan's *Jephtha* so highly, should have had no kind words in *The Scholemaster* for the parallel work of another old friend. Possibly the fact that Watson was still alive, while Christopherson, also a Marian bishop, had died in prison for his Romanist views occasioned the silence on his Greek *Jephtha*.

15. Mullinger, II, 74–76. Archbishop Matthew Parker preserved his correspondence with Gardiner concerning the performance of *Pammachius*; the exchange of letters shows that the council objected to the play because in purporting to expose the usurpations of the see of Rome, it had also attacked a number of doctrines still maintained by the established church (Corpus Christi College, Cambridge, MS. 106, pp. 437–53).

16. All that seems to remain of Ascham's version of the *Philoctetes* is a single line (v. 115) rendered into English trimeter: "Nor you without them, nor without you they do aught" (II, *Tox.*, 59).

17. Six years later, when Day had become Bishop of Chichester and returned to visit the college, the fellows were almost afraid to face him. They remembered, Ascham wrote to him, "the offense they had committed in the iniquity of those times," and they were still ashamed of their temerity in that unfortunate election (I, 323). Ascham, who places himself among the repentant offenders, sends as a compliment and peace offering a psalm "in senarian measures," which he had written recently on the threat of the Turks in Hungary. The psalm is now lost. Giles prints the letter, though by his own admission without much confidence, among those of 1552, when Charles V and his brother Ferdinand were at war with the Turk. Katterfeld, however, correctly dates it near the close of 1543, soon after Day's consecration and during a dismal period that found Francis I and Charles V at war, relations going badly between Catholics and Protestants in Germany, and the Turk making frightening military advances in Hungary (pp. 32–33).

18. Baker, p. 462.

19. I, 7. Giles, perhaps confused here as he certainly was elsewhere about old- and new-style dating, places the election and the letters concerning it in March 1539. Both Baker (p. 283) and Katterfeld (p. 24, n. 1) establish the correct date of the letter as March, 1539/40.

20. Three years later Ascham alluded to this coolness in a letter to Redman (I, 38–39). He tried to minimize the breach between them, and Redman did unbend enough to act as courier for him on one occasion in 1542 (I, 28). This letter shows, nonetheless, that during the following year, when Redman wanted a fine copy made of a manuscript that he was presenting to Henry

VIII, he was too proud, or unforgiving, though performing the task would have meant much to Ascham, to ask this favor of him (I, 46).

21. Bill, who eventually became Dean of Westminster, was both Ascham's close friend and a favorite of Cheke. One of Ascham's few surviving Latin poems is a New Year's gift in trimeters punningly addressed to "Bille belle . . . mi bellissime" (III, 286–87).

22. Ascham mentions in *Toxophilus* that he traveled southward over a road in Yorkshire at the time of "the great snow that fell four years ago" (II, *Tox.*, 154). Since he was revising his treatise for publication early in 1545, his journey home must have occurred late in 1540 or early in 1541.

23. The holograph of the *Titus* is preserved in Bodleian Library Rawlinson MS. D 1317. The dedication to Goodrich (fols. 3–5) has never been printed with Ascham's epistles. The autograph copy of *Philemon*, presented to Seton with an accompanying dedication (the latter is printed in I, 22–24), has been in the library of St. John's College since the eighteenth century (MS. L 3). In full, its title page runs "Expositiones quaedam antiquae in Epistolam Divi Pauli ad Philemonem ex diversis Sanctorum Patrum graece scriptis commentariis opera et diligentia Oecumenii collectae et nunc primum latine versae. Cantabrigiae Anno domini 1542 [i.e., 1543]." These are the handsomest of Ascham's surviving manuscripts, so evenly and cleanly written that the *Philemon* has been mistaken more than once for a printed book. Mullinger cites one such instance of an earlier scholar's misapprehension (II, 43, n. 3); the error led to an assumption by Giles (I, 22) and by Macray that the work was printed at Cambridge in 1542 (*Catologi Codicum Manuscriptorum Bibliothecae Bodleianae Partis Quintae Fasciculus Quartus*, ed. William D. Macray, Oxford, 1898, p. 413). The translations, however, were not printed until Grant included them, without the dedication, in a collection of Ascham's theological writings (*Apologia pro caena dominica, etc.*, London, 1577).

24. Their disagreement at this time did no harm to later relations between Ponet and Ascham. Early in 1545, Ponet having since become a canon of Canterbury, Ascham wrote to him of their long-standing friendship and asked him for the loan of a copy of Gregory of Nyssa (I, 71).

25. *De recta & emendata linguae Graecae pronuntiatione*, fol. 42.

26. *Athenae Oxonienses* and *Fasti*, ed. Philip Bliss (London, 1815), II, 114. Wood, sometimes an untrustworthy authority, may simply have invented this entry as a means of getting Ascham into his roll of prominent Oxonians; for criticism of his reliability as a source of biographical information, see William Riley Parker, "Wood's Life of Milton: Its Sources and Significance," *PBSA*, LII (1958), 3–4. On the other hand, since Wood did have access to the university archives and other manuscript records, his statement may be correct. C. H. Cooper and Thompson Cooper, *Athenae Cantabrigienses* (Cambridge, 1858), I, 264, give the date as 1542. Neither source, however, cites documentary authority for its entry; C. W. Boase likewise cites only Wood and Cooper in this connection (*Register of the University of Oxford, Vol. I (1449–63; 1505–71)*, Oxford, 1885, p. 302). If Ascham really did seek

incorporation at Oxford, the date 1542, in view of the unfortunate turn of events at Cambridge during that year, seems the likelier.

27. I, 404. Margaret Roper's death in 1544 sets a terminal date for her offer. It is possible, of course, that she had made it several years earlier, when the young Ascham's reputation was rising spectacularly at Cambridge.

28. Ascham's mention of this fact is a compliment not only to Cheke but also to Grindal, who had written the preface to Cheke's book.

29. Ascham seems to have attempted Latin verse only on rare occasions. Of the ten Latin poems he is known to have written, all but one date from before 1552. Eight were published by Grant with the *Epistolae* and were reprinted by Giles (III, 277–93). The other two are a distich on the tutors of Edward VI ("Inclyte ter felix est Anglia, rege Edoardo.. / Et ipse ter felix tribus didascalis") and the lost psalm against the Turks (see n. 17).

30. "In Anniversarium Natalem Diem Eduardi Principis," III, 279, ll. 9–16: "Begone, ill-boding things, avaunt, mournful ditties, hence away, complaints, sorrows, and discontents. Let all things abound in jests and jokings, pleasant talks and carouses, feasts and entertainments."

31. See, for example, Leland, *Laudatio Pacis* (London, 1546), and Haddon, "Angliae Prosopopoeia," in *Poematum . . . libri duo* (London, 1576), fols. [H_5^v–H_6^v]. Haddon extended the conception so that in his poem not only do the Tudor monarchs become Christ's true vicars upon earth, but England itself becomes in effect "the handmaiden of the Lord," with a mission to lead the rest of the world to a new Jerusalem.

32. Compare John Jortin, *The Life of Erasmus* (London, 1758), p. 581: "We have observed in many places that Erasmus could not endure even the smell of fish, and had a most Lutheran stomach."

33. I, 66. Compare Herodotus, II, para. 37.

34. See II, *Tox.*, 156–57, where Ascham speaks of his experiences in the butts at Norwich and outside the walls of York castle.

35. In his commemorative oration, Grant, too, felt called upon to vindicate Ascham's zeal for archery: "But this delight in shooting never lured him away from his books; on the contrary, it made his wit and will readier to return to his studies joyfully and with alacrity. . . . He had a valetudinarian body, afflicted with many illnesses, which in his condition, if he had not treated it with care and restored it by means of honest exercises, he would have been unable to preserve for long" (III, 320).

36. On Lee's death Ascham begged that he might be given, in place of one of the tardy installments due on his pension, some volumes from among the Greek orators, philosophers, or historians, preferably a copy of the *Decem Rhetores Graeci* (I, 59). To Cheke he spoke of Gregory Nazianzen and St. John Chrystostom (I, 43, 47), and there was the request to Ponet for some work of Gregory of Nyssa (see n. 24). It was also probably at this time or shortly afterwards that he began to gratify his taste for out-of-the-ordinary Greek authors, a taste evidenced not only by his translations of Oecumenius, but also by his reading in Polyaenus, "Leo the Emperor," and the *Theriaca; eiusdem Alexipharmaca* (Venice, 1499), a pair of treatises in hexameters on

venomous animals and poisons by Nicander, a physician of the second century B.C. On the final folio of a copy of this last-named work preserved in the Bodleian Library, appears a manuscript note, "Rogerus Aschamus dedit Ailando." This Ailand, or Eland, was probably Henry Ailand of St. John's (see Venn, Part I: ii, 59). Henry seems, further, to have been the brother of the William Eland at whose London house Ascham stayed in the autumn of 1550 (I, 208). The book is an especially good example of the rather esoteric nature of some of Ascham's reading in Greek.

37. Gertrude Noyes demonstrates that Ascham's interest in Greek literature was a continuing one and that his knowledge clearly exceeded that of such persons as depended mainly upon *florilegia* ("A Study of Roger Ascham's Literary Citations with Particular Reference to His Knowledge of the Classics," unpub. diss., Yale, 1937, p. 71). Ascham is himself the authority for the statement of later biographers that he possessed an extensive collection of Greek authors. His assertion in the published version of *The Scholemaster* that, of the extant Greeks, "even my poor study lacketh not one" (III, 134) may appear to imply that he had perused, not owned, them all. But in a manuscript version of an earlier draft of his treatise, the passage reads "even my poor library lacketh not one" (B.M. Royal MS. 18. B. XXIV, fol. 62ᵛ). This claim leaves no doubt that, in spite of financial difficulties in his later years, Ascham had managed to acquire a substantial private collection of Greek authors.

CHAPTER FOUR

1. I, 77–83, 84–85. The copy presented to Henry VIII became part of the old Royal Library. Edward VI's later turned up in the collection of Sir William Cope (*Reports of the Historical Manuscripts Commission*, 3d Report, London, 1872, III, 244) and is now in the Pierpont Morgan Library in New York. That sent to Parr, with Ascham's autograph dedication, is owned by the Folger Shakespeare Library.

2. "Non minus hic arcu est quam lingua clarus utraque; / Sic ornat patriam, sic iuvat ille suam" (quoted in Grant's oration, III, 316).

3. "Aschamus est auctor, magnum quem fecit Apollo / Arte sua, magnum Pallas et arte sua. / Docta manus dedit hunc, dedit hunc mens docta libellum" (I, cxiv).

4. II, 98. Although Giles provides separate pagination in his second volume for Ascham's letters and *Toxophilus*, citations of the latter will hereafter include only volume and page number, so long as the reference is clear.

5. G. G. Coulton, *Social Life in Britain from the Conquest to the Reformation* (Cambridge, 1918), p. 73. Translated from *The Ancient Laws of the Fifteenth Century for King's College, Cambridge, and for the Public School of Eton College*, ed. James Heywood and Thomas Wright (London, 1850). Opposition to archery continued at Cambridge even beyond Ascham's lifetime. In his revised statutes for Gonville and Caius College (1572), Dr. John

Caius forbade shooting along with bull- and bear-baiting and "hurling the axe" (Mullinger, II, 163–64).

6. The occasion of the section on the chase in *De Philologia* was remarkably similar to that of Ascham's work. Budé appears to be defending himself against the imputation that classical learning had suffered because he had deserted the schools for the idle pleasures of youth and of the field before assuming the mission of restoring Greek studies in France (see Pierre Bayle, *Dictionnaire historique et critique,* fourth edition, Paris, 1820, IV, 225).

7. II, 17. Though in his preface Ascham assumed that he was "the first, which hath said any thing in this matter" (II, 7 [*sic* for 5]), he had been anticipated by the anonymous French authors of *Lart Darcherie,* published *ca.* 1515, and of *Les Livres du Roy Modus et de la Royne Ratio,* a fourteenth-century treatise on hunting that includes a brief dialogue on pursuing game with the bow. Since there is no evidence, however, that Ascham was acquainted with either work, it is likely that his claim to priority was sincere.

8. *Journals of the House of Lords* (n.p., n.d.), I, 13, 15, 24–40 *passim,* 178, 193.

9. *The Boke for a Iustice of Peace* (London, 1539), fols. 24^r–25^r.

10. *The Sermons of Hugh Latimer,* ed. George Elwes Corrie (Parker Society; Cambridge, 1844), p. 196. Latimer by no means stood alone among distinguished clergymen in his esteem for shooting. James Pilkington, master of St. John's from 1559 to 1561 and thereafter Bishop of Durham, in his later years wrote an "Exposition upon Nehemiah" in which he commends both archery and the treatise of his old friend Ascham (*Works,* ed. James Scholefield; Parker Society; Cambridge, 1842, p. 429). In *Toxophilus* itself, Ascham adverts to still earlier episcopal sanction of the pastime. After citing a host of ancient authorities in its behalf, he continues, "If these old examples prove nothing for shooting, what say you to this, that the best learned and sagest men in this realm which be now alive, both love shooting and use shooting, as the best learned bishops that be?" (II, 33).

11. Clement C. Parker, *Compendium of Works on Archery* (Philadelphia, 1950), pp. 6–7. During the reign of Elizabeth I (1582), this fraternity was incorporated into the Honourable Artillery Company.

12. *The Holy State and the Profane State,* p. 176.

13. *The Archer's Craft* (London, 1951), p. 15.

14. See, for example, Dr. Robert P. Elmer, "Study of Correct Archery," *American Archery* (National Archery Association of the United States; [Columbus, Ohio?], 1917), p. 21.

15. *Certain Discourses . . . Concerning the formes and effects of divers sorts of weapons, . . . As also of the great sufficiencie, excellencie, and wonderful effects of Archers, etc.* (London, 1590).

16. Barwick's treatise bears the following self-explanatory and contentious title: *A Breefe Discourse, concerning the force and effect of all manuall weapons of fire, and the disability of the Long Bowe or Archery, in respect of others of greater force now in use* (London, n.d. [1594?]). Hayward's com-

mendation of archery occurs in *The Lives of the III. Normans, Kings of England* (London, 1613), pp. 77–79.

17. *De Studio Militari* (Rome, 1637), p. 538.

18. London, 1580, fols. $E_i{}^v$–$E_{ii}{}^r$.

19. Printed with *The Auncient Order, Societie, and Unitie Laudable, of Prince Arthure, etc.* (London, 1583).

20. For a discussion of Shotterel and D'Urfey's plagiarism, see my article, "Roger Ascham's *Toxophilus* in Heroic Verse," *HLQ*, XXII (1959), 119–24.

21. *The Civil Wars*, ed. Laurence Michel (New Haven, 1958), pp. 269–70; "Poly-Olbion," (XXVIth Song, ll. 327–28), *The Works of Michael Drayton*, ed. J. William Hebel *et al.* (Oxford, 1931–41), IV, 529.

22. "Discoveries," *Ben Jonson*, ed. C. H. Herford and Percy and Evelyn Simpson (Oxford, 1925–52), VIII, 589.

23. *The Anatomy of Melancholy*, ed. Floyd Dell and Paul Jordan-Smith (New York, 1948), p. 443.

24. *Complete Prose Works*, gen. ed. Don M. Wolfe (New Haven; London, 1953–), I, 354, 502.

25. See II, 102. Elizabeth's letter is cited in V. S. Lean, *Collectanea* (Bristol; London, 1902–4), III, 338.

26. *Astronomical Thought in Renaissance England* (Baltimore, 1937), pp. 91–92.

27. *The Institucion of a Gentleman*, second edition (London, 1568), fols. $E_{viii}{}^v$–$F_{iiii}{}^v$; Prologue, fol. $*_{vi}{}^{r-v}$.

28. Mulcaster, *Positions*, pp. 102–3; Cleland, ΗΡΩ-ΠΑΙΔΕΙΑ, *or The Institution of a Young Noble Man* (Oxford, 1607), pp. 218–19; Peacham, *The Compleat Gentleman* (London, 1622), p. 182.

29. *A Learned and True Assertion of . . . Prince Arthure, King of great Brittaine*, reprinted with Christopher Middleton, *The Famous Historie of Chinon of England*, ed. William Edward Mead (Early English Text Society, CLXV; London, 1925), p. 6.

30. C. F. Tucker Brooke, *A Literary History of England*, ed. Albert C. Baugh (New York, 1948), p. 389, n. 20.

31. *The Arte of Angling, 1577*, ed. Gerald Eades Bentley, second facsimile edition (Princeton, 1958).

32. *De amissa dicendi ratione*, fols. 33^v, 17^r.

33. *Wilson's Arte of Rhetorique 1560*, ed. G. H. Mair (Oxford, 1909), p. 159. Wilson's treatise first appeared in 1553, but since the 1560 edition is regarded as authoritative, all references will be to Mair's reprint.

34. For an account of the literary obligations of Ascham to Elyot, though it does not take into account all of the foregoing parallels, see Cornelius Benndorf, *Die englische Pädagogik im 16. Jahrhundert . . . in den Werken von T. Elyot, Roger Ascham und R. Mulcaster* (Vienna, 1905). Hogrefe observes that in many instances in which Ascham's humanistic ideals differ markedly from those of More and his friends, they resemble Elyot's closely (*The Sir Thomas More Circle*, pp. 134–35).

35. *The Boke Named the Governour,* ed. Henry Herbert Stephen Croft (London, 1883), I, 295–302.

36. *Ibid.,* p. 163.

37. *Ibid.,* pp. 38, 41.

38. *Ibid.,* p. 273.

39. Elyot first records this criticism of his efforts in *Of that knowlage whiche maketh a wise man,* second edition (London, 1534), fol. A₃ʳ⁻ᵛ.

40. *The Castel of Helthe (1541)* (Scholars' Facsimiles & Reprints; New York, 1937), fol. Aᵢᵥᵛ.

41. See Croft's glossary for tables and extensive discussion of Elyot's importations from Latin and Greek (*Governour,* II, 449–62).

42. *Arte of Rhetorique,* p. 162.

43. Baldassare Castiglione, *The Book of the Courtier,* trans. Sir Thomas Hoby (Everyman's Library; London; New York, 1928), p. 7. Cheke's version of Matthew and part of Mark was edited by James Goodwin (London, 1843); for further discussion, see Herbert D. Meritt, "The Vocabulary of Sir John Cheke's Partial Version of the Gospels," *JEGP,* XXXIX (1940), 450–55.

44. Lever's "Saxonized" vocabulary is discussed in James L. Rosier, "The Vocabulary of Ralph Lever's *Arte of Reason," Anglia,* LXXVI (1958), 505–9. See also Howell, *Logic and Rhetoric,* pp. 57–63; Richard Foster Jones, *The Triumph of the English Language* (Stanford, 1953), pp. 124–29.

45. III, 264–71. Wilson, in the preface to his English version of Demosthenes' Olynthian orations and Philippics (London, 1570), quotes Cheke as having asserted that because Demosthenes used the speech of the common people "none ever was more fit to make an Englishman tell his tale, praiseworthily in an open hearing, either in Parliament or pulpit, or otherwise, than this early orator was" (cited in John Strype, *The Life of the Learned Sir John Cheke, Kt.,* Oxford, 1821, p. 151).

46. II, 7. Interestingly enough, Stanford Lehmberg conjectures that the person Ascham speaks of in this anecdote may have been Elyot himself (*Sir Thomas Elyot Tudor Humanist,* Austin, 1960, p. 92).

47. *Orator,* xxiii, 76–xxvi, 90; xxix, 101.

48. *Rhetoric,* III, xi, 5–6.

49. Esther Cloudman Dunn, *The Literature of Shakespeare's England* (New York, 1936), p. 182.

50. See, for example, Noyes, pp. 216–17.

51. Kenneth O. Myrick, *Sir Philip Sidney as a Literary Craftsman* (Cambridge, Mass., 1935), pp. 46–83.

52. The arrangement is slightly different in the *Cynegeticus,* where discussion of nomenclature and technique precedes that of the beneficial effects of hunting the hare. In the Loeb Classical Library edition of Xenophon's *Scripta Minora,* trans. E. C. Marchant (London; New York, 1925), the three traditional divisions occupy, respectively, pp. 367–73, 443–57, 373–443.

53. *Ibid.* pp. 445–77 (xii, 10–16).

54. *The Master of Game,* ed. Wm. A. and F. Baillie Grohman (London, 1909), pp. 4–13.

55. *Boke of St. Albans* (Westminster, 1496), fols. $g_{iii}{}^v - i_{iv}{}^v$. In the introduction (p. 1) to Bentley's reprint of *The Arte of Angling, 1577*, Carl Otto von Kienbusch notes the ubiquity of the tripartite division in treatises on fishing ever since the appearance of the section on angling in the *Boke of St. Albans.*

56. Cicero, *De Inventione*, I, v, 7; *Rhetorica ad Herennium*, I, ii, 2.

57. *The Arte of Rhetorique*, p. 29.

58. Cicero, *De Inventione*, II, lii-lviii; Quintilian, *Institutio Oratoria*, III, viii, 22ff. The *Rhetorica ad Herennium* gives "advantage" as the chief topic, with "honor" and "security" among its subdivisions (III, iii). According to such a scheme, *Toxophilus* could be said to point out under this topic both kinds of advantage, since military safety and personal health, along with great esteem, accrue to a nation of diligent archers.

59. *De Inventione*, I, vii–lvi. The reference to digressions occurs in I, li, 97. Quintilian discusses the matter at somewhat greater length (IV, iii).

60. Aristotle, *Rhetoric*, III, 1415b; Cicero *De Inventione*, I, xv.

61. *Rhetoric*, I, 1356a.

62. See Quintilian, IV, iii, 15. Wilson also warns his readers to take heed "that (when we make any such digression) the same may well agree to the purpose, and so be set out that it confound not the cause, or darken the sense of the matter devised" (*The Arte of Rhetorique*, p. 182).

63. See Alfred Hettler, *Roger Ascham: sein Stil und seine Beziehung zur Antike* (Elberfeld, 1915), pp. 28ff.

64. After a brief introduction, the questioning in Cicero's treatise proceeds in the following manner:

C. Jun. Into how many parts should the whole doctrine of eloquence be divided?

C. Sen. Into three.

C. Jun. Let us hear what they are.

C. Sen. First into the orator's own resources, next into the oration, and then into the question.

C. Jun. In what do the orator's own resources consist?

C. Sen. In matter and words, etc. (*De Partitione Oratoria*, i, 3).

Compare the opening of *Toxophilus*, Book Two:

Phi. What is the chief point in shooting, that every man laboureth to come to?

Tox. To hit the mark.

Phi. How many things are required to make a man evermore hit the mark?

Tox. Two.

Phi. Which two?

Tox. Shooting straight, and keeping of a length.

Phi. How should a man shoot straight, and how should a man keep a length? (II, 98).

65. The main impetus seems to have come, though others had employed the form earlier, from the eighth-century English scholar Alcuin. While at

Charlemagne's court, Alcuin had composed a separate manual for each subject of the trivium, his *Grammatica, Dialogus de Rhetorica et Virtutibus,* and
De Dialectica; all are "master-pupil" dialogues (see *Patrologia Latina,* CI,
ed. J.-P. Migne, Paris, 1863, for the three works). Aelfric established the form
in texts for English schools, and it was widely adopted in the later Middle
Ages for treatises on sport, including the verse manual on hunting in the *Boke
of St. Albans.*

66. Although Ascham does not specify the season, Philologus would
hardly refer to "this fair wheat (God save it)" (II, 13) either early in the
year or after harvest. Nor is it likely that the season is high summer. Several
"good fellows" whom Philologus has observed on their way to shoot would
probably not be doing so at that time of year, since Toxophilus observes that
the weather is then too hot for the sport and that of the four seasons, only
"spring-time and fall of the leaf be those which we abuse in shooting" (II, 36).

67. II, 12. The allusion is to *Phaedrus,* 246E.

68. *De Officiis,* I, ch. 29. Although Ascham knew this work of Cicero's
intimately, he may have got the idea from Elyot's *Governour* (I, 287–88).

69. For such an identification, see Sir Sidney Lee's article on Ascham in
the *DNB.*

CHAPTER FIVE

1. See John LeNeve, *Fasti Ecclesiae Anglicanae* ([London], 1716), II,
413; *Grace Book B,* Part II, pp. 212–28 *passim.*

2. Mullinger, II, 7.

3. I, 116–17. See Cooper, *Annals of Cambridge,* I, 349. Archbishop
Parker preserved an interesting body of letters about various disputes between
the scholars and the townsmen, a number of which concern the extensive and,
to the townsfolk, annoying privileges of the university in connection with
Stourbridge Fair (Corp. Chr. Coll., Cambr., MS. 106, *passim*).

4. J. D. Mackie, *The Earlier Tudors 1485–1558* (Oxford, 1952), pp. 399–
400, 513–14, 573–74; Mullinger, II, 76.

5. Baker, p. 372. The letter is not in Giles, nor are two others, written to
Somerset and Denny in March [1548/9?]. Giles does print, besides the plea
to the Bishop of Llandaff, one to Denny written in March 1549 (I, 165–66)
and the one sent to Northampton (I, 180–81). The others are summarized by
Baker (p. 371).

6. I, 180–81. Compare *The Sedbergh School Register,* ed. Bernard Wilson (Leeds, 1895), pp. 7ff.

7. *Ibid.,* pp. 132, 575; Lever, *Sermons. 1550,* ed. Edward Arber (London, 1870), p. 81.

8. A. F. Torry, *Founders and Benefactors of St. John's College, Cambridge*
(Cambridge, 1888), p. 6.

9. Mullinger, II, 76–80, 86. For evidence that the middle years of the
sixteenth century actually saw some founding of new and re-establishing of

older schools although others were being despoiled, see Arthur F. Leach, *English Schools at the Reformation, 1546–8* (Westminster, 1896), *passim*.

10. *The Lyfe of Sir Thomas Moore, Knighte,* ed. James Mason Cline (New York, 1950), p. 50.

11. *Sermons,* pp. 121–22.

12. *Lucubrationes* (London, 1567), p. 12.

13. Mullinger, II, 88, n. 3.

14. Latimer, *Sermons,* I, 179. The fears expressed by English scholars at mid-century reflect, rather than an unmitigated decay of learning, an important change in the student body, a change that Ascham himself, when he came to write his *Scholemaster,* would recognize and approve as beneficial to the country. As modern historians have suggested, the sons of noblemen and the gentry were being sent to the universities to prepare for the careers in government service that now lay open to them (see Curtis, pp. 70–83; Fritz Caspari, *Humanism and the Social Order in Tudor England,* Chicago, 1954, pp. 132–56). For evidence that benefactions to the universities actually took a marked upturn at the time from the shameful low of the preceding decade, see W. K. Jordan, *Philanthropy in England 1480–1660* (London, 1959), pp. 291–95, 373.

15. Lever to Ascham (November 13, 1551), *Original Letters Relative to the English Reformation . . . Chiefly from the Archives of Zurich,* ed. Hastings Robinson (Parker Society; Cambridge, 1846), Part I, pp. 150–52. See also Strype, *Cheke,* pp. 67–69.

16. Mullinger, II, 36. Melanchthon was also inclined to believe that Ascham's patron, Bishop Gardiner, had been primarily responsible for the conservatism of the religious settlement under Henry VIII.

17. *Lucubrationes,* pp. 173–74.

18. Strype, *Cheke,* p. 35. At the beginning of 1548, Ascham registered in a letter to Cecil his annoyance at Day's having interfered with the fellows of King's: "Our common prayer is that Cambridge sometime, or rather very soon, may see John Cheke presiding over King's College. That bishop [Day] is of no profit to their studies; I could wish that he were not so mistaken, and I say this not to be snatching after favor for anyone, but for the advantage of the entire university" (I, 158).

19. I, 153. In letters that he wrote at the time to Bill and Cecil, Ascham epitomizes some of the developments in this controversy over the Eucharist (I, 153–58).

20. The language of the letter does not make clear whether he had composed the treatise alone or with the help of others. He does use the first person plural, "Scripsimus enim fere justum librum de Missa, quem brevi offerre instituimus Domino Protectori" (I, 157). Ascham, however, may simply have been employing the more formal plural here in speaking of his own individual effort.

21. *Apologia,* pp. 26, 1.

22. *Ibid.,* p. 136. In mentioning "this most famous college," Ascham

speaks as though he were present at St. John's. This reference, along with that to Somerset as chancellor of the university, narrows the possible time of composition to the period between December 1547 and October 1551, when Somerset was imprisoned by the privy council and deprived of his offices. During these four years, Ascham resided at Cambridge for only a few months in 1548 and for a slightly longer period in 1549–50. Though the question of transubstantiation continued to be debated throughout and beyond this period, internal evidence makes the beginning of 1548 the most likely date of composition of the *Apologia* and argues strongly for identifying it with the treatise intended for the Protector. Katterfeld doubts the identity of the works, though he does concede that the content of the latter must have been much like that of the *Apologia*. His objections to identification are that the *Apologia* is not addressed to Somerset but to "the grave fathers and most learned men," presumably of the university; that it contains the expression, "Understand, reader, whoever, you may be," whereas Somerset would have been addressed in the formal third person; and finally that the existing treatise is, despite its length of 148 pages, incomplete (pp. 64–65).

These arguments are unconvincing. Ascham merely told Cecil that the book was to be presented, not addressed, to Somerset, and its incompleteness does not contradict his mention of an "almost finished book." It is, further, quite conceivable that he originally composed the *Apologia* for delivery in the college and intended to revise it for dedication to Somerset but never found the time to make the appropriate changes. That he ever bothered to produce two distinct versions of the treatise, one for the Protector and another for his colleagues, seems unlikely, particularly since his interests were very shortly to be directed elsewhere. Even if he did plan two versions, his generally economic habits of literary production make it doubtful that he would have made them different in any significant respect.

23. *Apologia*, p. 63.

24. *Lords Journals*, I, 313; Strype, *Ecclesiastical Memorials, etc.* (Oxford, 1822), II: i, 97–99.

25. Pighius, who according to Ascham bore great sway among the Catholics at Cambridge (I, 68), had written a rejoinder to Henry VIII, *Hierarchiae ecclesiasticae assertio* (Cologne, 1538) and an *Apologia . . . Adversus M. Buceri Calumnias* (Mainz, 1543). More had supported Henry VIII's *Assertio septem sacramentorum* against Luther (London, 1521) with his own *Opus quo refellit Lutheri calumnias* (London, 1523). He had also engaged in a well-known controversy with the reformers John Frith and William Tyndale over their defense of "the supper of the Lord." Ascham prays that God will help his own party "so that the truth may neither be overthrown by the thunderbolts of Pighius, nor derided by the mockeries of Thomas More" (*Apologia*, p. 15). He scoffs at Pighius and More again on pages 65–66, and breaks off his treatise in the midst of an attack on Pighius as "the head of the papists" whom the opposition hold up as an oracle so that "the Babylonian beast, contrary to the gospel of Christ, may occupy the throne of the Most High in the holy of holies" (pp. 143–48). See also *The Schole-*

master, where Ascham links Pighius with Machiavelli as "two indifferent patriarchs" of the worst sorts of papistry and impiety (III, 163).

26. *Apologia*, p. 43.   27. *Ibid.*, fol. [¶ᵥᵛ].

28. *Ibid.*, p. 125.   29. *Ibid.*, p. 116; *Works*, III, 201.

30. *Ibid.*, pp. 66–69.   31. *Ibid.*, pp. 71ff.

32. *Ibid.*, pp. 88–109.   33. *Ibid.*, fol. ¶ ᵥᵢᵢʳ.

34. *Themata Theologica*, pp. 187, 195, 228; see also pp. 222, 221, 156.

35. *Ibid.*, p. 195.

36. *Ibid.*, p. 200.

37. *Ibid.*, p. 156.

38. For discussion of the "puritanism" of Ascham, and of the Cambridge humanists and reformers in general, see Walter F. Schirmer, *Antike, Renaissance und Puritanismus* (Munich, 1933), *passim*, but especially pp. 93–104. Although it may sound unnecessarily tendentious to say so, the rather strict moral view expressed in *The Scholemaster* is characteristic of many humanist treatises on the rearing of youth and does not prove that Ascham was strongly influenced by or sympathetic with Genevan theological doctrine.

39. Baker, I, 125–26.

CHAPTER SIX

1. The identity of this other "Grindal" is not known. He may have been a certain James Grindall but was probably not Edmund, the future Archbishop of Canterbury (Strype, *The History of the Life and Acts of the Most Reverend Father in God, Edmund Grindal*, Oxford, 1821, I, 5).

2. I, 86–87. Two other letters of Ascham to Mistress Astley, not included in Giles, are preserved in B.M. Add. MS. 33,271, fols. 37ᵛ–38ʳ, 39ᵛ. They have been reproduced in Hayes, "The English Letters of Roger Ascham," pp. 1–6, 16.

3. Wilfred Blunt, *Sweet Roman Hand* (London, 1952), pp. 22–23. Blunt prints specimens of both Ascham's and the young Elizabeth's fine handwriting. Ascham is also mentioned among the great teachers of penmanship in Ambrose Heal, *The English Writing-Masters and Their Copy-Books, 1570–1800* (Cambridge, 1931), p. 6.

4. *Calendar of State Papers, Domestic Series, of the Reigns of Edward VI, Mary, Elizabeth, 1547–1580*, ed. Robert Lemon (London, 1856), p. 14.

5. I, 167. Giles places the letter in 1549, but in it Ascham mentions John Whitney as living, though he was dead by July of that year. Further, Elizabeth moved back to Hatfield in the autumn after Ascham came to her at Chelsea. The letter must have been written in 1548.

6. The information on these pages concerning Seymour's intrigues, along with that which follows concerning his arrest and the subsequent interrogation of Elizabeth and the Astleys, is taken from *Acts of the Privy Council of England, A.D. 1547–1550, new series* (London, 1890), II, 236–40, 246–63, and *Cal. St. Pap. Domestic, 1547–1580*, pp. 12–14. These troubles of the prin-

cess are treated in J. E. Neale, *Queen Elizabeth I* (New York, 1957), pp. 17–27, and, with some confusion about the current role of Ascham in her household, in Elizabeth Jenkins, *Elizabeth the Great* (London, 1958), pp. 26–34.

7. *Cal. St. Pap. Domestic, 1547–1580,* pp. 13–14.

8. Margaret Irwin, *Young Bess* (New York, [1945]), pp. 159–60, even suggests that Ascham may have been in love with his pupil and that he had formerly aroused the jealousy of Seymour. Hatch warns that while Miss Irwin's story is "romance," it may not be totally discounted because she "has had access to the private papers of the Seymour family" (p. 315n).

9. Strype, *Cheke,* pp. 44–46.

10. *Acts of the Privy Council, 1547–1550,* pp. 393, 398, 407; Strype, *The Life of the Learned Sir Thomas Smith, Kt., D.C.L.* (Oxford, 1820), pp. 41–43.

11. On the occasion of Mary Cecil's death, Ascham composed a Latin epitaph in the form of a dialogue among Life, Death, and Mary herself (III, 284–86). It is of the same mediocre quality as his other efforts in verse.

12. Cambridge University Library MS. Dd. ix. 14, fols. 78^v, 79^v. In February 1552, both Lever and Cheke wrote to Ascham. Lever was confident of procuring for his friend "all liberty" (*ibid.,* fol. 77^v), and Cheke promised to do all that he could in the matter (*ibid.,* fol. 82^r).

13. Katterfeld believes that all three letters refer to the same woman, and that the one addressed to "Mistress N——" (II, 143–45), since it alludes to "mine absence," was probably written from abroad (pp. 83–86). Giles prints the letter under the year 1567 and heads it "A letter written by R. A. for a gent to a gentlewoman in way of marriage," this heading being taken from a copy of the letter in the library of the University of Cambridge (MS. Dd. ix. 14, fol. 44^{r-v}). Yet Ascham is clearly proposing to the lady in his own behalf ("I write to you, and of myself") and would scarcely have done so in 1567 when he had already been married for thirteen years. There is no evidence either that he was writing from abroad or that "Mistress N——" is to be identified with "Alice" or "A—— B——." The letter may have been composed at any time in Ascham's adult life before June 1, 1554, the date of his marriage.

14. A copy of Sturm's letter (I, 195–207) is preserved in Corp. Chr. Coll., Cambr., MS. 113, fols. 141^r–153^r. On fols. 3–4 of the same manuscript is a letter to Princess Elizabeth (October 20, 1550) composed to accompany a present of two books that Sturm was sending her, presumably by means of Bucer's wife. Though Montague Rhodes James (*A Descriptive Catalogue of the Manuscripts in the Library of Corpus Christi College, Cambridge,* Cambridge, 1912, I, 249) says that the second epistle seems to be by Ascham, it appears, from internal evidence, to have been written by Bucer.

CHAPTER SEVEN

1. *Acts of the Privy Council of England,* new series III (1550–1552), ed. John Roche Dasent (London, 1891), p. 45; *Calendar of State Papers, For-*

eign Series, of the Reign of Edward VI., 1547–1553, ed. William B. Turnbull (London, 1861), p. 52.

2. The interview is described in a letter to Sturm (I, 227) and in *The Scholemaster* (III, 117–19). Among the works inspired or influenced in part by the latter passage, apart from its importance to biographies of Lady Jane Grey, are paintings by I. Fradelle and J. C. Horsley; romances like Francis Hodgson's *Lady Jane Grey: A Tale in Two Books* (London, 1809), especially pp. 47–49; a French tragedy, "Jane Grey," by A. Soumet and G. Daltenheym, *Magasin Théatral,* XXXVII (Paris, 1844); lines in Samuel Rogers's poem, "Human Life" (*Poems,* London, 1834, pp. 72, 105); and, of course, Walter Savage Landor's famous "Imaginary Conversation." In the fourth act of *The Tragedy of Lady Jane Grey,* Nicholas Rowe draws upon Ascham's account for a scene between Jane and her husband, Guildford Dudley.

3. Richard Patrick, fellow of St. John's; the implication seems to be that Patrick was one of those who had remained Catholic or at least favored the mass (see Baker, p. 284).

4. *Chambers's Cyclopaedia of English Literature,* revised edition (Philadelphia, 1923), p. 144.

5. This work was *The Epistle that J. Sturmius . . . sent to the Cardynalles and prelates, etc.* (London, 1538).

6. *Calendar of State Papers. Spanish. Edward VI, 1550–1552,* ed. Royall Tyler (London, 1914), X, 187.

7. I, 285. The reference is to religious practices that "have indeed a show of wisdom in will-worship, and humility, and neglecting of the body; not in any honor to the satisfying of the flesh" (Colossians 2:23).

8. Morison's comments appear in *Cal. St. Pap. Foreign. Edw. VI,* pp. 144–45. Ascham wrote a similar account in a letter to Thomas Lever (August 11, 1551). The letter is lost except for the description of the granaries, which is preserved in Thomas Milles, *The Custumers Apology* ([London, 1601]), last leaf, verso. The visit of Ascham and Morison to Nürnberg parallels that of Sir Thomas Elyot during his embassy to Charles V in 1532. Elyot had also noted the remarkable provision in the municipal granary and had sent the Duke of Norfolk a sample "of rye, which was laid in there 190 years past, whereof there remaineth yet above 500 quarters" (B.M. MS. Cotton Vitellius B. XXI, fols. 58–59, cited by Lehmberg, p. 105).

9. *Acts of the Privy Council,* n.s. III, 126.

10. *Cal. St. Pap. Foreign. Edw. VI,* pp. 74–75.

11. *Cal. St. Pap. Spanish,* X, 237–41. Morison seems also to have been dismissed once, when, as a gentleman of the privy chamber, he expressed in his writings opinions that were too markedly Protestant to please Henry VIII (*ibid.,* pp. 176–77).

12. *Cal. St. Pap. Foreign. Edw. VI,* pp. 83–84, 261.

13. *Cal. St. Pap. Spanish,* X, 310–17.

14. *Cal. St. Pap. Foreign. Edw. VI,* p. 137.

15. After Morison returned to England, the imperial ambassadors, among them Scheyfve and Simon Renard, informed Queen Mary of his actions on the

Continent "so that she may trust or mistrust [him] accordingly" (*Cal. St. Pap. Spanish*, X, 242). When they spoke of him, "her reply showed that she thoroughly knew that merchant (*marchant*)" (ibid., p. 257).

16. *Cal. St. Pap. Foreign. Edw. VI*, pp. 64, 80. Morison, for example, cannot refrain from such puns in his dispatches as calling Pope Julius III "the hollow Father" and "his Hollowness." He also makes such comments on the rumors of impending war as that the Turkish fleet appears "to have the Jews' Messias for their loadsman, so is it still a-coming and never cometh" (*ibid.*, pp. 111, 115, 136).

17. *Ibid.*, p. 216. Apparently this spy within Morison's own household was John Bernardine, an unsavory political agent who had served the King of France and was now in the pay of the English (*ibid.*, pp. 101–3). Bernardine seems to have done his utmost throughout the three years that Morison was abroad to discredit the ambassador both at the imperial court and with the privy council at home (*ibid.*, pp. 209, 212, 213, 223; *Cal. St. Pap. Spanish*, XI, 307).

18. *Cal. St. Pap. Foreign. Edw. VI, passim*, especially pp. 157, 173, 181–85, 242–45, 267, 280.

19. I, 344, 330. Cecil thanked Ascham for the map of Germany in a letter from Basing dated September 7, 1552 (Cambridge Univ. Library MS. Dd. ix. 14, fol. 76^v).

20. Paolo Giovio, *Historiarum sui temporis tomus primus* (Florence, 1550); *Polybii Megalopolitani Historiarum libri, etc.* (Basel, 1549).

21. *Philonis Judaei . . . libri quatuor, etc.*, trans. J. Christopherson (Antwerp, 1553).

22. I, 294. The volume referred to by Ascham is *De obitu doctissimi et sanctissimi theologi doctoris Martini Buceri, etc.*, ed. Sir John Cheke (London, 1551). Bucer's *De regno Christi Jesu* was finally published by Oporinus (Basel, 1557).

23. John Hales to Ascham, Augsburg, December 3, 1551 (Cambridge Univ. Library MS. Dd. ix. 14, fols. 79^v–81^v).

24. I, 192; trans. Giles, I, lxiii–lxiv.

25. The identification was made by M. Guggenheim, "Beiträge zur Biographie des Petrus Ramus," *Zeitschrift für Philosophie und Philosophische Kritik*, CXXI (1903), 141–42, and is supported by Howell (*Logic and Rhetoric*, p. 175). But even in Elizabethan times at least one person knew whom Ascham meant by the name "Cephas Chlononius," which is clearly a Greek rendering of "Pierre de la Ramée." In a copy of Ascham's *Epistolae* (1576) preserved in the library of St. John's College, an early owner named Robert Dow noted that the person in question was Ramus (fol. 14^v).

26. *Cal. St. Pap. Foreign. Edw. VI*, pp. 186, 196.

27. *Ibid.*, p. 207.

28. I, 242–43. This letter appears without date or the name of the addressee. It was unquestionably written to Maximilian, in December 1551, or shortly thereafter, for the reference to moving on a wintry day points to this particular time and incident. Katterfeld dates the letter from Hall, December 26, 1551 (p. 170, n. 1).

29. Such is the account of the incident rendered by Scheyfve some months later in a dispatch to Mary of Hungary (*Cal. St. Pap. Spanish*, X, 533–34). Morison's sojourn in Hall lasted at least until April 9, 1552, on which date he wrote from that town to the privy council (B.M. MS. Cotton Galba B. xi., fols. 105ʳ–106ʳ).

30. *Vita dell'Invittisimo Imperator Carlo Quinto*, second edition (Venice, 1562), fol. 301ᵛ.

31. At no other time during his three years abroad, with the possible exception of July–August of the same summer, could Ascham have made this journey. Before going to Innsbruck, he had mentioned hoping at last to see Italy (I, 308); after the return from Villach, he was with or near the emperor constantly until his own departure for England in September 1553. Katterfeld also argues for June 1552 as the most likely time for the trip to Venice (pp. 185–86, n. 1).

32. I, 340. On September 20, Sleidan reported to Cecil this visit of Morison and Ascham (John Strype, *Memorials of Archbishop Cranmer*, Oxford, 1848, III, 666).

33. *Cal. St. Pap. Foreign. Edw. VI*, p. 223. Morison was, in fact, a busy correspondent; during his embassy, his dispatches to the council alone number more than one hundred and forty.

34. *Cal. St. Pap. Spanish*, XI, 8.

35. Apparently Hoby had once been Cheke's pupil, for in July Ascham wrote to Cheke that the accomplished "young man showed clearly from what master's workshop he had come forth" (I, 363). See also *The Travels and Life of Sir Thomas Hoby, Kt. of Bisham Abbey written by himself 1547–1564*, ed. Edgar Powell (Camden Miscellany, X; London, 1902) for information about Hoby's activities at this time. Although neither he nor Ascham mentions the substance of their talks during the summer of 1553, comparison of their travel writings and their comments on certain recent events reveals a more than coincidental similarity of viewpoint and turn of expression.

CHAPTER EIGHT

1. Ascham mentions the death of Duke Maurice, which occurred on July 11, two days after he was wounded at the battle of Sievershausen (III, 53–54).

2. III, 55, 62. Although no journal has ever been found, it is certain that Ascham kept one for at least five months. On October 20, 1552, he wrote to Sturm: "I have maintained a record of each day in uninterrupted order from the flight out of Innsbruck until yesterday" (I, 338). It is conceivable that he took the precaution of destroying the diary before returning to England.

3. Katterfeld does devote a large portion of his monograph to a translation of and commentary on the *Report*, and Walter F. Staton, Jr., "Roger Ascham's Theory of History Writing," *Studies in Philology*, LVI (1959), 125–37, has discussed the theory of history outlined in its opening pages. Isaac Disraeli, *Amenities of Literature*, ed. B. Disraeli (London, n.d.), p. 362, recognizes the value of the fragment and expresses surprise that it was

not better known to historians. Lily B. Campbell also credits Ascham with formulating "as clearly as anyone in England basic standards of judgment" for evaluating historical writing (*Shakespeare's "Histories": Mirrors of Elizabethan Policy*, San Marino, Calif., 1947, p. 65). At least two modern writers on German affairs of this period have drawn upon the work (see n. 8 below), but curiously, other historians and biographers of Charles V, among them Robertson, Brandi, and, most recently, Royall Tyler, do not mention its existence. Even in its own time it seems to have enjoyed no special regard. Only Gabriel Harvey, that helpful jotter of marginalia, recognized the potentialities of the *Report*. In his personal copy, now owned by the Huntington Library, of Michel Hurault's *An Excellent Discourse upon the now present estate of France* (trans. Edward Aggas, London, 1592), Harvey notes, "Prima pars politica. Qualis Aschami discursus Germanicus" (fol. 1^r). In the margin of the next leaf, he calls Hurault's work "politic, & pragmatic," and thus links Ascham's effort with the new "pragmatic" Continental historiography.

4. The credit is given to Hayward, for example, in James Westfall Thompson, *A History of Historical Writing* (New York, 1942), I, 610. Yet Hayward's works and Bacon's *Henry VII* are more truly biographies than histories. Bacon, in particular, is concerned with the character of his subject rather than with the causes underlying the important historical events of his reign. Ascham, though he concentrates on Charles's character, does so because he sees it as a significant factor in the political history of contemporary Germany.

5. Even Denys Hay, though he does much to vindicate the *Anglica Historia* as unusually objective for its time, admits that Vergil's wish to please Henry VIII led to distortion in some portions of the work (*Polydore Vergil Renaissance Historian and Man of Letters*, Oxford, 1952, p. 154).

6. In several details, Proctor's preface strikingly resembles Ascham's opening pages. His aim, too, is ethical: to warn men away from rebellion and praise the conduct of loyal Kentishmen who withstood Wyatt. Originally, Proctor had intended simply to transcribe notes of his conversations with witnesses and to leave the writing of the actual history to others better qualified, but inconsistent and even false reports (stemming from malice on the one side and adulation on the other) had induced him to undertake the work himself in order to set the record straight and clear the good name of Kentishmen. Although he did not compose a genuine political history and is not a very competent student of historical causes, Proctor does use firsthand reports and original documents, inserts Thucydidean orations, and shows himself more the historian than the mere chronicler. He also claims to be impartial and disavows any hatred of Wyatt. He admires, indeed, the rebel leader's rare, though misapplied, talents. To the Catholic Proctor, the manifest cause of Wyatt's misguided rebellion is "heresy," which in his judgment, incidentally, is also the true source of all the current subversion in Bohemia and Germany (1555 edition, fols. a_{iiii}^r–a_{viii}^r).

7. See George B. Parks, "The First Draft of Ascham's *Scholemaster*," *Huntington Library Quarterly*, I (1938), 324. Parks quotes from the MS. Ascham's announcement of this project, which he mentions nowhere else.

8. According to Voigt, Ascham's is the most informative contemporary account of Maurice (*Moritz von Sachsen, 1541–1547*, Leipzig, 1876, p. 4, n. 3). Leopold von Ranke praises the section on Albert of Brandenburg and makes it the basis of his own portrait of the Margrave (*Deutsche Geschichte im Zeitalter der Reformation*, Leipzig, 1881, V, 228ff.) Katterfeld, who admires the *Report* for a number of reasons, observes that besides being unusually impartial for his time, Ascham provides one of the few reliable accounts of Maurice's early years, the only accurate contemporary record of the original dissension between the emperor and Albert, and the first authentic analysis of the political relations between Charles and the Duke of Cleves (p. 232).

9. A summary of this correspondence appears in *Cal. St. Pap. Foreign. Edw. VI*, pp. 269–88 *passim*. During these weeks Ascham apparently kept in close touch with the imperial apothecary so that Morison and his colleagues might be constantly aware of the state of Charles's health, upon which the negotiations hinged (Hist. MSS. Comm. *Calendar of the Manuscripts of the Marquess of Salisbury*, London, 1883, Part I, 114).

10. See Cicero, *De Oratore*, II, xv, 62–64; Lucian, *How to Write History*. For an account of the influence of Ciceronian theory on Guarino and other early humanists, see Remigio Sabbadini, *Il Metodo degli Umanisti* (Florence, [1922], pp. 75–85).

11. See Geneva Misener, "Iconistic Portraits," *Classical Philology*, XIX (1924), 110ff.

12. *The Histories*, trans. W. R. Paton (Loeb Classical Library; New York and London, 1925), IV, 3–5.

13. *Ibid.*, V, 385.

14. *Ibid.*, IV, 267. Ascham refers several times in his writing to Polybius (e.g., I, 129; II, 179; III, 230). In the long letter to Raven describing his journey from Mechelen to Augsburg, he reports that in Speyer he saw Polybius "printed in Greek and Latin with twelve books moo than was printed afore" (I, 258).

15. W. H. Woodward was the first to point out this debt, remarking that although Ascham "would not have allowed it, we may safely affirm that Machiavelli's *Relazioni* had taught him more than the ancients" (*Cambridge History of English Literature*, Cambridge, 1908–16, III, 432). Woodward, however, does not elaborate.

16. Besides two scornful references in the *Report* to those who have unscrupulous "Machiavel's heads" (III, 59, 61), there is a pair of comments in Ascham's correspondence on Machiavelli's unfailing "great wit" but frequent lack of "sound judgment" in ridiculing true religion (I, 438, 442). In *The Scholemaster*, too, Ascham links Machiavelli with the Catholic theologian Albert Pighius as "two indifferent patriarchs" of impiety and papistry (III, 163). All of these comments were in print before Innocent Gentillet's *Discourse . . . contre Nicolas Machiavel Florentin* ([Geneva], 1576) appeared, and long before the printing of Simon Patrick's translation of Gentillet's work (London, 1602).

17. *The Prince and the Discourses* (New York, 1950), p. 30.

18. In his "Proem," or preface, Machiavelli takes issue with the histories of Leonardo Bruni and Poggio, saying that upon reading "their writings to see in what order and manner they had proceeded, I found that in their descriptions of the wars carried on by the Florentines with foreign princes and peoples they had been most diligent; but of their civil discords and internal dissensions, and of the effects resulting therefrom, they had in part been silent, and in part had described them very briefly, which to the reader could be neither useful nor agreeable. I believe they did so because these facts seemed to them so unimportant that they judged them unworthy of being recorded in history, or because they feared to offend the descendants of those who took part in them, and who by the narration of these facts might have deemed themselves calumniated. These two reasons (be it said with their leave) seemed to me wholly unworthy of such great men; because if any-thing delights or instructs in history, it is that which is described in detail; and if any lesson is useful to the citizens who govern republics, it is that which demonstrates the causes of the hatreds and dissensions in the republic, so that, having learned wisdom from the perils experienced by others, they may maintain themselves united" (*The Historical, Political, and Diplomatic Writings of Niccolo Machiavelli*, trans. Christian E. Detmold, Boston and New York, 1891, I, 7–8). The edition of the *Historie Fiorentine* with which Ascham was familiar was probably that published at Florence, 1537, in which the passage translated above appears on fol. $BB_{iii}{}^{r}$.

19. The harms of internal discord, and the evils that befall states when factions call in foreign aid, form almost a leitmotif for *The History of Florence* (see, for example, pp. 8, 88–89, 119–20, 126, 221, and 320–21 in Detmold's version).

20. Detmold trans., I, 330.

21. The *Oxford English Dictionary* (under def. 2 of the word) cites Elyot's *Governour:* "The most damnable vice . . . is ingratitude, commonly called unkindness." But significantly enough, it was Ascham's master, Morison, who best explained the Tudor meaning of the term: "This vice is much better named in our tongue, than it is, as me thinketh in any other. Unkindness, is a fit name for so unnatural a vice: they that fall into it, go from the kind of men, they lose that state and name, that nature put them in, and are turned into cruel and unnatural beasts" (*An Invective Ayenste the great and de-testable vice, treason, etc.* London, 1539, fol. $B_{ii}{}^{v}$).

22. Katterfeld charges Ascham with naiveté in making ingratitude the principal cause and says that the troubles resulted from the clash of the emperor's dynastic ambitions with the interests of other princes (p. 231). But Ascham, as evidence given later in this chapter is meant to show, was not so naive as Katterfeld assumes.

23. Detmold trans., I, 154; *Hist. Fior.*, fol. 79^{r}. Staton observes, correctly, that even "when Machiavelli gets down to cases, he nearly always gives the *virtù* or lack of it of the prince as the cause of historical events" (p. 133). Thompson expresses much the same view (I, 477).

24. Compare Cicero, *Ad Atticum,* VIII, xi; IX, iv, xix.

25. No documentary record remains of such a pledge by Charles, and here Ascham's memory may have failed him. Besides, in an earlier letter to the fellows of St. John's (October 12, 1551), in which he discusses the Turkish affairs that constitute the first section of the *Report,* he writes more doubtfully that "whether a promise of the delivery was either not made or not kept, I cannot tell" (I, 310). It is possible that by 1553 he had more accurate information, but Ulloa asserts in his biography of the emperor that once Charles had the strategic city in his hands, he paid little heed to Soliman's request (fol. 297).

26. III, 14. Although he claims to be impartial, "neither Imperial nor French, but flat English," Ascham can see nothing but duplicity in the conduct of Henry II. This viewpoint, however, does not substantially affect the comparative objectivity of the *Report,* since Ascham is mainly concerned with the quarrel between Charles and the German princes.

27. III, 13. Ascham had already extolled Soliman's honesty and firmness in the letter to St. John's (I, 308).

28. Charles apparently did have knowledge that Farnese might be assassinated, for in the national archives at Simancas is preserved a letter to him from Gonzaga in which the plot is mentioned (*Cal. St. Pap. Spanish,* IX, 125).

29. III, 15. In his *Commentaries,* Sleidan offers a different interpretation of Ottavio's behavior. He cites a communication from the imperial court accusing Farnese of fomenting trouble and pretending that he sought Henry II's aid out of fear of Gonzaga. "But that is confuted by this writing: For if there were any cause of fear, the occasion was given of himself, who hath ofttimes laid wait for the life of Gonzaga" (*A Famouse Cronicle of oure time,* trans. John Daus, London, 1560, fol. ccclxviii^v).

30. See Ranke, *Deutsche Geschichte,* V, 123–25; *The History of the Popes,* trans. E. Foster (London, 1913), I, 214–19, and Wilhelm Maurenbrechen, *Karl V und die deutschen Protestanten, 1545–1555* (Düsseldorf, 1865), pp. 285–87, for evidence that Julius's advice was in fact strongly against Ottavio's appealing for French assistance.

31. III, 22. Katterfeld notes that Ascham's critical sense was overridden by this *mot,* the neatness of which led him to attribute to Julius unmerited cleverness: "Der Schurke, als welchen Pyramus ihn characterisirt, war er wohl, aber nicht der geniale Schurke, als welchen Ascham ihn zeichnet" (p. 243). Peter Vannes, furthermore, in at least two dispatches written to the privy council during July 1551, remarked that the pope got into political predicaments by his "great timidity and unadvised hastiness in determination" (*Cal. St. Pap. Foreign. Edw. VI,* pp. 143, 148). Yet in November of the same year Vannes also reported that at Venice "men of all sorts, as well temporal as spiritual, charge the Bishop of Rome as author of all the mischief, and men judge this to be the time that he shall be scourged with his own rod" (*ibid.,* p. 191).

32. See, for example, Royall Tyler, *The Emperor Charles the Fifth* (Lon-

don, 1956), p. 79, and Karl Brandi, *Kaiser Karl V*, third edition (Munich, 1941), I, *passim*.

33. III, 28. On Christmas Eve 1552, Vannes reported to the council that the Prince of Salerno was in Constantinople and had been well received by Soliman. But Vannes doubted that he would "prevail on the Turk to send his army in the spring to help forward the enterprise of Naples" (*Cal. St. Pap. Foreign. Edw. VI*, p. 234).

34. *Ibid.*, p. 240. I have transcribed the quotation at somewhat greater length from P.R.O. State Papers. Foreign. Edward VI, January–March, 1552–1553, XI, 55.

35. Brandi, who takes a different view of Albert, says that in the events leading up to the battle of Sievershausen Maurice, finding himself now opposed to his sometime ally, believed that in fighting Albert he was ridding Germany of the destructive and outworn forces of the robber-barons, who were an anachronism in Reformation Germany ("er bekämpfte und besiegte in ihm die zerstörenden Kräfte des alten, schliesslich käuflich gewordenen Raubrittertums, das für den Aufbau des Fürstenstaates der Reformation untragbar geworden war," I, 535).

36. According to Katterfeld, Ascham misapplies this epithet to Casimir, when it had actually been assigned to Prince Albert of Brandenburg, the Margrave's grandfather (p. 252, n. 2).

37. III, 37. Ascham's mention of Schwendi's handsome personal appearance is confirmed by a contemporary portrait preserved at Schloss Ambras, near Innsbruck.

38. The original Spanish version was printed at Amsterdam in 1547; in 1548 editions appeared at Venice and Madrid. In 1550 a rather free Latin rendering by W. von Male appeared at Antwerp, and in 1555 at London, an English translation by J. Wilkinson (*The Comentaries of Don Lewes de Avila, and Suniga, etc.*). Ascham may have known Avila, who commanded the emperor's cavalry at the siege of Metz.

39. Ascham has little support by other authors in these accusations of flattery and spite. Thompson calls Avila "the stellar historian under Charles V" and asserts that the *Commentarios* "ranks high in Spanish prose literature" (*A History of Historical Writing*, I, 581). Katterfeld also defends Avila, saying that the charge against Albert is correct and that in the original Spanish text the author is guilty of almost no "unbegründeter Schmähungen gegen die deutsche Nation." Whatever offense he may have given is of the kind that can come from any history in which the author has the military glory of his own people at heart. As for the alleged slanders, Katterfeld conjectures that Ascham must have seen, and Albert must have been referring to, the Latin version, in which the freedom of the rendering may have made Avila appear to be reviling the German people (p. 245, n. 2). In Wilkinson's translation, made directly from the Spanish, rather than the Latin, one finds only praise for the Germans as hardy soldiers (fols. $F_{viii}{}^{r-v}$, $H_{vii}{}^{v}$). Sleidan, on the other hand, agrees with his friend Ascham that the book offended the German princes because Avila, "a naughty and a lying fellow, . . . speaketh

of all Germany so coldly, so disdainfully and strangely, as though it were some barbarous or vile nation, whose original were scarcely known" (*A Famouse Cronicle*, fol. cccxciii^v).

40. Ascham cannot believe that John Frederick would have left Maurice's army behind him in Saxony if he had suspected treachery. He claims as well that he had "heard skilful men say" that Maurice "was ready with his counsel, and promised his aid, to help forward the enterprise" (III, 45). That Maurice's betrayal of John Frederick was unexpected is also reported by Sleidan (fol. cclxx^r) and Johann Carion, *The thre bokes of Cronicles,* trans. Walter Lynne (London, 1550), under A.D. 1546 (fols. cclxvii^v–cclxviii^r).

41. II, 42. Ranke was sufficiently impressed with the authenticity of this anecdote to take it over from Ascham in his *Deutsche Geschichte* (IV, 380).

42. The substance of the foregoing paragraph is taken from III, 41–44, and from a letter to Raven in which Ascham sharply contrasts John Frederick's good character with the untrustworthy deportment of the Landgrave (I, 244). Avila draws a strikingly similar contrast (Wilkinson trans., fol. T$_{ii}$$^{r-v}$). Falletti, though decidedly anti-Protestant and especially anti-Mauritian in his history, expresses ungrudging admiration for John Frederick (*Della guerra di Alamagna,* Venice, 1552, pp. 281ff).

43. III, 47–48. In his lament over England, Ascham may have had in mind not only the recent example of the Seymours but also an incident in More's *Richard III.* His words are remarkably suggestive of the deathbed speech of King Edward IV in More's history; see *The English Works of Sir Thomas More,* ed. W. E. Campbell (London; New York, 1931–), I, 38–39.

44. The neat trick of pen reported by Ascham calls to mind the device of omitted punctuation by which the king's execution is ordered in Christopher Marlowe's tragedy, *Edward II* (V, v, 16–17). Fascinating as it is, other contemporary historians on both sides fail to mention the incident. Avila, who was actually present on the occasion, writes that Charles promised the Landgrave only that he would not be punished "with perpetual prison" and that the desperate Philip gladly submitted himself to the emperor's discretion, "entreating of no other thing, but to be a prisoner perpetual or temporal" (Wilkinson trans., fols. S$_{viii}$^{r}, T$_i$^{v}). According to Sleidan, the suppliants who appeared before Charles admitted that the sole promise had been not to imprison Philip forever, but the Elector of Brandenburg and Maurice had nevertheless brought him to Halle out of hope that his coming would lead to a reconciliation with the emperor (fol. 375^r). Ranke will have no part of the "einig-ewig" tale. He says that if Maurice and others were amazed at the arrest, their misunderstanding was their own fault, since Charles had made clear his intention of detaining Philip, at least temporarily, for the imperial safety (*Deutsche Geschichte,* IV, 382–88). Brandi claims that Joachim and Maurice, by pretending to read into the agreement something that was not there, had duped the Landgrave into believing that he would not be arrested (I, 572).

45. III, 61. Compare Ranke (V, 177) for the contrary opinion that Maurice really intended to go further than he found himself capable of doing.

46. III, 61–62. In his preface Appian explains why he did not order his history according to a strict chronology: "Thinking that the public would like to learn the history of the Romans in this way, I am going to write the part relating to each nation separately, omitting what happened to the others in the meantime, and taking it up in its proper place" (*Appian's Roman History*, trans. Horace White; Loeb Classical Library; London, 1912, I, 21).

47. Cicero, *De Oratore*, IV, xv, 64 ("fusum et tractum"). Compare the treatise on historiography by the Jacobean writer Edmund Bolton, who declares that the style of the historian "should have gloss and luster, but otherwise rather solidity and fluency, than singularity of oratorical or poetical notions" ("Hypercritica," in *Critical Essays of the Seventeenth Century*, ed. J. E. Spingarn, Bloomington, 1957, I, 107).

48. *How to Write History*, para. 44. This precept is a variation of the Aristotelian commonplace paraphrased by Ascham in *Toxophilus*: "To speak as the common people do, to think as wise men do" (II, 7). In the preface to his translation of Livy, Philemon Holland expresses the same intention of making his effort "profitable to the most" by framing his "pen, not to any affected phrase, but to a mean and popular style" ("To the Reader," *The Romane Historie*, London, 1600).

49. *The Historie of Guicciardin*, trans. Geoffrey Fenton (London, 1579), especially pp. 1, 729.

50. Machiavelli, *The Prince and the Discourses*, pp. 191–93.

CHAPTER NINE

1. Not one item in the first volume of state papers for Mary's reign appears to be in Ascham's hand (Public Record Office, State Papers, Mary, July–October, 1553).

2. James Anthony Froude, *History of England*, London, 1870–72, V, 212; Conyers Read, *Mr. Secretary Cecil and Queen Elizabeth* (London, 1955), pp. 97–103.

3. I, 318. During his three years abroad, Raven and Ireland and possibly Walter Haddon served as his proxies. Haddon appears to have composed much of the official correspondence for the university during Ascham's absence, including the invitation to Northumberland in 1552 to replace Somerset as chancellor (*Lucubrationes*, pp. 159–62).

4. *Cal. St. Pap. Foreign. Mary, 1553–1558*, p. 8; *The Travels and Life of . . . Hoby*, p. 96.

5. Baker, I, 137.

6. III, 236. "Aper de Silva" is the "boar out of the wood" that laid waste the vine planted by the Lord in Israel (Psalms 80: 13; Vulgate 79: 14). Here it signifies papistry, revival of which led to the Marian persecutions. Ironically, Pope Leo X, in his bull *Exsurge, Domine*, had applied this same figure to Luther.

7. Charles Henry Hopwood, *Middle Temple Records* (London, 1904–5), I, 98. A "Roger Askam" is also listed among those admitted to the society between 1525 and 1551, but since the volume containing the records for those years has been lost, it is not certain that the person named is the subject of this study (*Register of Admissions to the Honourable Society of the Middle Temple*, ed. Sir Henry F. MacGeagh, London, 1949, I, 12).

8. *Cal. Pat. Rolls. Philip and Mary. 1553–1554* (London, 1937), I, 278.

9. *Reformatio Angliae ex Decretis Reginaldi Poli Cardinalis, Sedis Apostolicae Legati, Anno M.D.LVI.* (Rome, 1562), fols. 12^v, 19^r.

10. Ascham remained silent about the *Report* and did not reveal its existence even to his trusted patron Gardiner. He did mention to the bishop that his sojourn at the emperor's court *would have* made him capable of writing such a work, had not the springs of eloquence dried up within him because of his long absence from the sources of learning and his worries about his own future (I, 384).

11. For some reason the epigraph, along with Haddon's commendatory verses, appears in Giles's edition not before *Toxophilus*, but immediately after the title page of vol. I.

12. Froude, V, 292–93; James Arthur Muller, *Stephen Gardiner and the Tudor Reaction* (New York, 1926), p. 223.

13. *Cal. Pat. Rolls. Philip and Mary*, I, 383. Giles places the letter in which Ascham mentions the difficulties over the wording of the appointment at the end of 1554, but since the patent was issued on May 7, the letter (I, 417–19) must have been written at about the same time.

14. The Howe family was prominent among the gentry of Essex until well into the seventeenth century (See *The Visitations of Essex*; Harleian Society, XIII; London, 1878, Part I, 425).

15. *Transactions of the Essex Archaeological Society*, new series (Colchester, 1898), VI, 49, gives the descent of the Harlestons of South Ockenden.

16. I, 447. The "R." is obviously a scribal error. The Walop mentioned by Sturm was Sir John. Ascham's comparison is certainly meant to afford an exact guide to Margaret Howe's appearance, which Sturm could easily surmise from his memory of her aunt. Inadvertently confusing the matter of this person's Christian name even further, the author of the article on Ascham in the eleventh edition of the *Encyclopaedia Britannica* calls him Sir *Henry* Walop (II, 721).

17. Nowhere is the year of Margaret's birth given, but the evidence suggests that she was quite young, and in all likelihood a minor, when she married Ascham. Grant calls her *adolescentulam* ("a young maiden," III, 333), and in 1567 Ascham reminded himself of the difference in their ages: "You are well stepped into years; your wife is young" (II, 156).

18. II, 170–73. Giles, believing that the letter refers to the death of Ascham's son Sturm (*ca.* 1567) includes it tentatively in the correspondence for 1568. But Katterfeld infers from the context, in which the Aschams' disappointed hope of being "made vessels to increase the world" is mentioned, that it followed upon the loss of a first-born child (p. 297, n. 2). Since several other children had been born by then, he rejects 1568 as an unlikely date.

324 *Notes to Pages 203–6*

Hayes, though with the reservation that the internal evidence does not absolutely preclude the existence of other children, agrees substantially with Katterfeld and offers a conjectural date of 1555 (p. 217). While the grounds are insufficient for assigning so early a date, the letter, because its wording does suggest the loss of an only child, was probably written between 1555 and 1562, by which time Giles, eldest among the sons who survived infancy, had been born.

19. In the version printed by Giles, only three of the four points are taken up, and the third is disposed of in a slapdash manner. Giles, as both Katterfeld and Hayes have noted, followed the text printed in Whitaker's *Richmondshire*, which is based on the inferior Hopkinson MS. The copy in B.M. Add. MS. 33,271, fol. 39^v, is similarly truncated. A version almost twice as long, proving how the parents' hopes had been fulfilled in all respects, is preserved in Cambridge University Library MS. Ee.V.23, pp. 455–57. Because Ascham would never have been guilty of the logically incomplete version printed by Giles, I have varied here from my usual practice in citation and have followed the superior text of the Cambridge manuscript.

20. III, 332. The letter to Raven has been lost, but copies of more than one hundred epistles written for Philip and Mary, among them many of the forty-seven alluded to by Grant, are preserved in one of Ascham's letter books among the Hardwicke papers (B.M. Add. MS. 35,840). Giles prints but a few of these.

21. I, 421–22. The probable identification of the correspondent has been made by Hatch (p. 608n).

22. I, 429–30. Giles conjectures 1555; Hatch, 1556 (p. 632n). Hatch is more probably correct since the council ordered a stay of seizure of the Dudleys' goods on April 18, 1556 (*Acts of the Privy Council, 1554–1556*, ed. John Roche Dasent, new series, London 1892, V, 263).

23. Without offering any evidence, some earlier writers have assumed that Ascham's wife had "a considerable fortune" (see, for example, George Ballard, *Memorials of Several Ladies of Great Britain, etc.*, Oxford, 1752, p. 153). But Ascham's letters and official contemporary documents show that in fact he spent a good deal of his own time and money on helping his wife's family out of financial difficulties.

24. I, 413. Giles, following the ascription made by Whitaker (*Richmondshire*, p. 275), assumes that the recipient was William Paulet, Marquis of Winchester. The copy of the letter in B.M. Add. MS. 33,271, fol. 5^v, is undated and is addressed simply "To Sir W.P." It is not likely that Ascham would have saluted Winchester as though he were a mere knight, or begun, as he does, with a crisp "Sir." He also twice uses "your," never "your lordship's," in the text. Though the addressee could have been Paget, the likeliest candidate is Petre, with whom Ascham had been corresponding about his patents and whom he credits elsewhere with having helped to secure another important grant for him (II, 48). Giles, in order to eliminate an apparent anachronism, corrects the date, given by Whitaker as January 18, 1554, to June 18 of the same year. But since the date may have been written old style,

January 18, 1554 (that is, 1555), there is no significant chronological problem.

25. *Cal. Pat. Rolls. Philip and Mary*, III, 259.

26. See "The tenoure of Cardinall Pooles Oration," printed by John Foxe in his *Actes and Monuments* (London, 1563), pp. 1008–10.

27. The copies presented to Tunstall and the cardinal, with Ascham's autograph inscriptions on the flyleaves, are in the library of St. John's College, Cambridge. The letter to Tunstall, printed by none of Ascham's editors, is dated March 12, 1554 (that is, 1555), nearly a month earlier than the other. Because a large part of the dedication to Pole (I, 440–42) is copied almost verbatim from that to Petre (I, 436–39), Giles places the latter epistle, which is undated, with the correspondence for 1555. But since this is the letter in which Ascham complained of having spent £40 in five months of waiting about for his commission as secretary, it obviously belongs to the winter of 1553–54.

28. III, 185, 204–5. Ascham's later judgment of Osorio is more tempered, for this is that same writer whose "flowing and watery vein" Bacon disparages, along with Ascham's own Ciceronianism, in the well-known attack in *The Advancement of Learning* on the idle pursuit of "words more than matter." Ascham may have revised his opinion of Osorio's style in after years because of Osorio's attack on the English Reformation, which involved him in a running controversy with Walter Haddon and John Foxe; see my article, "The Haddon–Osorio Controversy (1563–1583)," *Church History*, XXII (1953), 142–54.

29. II, 50–51, 53–55. Giles erroneously places the former letter among those of 1561, but since Osorio mentions in it having met Thomas Wilson, the English ambassador, it belongs to 1567, the year in which Wilson's embassy began (Hatch, p. 847n).

30. I, 447–48. Ascham became devoted to Priuli and in 1561 lamented his passing in an epistle to Osorio (not in Giles; printed in Osorio, *Opera Omnia*, Rome, 1592, I, 1143).

31. B.M. MS. Cole 5807, fol. [i^r].

32. Johnson, "Life of Ascham," in Bennet's edition of *The English Works*, p. xii; Hartley Coleridge, *Biographia Borealis* (London, 1833), pp. 321–24. Johnson observes that it is vain to try to comprehend the "motives of discrimination and partiality" of another age.

33. See also the letters to his young brother-in-law Christopher Howe (II, 27–30) and to Richard Goodrich (II, 20–25). Katterfeld mentions having seen at St. John's an evening prayer composed by Ascham on a flyleaf of Conrad Heresbach, *De laudibus Graecarum literarum oratio* (Strasbourg, 1551), the work with which his and Sturm's *De Nobilitate Anglicana* had been bound. Unfortunately, the volume seems to have disappeared from the college.

34. "Mereri est proficere ad vitam aeternam per fidem quemadmodum ego colligi ex his locis" (bottom of p. 47).

35. Christina H. Garrett, *The Marian Exiles: A Study in the Origins of*

Elizabethan Puritanism (Cambridge, 1938), *passim;* Porter, *Reformation and Reaction in Tudor Cambridge,* pp. 76–82.

36. Strype, *Cheke,* pp. 107–31.

37. Froude, V, 561.

38. Letter to Aylmer (not in Giles; cited in Jenkins, p. 57).

39. *Cal. St. Pap. Foreign. Mary,* p. 172. So certain was the queen of her pregnancy that two of the prematurely drafted letters bear her sign manual as well as Ascham's countersign.

40. I, 446. Although Wolfgang Werter visited Paolo Manuzio at this time, he seems not to have shown or mentioned Sturm's work to the famous Italian humanist. When Manuzio wrote later to a friend at Brescia that he had seen Werter, he did not allude to the manuscript. Having heard, in fact, that his friend was preparing a commentary of his own on the *Rhetoric,* Manuzio urged him to finish this useful and sorely needed work (*Paulli Manutii Epistolarum Libri XII Uno nuper addito,* Venice, 1582, pp. 89–90).

CHAPTER TEN

1. "Carmen consolatorium in rebus afflictis S. Principis Elisabethae," in Haddon, *Poematum libri duo,* fols. H_4^v–[H_5^r].

2. *Cal. St. Pap. Foreign. Mary, 1553–1558,* pp. 345, 374, 380; *Arte of Rhetorique,* preface.

3. Brief of Edward Raven's Will (B.M. MS. Harleian 7039, fol. 218^r), reproduced by Hayes, p. 359.

4. B.M. Royal MS. 13. B. I, fol. 215. Also preserved in the British Museum is a copy of Englefield's own petition to the queen for forgiveness, written in 1563. It is somewhat ironic that the manuscript in which the supplication appears is a collection of model epistles dominated by examples taken from the correspondence of Ascham (Add. MS. 33,271).

5. II, 62–64. This epistle, and also Ascham's next to Sturm, in which he further praises Elizabeth as a monarch (II, 71–73), are translated in full in *The Zürich Letters,* second series, ed. Hastings Robinson (Parker Society; Cambridge, 1845), pp. 64–72, 90–93.

6. How he typically performed his function as secretary is shown not only by surviving copies of both the English and the Latin versions of individual letters (for example, a safe-conduct for certain Portuguese subjects, P.R.O. State Papers. Foreign. Elizabeth, April–June, 1561, nos. 138–39), but also by a revealing note preserved in the domestic state papers for 1565. There, under the preliminary draft of a pension for the Marquis of Baden, Cecil has scribbled the following hurried instructions: "Mr. Ascham, I pray you draw out for the Marquis of Baden patents according as I have Englished it." He requests, moreover, that the task be finished speedily, "because there is another which you must write to the King of Denmark" (P.R.O. State Papers. Domestic. Elizabeth, August–November, 1565, fol. 197^r).

7. Copies of more than two hundred letters composed by Ascham appear

on the first 257 folios of B.M. Royal MS. 13. B. I, which is almost certainly his personal register of state correspondence for the period from November 26, 1558, to October 8, 1568. Most of the transcripts seem to have been made by scribes, perhaps by his own staff of underlings. Those on fols. 1–6, 10ʳ, and 16–24, however, are in his own hand, as are a number of marginal notes, additions, and corrections appearing elsewhere in the volume (see Sir George F. Warner and Julian P. Gilson, *Catalogue of Western Manuscripts in the Old Royal and King's Collections,* London, 1921, II, 88–92). Other official letters written by Ascham are preserved in B.M. MS. Lansdowne 98, fols. 49–101, and among the volumes of state papers for the decade 1558–68 in the Public Record Office. Giles gives a fair sample of this extensive correspondence, in all about fifty specimens from William Elstob's edition of Ascham's epistles (Oxford, 1703) and from MS. Lansdowne 98.

8. B.M. Royal MS. 13. B. I, fol. 217. Ascham was also supposed to draw up a second request when Murray, Regent of Scotland, came to London late in 1568, but death prevented his doing so (Murray to Cecil, *Calendar of State Papers. Foreign. Elizabeth, 1569–1571,* ed. Allan James Crosby, London, 1874, p. 35).

9. II, 16–20, 43, 51–53, 135–38; B.M. Royal MS. 13. B. I, fols. 44ᵛ, 108, 113. A firm threat of reprisals against Spanish merchants if wrongs against certain English seamen are not redressed occurs in Folger Shakespeare Library MS. X. d. 138 (2).

10. For example, II, 40–45, 78–83; B.M. Royal MS. 13. B. I, fols. 3, 39ᵛ, 47, 49, 56ᵛ, 123ᵛ, 198ᵛ, 230.

11. II, 43–45; B.M. Royal MS. 13. B. I, fol. 56ᵛ.

12. II, 41–42; B.M. Royal MS. 13. B. I, fols. 47, 49.

13. II, 83–87; B.M. Royal MS. 13. B. I, fols. 12, 18, 94. Another letter to the landgrave, in Ascham's italic hand, is preserved in Folger Shakespeare Library MS. X. d. 138 (1).

14. *Calendar of State Papers. Foreign. Elizabeth, 1558–1559,* ed. Joseph Stevenson (London, 1863), p. 134.

15. *Calendar of State Papers. Foreign. Elizabeth, 1562,* ed. Joseph Stevenson (London, 1867), pp. 608–9.

16. H.M.C., *Marquess of Salisbury MSS.,* Part. I, 294. In 1561 Ascham wrote a letter for the queen, asking the Duke of Tuscany to protect Hertford, who meant to travel to Italy (II, 45).

17. Letters from the Hapsburg archives, cited in *Queen Elizabeth and Some Foreigners,* ed. Victor von Klarwill and trans. T. H. Nash (New York, 1928), p. 112. Although Ascham supported the King of Sweden in 1559, three years later he was in favor of Elizabeth's marrying one of her own countrymen, perhaps, though he does not say so, Lord Robert Dudley (II, 64).

18. The fact is recorded in the letter book in Ascham's own hand (B.M. Royal MS. 13. B. I, fol. 33ᵛ). This favor by Cecil was first noted by Warner and Gilson (II, 88).

19. *Return Members of Parliament* ([London], 1878), Part I, 403–4; W. Duncombe Pink and Alfred B. Beaven, *The Parliamentary Representa-*

tion of Lancashire, (County and Borough), 1258–1885, etc. (London, 1889), p. 144.

20. "Cum tamen alea et Alectryomachia plus nimio oblectatur, re tenui vixit et obiit" (*Annales Rerum Anglicarum, et Hibernicarum, Regnante Elizabetha, ad annum Salutis M.D.LXXXIX.*, London, 1615, p. 150).

21. Fuller, *The History of the Worthies of England*, ed. P. Austin Nuttall (London, 1840), III, 430; Lloyd, *The States-Men and Favourites of England Since the Reformation, etc.* (London, 1665), p. 429. Among other places where Camden's comment has been repeated are Wood, *Athenae Oxonienses*, I, 695; Johnson's sketch in Bennet's edition of the *English Works*, p. xiii; *Critical Review*, XVI (1763), 27; and *Biographia Britannica* (1747), I, 217. Some skepticism about the charge accompanies its reiteration in Archbishop William Nicolson, *The English, Scotch, and Irish Historical Libraries*, new edition (London, 1776), Part I, p. 203; *The Imperial Dictionary of Universal Biography*, ed. John Eadie *et al.* (London, n.d.), I, 252; Disraeli, *Amenities of Literature*, p. 365; and *The Oxford Companion to English Literature*, ed. Sir Paul Harvey (Oxford, 1932), p. 43.

22. III, 140, 225. The treatise on cockfighting, which has never come to light, has tantalized scholars and antiquarians ever since publication of *The Scholemaster*. Probably, like the Latin version of the *Philoctetes* and the German diary, it was one of those works that Ascham projected and either never completed or destroyed.

23. II, 134. Ascham credits Cecil with having brought about this appointment without his own knowledge, "I being sick in my bed, not suiting nor knowing any such matter" (II, 48).

24. Sir Robert Naunton, *Fragmenta Regalia*, ed. Horace Walpole (London, 1797), p. 95.

25. B.M. Add. MS. 33,271, fol. 44; also MS. Hopkinson 18, fols. 127ᵛ–128ʳ. Not in Giles, but reproduced in Hayes, pp. 273–75.

26. II, 175. Thomas Ascham's relationship to Roger went unsuspected until Katterfeld (p. 353) picked up a hint about the connection from the Coopers' *Athenae Cantabrigienses* (I, 263). Although Katterfeld did not investigate the clue, in 1886 Ernest G. Atkinson deduced from certain documents which he had examined that Ascham's second surviving son was really named Thomas, and not Dudley after all. Sir Sidney Lee replied immediately that Ascham's own letters and a number of entries in the patent rolls supplied incontrovertible proof of Dudley's existence; relying too heavily on the final letter to Sturm, he refused to admit the possibility that Ascham might have had a posthumous son. His final conclusion was that contemporary lawyers may have been confused by the existence of some near relation named Thomas, the son, perhaps, not of Elizabeth's Latin secretary, but of that other Roger Ascham, her yeoman of the bears (for the Atkinson–Lee controversy, see *Athenaeum*, July–Dec., 1886, pp. 304–5, 399, 432–33, 499–500). In 1932, B. F. C. Atkinson proved conclusively that Thomas was Roger's son by tracing the family relationships through a group of legal documents acquired early in the present century by the Cambridge University Library; see "Whit-

tlesford Rectory & the Ascham Family," *Proceedings of the Cambridge Antiquarian Society*, XXXII (1932), 47–50. The article is based on original indentures and leases (C.U.L. Documents 441–56) that give the story of the Aschams' long connection with Whittlesford.

27. II, 47. See *Cal. Pat. Rolls. Elizabeth* (London, 1939), I, 432, for a grant on August 2, 1560, of the reversion and rents of Ascham's lease to various Londoners. Why a similar grant of the reversion was made to certain other persons in the last year of Mary's reign is not explained (*Cal. Pat. Rolls. Philip and Mary*, London, 1939, IV, 406–9).

28. I, 409–10. With some hesitation, Giles dates the letter shortly before Palm Sunday 1554. But if the "dearest brother John H." mentioned therein is a brother-in-law of Ascham's, the earliest possible date is 1555, after his marriage.

29. II, 27–30. Though Giles places this letter conjecturally among those of 1559, Hayes dates it more accurately between December 26, 1561, and October, 1562 (p. 246).

30. II, 48; also II, 151 (Ascham's rendering of Sophocles, *Oedipus at Colonus*, l. 1129). He had twice cited the same text in expressing gratitude to his earlier patron, Gardiner (I, 407, 409).

31. *Cal. Pat. Rolls. Elizabeth*, I, 45.

32. *Valor Ecclesiasticus, Temp. Henr. VIII.* ([London], 1817–1834), V, 2.

33. Quoted in Thomas Wright, *Queen Elizabeth and Her Times* (London, 1838), I, 145–46. Although it is not absolutely certain that the bearer mentioned was Roger Ascham, the "Master" prefixed to the name, the likelihood that the affair of the prebend would have taken him to the north at some time, and his suitability as a courier because of his direct access to Cecil argue for the identification.

34. *Lucubrationes*, p. 311.

35. III, 69. Ascham stresses the appropriateness of his gift by pointing out that Elizabeth has been to him like another David, the pattern of just monarchy. Giles, finding the letter prefixed to *The Scholemaster* in Bennet's edition, mistakenly prints it as Ascham's dedicatory epistle to the queen, even though its contents and intention obviously have no relation to the treatise.

36. Muniments Room, St. John's College, Drawer 16, Document 18; see also Baker I, 393.

37. Baker, pp. 396–97.

38. II, 152–61. The letter is included as a model of supplication in B.M. Add. MS. 33,271, fols. 3^r–4^r.

39. See, for example, the discussion of "suasory" epistles in Erasmus's *Opus de conscribendis epistolis* (Paris, 1530), or, better, his *Brevissima maximeque compendiaria conficiendarum epistolarum formula* (Paris, 1526), fol. a$_{vii}$^{r}–b$_i$^{r}.

40. Buchanan, *Opera Omnia*, ed. Thomas Ruddiman (Leyden, 1725), II, 762.

41. *Ibid.*, p. 369.

42. Wilson, *Arte of Rhetorique,* p. 123. Compare Ascham, II, 104; III, 203, 225–26, where the "one-winged" classicist mentioned is unquestionably Haddon, who freely admitted his incompetence in Greek (*Lucubrationes,* p. 168). John E. B. Mayor's conjecture that Ascham may have been referring to Leicester is unsupported by any evidence (*The Scholemaster,* London, 1863, p. 244).

43. B.M. Royal MS. 18. B. xxiv, Item 3. Haddon's verses, extolling Norton for revealing the hidden sources of gold and for the more preciously golden literary work in which he has disclosed such riches, appear on fol. 79^v and are printed in his *Poematum libri duo,* fol. H$_2$^{v}.

44. Haddon, *Lucubrationes,* pp. 307–8. The pun on *gallus* (cock) and *Gallus* (Frenchman) seems to refer to the projected treatise on the cockpit and probably owes something to the similar play upon words in More's epigram "In Anglum Gallicae Linguae Affectatorum," *The Latin Epigrams of Thomas More,* ed. and trans. Leicester Bradner and Charles Arthur Lynch, Chicago, 1953, p. 45.

45. *Lucubrationes,* p. 311.

46. Marginal annotations in his copy of St. Ambrose, *De vocatione,* pp. 38–39.

47. See Chapter Three, n. 37.

48. *Three morall treatises, etc.* (London, 1561), fol. A$_{11}$^{r} of the "Fruites of Foes" section (not in Giles).

49. Translator's preface, addressed to Thomas Cecil, *Ten Books of Homers Iliades, translated out of French* (London, 1581), fol. A$_{11}$^{v}.

50. Osorio, *Opera Omnia* (Rome, 1592), I, 1143–44 (not in Giles).

51. *Aeschinis et Demosthenis orationes duae contrariae, etc.* (Strasbourg, 1550); an edition entitled *Aeschinis contra Ctesiphontem et Demosthenis pro corona, etc.* was published at London in 1624.

52. II, 175. The letter extends over pp. 174–91. Giles dates it "about Dec. 1568," but internal evidence suggests that it was composed over a period of several months, beginning in July or August. Ascham accounts for his leisure to write at such length by remarking that the queen was away from the city, not serving Athena, "as she does all the rest of the year," but rather following Diana in the forest (II, 190). This seems to allude to Elizabeth's long summer progress after the middle of July, which took her, among other places, to the Earl of Oxford's beautiful park and wood at Havering Bower in Essex (Joseph Nichols, *Progresses of Queen Elizabeth,* London, 1788, I, 115). Ascham's mentioning his son Sturm's death, however, seems to be in response to a worried inquiry about his health sent by his godfather on October 1 (II, 169). It is conceivable that the letter, begun apparently before the end of July, was not finished, in spite of the leisure at Ascham's disposal, until autumn. Since Ascham soon became mortally ill, it may never have been sent to Sturm.

53. Compare Haddon, "Angliae Prosopopoeia," *Poematum libri duo,* fols. [H$_5$^{v}–H$_6$^{r}].

54. The absence of a written will is confirmed, and Grant's account authenticated, by a memorandum preserved in Somerset House that records

the substance of the testament, the time of the declaration, and the names of the witnesses, as sworn before William Ireland on January 3, 1569, by Margaret Ascham (Sheffield MS. 1, fol. 1ʳ).

55. Although the church was gutted by the fire of 1666, one monument along the north wall was left intact. A tradition of St. Sepulchre's, unsubstantiated by any inscription or other evidence, holds this to be Ascham's resting place.

56. *Opera Omnia,* II, 384; reprinted by Giles, I, cxii. Translations of the epigram appear in Bayle's *Dictionary* and in *Biographia Britannica,* but Hartley Coleridge's (*Biographia Borealis,* p. 333), is somewhat more accurate than either of these:

> The native Muses join with those of Greece
> And mighty Rome, in pious grief for Ascham,
> Whom Princes valued, and his friends beloved;
> With little wealth he lived, and spotless fame.

In the Huntington Library copy of Coleridge's work, an irreverent parody of the epigram is scribbled in pencil at the bottom of the page:

> The Latin muses and Grecian muses
> For Ascham Blubber and Bawl—
> A Pleasant Fellow who with Princes got mellow
> Although his means were small—
> And as for his morals, he little loses
> . . . . them . . . . . .

Perhaps fortunately, the remainder is cropped.

CHAPTER ELEVEN

1. "Mr. Nicasius" is not identified by Ascham or any of his editors. In B.M. Royal MS. 13. B. I, however, he is mentioned by his full name in a letter that Ascham wrote for Cecil in 1565 to the mayor of Dunkirk (fol. 138ᵛ).

2. Some uncertainty remains about the identity of this "best schoolmaster" and "greatest beater" of the time. The Tudor headmaster of Eton with the outstanding reputation as both teacher and strict disciplinarian was the playwright Nicholas Udall, named by Mayor (p. 205), Giles (III, 80n), and others on evidence provided by Bishop John Bale and some verses of Thomas Tusser as the subject of this passage. But since the compliment about the scholar is almost certainly meant for Haddon, it is more likely that the teacher in question was the incumbent Bishop of Ely, Richard Cox, who had been master of Eton during Haddon's schooldays there. Haddon went up to King's College in 1533, and Udall did not become master of Eton until the following year. An affectionate exchange of elegiac distichs between Cox and Haddon occurs in the latter's *Poematum libri duo,* fol. H₁ʳ⁻ᵛ.

3. This draft appears in the already cited B.M. Royal MS. 18. B. xxiv, art.

2, fols. 47ʳ–78ʳ, formerly in the library of John, Lord Lumley. Parks concludes that the manuscript, which is entitled, in different and slightly later hand-writing, "[Asch]ams institution [for] hys chylde," is "a progressive first draft," somewhere between a rough version and a fair copy, with "no intervening revision" before the text that finally went to the printer (*HLQ*, I, 316). Katter-feld (p. 321, n. 1) suggests that parts (evidently the passages in italic script) were transcribed by Ascham himself. After examining the manuscript, I am convinced that it is not a holograph but a copy made for the author by a scribe who alternates for some reason between an italic and a cursive hand. Parks believes that Ascham may have interrupted composition before the end of 1564 and presents evidence to support his claim that the manuscript probably dates from this time (pp. 314–17). A draft may even have been ready quite early in 1564, for in an allusion (fol. 73ʳ) that is deleted in the published version, Ascham mentions that Sir Thomas Lodge has been Lord Mayor of London "this last year" (that is, 1561–62).

4. Although Giles believes that death prevented Ascham's finishing the treatise (III, 275–76), Katterfeld assumes that he had completed it and that between his death and publication a part of the manuscript was lost (pp. 330–35). From the letter to Sturm it appears that Ascham was finished but wanted to see what his friend had to say in the long-awaited *De Imitatione Oratoria* before publishing his own work (II, 189–90). One may reasonably surmise from the manner in which the published version breaks off that the missing sheets included the long discussion of Cicero as the one perfect model of Latinity (III, 274). Also probably missing is a section on *declamatio,* listed early in Book Two as one of the "six ways appointed by the best learned men, for the learning of tongues and increase of eloquence"(III, 174). In the letter to Sturm, Ascham mentions two other necessary steps in learning languages, *commentatio* and *scriptio* (II, 177). There is no way of knowing whether he included these in the final version.

5. Budé, whose opinion Ascham cites (III, 92), also disapproved of too early exercise in Latin conversation. The important grammarian Petrus Mosellanus, moreover, wrote his colloquies specifically to correct the vulgar errors occasioned by the current practice of encouraging pupils to speak the language at too early an age (*Paedologia,* trans. Robert Francis Seybolt, Urbana, 1927, pp. 1–2).

6. Cicero, *De Oratore,* I, xxxiv; Pliny, *Epistolae,* VII, ix.

7. The work recommended by Ascham is *Ciceronis Epistolarum libri IV, a J. Sturmio puerili educationi confecti* (Strasbourg, 1539).

8. The necessity of teaching by means of examples had been from the beginning one of the central topics in Ascham's correspondence with Sturm (I, 186). In the last letter, the stress on example is particularly prominent because of the long discussion of imitation. Ascham wants to have many—"nor will I be content with one or two"—examples showing how Cicero imitated his Greek models (II, 178–79).

9. Although Ascham really directs his attack against narrow-minded mathematical specialization, this passage evoked an amazed rejoinder from

Mulcaster, who wondered how the close friend of Cheke, a great fosterer of the subject, could so thoroughly "mislike the *mathematical* sciences" (*Positions*, p. 241).

10. III, 99. According to Mrs. Thrale, Samuel Johnson especially liked this phrase and applied it, with a change upon the meaning of "wit," to the host of inferior scribblers of his own age (See *Thraliana: The Diary of Mrs. Hester Lynch Thrale [Later Mrs. Piozzi], 1776–1809*, ed. Katherine C. Balderston, Oxford, 1942, II, 927).

11. Although this contrast between "quick" and "hard" wits is commonplace, worth noting is the manner in which it is phrased in More's translation of *The Lyfe of Johan Picus Erle of Myrandula* (London, [1510?]), where wonder is expressed that Pico enjoyed both ready wit and an astonishingly retentive memory: "For they that are swift in taking be oftentimes slow in remembering / and they that with more labor and difficulty receive it: more fast and surely hold it" (fol. $A_{iv}{}^v$).

12. Socrates does not himself express, as Ascham implies he does, all of these marks in order. Ascham has extracted them mainly from the *Republic*, VII, xv, 535B–D, and III, xii, 402D, with supplemental details from the *Symposium*, 209B–C, and the *Phaedrus*, 252E.

13. *Elizabethan Critical Essays*, I, 161.

14. *Governour*, I, 36.

15. Ascham's discussion of the queen's accomplishments (III, 142–44) is much condensed from the manuscript. A number of the other revisions improved the treatise noticeably, but alteration of this passage, obviously to stress the indispensability of learning to the highly born, sacrifices Elizabeth the royal woman to Elizabeth the bluestocking. In the earlier version, she is presented more expansively as the cynosure of all courtly behavior. She is not only "an example of learning to all gentlemen, but a mistress of womanhood to all women, and a mirror of comely and orderly living to all her court. And yet in her other excellent qualities, fit for a noblewoman, she is still like herself, that is above all the rest, as in riding most trimly, in dancing most comely, in playing of instruments most excellently, in all cunning needlework, and finest portraiture, yea, and to descend to those so housewifelike properties, which were so commended in Lady Mary late Queen of Hungary, and Regent of Flanders, she shall appear a Diana amongst all the nymphs, in what company of ladies so ever she shall be" (fol. 70^{r-v}).

16. Among the "corrupted" friends whom Ascham may have had in mind was Robert Stafford, who had made a nuisance of himself while abroad in 1549–50. For comment on other Italianated Englishmen of the time, see George B. Parks, "The First Italianate Englishmen," *Studies in the Renaissance*, VIII (1961), 197–216.

17. III, 166. Ascham may also have been influenced by Erasmus's mistrust of exposure to the corruption of the Italians. So marked was Erasmus's prejudice that, disregarding his own pleasant experiences there, he disapproved William Latimer's suggestion that a Greek tutor be secured from Italy for even so mature and saintly a person as John Fisher. (Cited in Mayor's

edition of *The Scholemaster*, p. 222. Mayor also notes that when Cecil thought of permitting his son Thomas to go to Italy, a friend dissuaded him "by reason of the enticements to pleasure and wantonness there.")

18. The literary allusions in *The Scholemaster*, estimated at some two hundred, have been studied in Gertrude Noyes's dissertation and in Herbert Patterson's article, "The Humanism of Roger Ascham," *Pedagogical Seminary*, XXII (1915), 546–51. Patterson's analysis is somewhat vitiated by his failure to distinguish among authors and nonauthors in his list of persons cited by Ascham.

19. *The Education or bringing up of children*, trans. Sir Thomas Elyot (London, [1531?]).

20. "Defence," *Elizabethan Critical Essays*, I, 160.

21. Hogrefe, p. 143.

22. For further discussion of Elyot's and Ascham's program for the aristocracy and its differences from that of More and his circle, see Hogrefe, pp. 59–62. Among writers who shared their worry about the decay of gentlemen and the consequent disordering of English society were Edmund Dudley, in *The Tree of Commonwealth* (1509–10), and the anonymous author of another of Ascham's unacknowledged sources, *The Institucion of a Gentleman* (London, 1555).

23. Sturm, *De litterarum ludis recte aperiendis liber* (Strasbourg, 1543), fol. 15^r. On fol. 32^r Sturm again asserts that he considers piety the true end of learning ("pietatem finem statuimus studiorum").

24. Compare Ascham's imitation of this metaphor: quick wits "be like trees, that show forth fair blossoms and broad leaves in spring-time, but bring out small and not long lasting fruit in harvest-time; and that only such as fall and rot before they be ripe, and so never, or seldom, come to any good at all" (III, 99).

25. The charge of undue emphasis on form, made first by Bacon, has been reiterated in modern times, notably by Katterfeld in his "Roger Aschams pädagogische Ansichten," *Paedagogium*, V (1883), 476–504, and by Sturm's biographer Charles Schmidt, who concludes that "Tout le zèle de Sturm était tourné du côté du bien parler" (*La Vie et les travaux de Jean Sturm*, Strasbourg, 1855, p. 239).

26. *De litterarum ludis, passim; De amissa dicendi ratione*, fols. 30^v, 34^r.

27. *De amissa dicendi ratione*, fols. 12, 32^v.

28. *De litterarum ludis*, fol. 23^r.

29. *Ibid., passim.* Compare *The Scholemaster* (III, 239, 246–48, 274). Both Sturm and Ascham derive their views of Caesar from Quintilian, X, i, 114.

30. See Friedrich August Arnstädt, *Roger Ascham, ein englischer Pädagog des XVI. Jahrhunderts, und seine Geistesverwandschaft mit Johannes Sturm* (Plauen, 1881). Arnstädt's is the most detailed study of Ascham's intellectual indebtedness to Sturm.

31. III, 211–13. Compare Sturm: "But knowledge of things without grace in speech is wont to be barbarous and vile, and likewise with the corruption of speech we observe that a kind of captious conviction of their own

wisdom steals into men. Whence it may be seen, that the first tender age of children ought to be given over to instruction in proper speaking" (*De litterarum ludis,* fol. 4ᵛ).

32. III, 174. Though Cicero also comments on these methods in *De Oratore* and *Brutus,* the model for Ascham's discussion is the *Elementa Rhetorica* (1551) of Joachim Camerarius, which provided both the phrasing for a number of statements in *The Scholemaster* about all but the first and last topics, and also most of the examples used by Ascham in treating *paraphrasis* and *metaphrasis.*

33. *De Oratore,* I, xxii, 90–92; xxxiv, 154–55. Ascham may never have covered, though he lists, *declamatio* because, in the same book of *De Oratore* (xxxiii, 150), Crassus had discommended too early speaking and insisted that "the pen is the best and most excellent producer and teacher of eloquence."

34. III, 213. A comprehensive account of this long-extended debate is Izora Scott's *Controversies over The Imitation of Cicero* (New York, 1910). For the period up to 1530, see also Remigio Sabbadini, *Storia del Ciceronianismo e di altre questioni letterarie nell'età della Rinascenza* (Turin, 1885).

35. Ascham's judgments on the various writers cited above occur on III, 221–22. Miss Scott has called attention to the practical, though not theoretical, strictness of the Ciceronianism of Melanchthon, Camerarius, and Sturm (*Controversies,* Part I, pp. 106–11).

36. A useful outline of Ascham's system for studying Latin is provided in the introduction to Edward Arber's edition of *The Scholemaster* (Birmingham, 1870), pp. 9–11. T. W. Baldwin examines the method in detail in *William Shakspere's Small Latine & Lesse Greeke* (Urbana, 1944), I, 261–75.

37. *A History of Literary Criticism in the Renaissance* (New York, 1899), p. 255.

38. III, 228–29. Ascham's earlier intention of imitating Seneca's verse in his proposed translation of the Philoctetes should be recalled here (I, 32).

39. Compare *Poetics,* 1453ᵃ.

40. Ascham calls tragedies "the goodliest argument of all, and for the use either of a learned preacher, or a civil gentleman, more profitable than Homer, Pindar, Virgil, and Horace" (III, 228). Compare *Poetics,* 1461ᵇ–1462ᵇ.

41. For example, C. S. Lewis, *English Literature in the Sixteenth Century Excluding Drama* (Oxford, 1954), pp. 281–82.

42. G. D. Willcock, "Passing Pitefull Hexameters: A Study of Quantity and Accent in English Renaissance Verse," *MLR,* XXIX (1934), 2.

43. *Ibid.,* pp. 3–5, 8, 17. Hence Ascham is scarcely blameworthy for being unable to discern any formal constant in vernacular poetry other than the rhyme to which he was objecting. As a rhetorician, moreover, he may have looked upon rhyme simply as a variation of the figure called *similiter desinens* (a likeness of word endings), agreeable enough as an ornament if used by the orator in moderation, but in no way essential to structure (see III, 250–51).

44. For Spenser's and Harvey's exchange of views about classical meters, see *Elizabethan Critical Essays,* I, 87–122. Harvey, incidentally, believes (pp.

101, 109) that with all due respect to the author of *The Scholemaster*, the experiment in quantitative versifying by Sidney and Dyer would prove to be of greater consequence "than the dead advertisement and persuasion of Mr. Ascham."

45. See Harvey's protest against Spenser's attempt, on quantitative principles, to make English cárpentĕr read cārpēntĕr (*ibid.*, p. 117).

46. Such efforts as this led Gregory Smith to assume, quite wrongly, that the efforts of Ascham and his disciples are purely "accentual hexameters" (*ibid.*, p. 1).

47. III, 155, rendering *Odyssey*, X, 305–6.

48. Fleming, who also translated several of Ascham's Latin letters as models of style in his *A Panoplie of Epistles*, made English versions of the *Eclogues* (1575) and the *Georgics* (1589) in classical meters. Webbe, in *A Discourse of English Poetrie* (1586), and Fraunce, in *The Lawiers Logike* (1588), rendered individual eclogues into English quantitative measures; he did likewise with the Latin *Amyntas* (1587) of Thomas Watson (not to be confused with Ascham's friend). In 1582 Stanyhurst published *Thee First Foure Bookes of Virgil his Aeneis*, in which he stated explicitly that his inspiration had been Ascham's wish that scholars would "apply their wits in beautifying our English language with heroical verses" (*Elizabethan Critical Essays*, I, 137).

49. For discussion of Sturm's influence on Ascham's critical ideas, see M. A. Emkes, *Das Erziehungsideal bei T. More, Roger Ascham, T. Elyot, und J. Lyly* (Marburg, 1904), pp. 51–54; for Cheke's influence, see Walter Ludwig Nathan, *Sir John Cheke und der englische Frühhumanismus* (Bonn, 1928), pp. 84–99.

50. III, 184. Ascham admittedly takes over these points from Quintilian's chapter "De emendatione" (X, iv, 1).

51. Compare Melanchthon's objection to Sallust's writings as "dry, uncouth, and obscure" (*Opera Quae Supersunt Omnia*, ed. Carolus Gottlieb Bretschneider; Corpus Reformatorum; Halle, 1846, XIII, 505). "E.K." appears to have this passage in *The Scholemaster* in mind when, in defending Spenser's antiquated language in *The Shepheardes Calender*, he cites the objections to archaisms "of Valla against Livy, and of other against Sallust" (*Elizabethan Critical Essays*, I, 128–29).

52. *A History of Criticism and Literary Taste* (New York, 1902), pp. 151–52.

53. Donald Lemen Clark, *Rhetoric and Poetry in the Renaissance* (New York, 1922), p. 77.

54. III, 239. These conclusions disagree to some extent with those of Jones, who interprets these same passages as evidence that Ascham still considered English to be an "uneloquent language" (*The Triumph of the English Language*, pp. 14–15).

55. "Defence," *Elizabethan Critical Essays*, I, 164.

56. III, 116. Although in this and the ensuing quotations illustrating Ascham's prose style, I have adhered to my practice of retaining Giles's

modernized spelling and punctuation, the reader would do well to compare Wright's edition of the *English Works*, which reproduces the 1570 text of *The Scholemaster*. For both Giles and Mayor lighten Ascham's customarily heavy pointing, by means of which he vividly brings out the structural relationships among his words and phrases.

57. The Gorgianic figures, which appear also in a lesser degree in *Toxophilus*, *A Report of Germany*, and the Latin and English correspondence, would have been familiar to Ascham from his early grammatical training as well as from pulpit oratory. In the *Barbarismus*, a standard text in the schools, Donatus treats them among the sixteen figures of words (*schemata lexeos*) belonging to the art of the grammarian, and Morris Croll finds them in the highly patterned prose of the sermons of Bishop John Jewel and Ascham's friend Thomas Lever (introduction to John Lyly, *Euphues*, New York, 1916, pp. xlix–l). Ascham's familiarity with such patristic authors as Sts. Augustine, Cyprian, and Basil, all of whom he quotes in *The Scholemaster* (III, 197), would have exposed him further to the figures. Finally, throughout his correspondence he had shown an exceptionally keen interest in Cicero's rather Gorgianic *Pro Quinctio* and in the *Gorgias* itself, and for eighteen years he kept by him, as the best work he knew on philosophical imitation, a manuscript copy of Sturm's unpublished commentary on Plato's dialogue (I, 183; III, 243).

58. *Arte of Rhetorique*, p. 168.

59. Eduard Norden was the first to argue that Isocrates, popularized in England by Ascham, exerted the main influence on the development of euphuism (*Die antike Kunstprosa*, Leipzig, 1898, II, 799–802). In 1916, both Croll (*Lyly's Euphues*, pp. xxiv–liv) and T. K. Whipple ("Isocrates and Euphuism," *MLR*, XI, 15–27, 129–35) took issue with this view. Whipple believed that the influence of Isocrates "ran directly counter to the tendency which culminated in *Euphues*. Isocrates explains the difference between Ascham and Lyly—but not the similarities." Croll went further and argued that the well-known medieval development of Gorgianic and other schemes beyond their use in classical oratory led directly to the peculiar stylistic features of euphuism. In 1938 William Ringler lent Croll support by offering as the direct link between medieval practice and euphuism the highly schematic Latin orations delivered at Oxford in the 1570's by John Rainolds ("The Immediate Source of Euphuism," *PMLA*, LIII, 678–86).

60. *Gabriel Harvey's Marginalia*, ed. G. C. Moore Smith (Stratford-upon-Avon, 1913), pp. 217, 127.

61. *A New Letter of Notable Contents* (1593), in *Elizabethan Critical Essays*, II, 282–83.

62. *Ibid.*, p. 274.

63. *Pierces Supererogation, ibid.*, p. 277. Here Harvey seems to have in mind Cicero's remark that whereas the eloquent orator carefully articulates his thought and periods, the ignorant speaker "spews out his ill-ordered matter helter-skelter, and ends his sentences not according to artistic considerations but when he runs out of breath" (*De Oratore*, III, xliv, 175–76).

64. II, 188. Rapicio's *De Numero Oratorio Libri Quinque* (Venice, 1554) was dedicated, incidentally, to Cardinal Pole.

65. *The Doctrinall of Princes made by the noble orator Isocrates,* third edition (London, [1548?]), fol. A$_{ii}$$^{r-v}$. How sound Elyot's opinion was may be tested by comparing his effort with Thomas Forrest's version of Isocrates' three Cyprian orations (*A Perfite Looking Glasse for all Estates,* London, 1580). Forrest, working from a Latin translation by Hieronymus Wolf, comes up with a rendering that is wordier, looser in syntax, much less firm in phrasing than Elyot's. Another Tudor translator of Isocrates with whose work Ascham may have been familiar was a Cantabrigian named John Bury. Like Elyot, Bury, in his *The Godly advertisement or good counsell of the famous orator* Isocrates, *intitled* Paraenesis *to* Demonicus (London, 1557), closely imitates the measured and comparatively succinct phrasing of the Greek rather than the longer periods of the Latin style.

66. *A History of English Prose Rhythm* (London, 1912), pp. 120–23; *A History of Elizabethan Literature* (London, 1891), p. 32.

67. *A History of Criticism and Literary Taste,* II, 156. Though Hooker does share several characteristics of style with Ascham, only an occasional passage in Jonson suggests any literary kinship. Perhaps the soundest estimate of Ascham's worth as a writer of prose remains that of George Philip Krapp. To Krapp, Ascham's most noteworthy characteristics are an Isocratean working of plain diction into "solidly dignified and elevated" composition, a careful articulation of elements that "served as a useful corrective of the loose, popular style of writing," and awareness of form and of the writing of vernacular prose as a serious endeavor of art. He provided a model not only for excessively ornate authors like Lyly, but also for those who recognized him as the harbinger of a truly "polished and refined eloquence" in the English tongue (*The Rise of English Literary Prose,* New York, 1915, pp. 296–99).

68. Jones, pp. 182–83.

69. *Marginalia,* p. 158.

70. *Nashes Lenten Stuffe* (1599), *Works,* ed. R. B. McKerrow (London, 1904–10), III, 181.

71. "The Pilgrimage to Parnassus," ll. 291, 298–99, *The Three Parnassus Plays,* ed. J. B. Leishman (London, 1949), p. 111.

72. Louise Brown Osborne, *The Life, Letters, and Writings of John Hoskyns 1566–1638* (New Haven, 1937), p. 4.

73. *The Critical Opinions of Samuel Johnson,* ed. Joseph Epes Brown (Princeton, 1926), pp. 281–82.

74. Another debtor, curiously enough, is Bacon, for in spite of his disparagement of Ascham's Latin Ciceronianism, his own English prose appears to owe as much to the style of *The Scholemaster* as it does to that of Tacitus or to the "amble" of Seneca. From among several examples, only the following need be quoted to underscore the relationship: "The joys of parents are secret; and so are their griefs and fears. They can not utter the one; nor will they utter the other. Children sweeten labours; but they make misfortune more bitter. They increase the cares of life, but they mitigate the remem-

brance of death" (*Works*, VI, 390). Besides this instance, which out-Aschams Ascham or Isocrates in its highly balanced antitheses, Bacon has many others in which, like Ascham's, his sentences tend to weigh possible alternatives in exactly paralleled phrases before adding an asymmetrical *colon* to resolve the issue. This is another of Ascham's typical sentence patterns, easily distinguishable from those of Lyly, who almost invariably maintains absolute balance of members to the end of his periods.

75. *Pierces Supererogation* (*Elizabethan Critical Essays*, II, 258, 249).

76. *Elizabethan Critical Essays*, I, 203.

77. *Ibid.*, p. 194.

78. *Ibid.*, p. 193.

79. Madeleine Doran, *Endeavors of Art* (Madison, 1954), p. 40. For an excellent analysis of the rhetorical design of Sidney's *Defence*, see Kenneth O. Myrick, *Sir Philip Sidney as a Literary Craftsman* (Cambridge, Mass., 1935), Ch. 2.

80. *Elizabethan Critical Essays*, I, 203–4.

CHAPTER TWELVE

1. *Allegations for Marriage Licenses Issued by the Bishop of London, 1520 to 1610*, ed. Joseph Lemuel Chester and Geo. J. Armitage (Harleian Society XXV; London, 1877), I, 43.

2. P. H. Reaney, "Roger Ascham, Margaret Rampston and Salisbury Manor," *Notes & Queries*, n.s. IV (1957), 332–33; G. F. Bosworth, *Manors of Low Hall and Salisbury Hall, Walthamstow* (Walthamstow Antiquarian Society, VII; [Walthamstow], 1920), pp. 13ff.

3. In April 1590, Ann's husband, Robert Symons, Junior, arranged to purchase Salisbury Manor from the crown upon expiration of Margaret's current lease, which had been renewed in 1586 (P.R.O. State Papers Domestic. 28° Elizabeth, January 27, 1586, Document 61; 32° Elizabeth, April 1, 1590, fols. 122–45).

4. P.R.O. Patent Roll. 21° Elizabeth, June 1579, Part iii, item 53.

5. H.M.C., *Marquess of Salisbury MSS.* (London, 1888), Part II, pp. 501–2. Presumably at least two of the children mentioned were her daughters by Rampston. It cannot be said with certainty that all of the other six were fathered by Ascham since he mentions the birth or expected birth of only four children in all his correspondence. The endorsement on this petition states that Giles was to receive the pension for only eight years.

6. Cambridge University Library, Document 441.

7. Note appended to P.C.C. MS. 1 Sheffield, fol. 1, the oath of Giles Ascham regarding his mother's will.

8. B.M. Lansdowne MSS. 34 (p. 67); 39 (p. 76), two letters; 46 (p. 87); 54 (p. 103); 71 (p. 136); and 107 (p. 205). All but that occurring in MS. 54, which is a copy, are autographs. They have been transcribed in C.U.L. Baker MS. A (Mm. 2. 22. No. 7) and are printed by Giles (III, 356–65).

Further information about Giles Ascham's career appears in Venn, I, 43; Cooper, II, 207; and Joseph Foster, *Alumni Oxonienses* (Oxford, 1891), I, 34.

9. *Register of the University of Oxford,* ed. Andrew Clark, II: Part I, pp. 352–53).

10. P.R.O. Patent Rolls. 29° Elizabeth, September 28, 1587, Part XV, p. 42 (fourth member from bottom of roll).

11. C.U.L., Doc. 442 (original indenture, March 4, 1594).

12. Elstob wrongly gives the year as 1615 (Ascham's *Works,* I, cxi); the earlier date is from Venn, I, 43.

13. C.U.L., Doc. 443 (original indenture).

14. P.R.O. Exchequer Bills and Answers. Elizabeth. Cambridge, No. 107.

15. P.R.O. Originalia Roll. 42° Elizabeth. Part I, Roll 21. Two copies are preserved in C.U.L., Docs. 444, 445.

16. C.U.L., Doc. 441 (copy of patent). See also *Calendar of State Papers Domestic. Elizabeth, 1581–1590* (London, 1865), p. 682.

17. C.U.L., Doc. 456 (copy of bill, June 1, 1633).

18. P.R.O. Exchequer Bills and Answers. Elizabeth. Cambridge, No. 107.

19. C.U.L., Doc. 444.

20. C.U.L., Doc. 446 (original indenture).

21. C.U.L., Docs. 447–49.

22. C.U.L., Docs. 451–52 (original indentures).

23. Preserved in B.M. Harleian MSS. 168, art. 117; 295, art. 231b; Bodleian Library Rawlinson MS. C. 680. 84.

24. *The Original Lists of Persons . . . Who Went from Great Britain to the American Plantations, 1600–1700,* ed. John Camden Hotten (London, 1874), p. 225.

25. Thomas Fuller, for instance, admired the "facile and fluent Latin-style" of the letters (*Worthies,* III, 430–31), and in the eighteenth century Thomas Warton praised their "terseness" (*A History of English Poetry,* London, 1871, IV, 399) while Archbishop Nicolson valued them for their historical content as well as "the fine variety" of their language (*The English, Scotch, and Irish Historical Libraries,* new edition, London, 1776, Part I, p. 203). Isaac Disraeli ranked them for their personal interest with those "of Gray and Shenstone" (*Amenities of Literature,* p. 367), and in the present century E. N. S. Thompson has found in them "a real gift for familiar correspondence" (*Literary Bypaths of the Renaissance,* New Haven, 1924, p. 104).

INDEX

Index